THE HEROIC LEGEND OF
ARSLAN

STORY BY
YOSHIKI TANAKA

MANGA BY
HIROMU ARAKAWA

10

THE HEROIC LEGEND OF
ARSLAN

TABLE OF CONTENTS

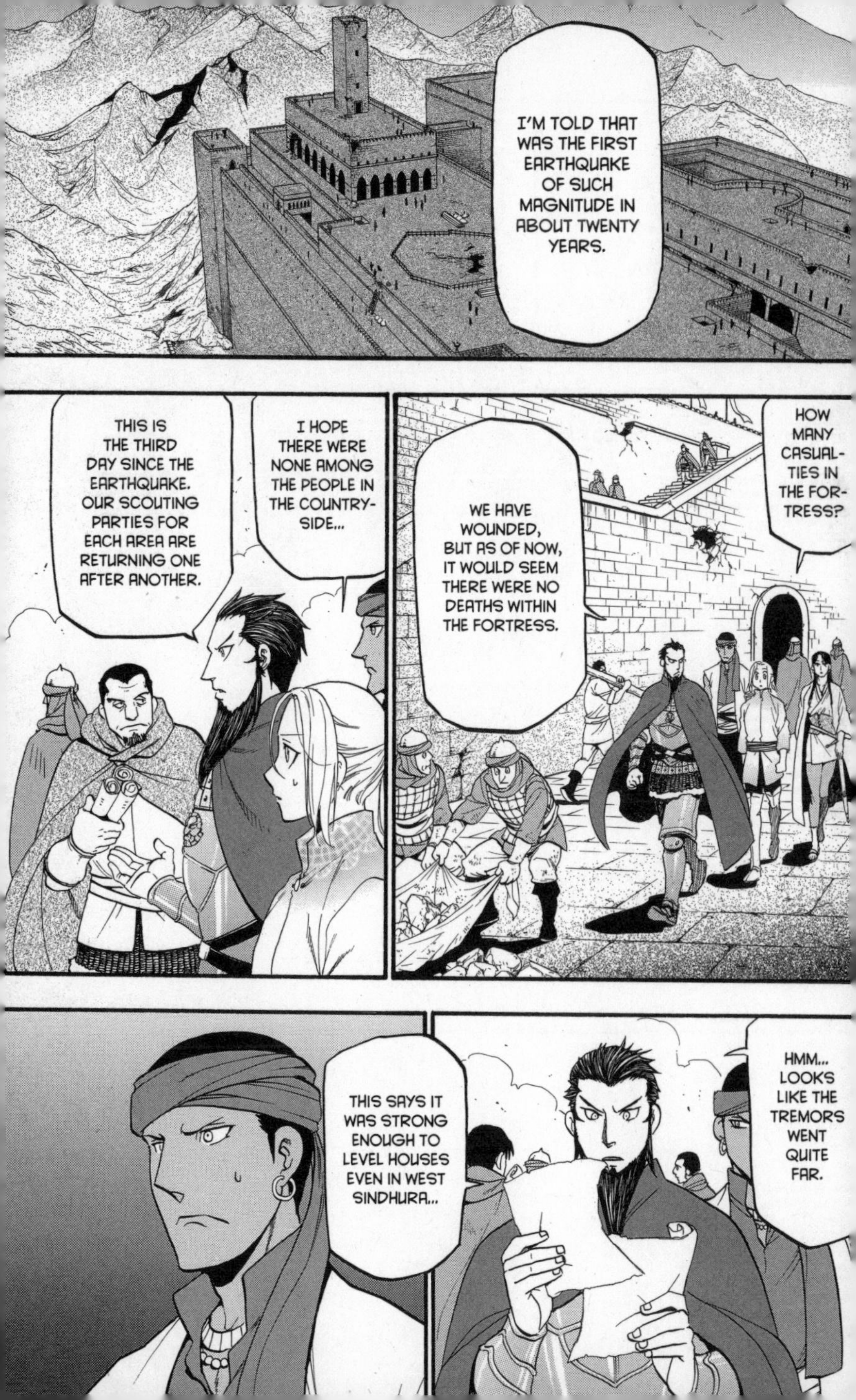
I'M TOLD THAT WAS THE FIRST EARTHQUAKE OF SUCH MAGNITUDE IN ABOUT TWENTY YEARS.
HOW MANY CASUALTIES IN THE FORTRESS?
WE HAVE WOUNDED, BUT AS OF NOW, IT WOULD SEEM THERE WERE NO DEATHS WITHIN THE FORTRESS.
I HOPE THERE WERE NONE AMONG THE PEOPLE IN THE COUNTRYSIDE...
THIS IS THE THIRD DAY SINCE THE EARTHQUAKE. OUR SCOUTING PARTIES FOR EACH AREA ARE RETURNING ONE AFTER ANOTHER.
HMM... LOOKS LIKE THE TREMORS WENT QUITE FAR.
THIS SAYS IT WAS STRONG ENOUGH TO LEVEL HOUSES EVEN IN WEST SINDHURA...

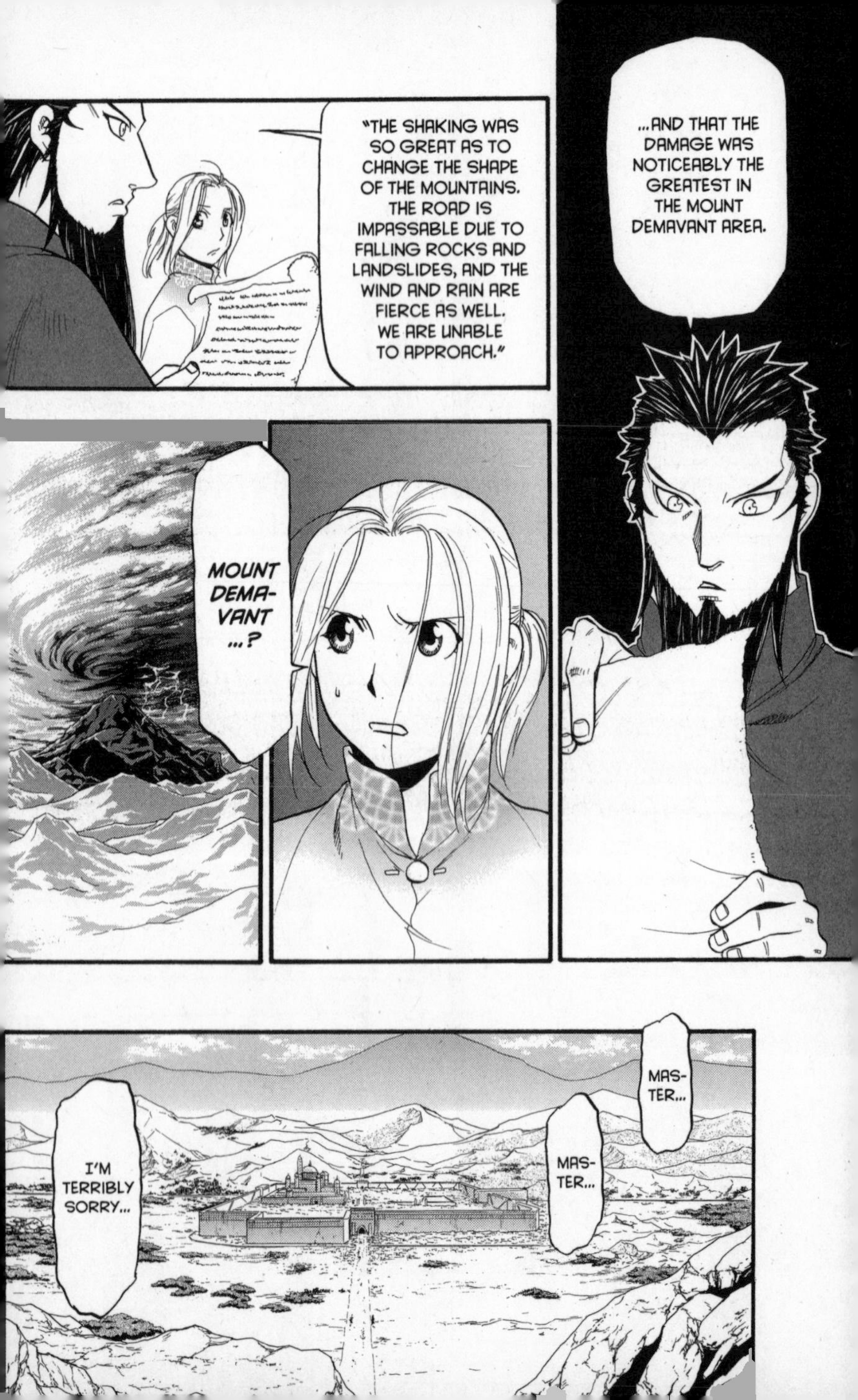
...AND THAT THE DAMAGE WAS NOTICEABLY THE GREATEST IN THE MOUNT DEMAVANT AREA.
"THE SHAKING WAS SO GREAT AS TO CHANGE THE SHAPE OF THE MOUNTAINS. THE ROAD IS IMPASSABLE DUE TO FALLING ROCKS AND LANDSLIDES, AND THE WIND AND RAIN ARE FIERCE AS WELL. WE ARE UNABLE TO APPROACH."
MOUNT DEMA-VANT ...?
MAS-TER...
MAS-TER...
I'M TERRIBLY SORRY...

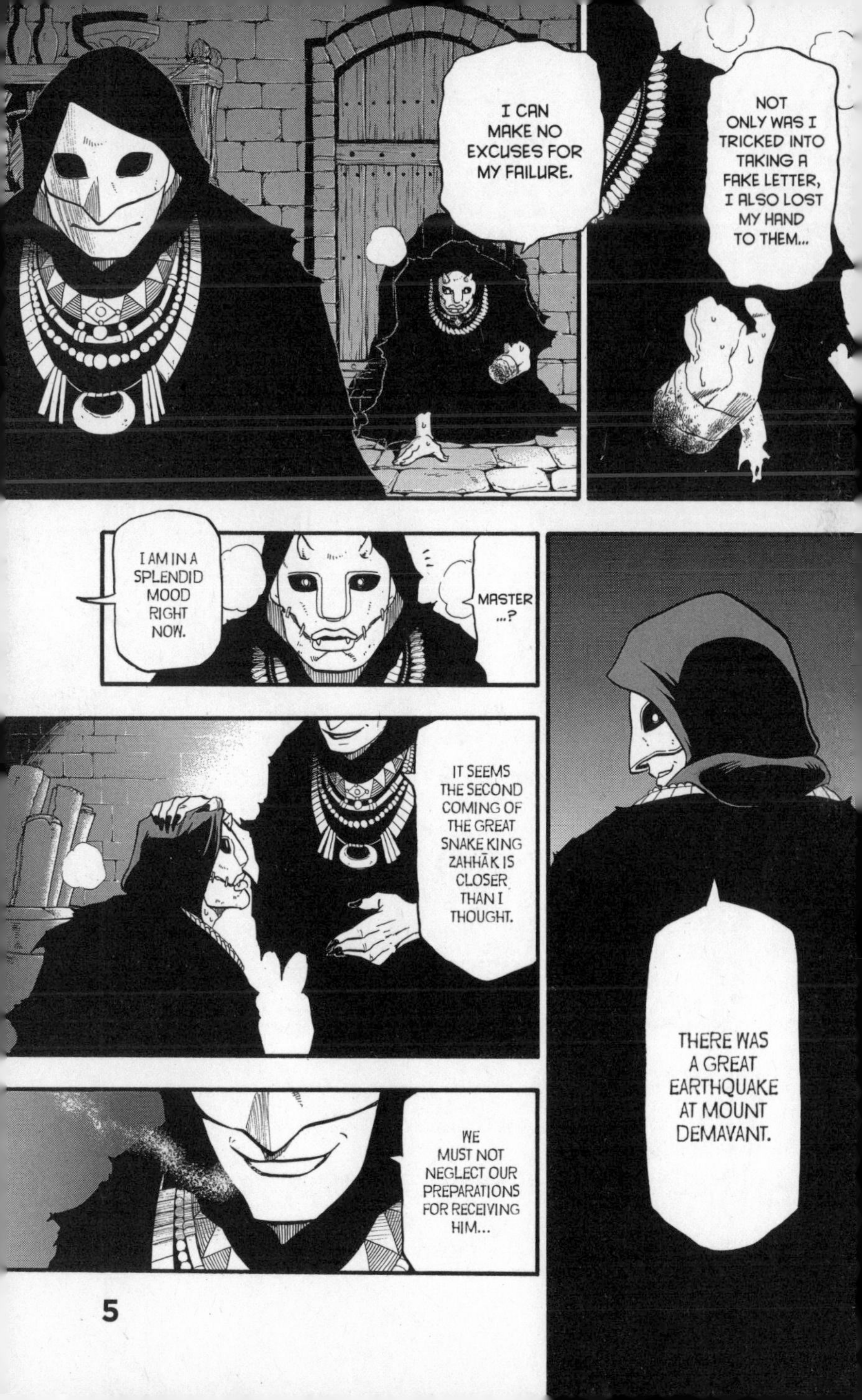
NOT ONLY WAS I TRICKED INTO TAKING A FAKE LETTER, I ALSO LOST MY HAND TO THEM...
I CAN MAKE NO EXCUSES FOR MY FAILURE.
THERE WAS A GREAT EARTHQUAKE AT MOUNT DEMAVANT.
MASTER ...?
I AM IN A SPLENDID MOOD RIGHT NOW.
IT SEEMS THE SECOND COMING OF THE GREAT SNAKE KING ZAHHĀK IS CLOSER THAN I THOUGHT.
WE MUST NOT NEGLECT OUR PREPARATIONS FOR RECEIVING HIM...

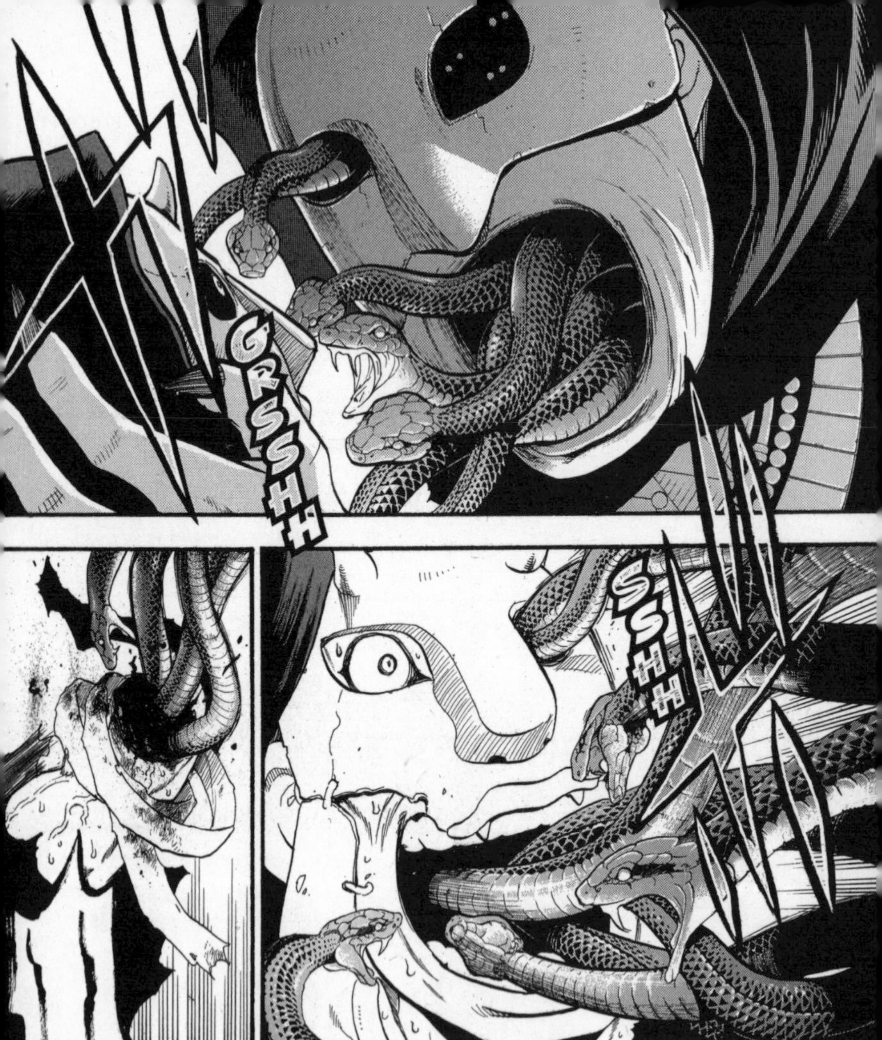
GRSSHH
SSHH

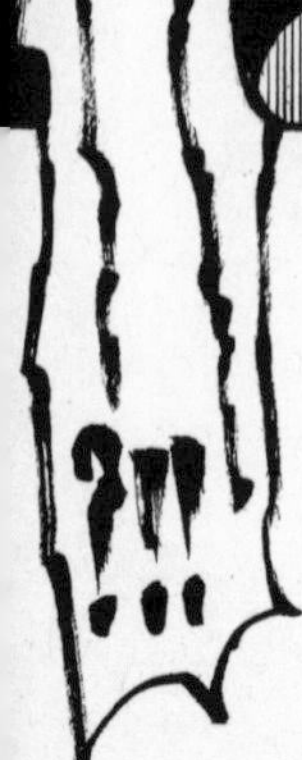
?!!

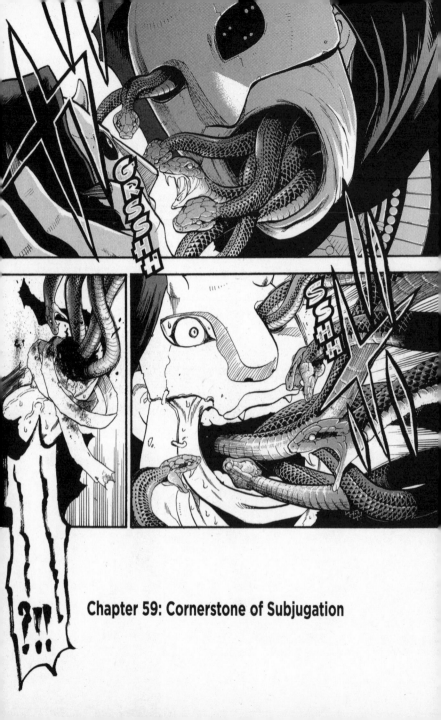

Chapter 59: Cornerstone of Subjugation

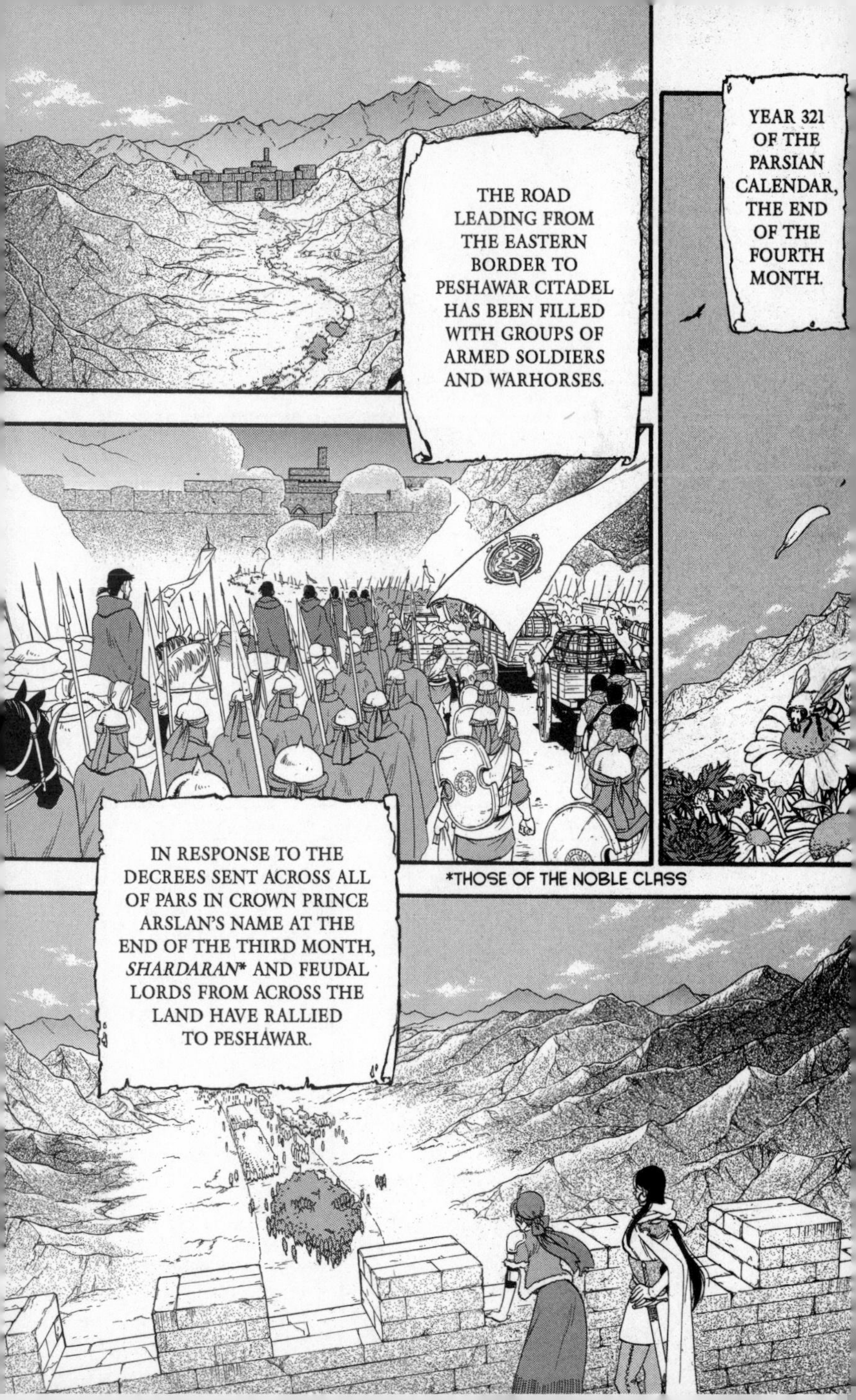
YEAR 321 OF THE PARSIAN CALENDAR, THE END OF THE FOURTH MONTH.
THE ROAD LEADING FROM THE EASTERN BORDER TO PESHAWAR CITADEL HAS BEEN FILLED WITH GROUPS OF ARMED SOLDIERS AND WARHORSES.
IN RESPONSE TO THE DECREES SENT ACROSS ALL OF PARS IN CROWN PRINCE ARSLAN'S NAME AT THE END OF THE THIRD MONTH, *SHARDARAN** AND FEUDAL LORDS FROM ACROSS THE LAND HAVE RALLIED TO PESHAWAR.
*THOSE OF THE NOBLE CLASS

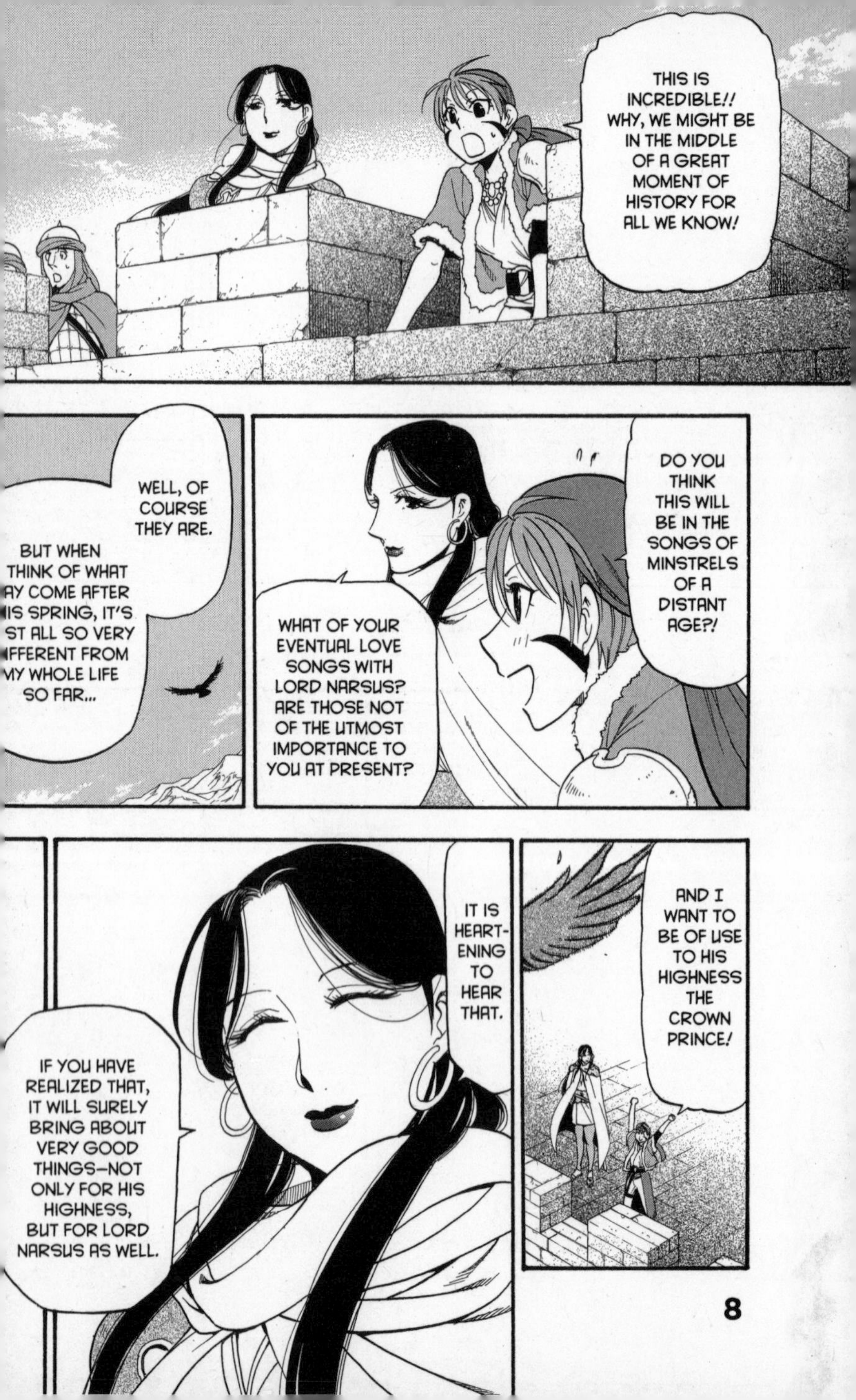
THIS IS INCREDIBLE!! WHY, WE MIGHT BE IN THE MIDDLE OF A GREAT MOMENT OF HISTORY FOR ALL WE KNOW!
DO YOU THINK THIS WILL BE IN THE SONGS OF MINSTRELS OF A DISTANT AGE?!
WHAT OF YOUR EVENTUAL LOVE SONGS WITH LORD NARSUS? ARE THOSE NOT OF THE UTMOST IMPORTANCE TO YOU AT PRESENT?
WELL, OF COURSE THEY ARE.
BUT WHEN THINK OF WHAT AY COME AFTER IS SPRING, IT'S ST ALL SO VERY IFFERENT FROM MY WHOLE LIFE SO FAR...
AND I WANT TO BE OF USE TO HIS HIGHNESS THE CROWN PRINCE!
IT IS HEARTENING TO HEAR THAT.
IF YOU HAVE REALIZED THAT, IT WILL SURELY BRING ABOUT VERY GOOD THINGS—NOT ONLY FOR HIS HIGHNESS, BUT FOR LORD NARSUS AS WELL.

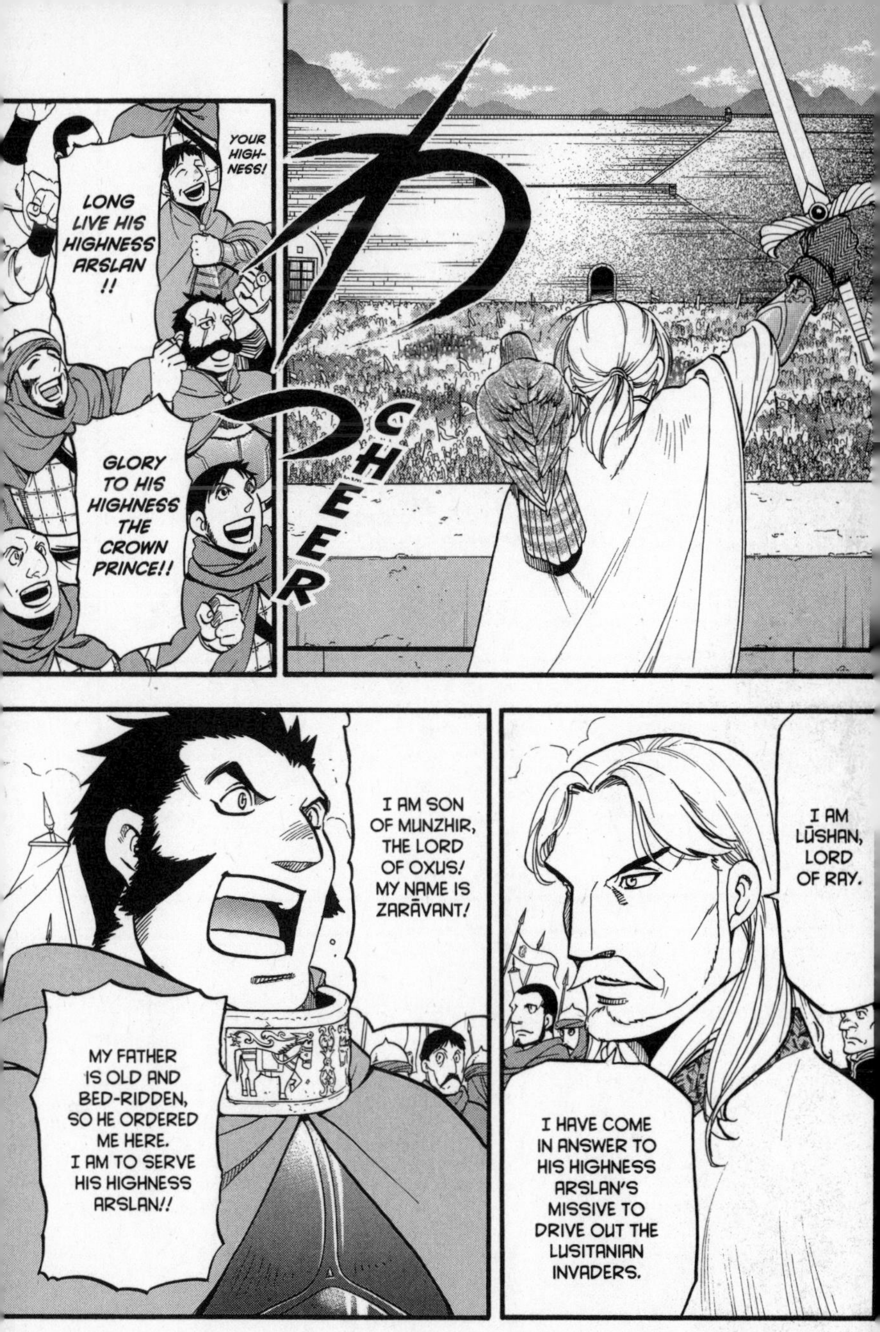
CHEER
YOUR HIGH-NESS!
LONG LIVE HIS HIGHNESS ARSLAN !!
GLORY TO HIS HIGHNESS THE CROWN PRINCE!!
I AM LŪSHAN, LORD OF RAY.
I HAVE COME IN ANSWER TO HIS HIGHNESS ARSLAN'S MISSIVE TO DRIVE OUT THE LUSITANIAN INVADERS.
I AM SON OF MUNZHIR, THE LORD OF OXUS! MY NAME IS ZARĀVANT!
MY FATHER IS OLD AND BED-RIDDEN, SO HE ORDERED ME HERE. I AM TO SERVE HIS HIGHNESS ARSLAN!!

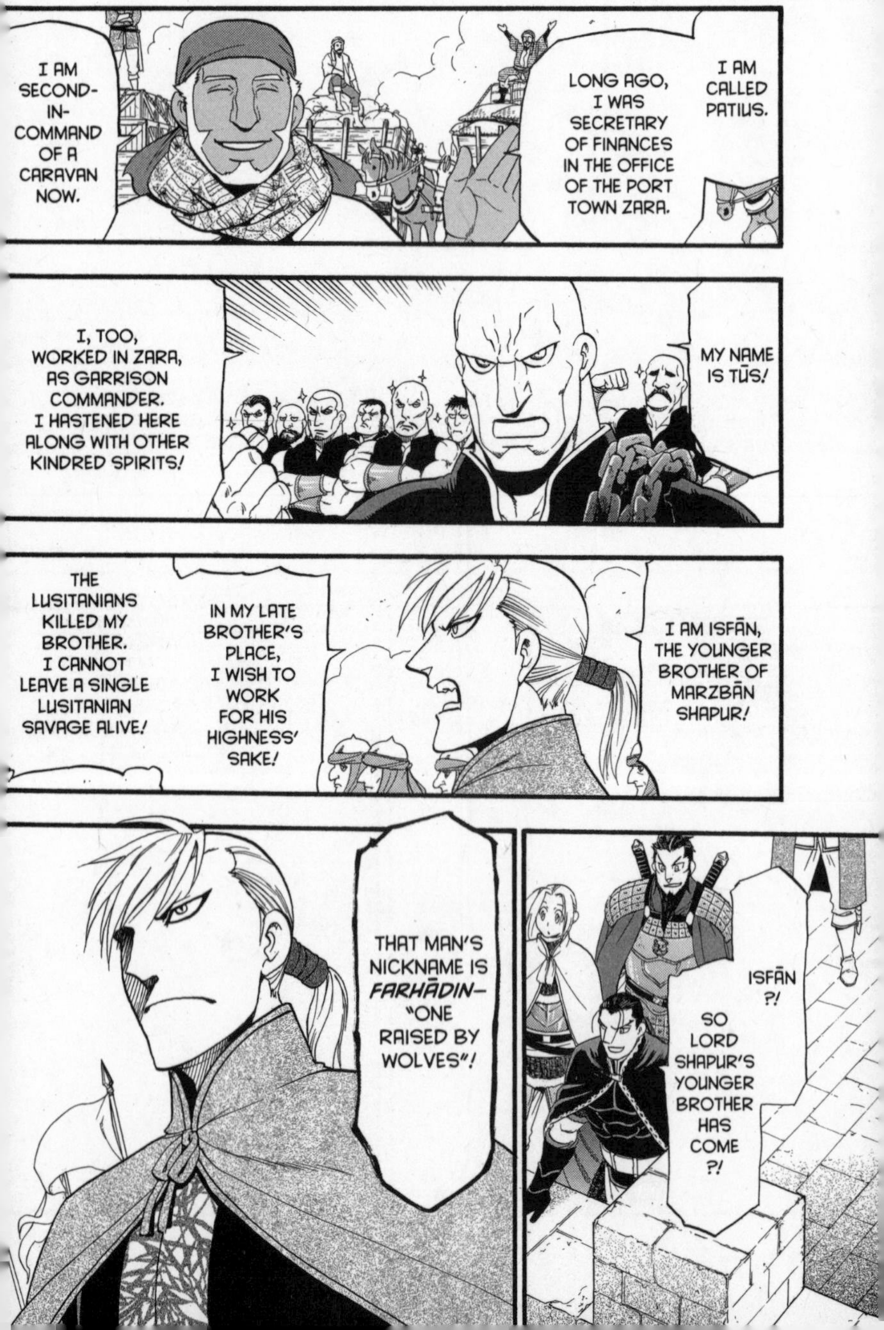
I AM CALLED PATIUS.
LONG AGO, I WAS SECRETARY OF FINANCES IN THE OFFICE OF THE PORT TOWN ZARA.
I AM SECOND-IN-COMMAND OF A CARAVAN NOW.
MY NAME IS TŪS!
I, TOO, WORKED IN ZARA, AS GARRISON COMMANDER. I HASTENED HERE ALONG WITH OTHER KINDRED SPIRITS!
I AM ISFĀN, THE YOUNGER BROTHER OF MARZBĀN SHAPUR!
IN MY LATE BROTHER'S PLACE, I WISH TO WORK FOR HIS HIGHNESS' SAKE!
THE LUSITANIANS KILLED MY BROTHER. I CANNOT LEAVE A SINGLE LUSITANIAN SAVAGE ALIVE!
ISFĀN ?!
SO LORD SHAPUR'S YOUNGER BROTHER HAS COME ?!
THAT MAN'S NICKNAME IS *FARHĀDIN*— "ONE RAISED BY WOLVES"!

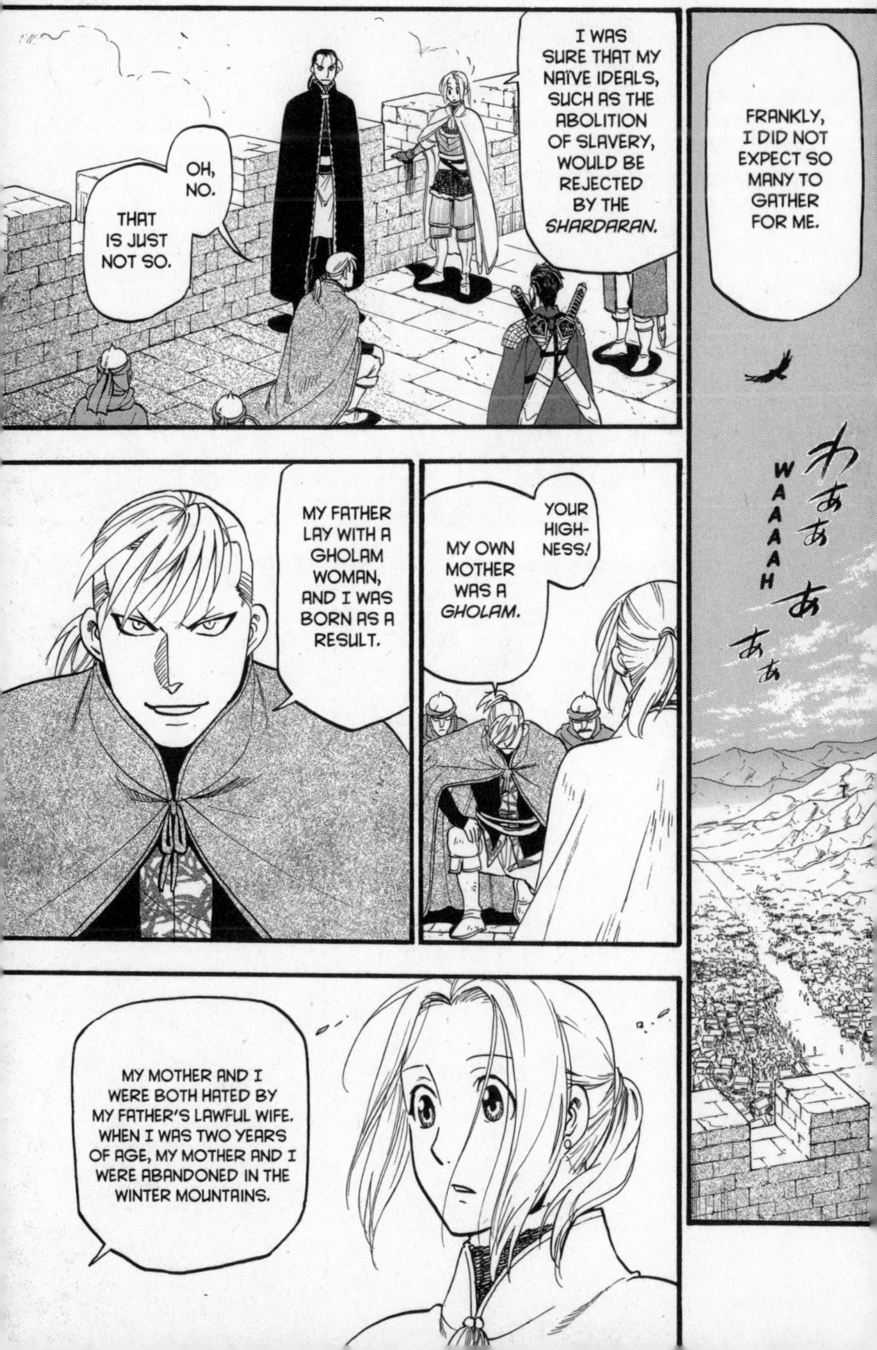

FRANKLY, I DID NOT EXPECT SO MANY TO GATHER FOR ME.
わあああああ
WAAAAH
I WAS SURE THAT MY NAÏVE IDEALS, SUCH AS THE ABOLITION OF SLAVERY, WOULD BE REJECTED BY THE *SHARDARAN.*
OH, NO.
THAT IS JUST NOT SO.
YOUR HIGHNESS!
MY OWN MOTHER WAS A *GHOLAM.*
MY FATHER LAY WITH A GHOLAM WOMAN, AND I WAS BORN AS A RESULT.
MY MOTHER AND I WERE BOTH HATED BY MY FATHER'S LAWFUL WIFE. WHEN I WAS TWO YEARS OF AGE, MY MOTHER AND I WERE ABANDONED IN THE WINTER MOUNTAINS.

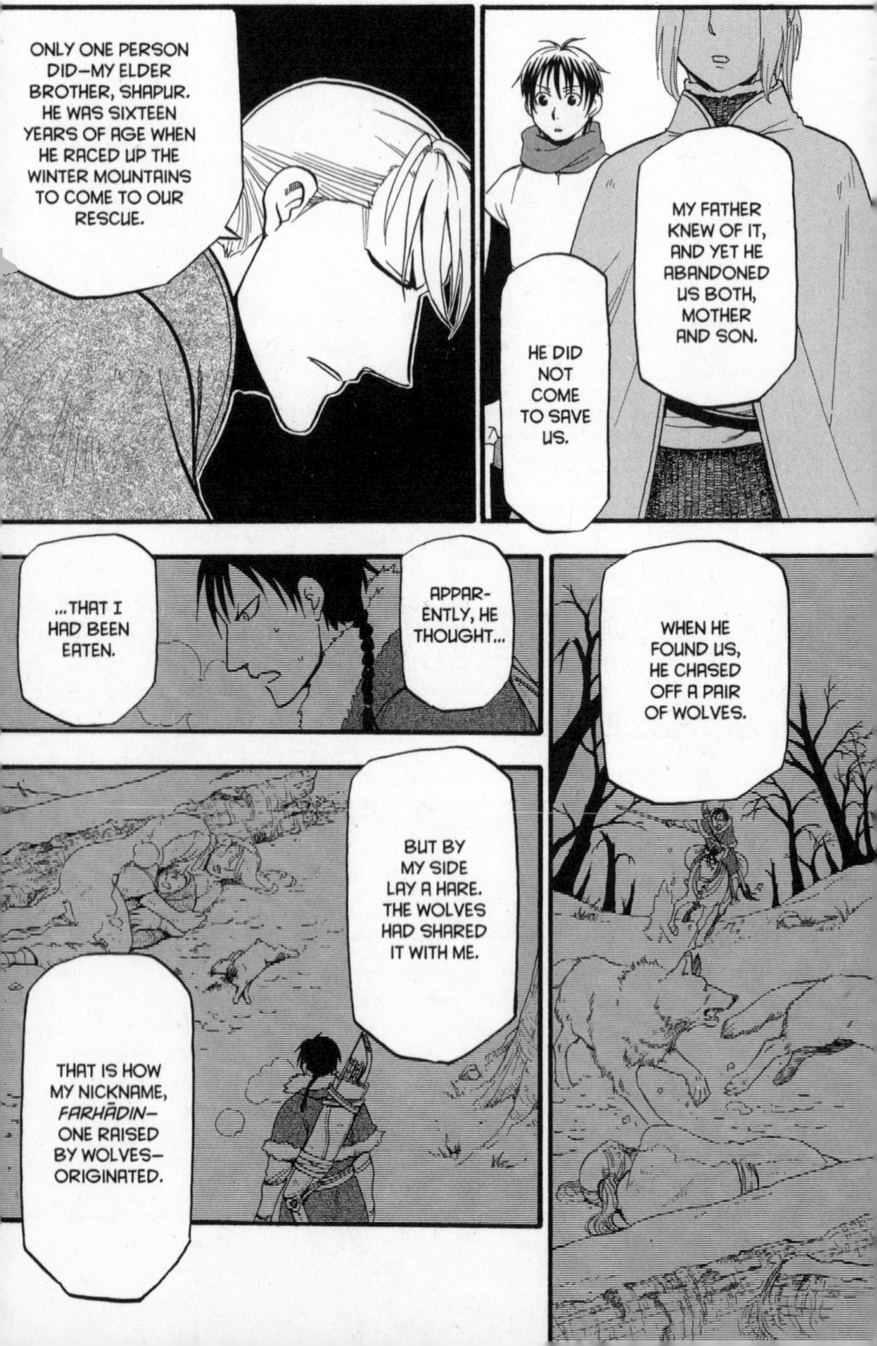
MY FATHER KNEW OF IT, AND YET HE ABANDONED US BOTH, MOTHER AND SON.
HE DID NOT COME TO SAVE US.
ONLY ONE PERSON DID—MY ELDER BROTHER, SHAPUR. HE WAS SIXTEEN YEARS OF AGE WHEN HE RACED UP THE WINTER MOUNTAINS TO COME TO OUR RESCUE.
WHEN HE FOUND US, HE CHASED OFF A PAIR OF WOLVES.
APPARENTLY, HE THOUGHT...
...THAT I HAD BEEN EATEN.
BUT BY MY SIDE LAY A HARE. THE WOLVES HAD SHARED IT WITH ME.
THAT IS HOW MY NICKNAME, *FARHĀDIN*—ONE RAISED BY WOLVES—ORIGINATED.

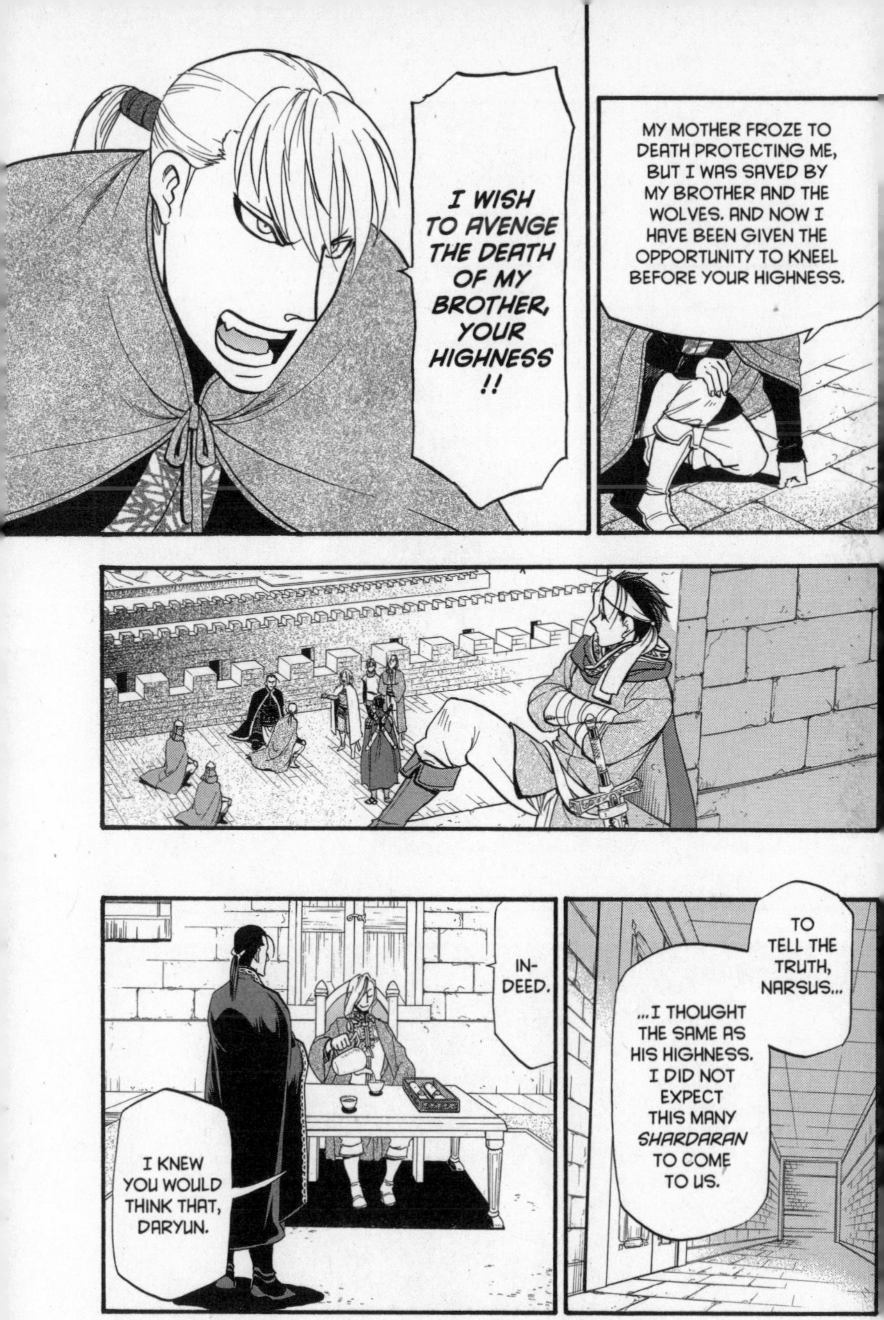
MY MOTHER FROZE TO DEATH PROTECTING ME, BUT I WAS SAVED BY MY BROTHER AND THE WOLVES. AND NOW I HAVE BEEN GIVEN THE OPPORTUNITY TO KNEEL BEFORE YOUR HIGHNESS.
I WISH TO AVENGE THE DEATH OF MY BROTHER, YOUR HIGHNESS!!
TO TELL THE TRUTH, NARSUS...
...I THOUGHT THE SAME AS HIS HIGHNESS. I DID NOT EXPECT THIS MANY SHARDARAN TO COME TO US.
IN-DEED.
I KNEW YOU WOULD THINK THAT, DARYUN.

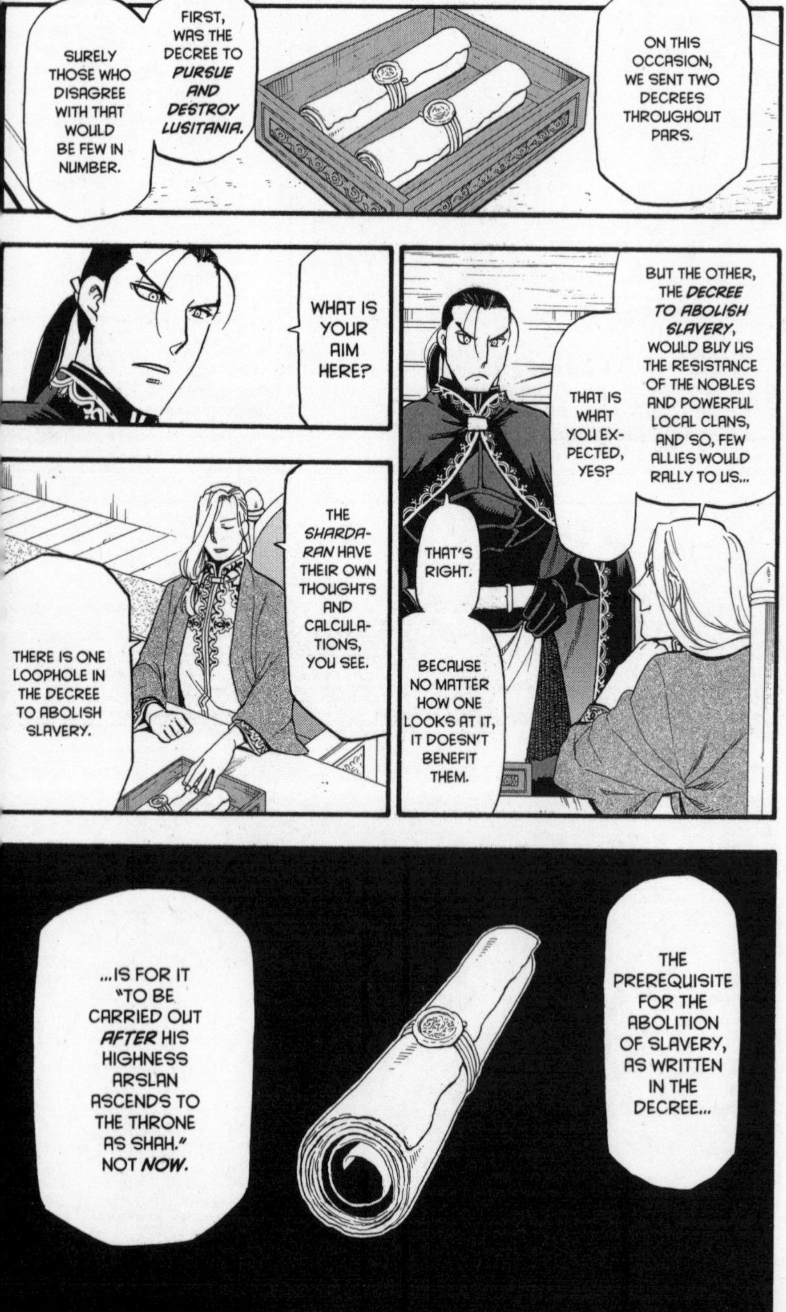
ON THIS OCCASION, WE SENT TWO DECREES THROUGHOUT PARS.
FIRST, WAS THE DECREE TO *PURSUE AND DESTROY LUSITANIA.*
SURELY THOSE WHO DISAGREE WITH THAT WOULD BE FEW IN NUMBER.
BUT THE OTHER, THE *DECREE TO ABOLISH SLAVERY*, WOULD BUY US THE RESISTANCE OF THE NOBLES AND POWERFUL LOCAL CLANS, AND SO, FEW ALLIES WOULD RALLY TO US...
THAT IS WHAT YOU EX-PECTED, YES?
THAT'S RIGHT.
BECAUSE NO MATTER HOW ONE LOOKS AT IT, IT DOESN'T BENEFIT THEM.
WHAT IS YOUR AIM HERE?
THE *SHARDA-RAN* HAVE THEIR OWN THOUGHTS AND CALCULA-TIONS, YOU SEE.
THERE IS ONE LOOPHOLE IN THE DECREE TO ABOLISH SLAVERY.
THE PREREQUISITE FOR THE ABOLITION OF SLAVERY, AS WRITTEN IN THE DECREE...
...IS FOR IT "TO BE CARRIED OUT *AFTER* HIS HIGHNESS ARSLAN ASCENDS TO THE THRONE AS SHAH." NOT *NOW*.

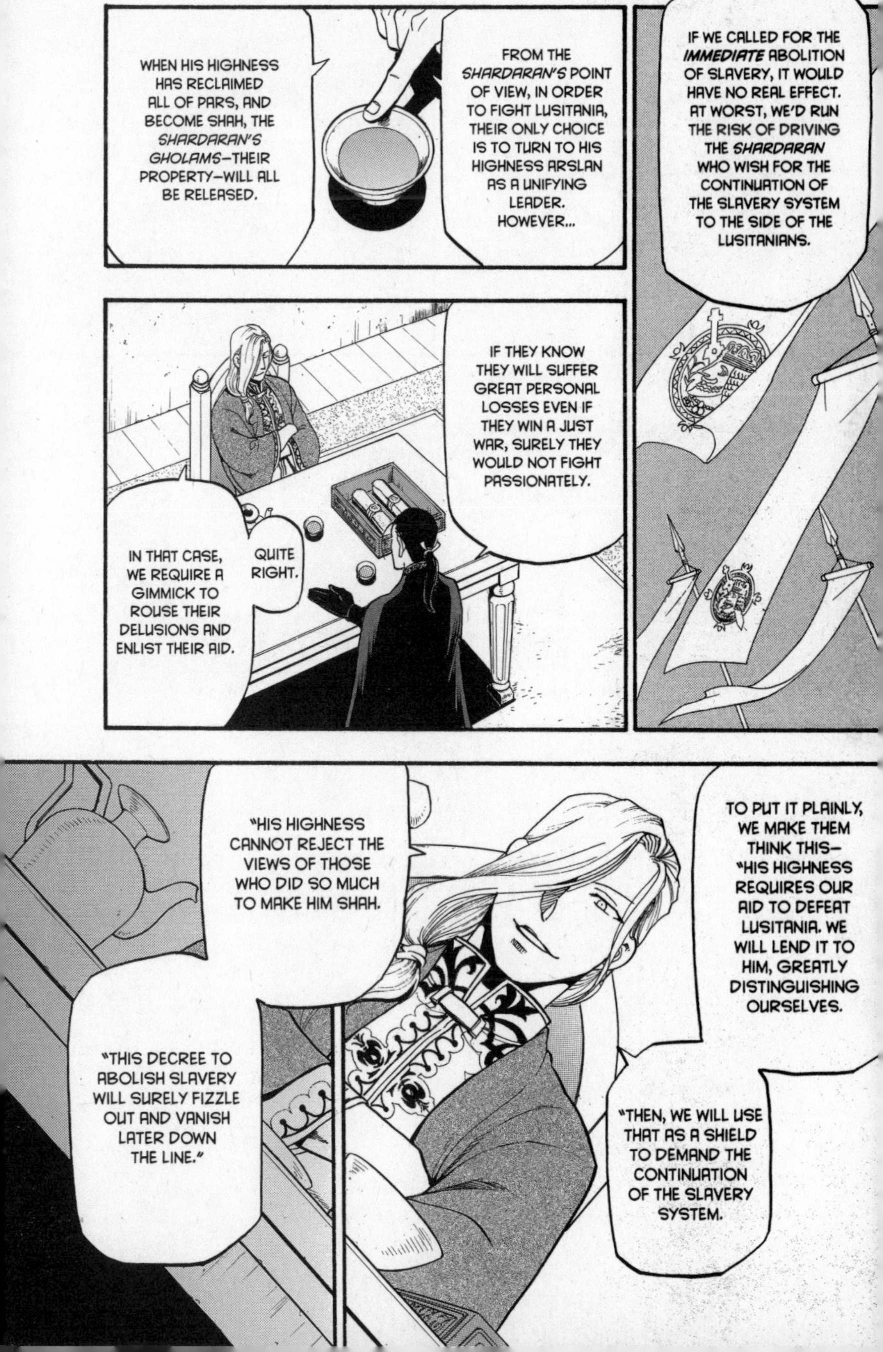
IF WE CALLED FOR THE *IMMEDIATE* ABOLITION OF SLAVERY, IT WOULD HAVE NO REAL EFFECT. AT WORST, WE'D RUN THE RISK OF DRIVING THE *SHARDARAN* WHO WISH FOR THE CONTINUATION OF THE SLAVERY SYSTEM TO THE SIDE OF THE LUSITANIANS.
FROM THE *SHARDARAN'S* POINT OF VIEW, IN ORDER TO FIGHT LUSITANIA, THEIR ONLY CHOICE IS TO TURN TO HIS HIGHNESS ARSLAN AS A UNIFYING LEADER. HOWEVER...
WHEN HIS HIGHNESS HAS RECLAIMED ALL OF PARS, AND BECOME SHAH, THE *SHARDARAN'S GHOLAMS*—THEIR PROPERTY—WILL ALL BE RELEASED.
IF THEY KNOW THEY WILL SUFFER GREAT PERSONAL LOSSES EVEN IF THEY WIN A JUST WAR, SURELY THEY WOULD NOT FIGHT PASSIONATELY.
QUITE RIGHT.
IN THAT CASE, WE REQUIRE A GIMMICK TO ROUSE THEIR DELUSIONS AND ENLIST THEIR AID.
TO PUT IT PLAINLY, WE MAKE THEM THINK THIS— "HIS HIGHNESS REQUIRES OUR AID TO DEFEAT LUSITANIA. WE WILL LEND IT TO HIM, GREATLY DISTINGUISHING OURSELVES.
"HIS HIGHNESS CANNOT REJECT THE VIEWS OF THOSE WHO DID SO MUCH TO MAKE HIM SHAH.
"THEN, WE WILL USE THAT AS A SHIELD TO DEMAND THE CONTINUATION OF THE SLAVERY SYSTEM.
"THIS DECREE TO ABOLISH SLAVERY WILL SURELY FIZZLE OUT AND VANISH LATER DOWN THE LINE."

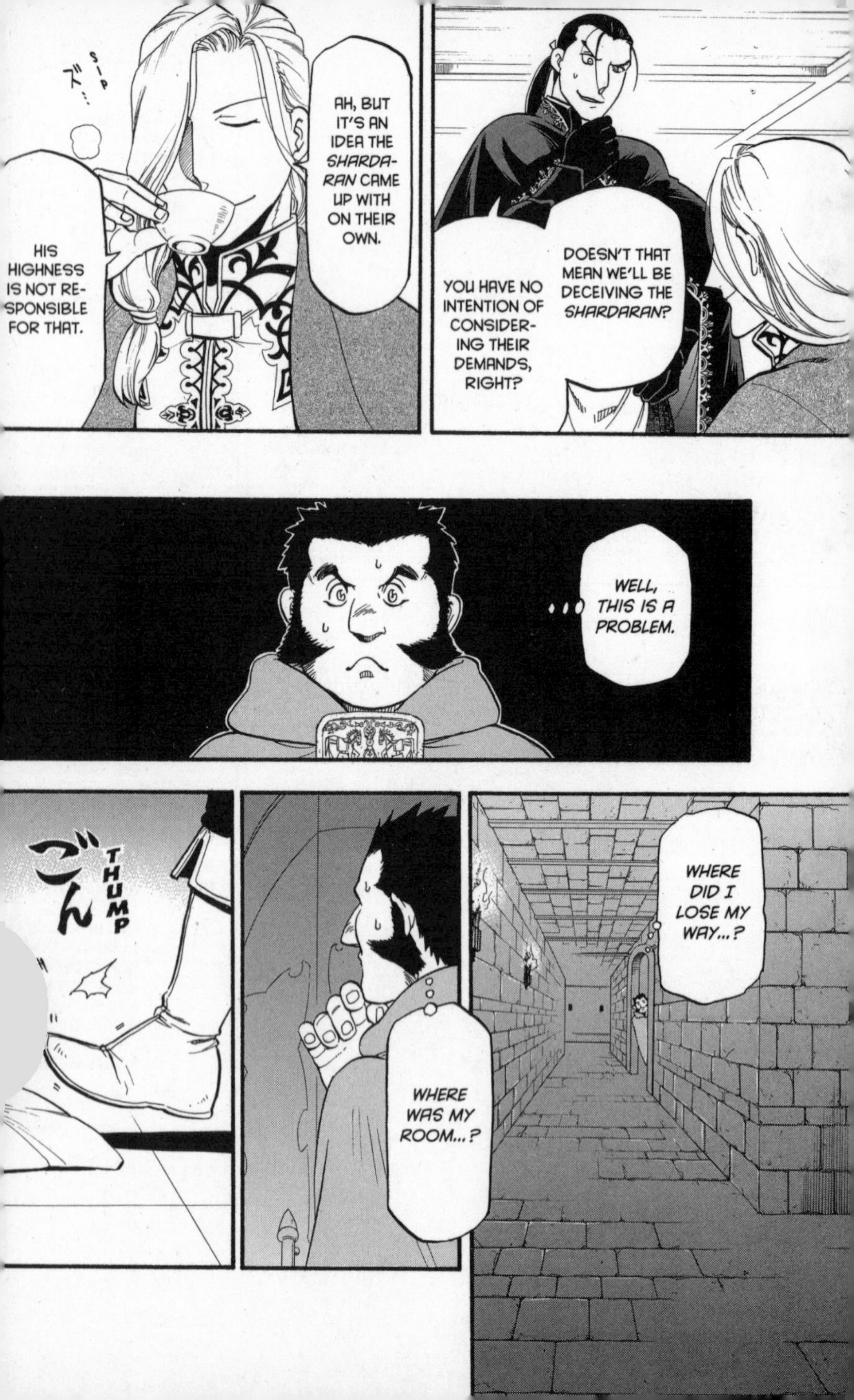
DOESN'T THAT MEAN WE'LL BE DECEIVING THE SHARDARAN?
YOU HAVE NO INTENTION OF CONSIDER-ING THEIR DEMANDS, RIGHT?
AH, BUT IT'S AN IDEA THE SHARDA-RAN CAME UP WITH ON THEIR OWN.
HIS HIGHNESS IS NOT RE-SPONSIBLE FOR THAT.
ズ… SIP
...WELL, THIS IS A PROBLEM.
WHERE DID I LOSE MY WAY...?
WHERE WAS MY ROOM...?
ごん THUMP

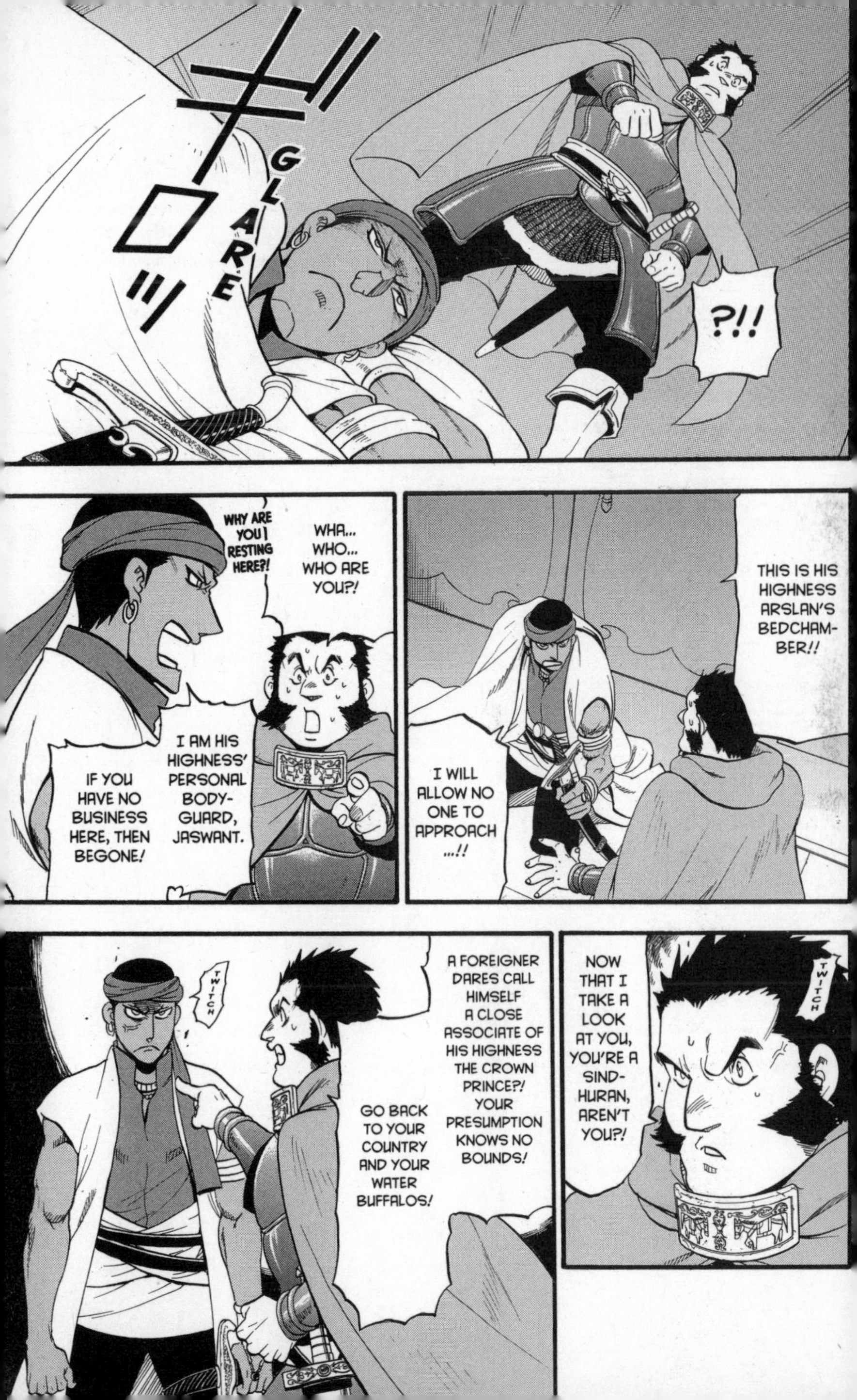
?!!
GLARE
THIS IS HIS HIGHNESS ARSLAN'S BEDCHAMBER!!
I WILL ALLOW NO ONE TO APPROACH ...!!
WHA... WHO... WHO ARE YOU?!
WHY ARE YOU RESTING HERE?!
I AM HIS HIGHNESS' PERSONAL BODYGUARD, JASWANT.
IF YOU HAVE NO BUSINESS HERE, THEN BEGONE!
TWITCH
NOW THAT I TAKE A LOOK AT YOU, YOU'RE A SINDHURAN, AREN'T YOU?!
A FOREIGNER DARES CALL HIMSELF A CLOSE ASSOCIATE OF HIS HIGHNESS THE CROWN PRINCE?! YOUR PRESUMPTION KNOWS NO BOUNDS!
GO BACK TO YOUR COUNTRY AND YOUR WATER BUFFALOS!
TWITCH

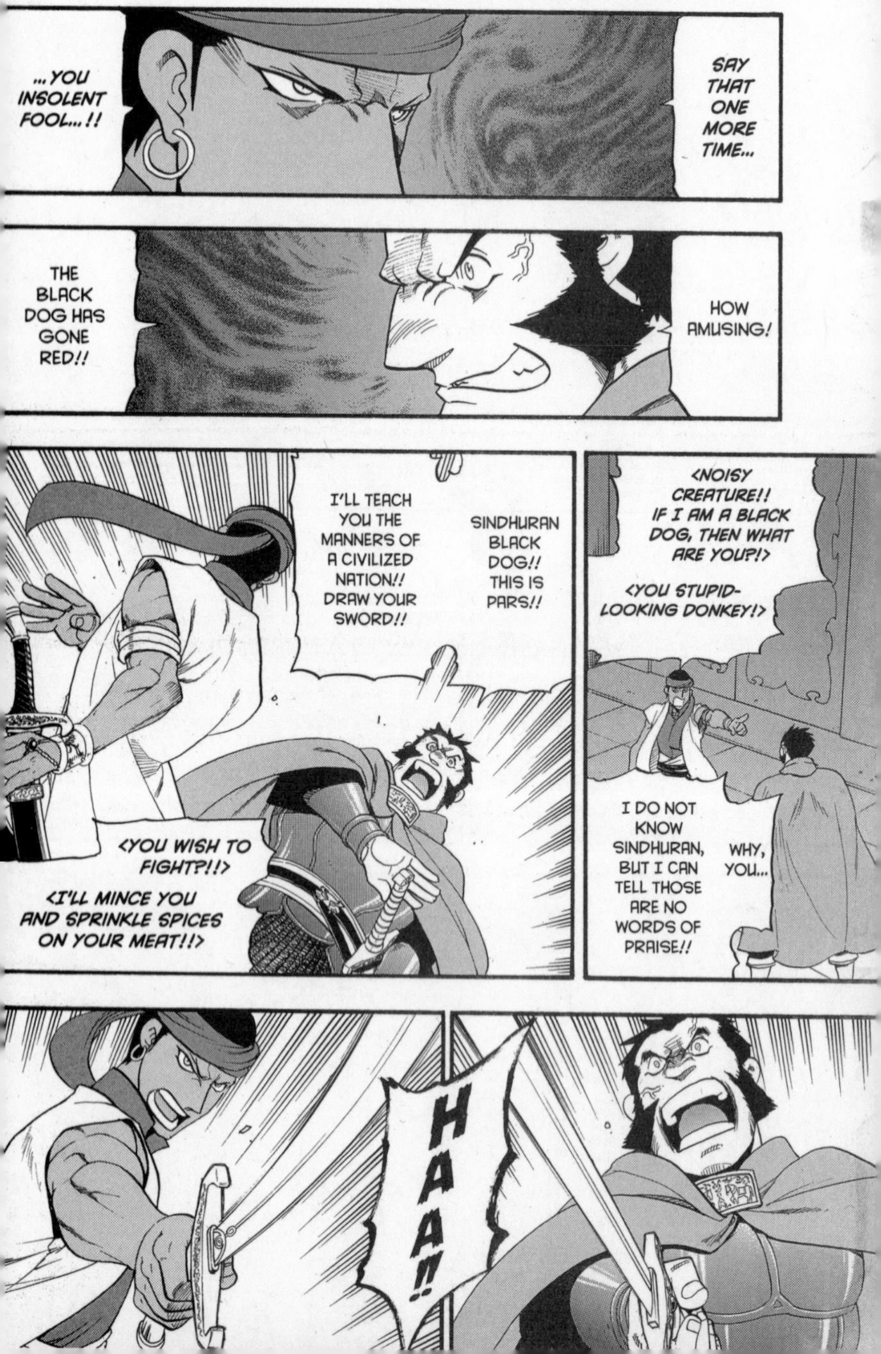

SAY THAT ONE MORE TIME...
...YOU INSOLENT FOOL...!!
HOW AMUSING!
THE BLACK DOG HAS GONE RED!!
<NOISY CREATURE!! IF I AM A BLACK DOG, THEN WHAT ARE YOU?!>
<YOU STUPID-LOOKING DONKEY!>
WHY, YOU...
I DO NOT KNOW SINDHURAN, BUT I CAN TELL THOSE ARE NO WORDS OF PRAISE!!
SINDHURAN BLACK DOG!! THIS IS PARS!!
I'LL TEACH YOU THE MANNERS OF A CIVILIZED NATION!! DRAW YOUR SWORD!!
<YOU WISH TO FIGHT?!!>
<I'LL MINCE YOU AND SPRINKLE SPICES ON YOUR MEAT!!>
HAAA!!

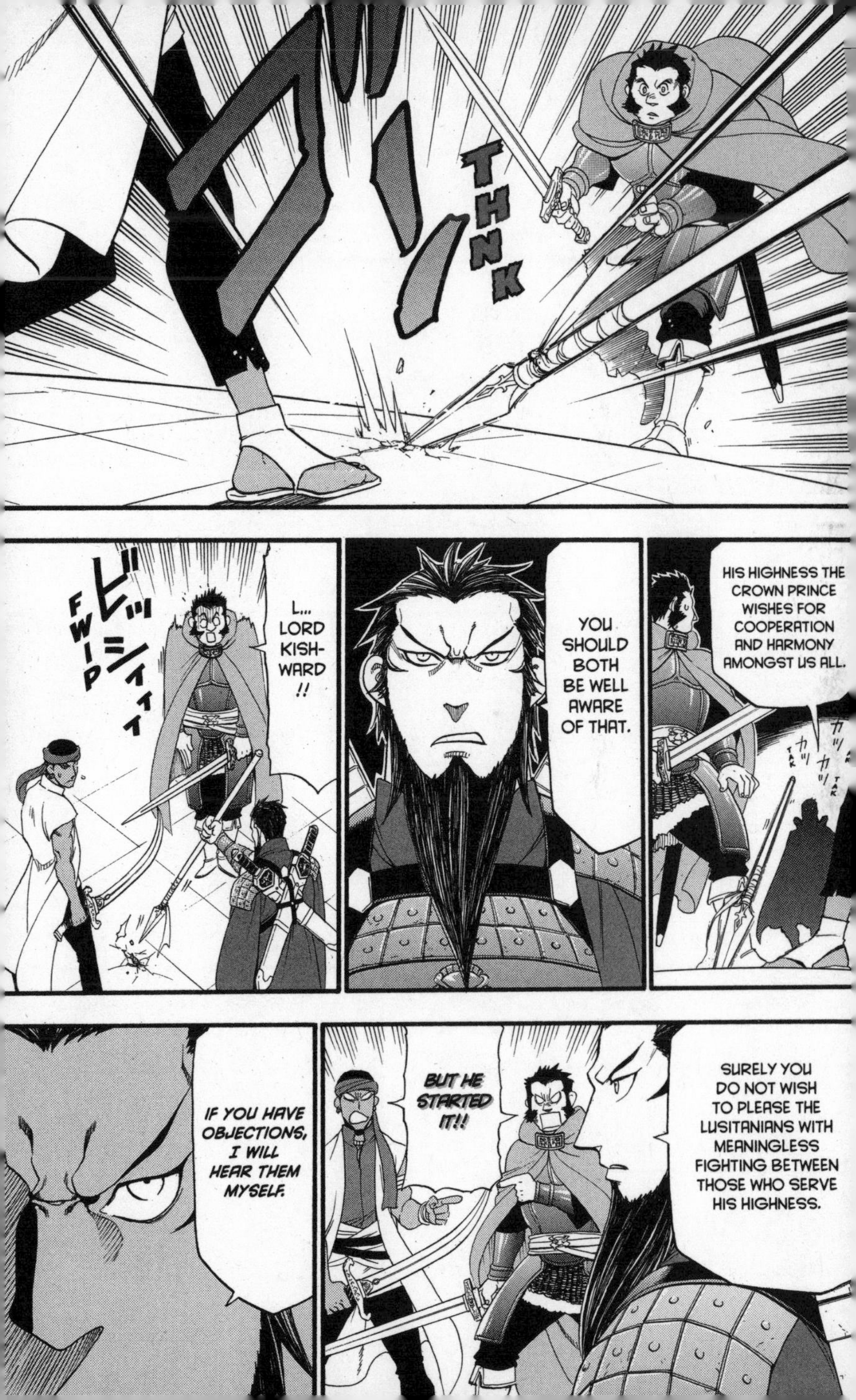
THNK
HIS HIGHNESS THE CROWN PRINCE WISHES FOR COOPERATION AND HARMONY AMONGST US ALL.
TAK
TAK
YOU SHOULD BOTH BE WELL AWARE OF THAT.
L... LORD KISHWARD!!
FWIP
SURELY YOU DO NOT WISH TO PLEASE THE LUSITANIANS WITH MEANINGLESS FIGHTING BETWEEN THOSE WHO SERVE HIS HIGHNESS.
BUT HE STARTED IT!!
IF YOU HAVE OBJECTIONS, I WILL HEAR THEM MYSELF.

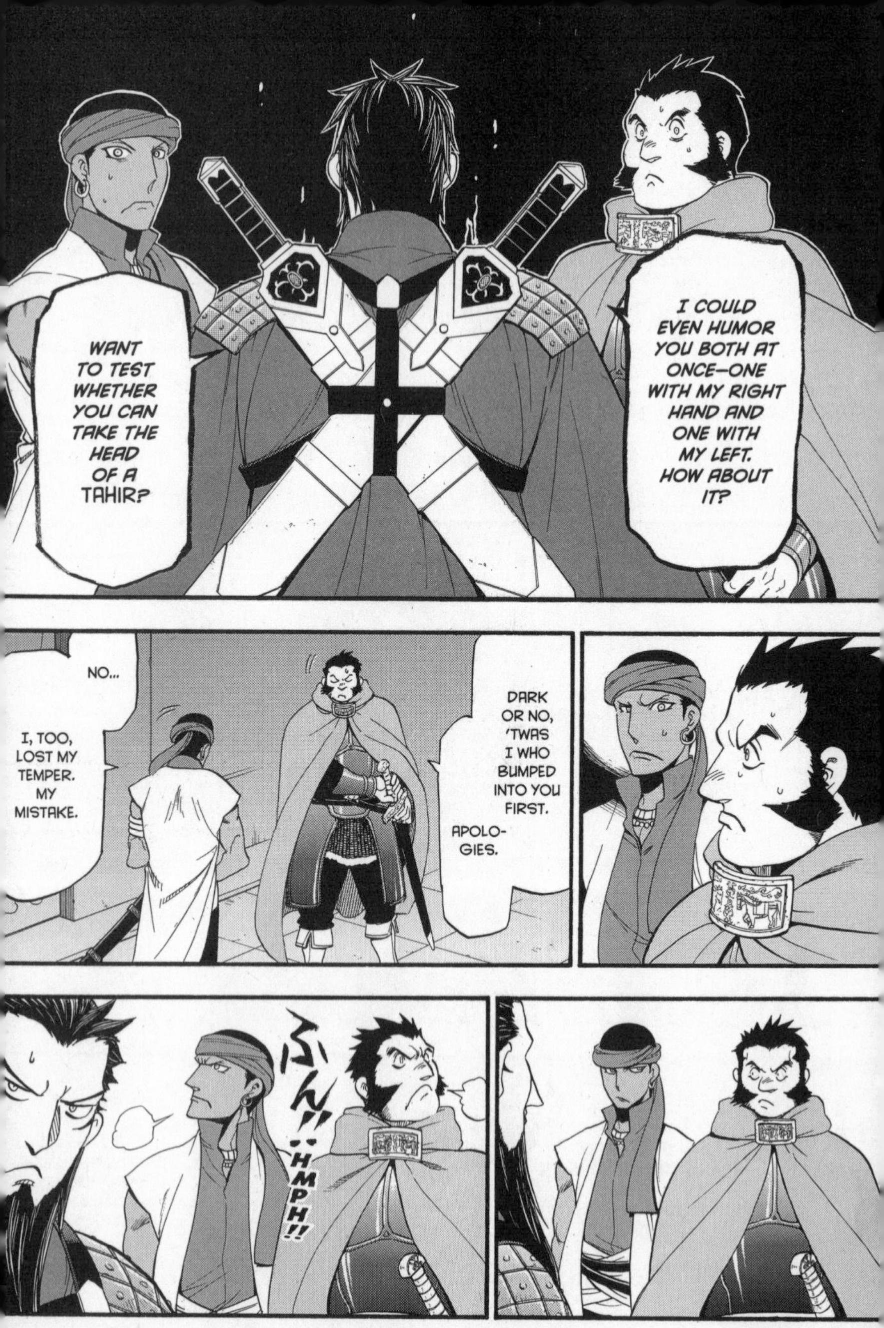
I COULD EVEN HUMOR YOU BOTH AT ONCE—ONE WITH MY RIGHT HAND AND ONE WITH MY LEFT. HOW ABOUT IT?
WANT TO TEST WHETHER YOU CAN TAKE THE HEAD OF A TAHIR?
DARK OR NO, 'TWAS I WHO BUMPED INTO YOU FIRST.
APOLOGIES.
NO...
I, TOO, LOST MY TEMPER. MY MISTAKE.
ふん!!
HMPH!!

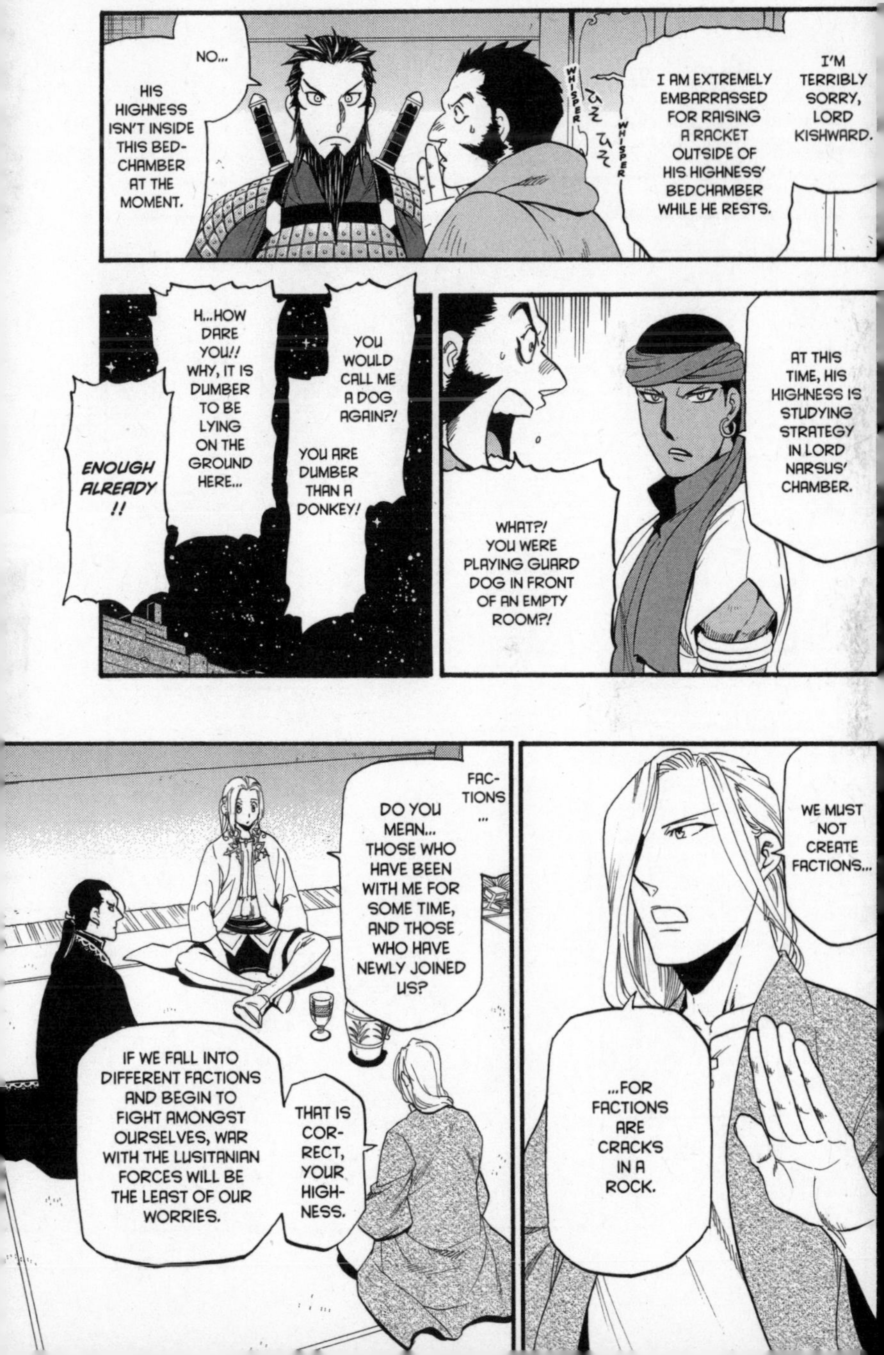
I'M TERRIBLY SORRY, LORD KISHWARD.
I AM EXTREMELY EMBARRASSED FOR RAISING A RACKET OUTSIDE OF HIS HIGHNESS' BEDCHAMBER WHILE HE RESTS.
WHISPER ひそ
WHISPER ひそ
NO...
HIS HIGHNESS ISN'T INSIDE THIS BED-CHAMBER AT THE MOMENT.
AT THIS TIME, HIS HIGHNESS IS STUDYING STRATEGY IN LORD NARSUS' CHAMBER.
WHAT?! YOU WERE PLAYING GUARD DOG IN FRONT OF AN EMPTY ROOM?!
YOU WOULD CALL ME A DOG AGAIN?!
YOU ARE DUMBER THAN A DONKEY!
H...HOW DARE YOU!! WHY, IT IS DUMBER TO BE LYING ON THE GROUND HERE...
ENOUGH ALREADY !!
WE MUST NOT CREATE FACTIONS...
...FOR FACTIONS ARE CRACKS IN A ROCK.
FAC-TIONS ...
DO YOU MEAN... THOSE WHO HAVE BEEN WITH ME FOR SOME TIME, AND THOSE WHO HAVE NEWLY JOINED US?
THAT IS COR-RECT, YOUR HIGH-NESS.
IF WE FALL INTO DIFFERENT FACTIONS AND BEGIN TO FIGHT AMONGST OURSELVES, WAR WITH THE LUSITANIAN FORCES WILL BE THE LEAST OF OUR WORRIES.

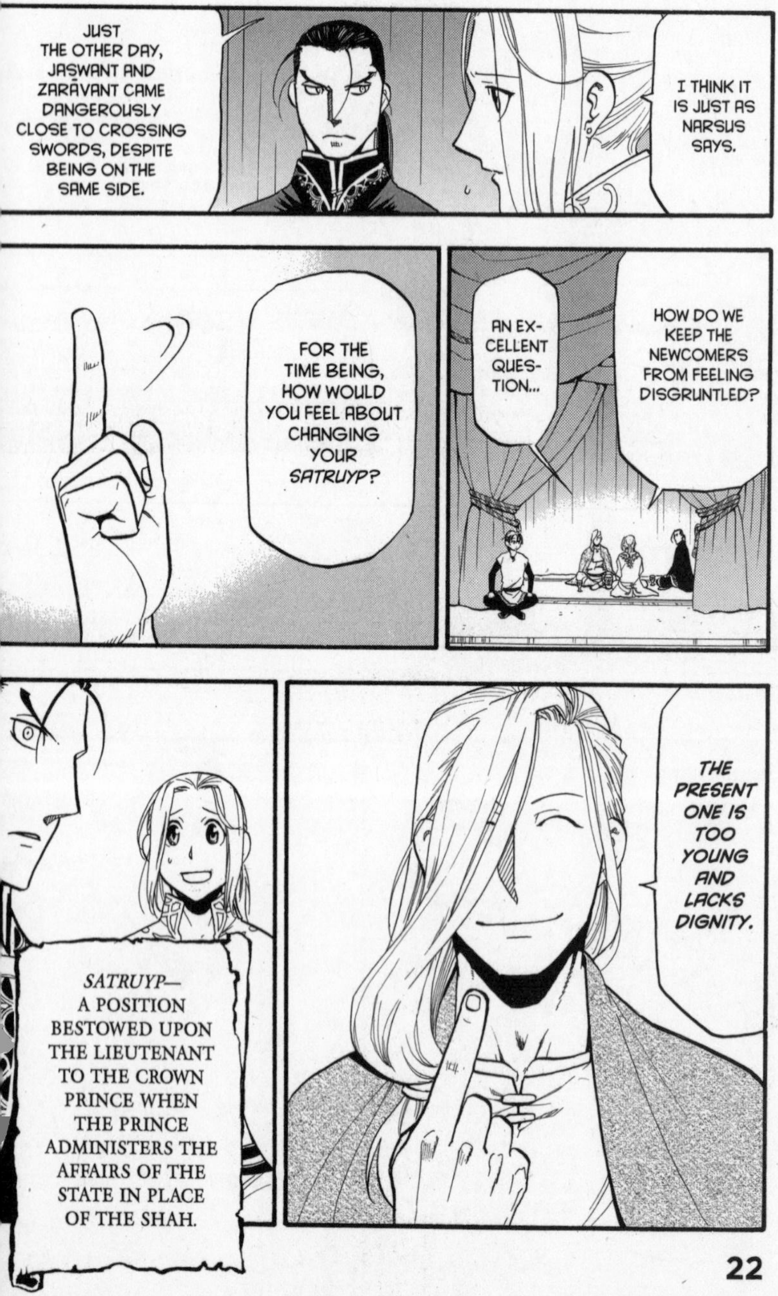
I THINK IT IS JUST AS NARSUS SAYS.
JUST THE OTHER DAY, JASWANT AND ZARĀVANT CAME DANGEROUSLY CLOSE TO CROSSING SWORDS, DESPITE BEING ON THE SAME SIDE.
HOW DO WE KEEP THE NEWCOMERS FROM FEELING DISGRUNTLED?
AN EX-CELLENT QUES-TION...
FOR THE TIME BEING, HOW WOULD YOU FEEL ABOUT CHANGING YOUR *SATRUYP*?
THE PRESENT ONE IS TOO YOUNG AND LACKS DIGNITY.
SATRUYP—A POSITION BESTOWED UPON THE LIEUTENANT TO THE CROWN PRINCE WHEN THE PRINCE ADMINISTERS THE AFFAIRS OF THE STATE IN PLACE OF THE SHAH.

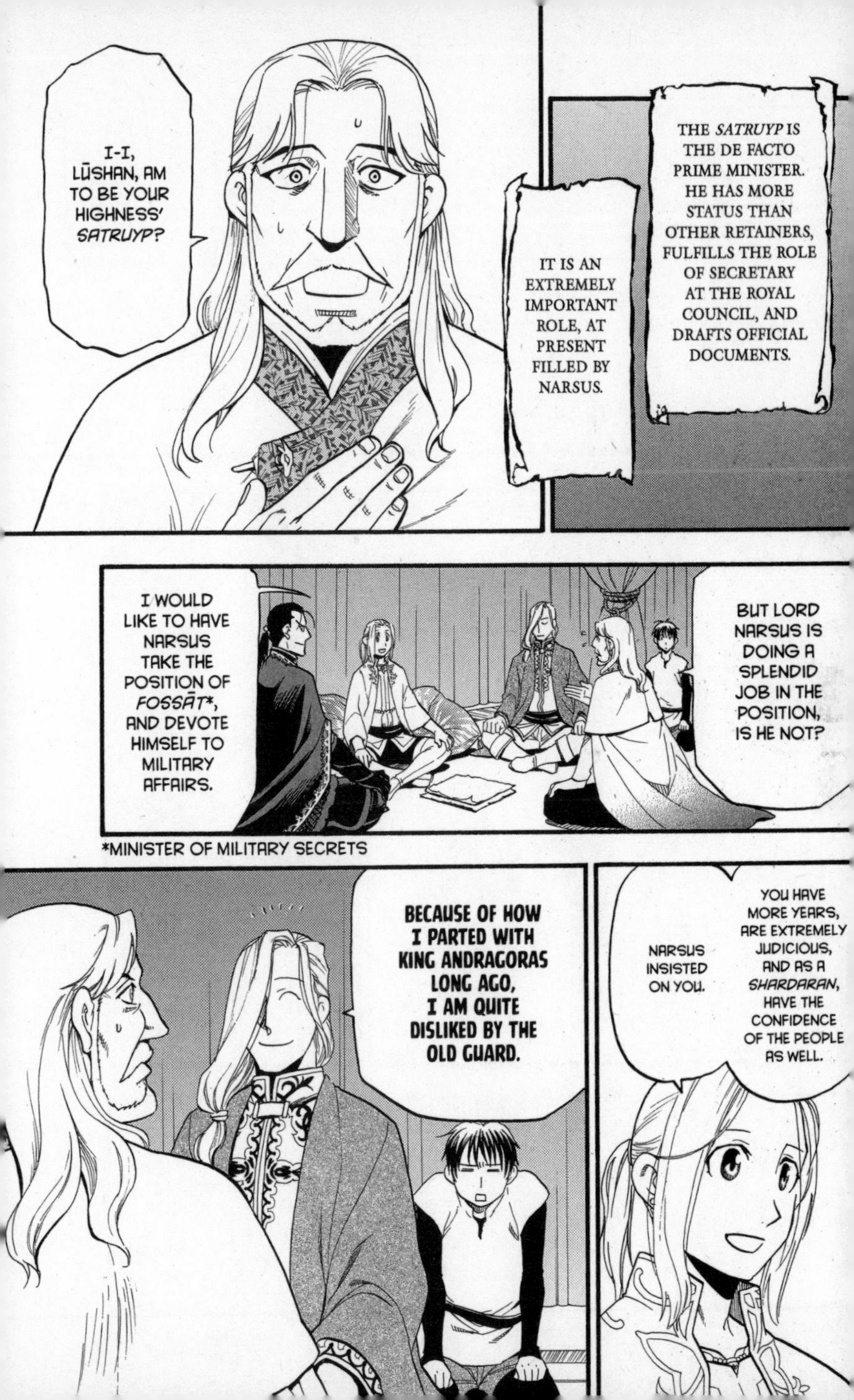
THE *SATRUYP* IS THE DE FACTO PRIME MINISTER. HE HAS MORE STATUS THAN OTHER RETAINERS, FULFILLS THE ROLE OF SECRETARY AT THE ROYAL COUNCIL, AND DRAFTS OFFICIAL DOCUMENTS.
IT IS AN EXTREMELY IMPORTANT ROLE, AT PRESENT FILLED BY NARSUS.
I-I, LŪSHAN, AM TO BE YOUR HIGHNESS' *SATRUYP*?
BUT LORD NARSUS IS DOING A SPLENDID JOB IN THE POSITION, IS HE NOT?
I WOULD LIKE TO HAVE NARSUS TAKE THE POSITION OF *FOSSĀT**, AND DEVOTE HIMSELF TO MILITARY AFFAIRS.
*MINISTER OF MILITARY SECRETS
YOU HAVE MORE YEARS, ARE EXTREMELY JUDICIOUS, AND AS A *SHARDARAN*, HAVE THE CONFIDENCE OF THE PEOPLE AS WELL.
NARSUS INSISTED ON YOU.
BECAUSE OF HOW I PARTED WITH KING ANDRAGORAS LONG AGO, I AM QUITE DISLIKED BY THE OLD GUARD.

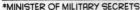

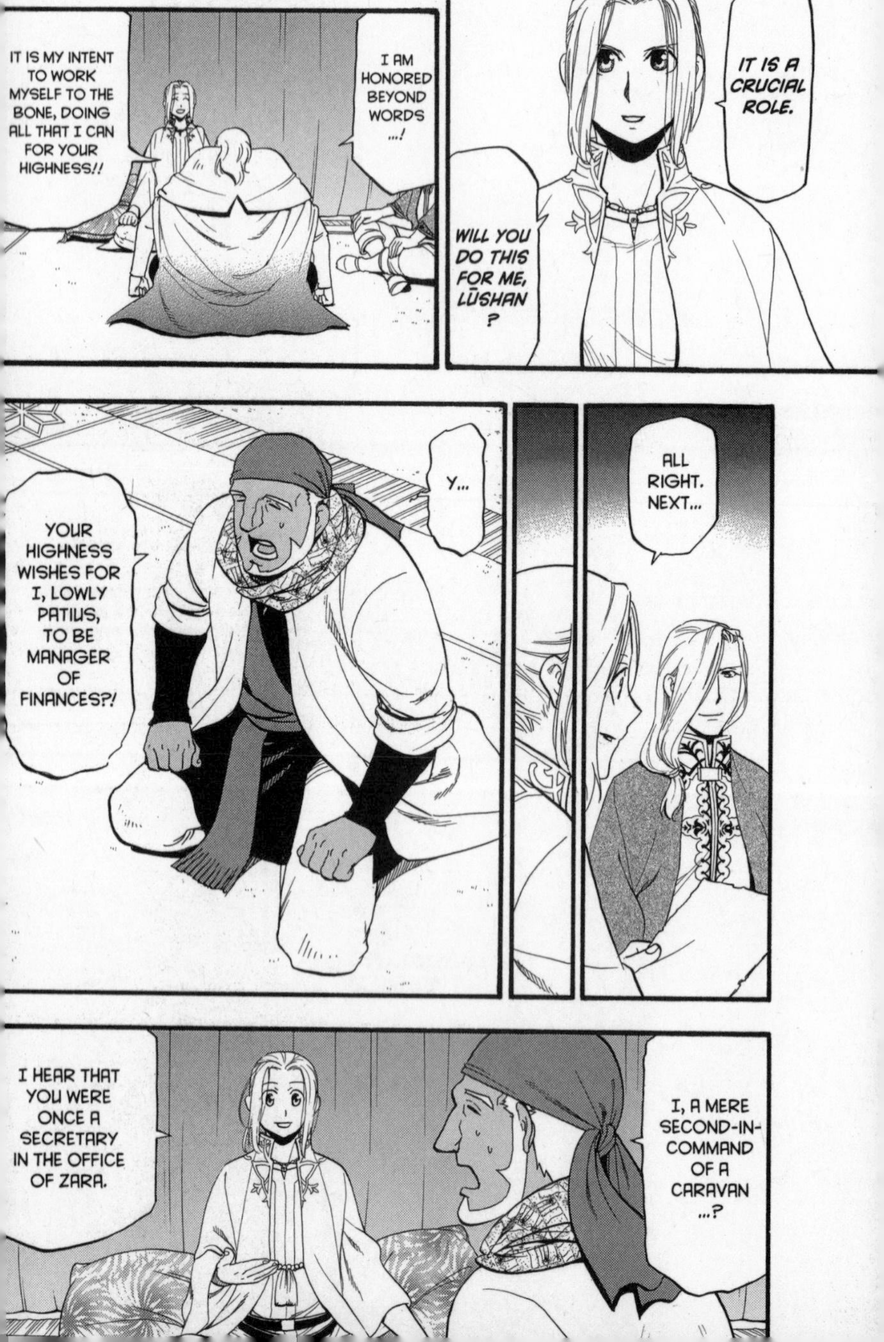
IT IS A CRUCIAL ROLE.
WILL YOU DO THIS FOR ME, LŪSHAN?
I AM HONORED BEYOND WORDS ...!
IT IS MY INTENT TO WORK MYSELF TO THE BONE, DOING ALL THAT I CAN FOR YOUR HIGHNESS!!
ALL RIGHT. NEXT...
Y...
YOUR HIGHNESS WISHES FOR I, LOWLY PATIUS, TO BE MANAGER OF FINANCES?!
I, A MERE SECOND-IN-COMMAND OF A CARAVAN ...?
I HEAR THAT YOU WERE ONCE A SECRETARY IN THE OFFICE OF ZARA.

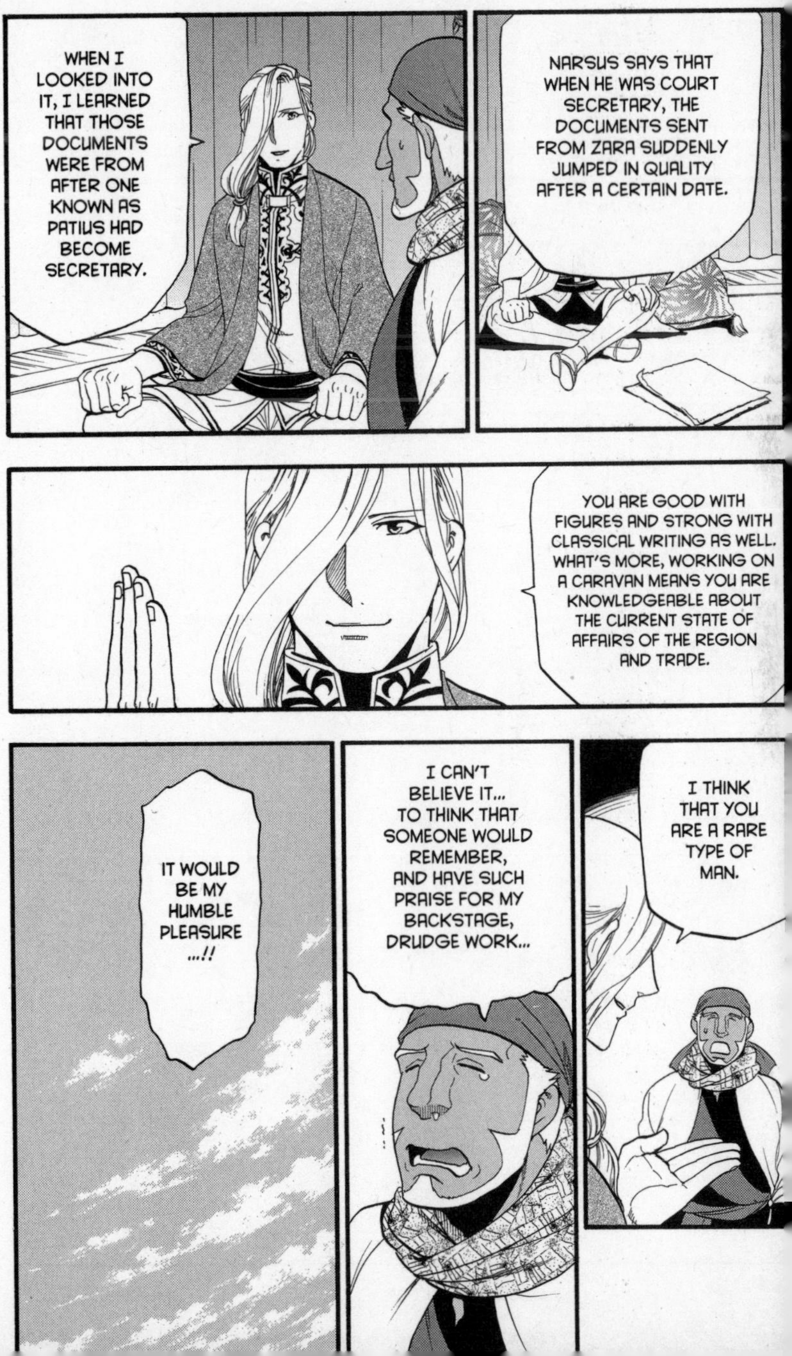
NARSUS SAYS THAT WHEN HE WAS COURT SECRETARY, THE DOCUMENTS SENT FROM ZARA SUDDENLY JUMPED IN QUALITY AFTER A CERTAIN DATE.
WHEN I LOOKED INTO IT, I LEARNED THAT THOSE DOCUMENTS WERE FROM AFTER ONE KNOWN AS PATIUS HAD BECOME SECRETARY.
YOU ARE GOOD WITH FIGURES AND STRONG WITH CLASSICAL WRITING AS WELL. WHAT'S MORE, WORKING ON A CARAVAN MEANS YOU ARE KNOWLEDGEABLE ABOUT THE CURRENT STATE OF AFFAIRS OF THE REGION AND TRADE.
I THINK THAT YOU ARE A RARE TYPE OF MAN.
I CAN'T BELIEVE IT... TO THINK THAT SOMEONE WOULD REMEMBER, AND HAVE SUCH PRAISE FOR MY BACKSTAGE, DRUDGE WORK...
IT WOULD BE MY HUMBLE PLEASURE ...!!

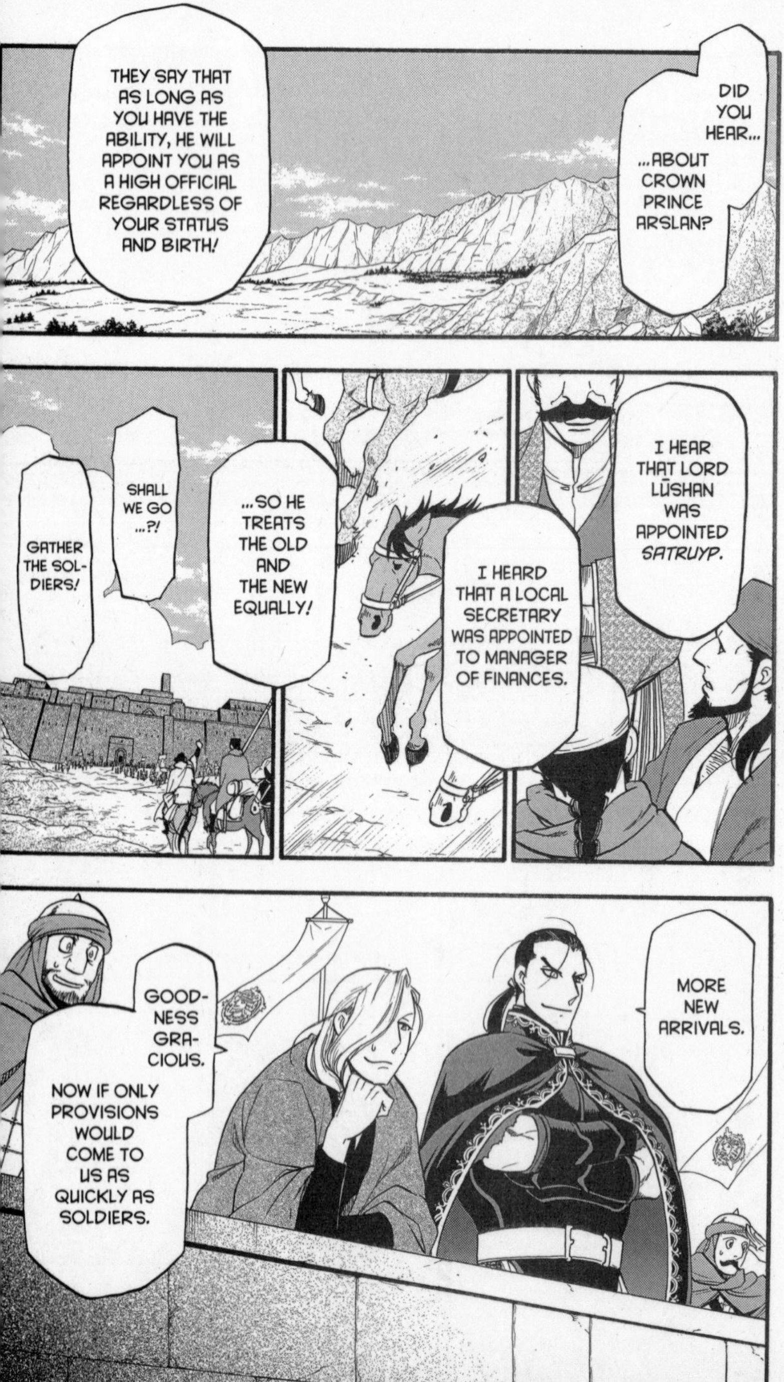
DID YOU HEAR...
...ABOUT CROWN PRINCE ARSLAN?
THEY SAY THAT AS LONG AS YOU HAVE THE ABILITY, HE WILL APPOINT YOU AS A HIGH OFFICIAL REGARDLESS OF YOUR STATUS AND BIRTH!
I HEAR THAT LORD LŪSHAN WAS APPOINTED *SATRUYP*.
I HEARD THAT A LOCAL SECRETARY WAS APPOINTED TO MANAGER OF FINANCES.
...SO HE TREATS THE OLD AND THE NEW EQUALLY!
SHALL WE GO ...?!
GATHER THE SOLDIERS!
MORE NEW ARRIVALS.
GOODNESS GRACIOUS.
NOW IF ONLY PROVISIONS WOULD COME TO US AS QUICKLY AS SOLDIERS.

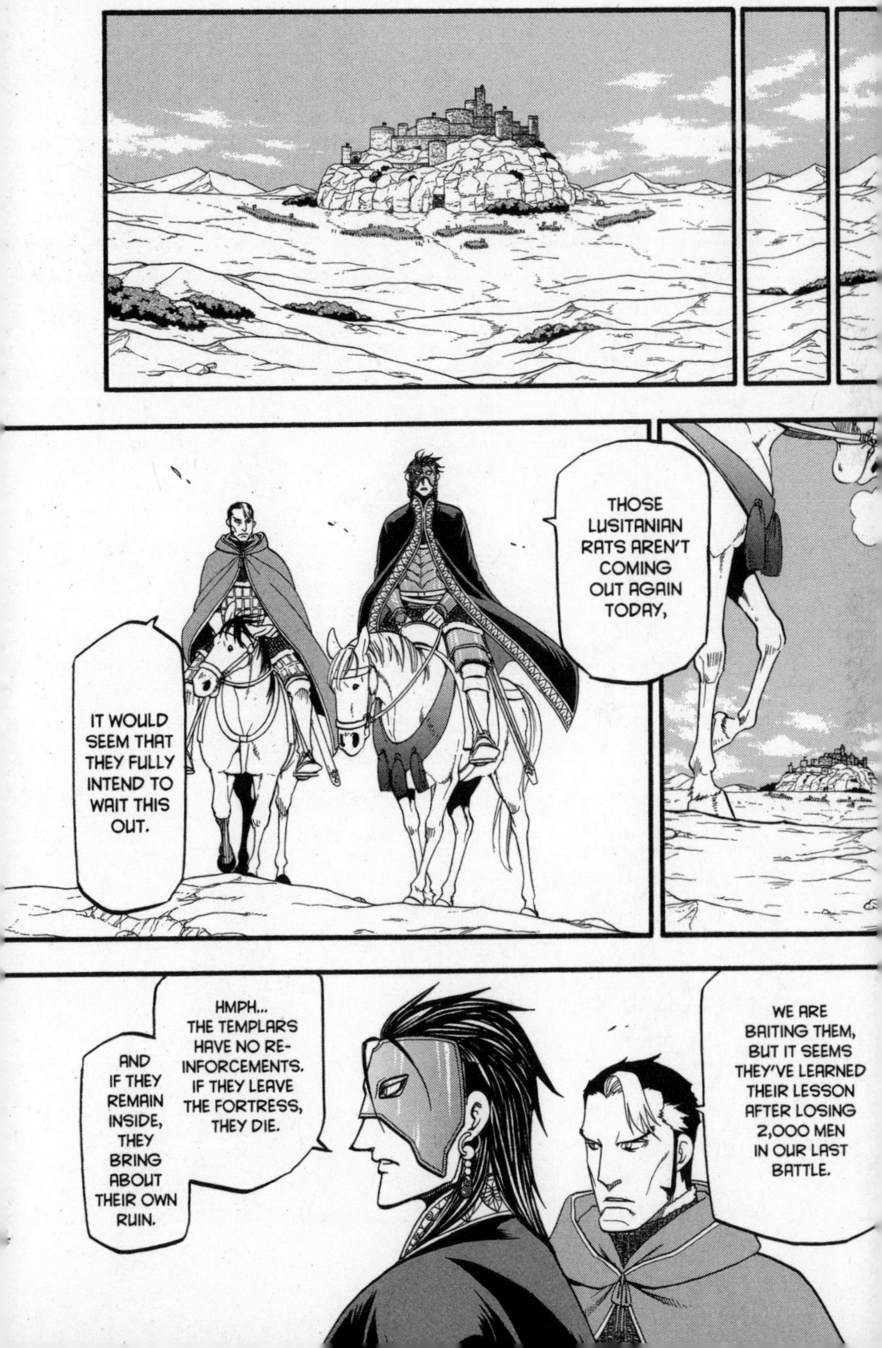
THOSE LUSITANIAN RATS AREN'T COMING OUT AGAIN TODAY,
IT WOULD SEEM THAT THEY FULLY INTEND TO WAIT THIS OUT.
WE ARE BAITING THEM, BUT IT SEEMS THEY'VE LEARNED THEIR LESSON AFTER LOSING 2,000 MEN IN OUR LAST BATTLE.
HMPH... THE TEMPLARS HAVE NO RE-INFORCEMENTS. IF THEY LEAVE THE FORTRESS, THEY DIE.
AND IF THEY REMAIN INSIDE, THEY BRING ABOUT THEIR OWN RUIN.

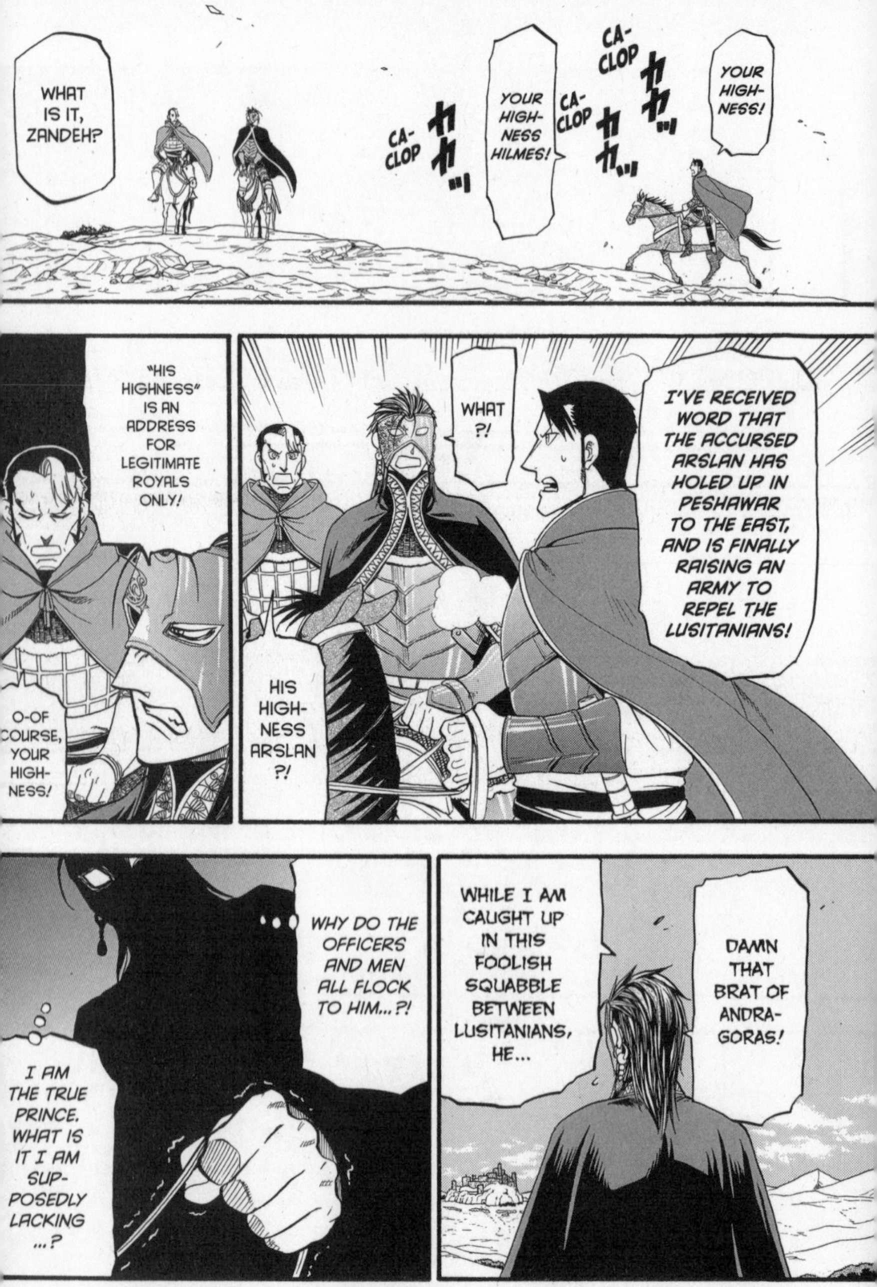
CA-CLOP
YOUR HIGHNESS!
CA-CLOP
YOUR HIGHNESS HILMES!
CA-CLOP
WHAT IS IT, ZANDEH?
I'VE RECEIVED WORD THAT THE ACCURSED ARSLAN HAS HOLED UP IN PESHAWAR TO THE EAST, AND IS FINALLY RAISING AN ARMY TO REPEL THE LUSITANIANS!
WHAT ?!
HIS HIGHNESS ARSLAN ?!
"HIS HIGHNESS" IS AN ADDRESS FOR LEGITIMATE ROYALS ONLY!
O-OF COURSE, YOUR HIGHNESS!
DAMN THAT BRAT OF ANDRAGORAS!
WHILE I AM CAUGHT UP IN THIS FOOLISH SQUABBLE BETWEEN LUSITANIANS, HE...
WHY DO THE OFFICERS AND MEN ALL FLOCK TO HIM...?!
I AM THE TRUE PRINCE. WHAT IS IT I AM SUPPOSEDLY LACKING ...?

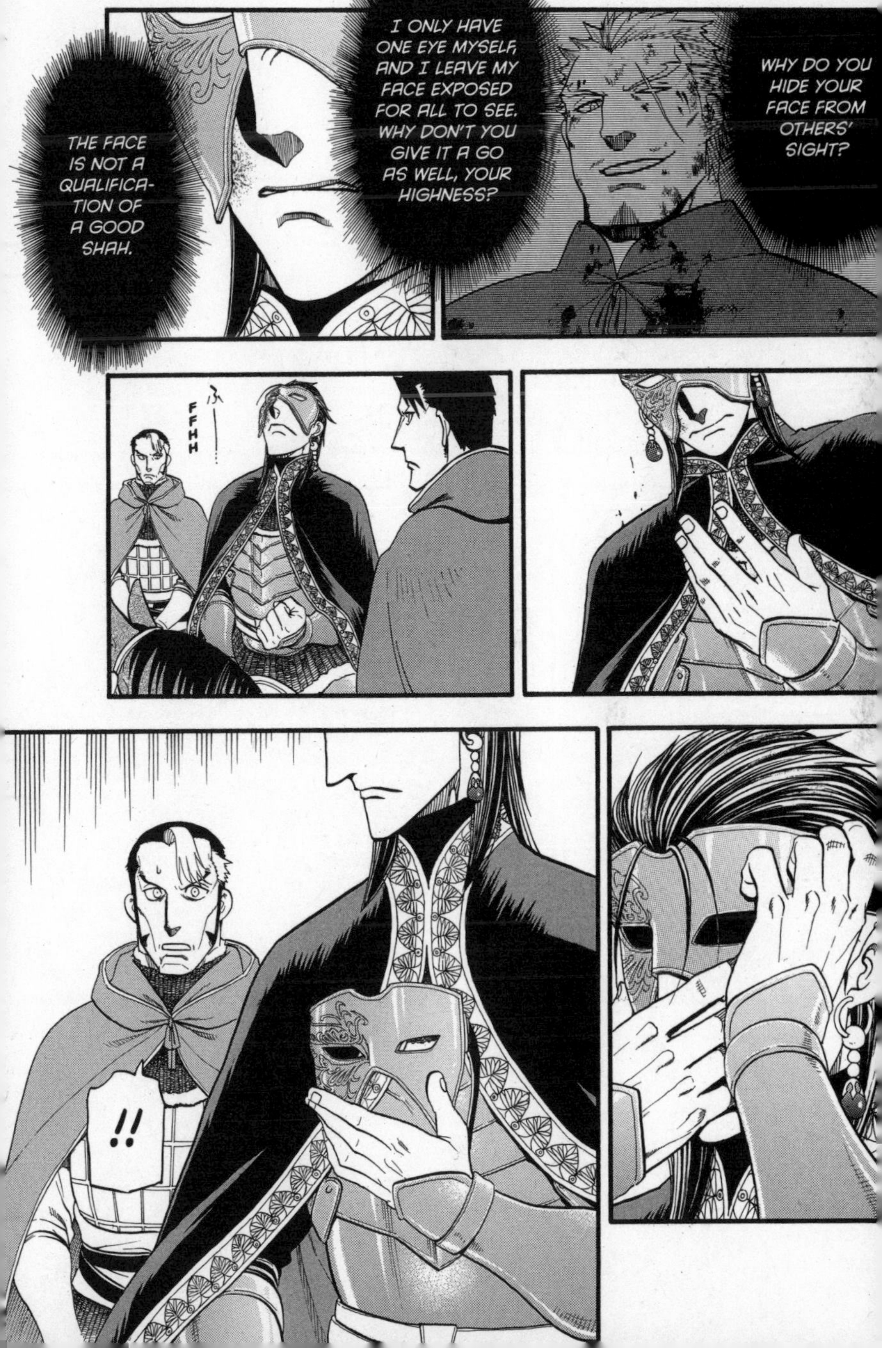
WHY DO YOU HIDE YOUR FACE FROM OTHERS' SIGHT?
I ONLY HAVE ONE EYE MYSELF, AND I LEAVE MY FACE EXPOSED FOR ALL TO SEE. WHY DON'T YOU GIVE IT A GO AS WELL, YOUR HIGHNESS?
THE FACE IS NOT A QUALIFICATION OF A GOOD SHAH.
!
FFHH
!!

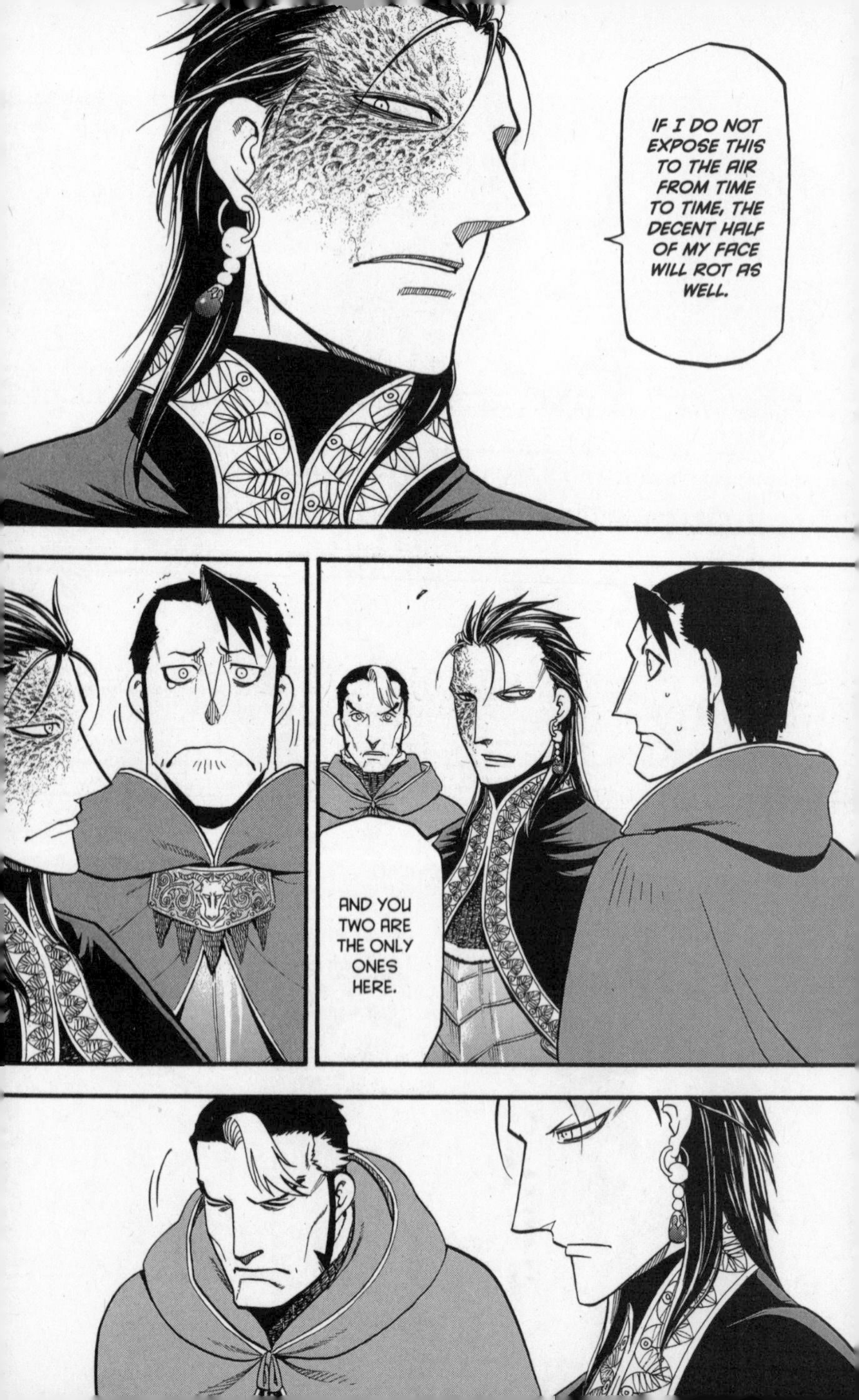
IF I DO NOT EXPOSE THIS TO THE AIR FROM TIME TO TIME, THE DECENT HALF OF MY FACE WILL ROT AS WELL.
AND YOU TWO ARE THE ONLY ONES HERE.

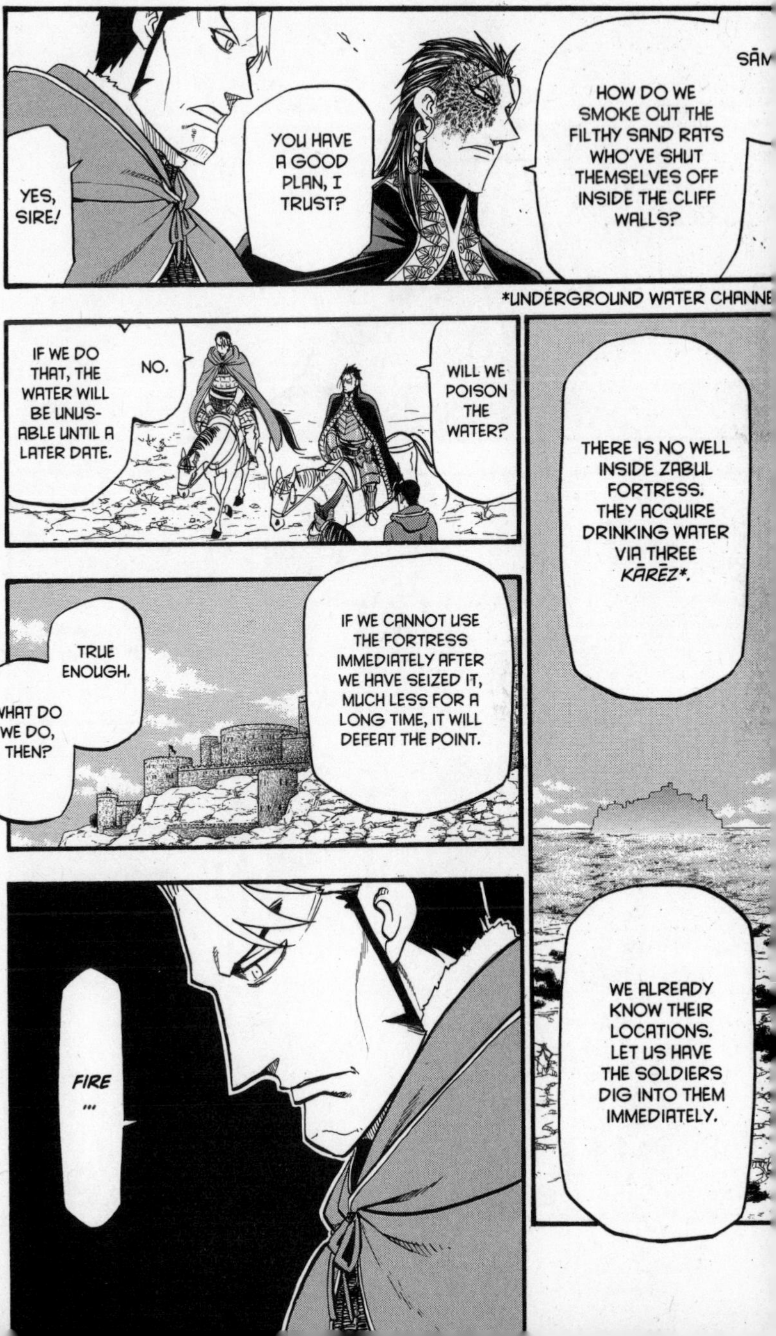
HOW DO WE SMOKE OUT THE FILTHY SAND RATS WHO'VE SHUT THEMSELVES OFF INSIDE THE CLIFF WALLS?
YOU HAVE A GOOD PLAN, I TRUST?
YES, SIRE!
THERE IS NO WELL INSIDE ZABUL FORTRESS. THEY ACQUIRE DRINKING WATER VIA THREE *KĀRĒZ**.
WE ALREADY KNOW THEIR LOCATIONS. LET US HAVE THE SOLDIERS DIG INTO THEM IMMEDIATELY.
WILL WE POISON THE WATER?
NO.
IF WE DO THAT, THE WATER WILL BE UNUSABLE UNTIL A LATER DATE.
IF WE CANNOT USE THE FORTRESS IMMEDIATELY AFTER WE HAVE SEIZED IT, MUCH LESS FOR A LONG TIME, IT WILL DEFEAT THE POINT.
TRUE ENOUGH.
WHAT DO WE DO, THEN?
FIRE ...

*UNDERGROUND WATER CHANNE

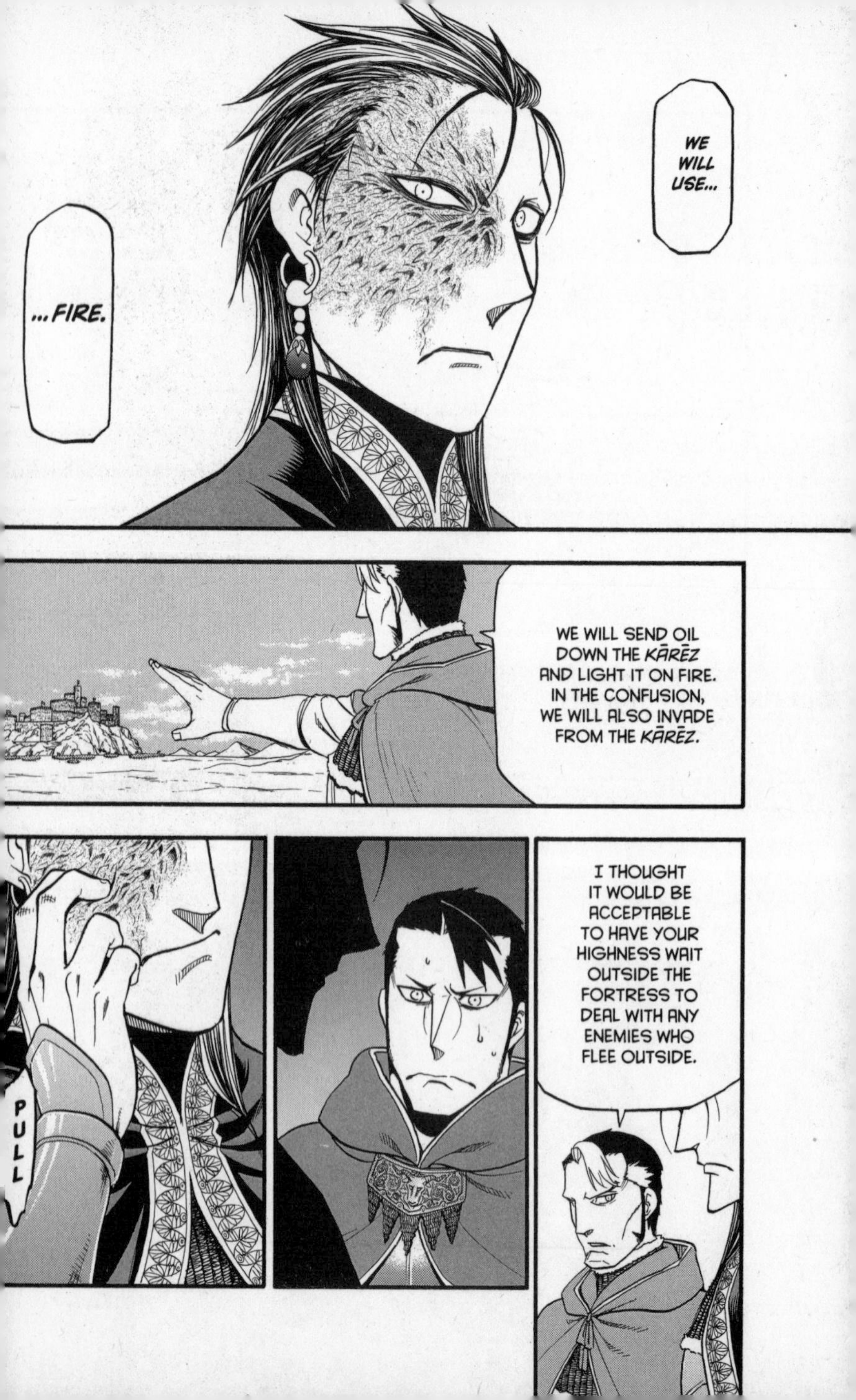

WE WILL USE...
...FIRE.
WE WILL SEND OIL DOWN THE *KĀRĒZ* AND LIGHT IT ON FIRE. IN THE CONFUSION, WE WILL ALSO INVADE FROM THE *KĀRĒZ*.
I THOUGHT IT WOULD BE ACCEPTABLE TO HAVE YOUR HIGHNESS WAIT OUTSIDE THE FORTRESS TO DEAL WITH ANY ENEMIES WHO FLEE OUTSIDE.
PULL

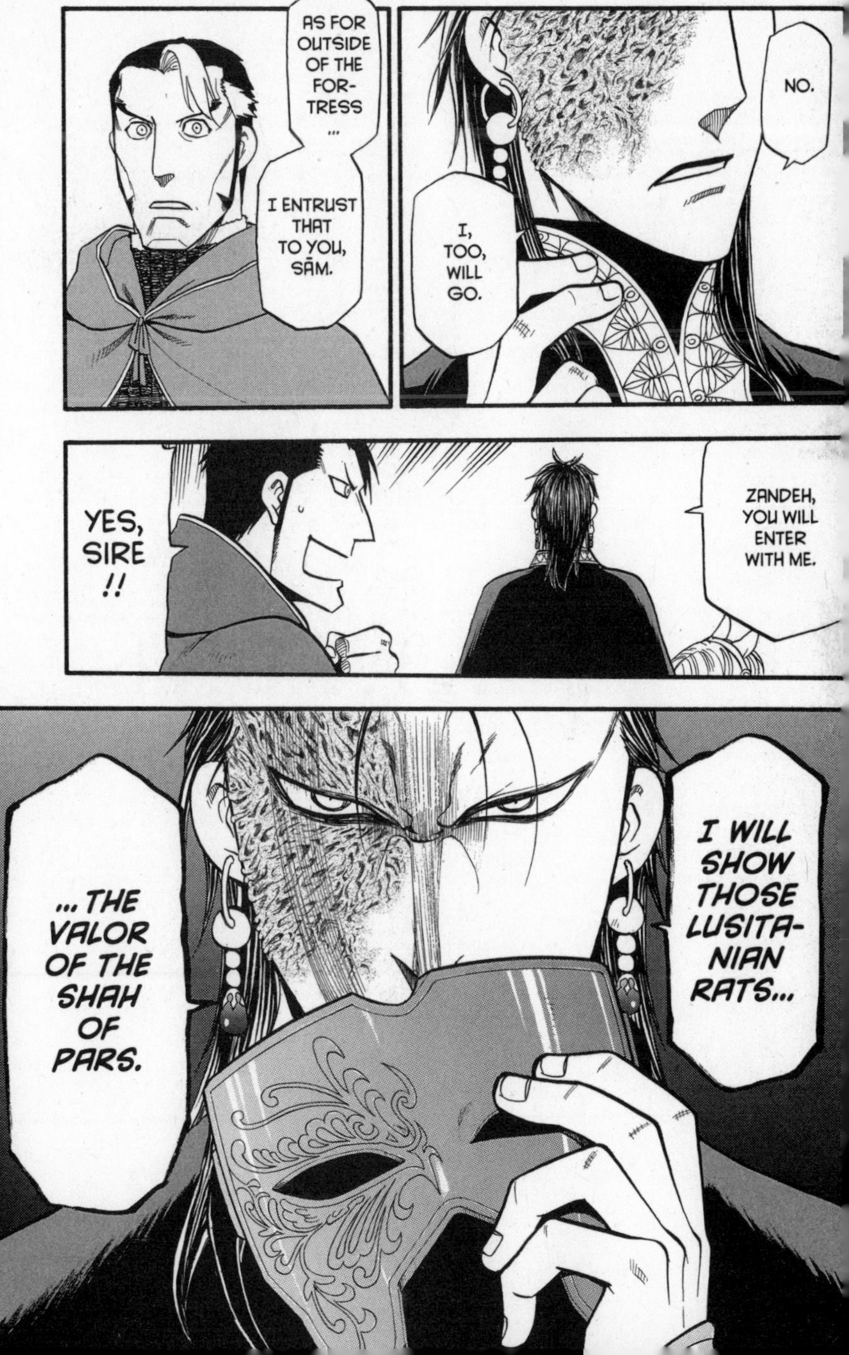
NO.
I, TOO, WILL GO.
AS FOR OUTSIDE OF THE FOR-TRESS ...
I ENTRUST THAT TO YOU, SĀM.
ZANDEH, YOU WILL ENTER WITH ME.
YES, SIRE !!
I WILL SHOW THOSE LUSITA-NIAN RATS...
...THE VALOR OF THE SHAH OF PARS.

THE HEROIC LEGEND OF
ARSLAN

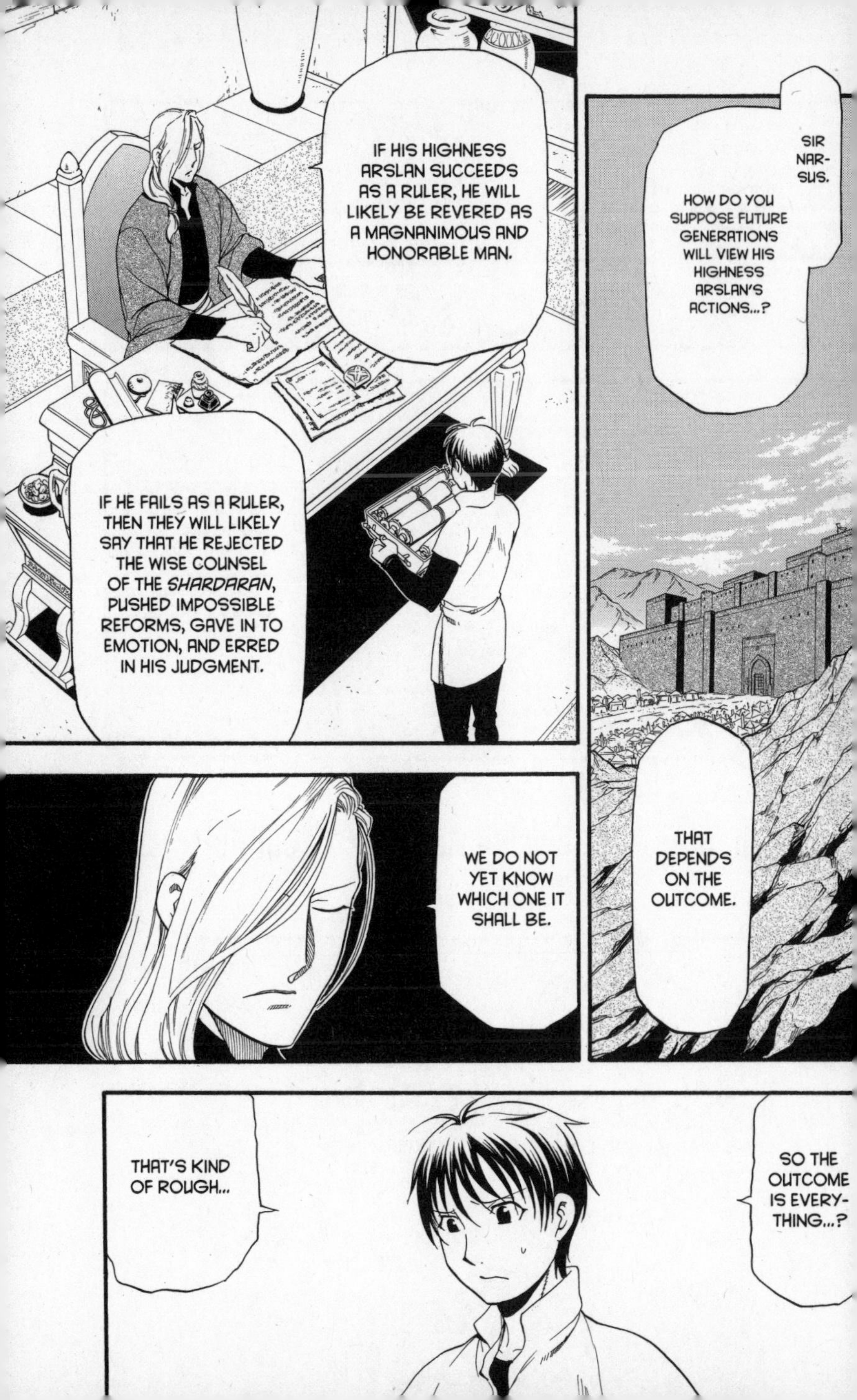
SIR NARSUS.
HOW DO YOU SUPPOSE FUTURE GENERATIONS WILL VIEW HIS HIGHNESS ARSLAN'S ACTIONS...?
THAT DEPENDS ON THE OUTCOME.
IF HIS HIGHNESS ARSLAN SUCCEEDS AS A RULER, HE WILL LIKELY BE REVERED AS A MAGNANIMOUS AND HONORABLE MAN.
IF HE FAILS AS A RULER, THEN THEY WILL LIKELY SAY THAT HE REJECTED THE WISE COUNSEL OF THE *SHARDARAN*, PUSHED IMPOSSIBLE REFORMS, GAVE IN TO EMOTION, AND ERRED IN HIS JUDGMENT.
WE DO NOT YET KNOW WHICH ONE IT SHALL BE.
SO THE OUTCOME IS EVERYTHING...?
THAT'S KIND OF ROUGH...

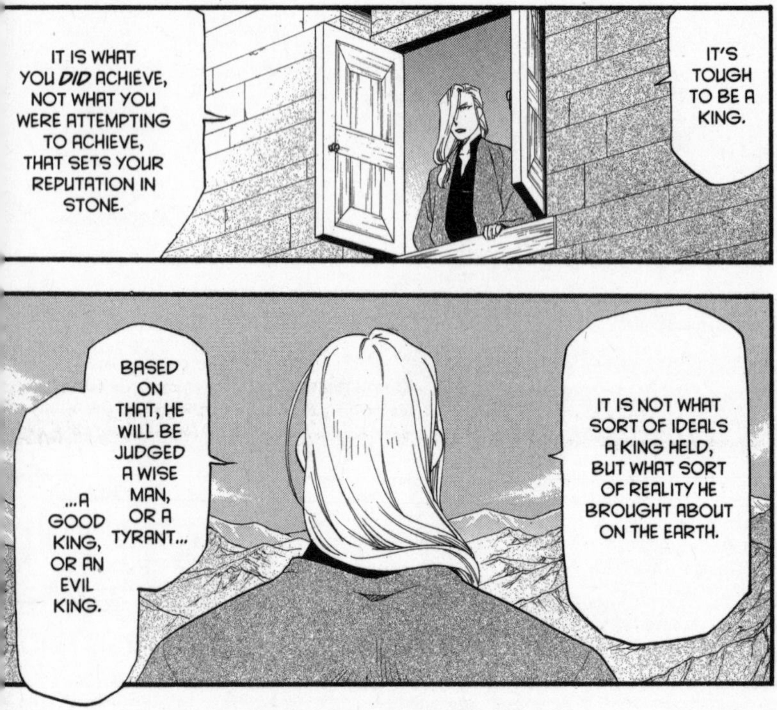
IT'S TOUGH TO BE A KING.
IT IS WHAT YOU *DID* ACHIEVE, NOT WHAT YOU WERE ATTEMPTING TO ACHIEVE, THAT SETS YOUR REPUTATION IN STONE.
IT IS NOT WHAT SORT OF IDEALS A KING HELD, BUT WHAT SORT OF REALITY HE BROUGHT ABOUT ON THE EARTH.
BASED ON THAT, HE WILL BE JUDGED A WISE MAN, OR A TYRANT...
...A GOOD KING, OR AN EVIL KING.

Chapter 60: Decisive Battle at Zabul Fortress

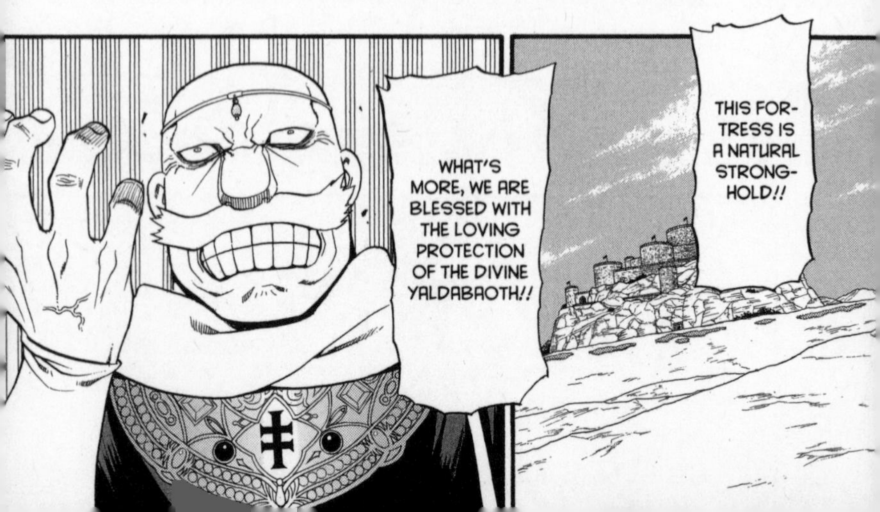
THIS FOR-TRESS IS A NATURAL STRONG-HOLD!!
WHAT'S MORE, WE ARE BLESSED WITH THE LOVING PROTECTION OF THE DIVINE YALDABAOTH!!

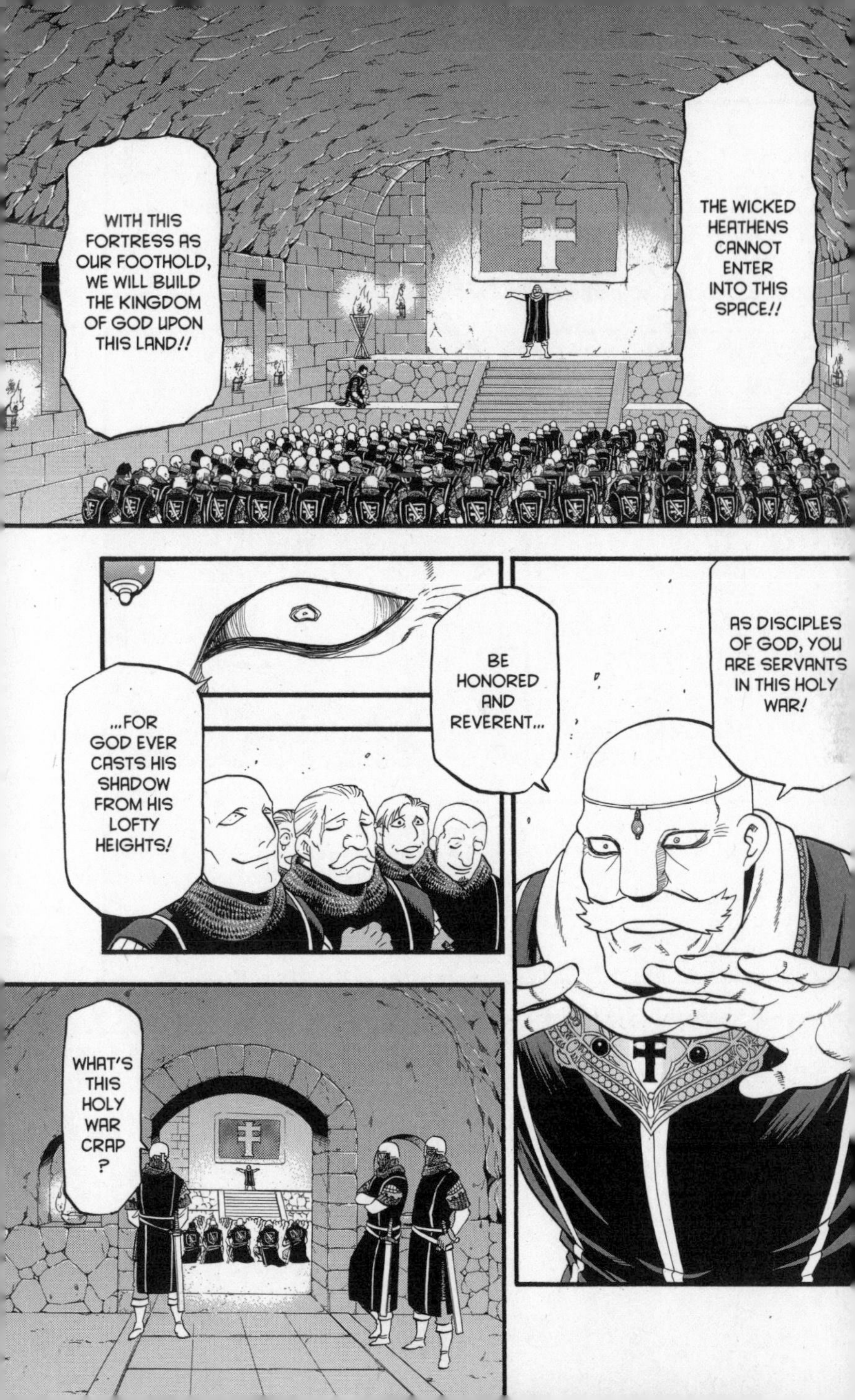
THE WICKED HEATHENS CANNOT ENTER INTO THIS SPACE!!
WITH THIS FORTRESS AS OUR FOOTHOLD, WE WILL BUILD THE KINGDOM OF GOD UPON THIS LAND!!
AS DISCIPLES OF GOD, YOU ARE SERVANTS IN THIS HOLY WAR!
BE HONORED AND REVERENT...
...FOR GOD EVER CASTS HIS SHADOW FROM HIS LOFTY HEIGHTS!
WHAT'S THIS HOLY WAR CRAP?

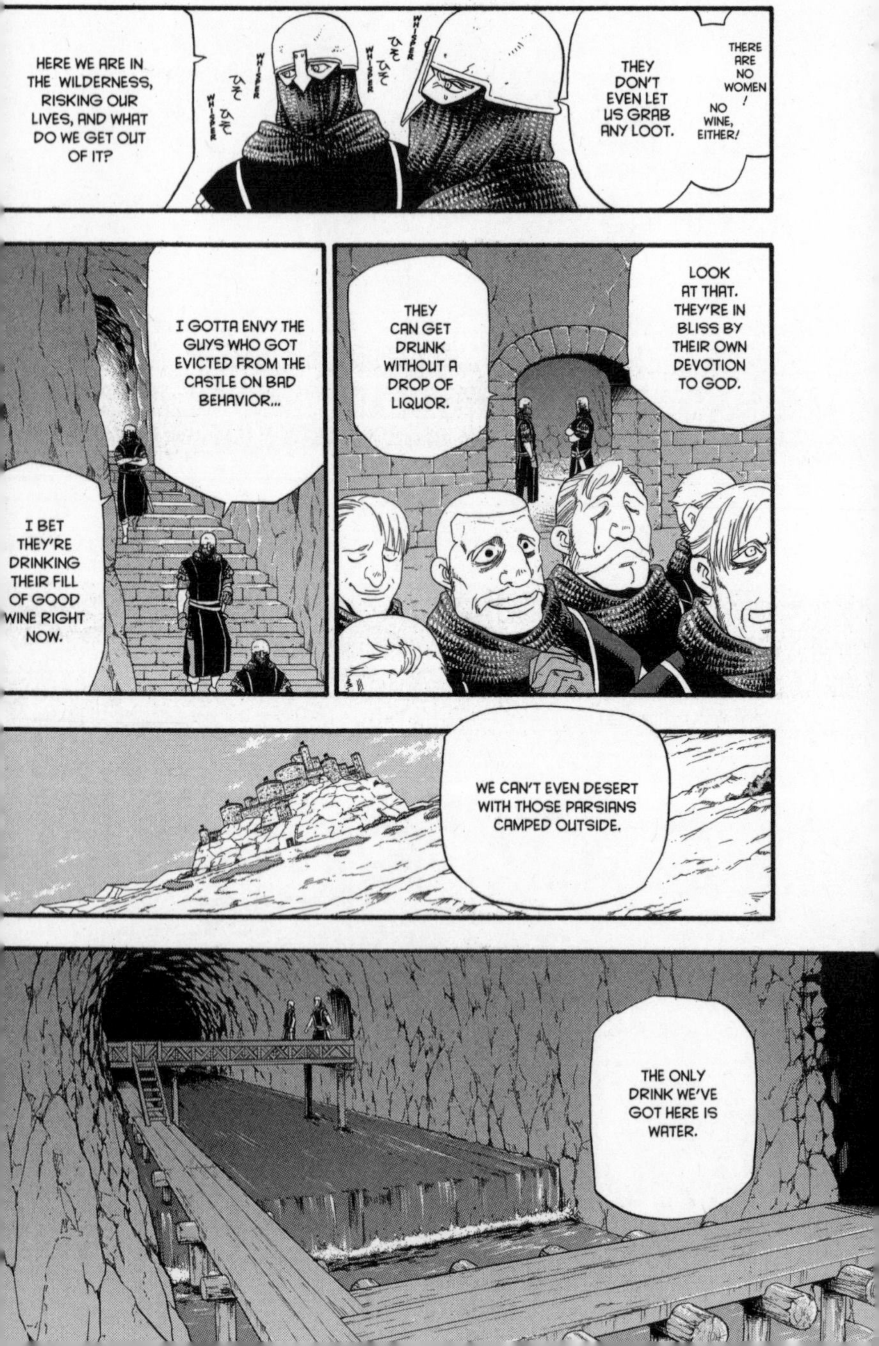
THERE ARE NO WOMEN!
NO WINE, EITHER!
THEY DON'T EVEN LET US GRAB ANY LOOT.
ひそ WHISPER
ひそ WHISPER
ひそ WHISPER
ひそ WHISPER
HERE WE ARE IN THE WILDERNESS, RISKING OUR LIVES, AND WHAT DO WE GET OUT OF IT?
LOOK AT THAT. THEY'RE IN BLISS BY THEIR OWN DEVOTION TO GOD.
THEY CAN GET DRUNK WITHOUT A DROP OF LIQUOR.
I GOTTA ENVY THE GUYS WHO GOT EVICTED FROM THE CASTLE ON BAD BEHAVIOR...
I BET THEY'RE DRINKING THEIR FILL OF GOOD WINE RIGHT NOW.
WE CAN'T EVEN DESERT WITH THOSE PARSIANS CAMPED OUTSIDE.
THE ONLY DRINK WE'VE GOT HERE IS WATER.

SMELLS LIKE OIL.

SNIFF
SNIFF
SNIFF

THAT'S ODD.

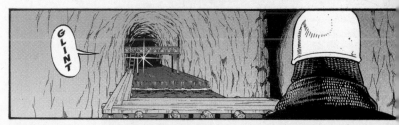
GLINT

FWOOM

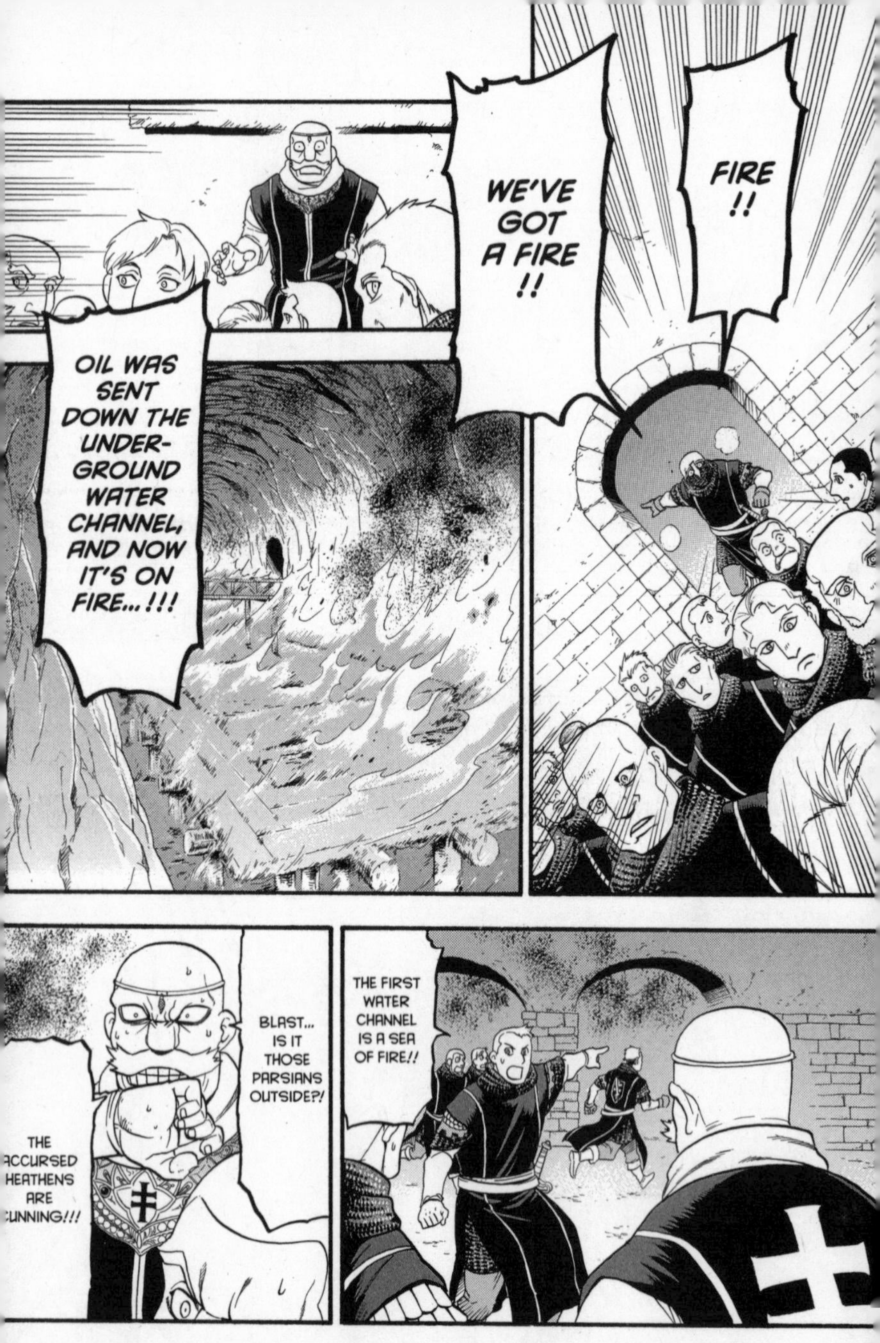
FIRE!!
WE'VE GOT A FIRE!!
OIL WAS SENT DOWN THE UNDER-GROUND WATER CHANNEL, AND NOW IT'S ON FIRE...!!!
THE FIRST WATER CHANNEL IS A SEA OF FIRE!!
BLAST... IS IT THOSE PARSIANS OUTSIDE?!
THE ACCURSED HEATHENS ARE CUNNING!!!

PUT OUT THE FIRE!!
WHAT ARE YOU WAITING FOR?!
EASIER SAID THAN DONE...
IF WE THROW WATER ON AN OIL FIRE, IT WILL SPREAD EVEN FURTHER...
GLINT
THOK
RUSH

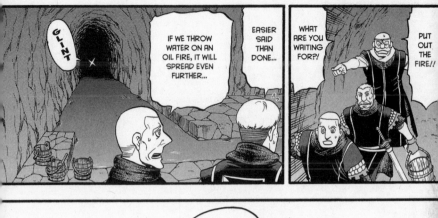

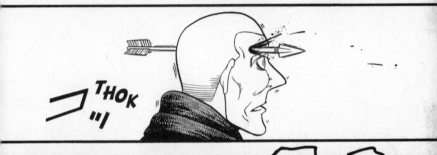

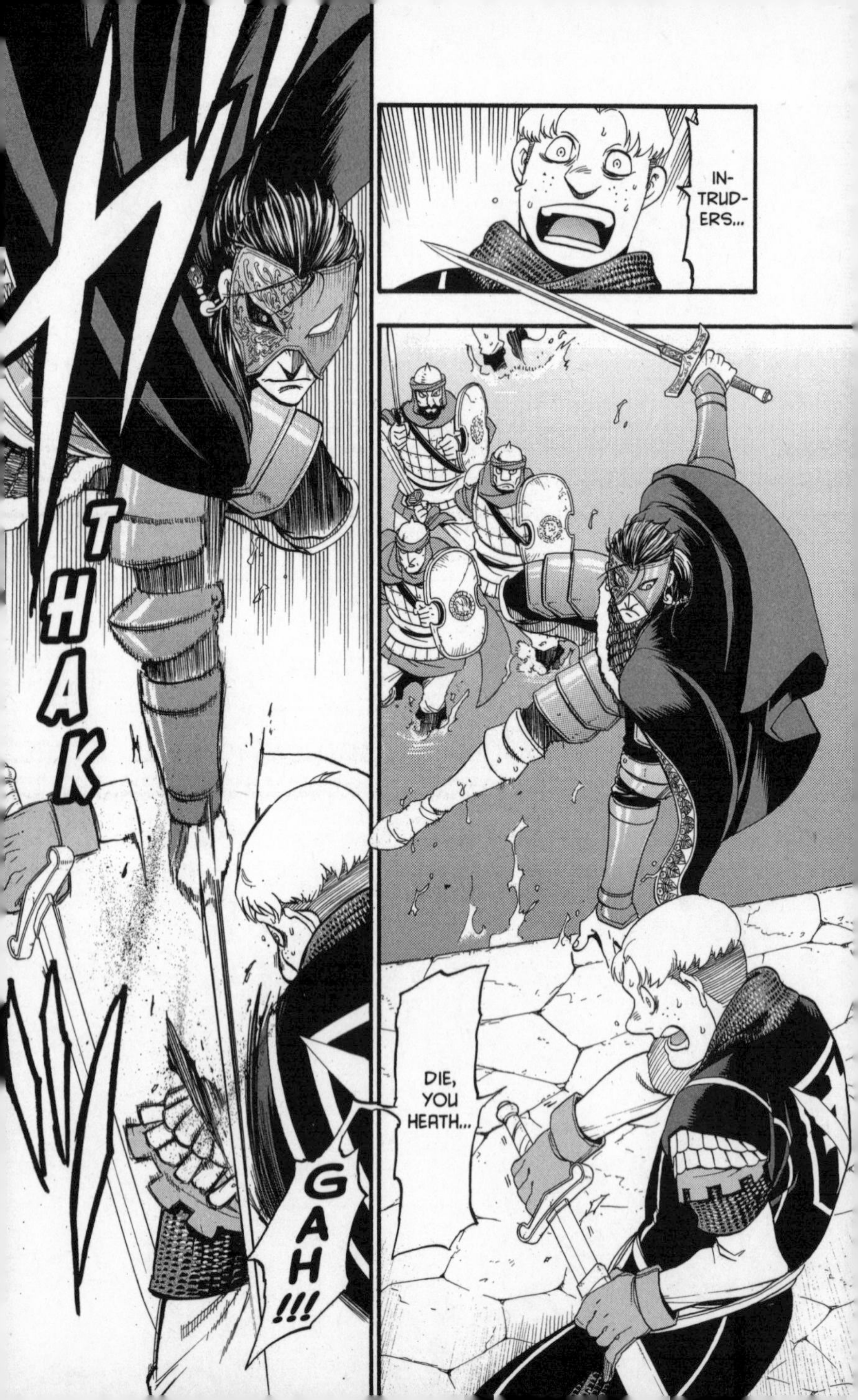
IN-TRUDERS...
DIE, YOU HEATH...
THAK
GAH!!!

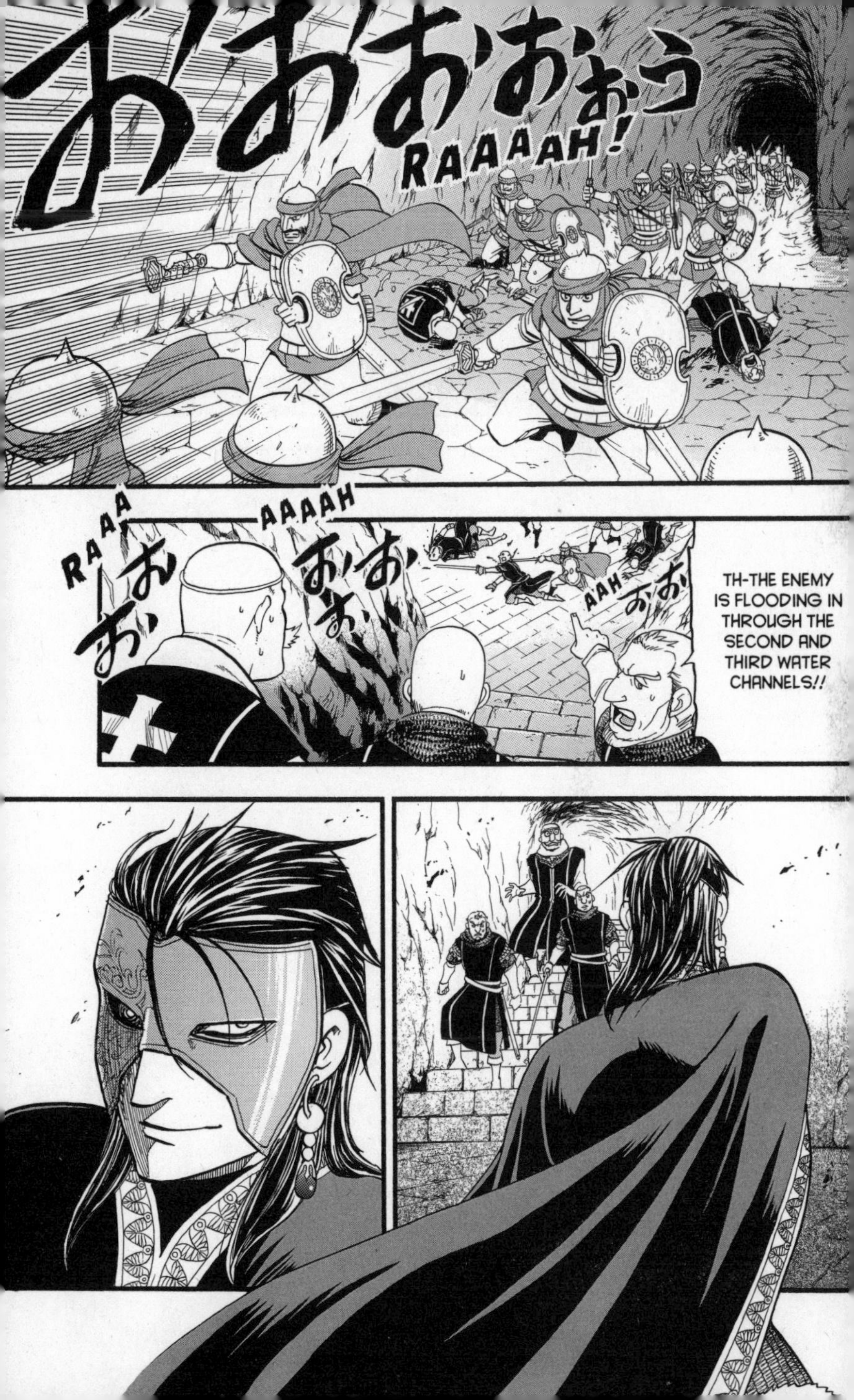

おおおおぉう
RAAAAH!
TH-THE ENEMY IS FLOODING IN THROUGH THE SECOND AND THIRD WATER CHANNELS!!
AAH
おぉ
AAAAH
おおおお
RAAA
おおお

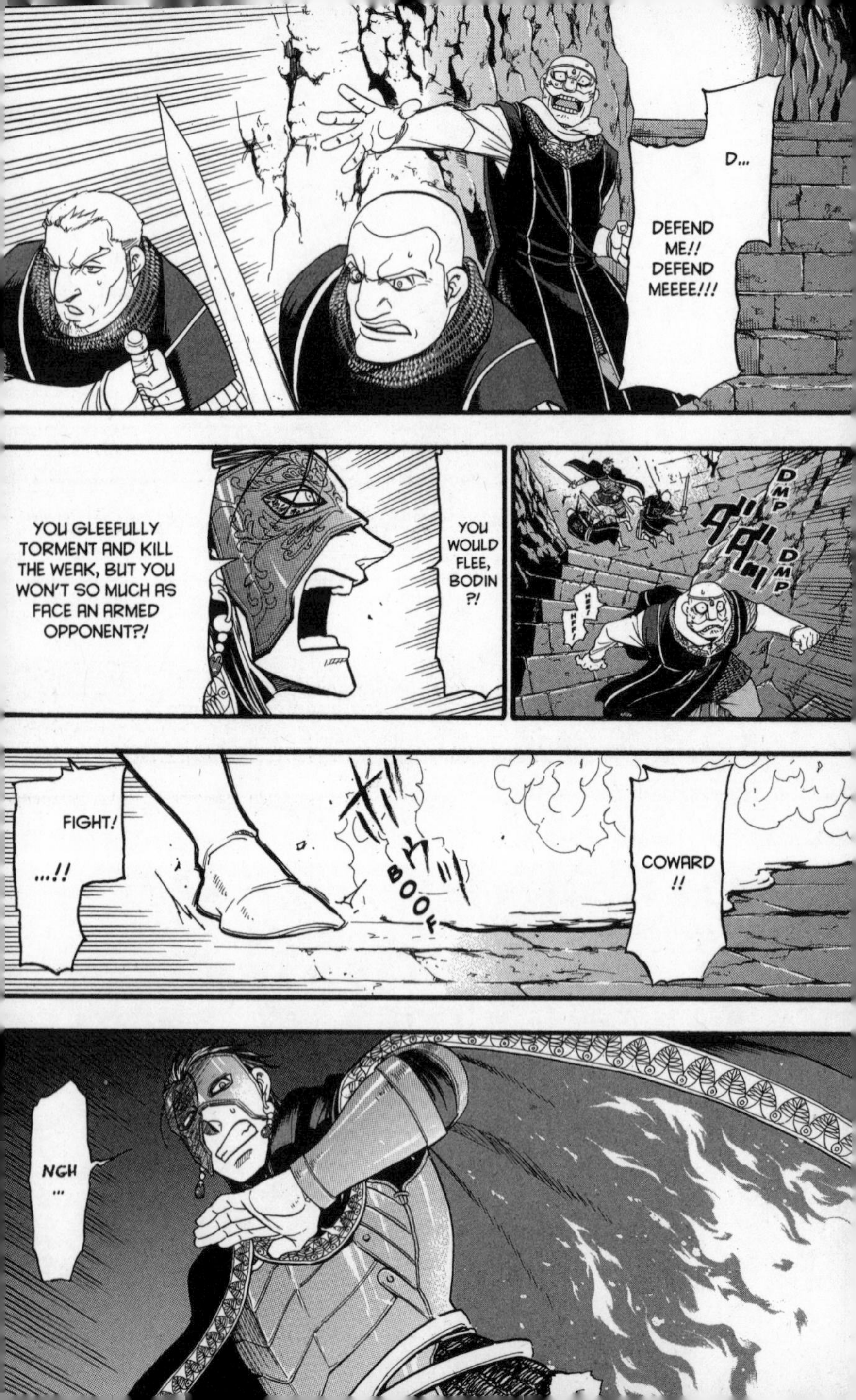
D...
DEFEND ME!! DEFEND MEEEE!!!
DMP DMP
YOU WOULD FLEE, BODIN?!
YOU GLEEFULLY TORMENT AND KILL THE WEAK, BUT YOU WON'T SO MUCH AS FACE AN ARMED OPPONENT?!
COWARD!!
BOOF
FIGHT!
...!!
NGH...

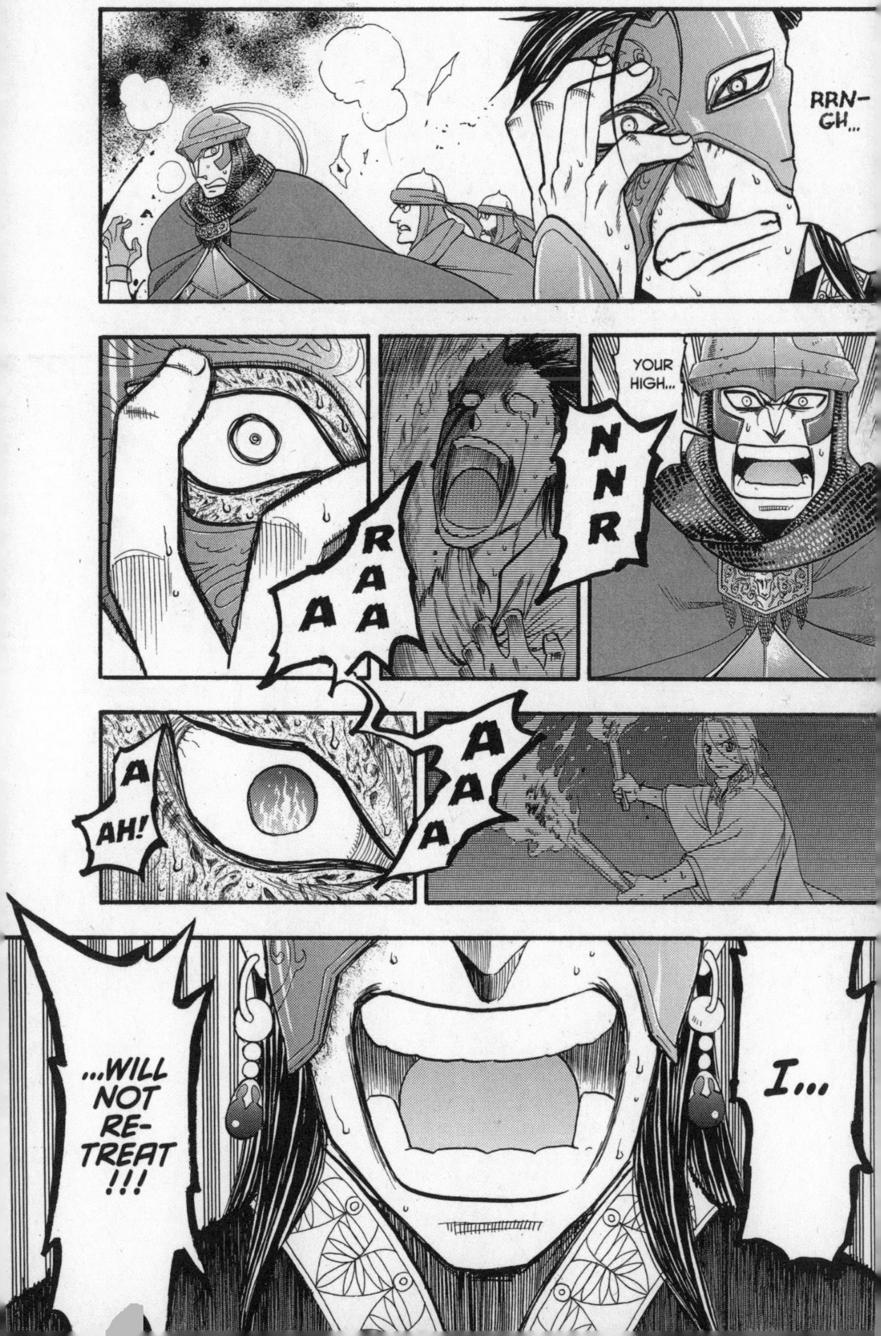
RRN-GH...
YOUR HIGH...
NNR
RAAAA
AAAA
A AH!
I...
...WILL NOT RE-TREAT!!!

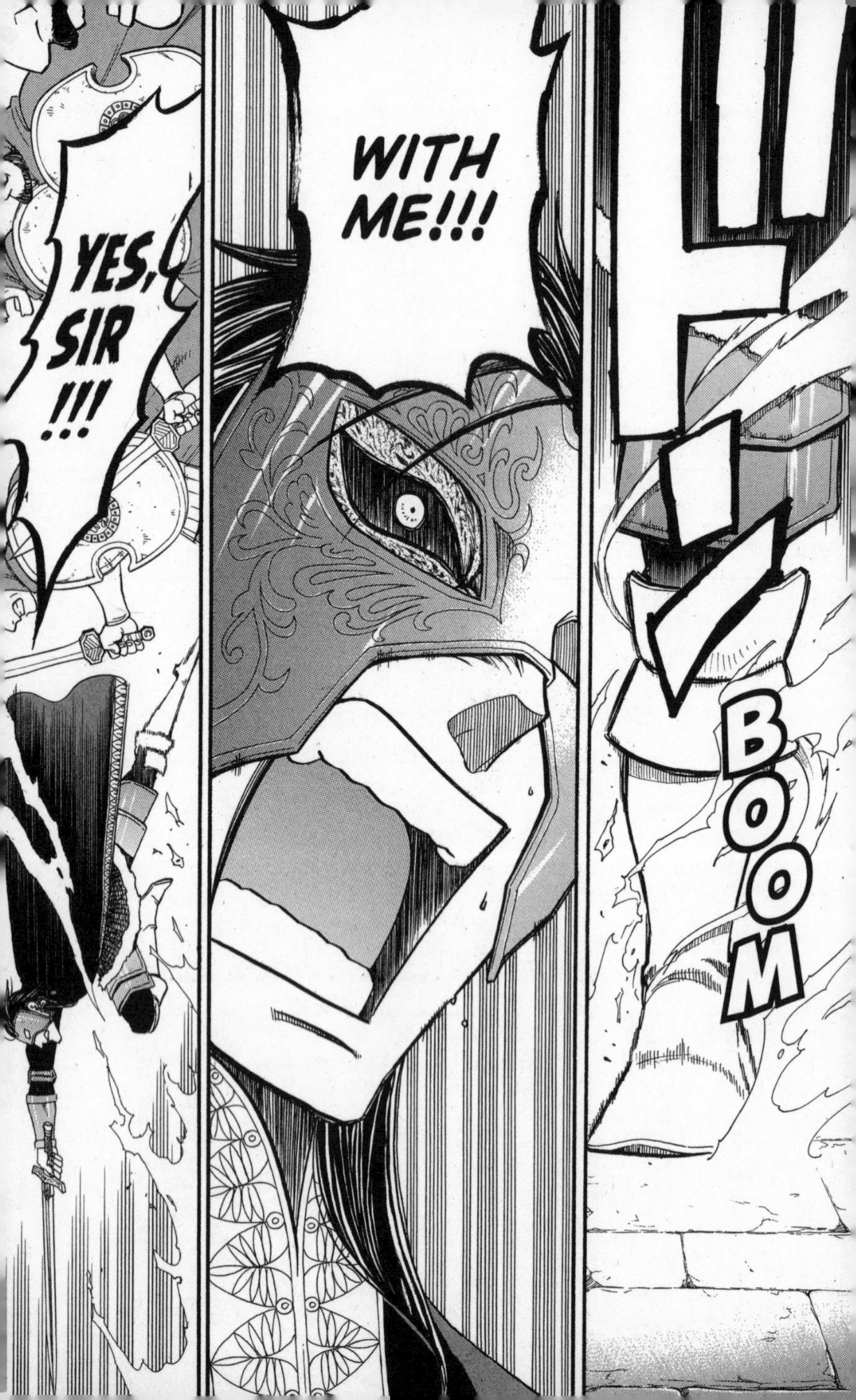
BOOM
WITH ME!!!
YES, SIR!!!

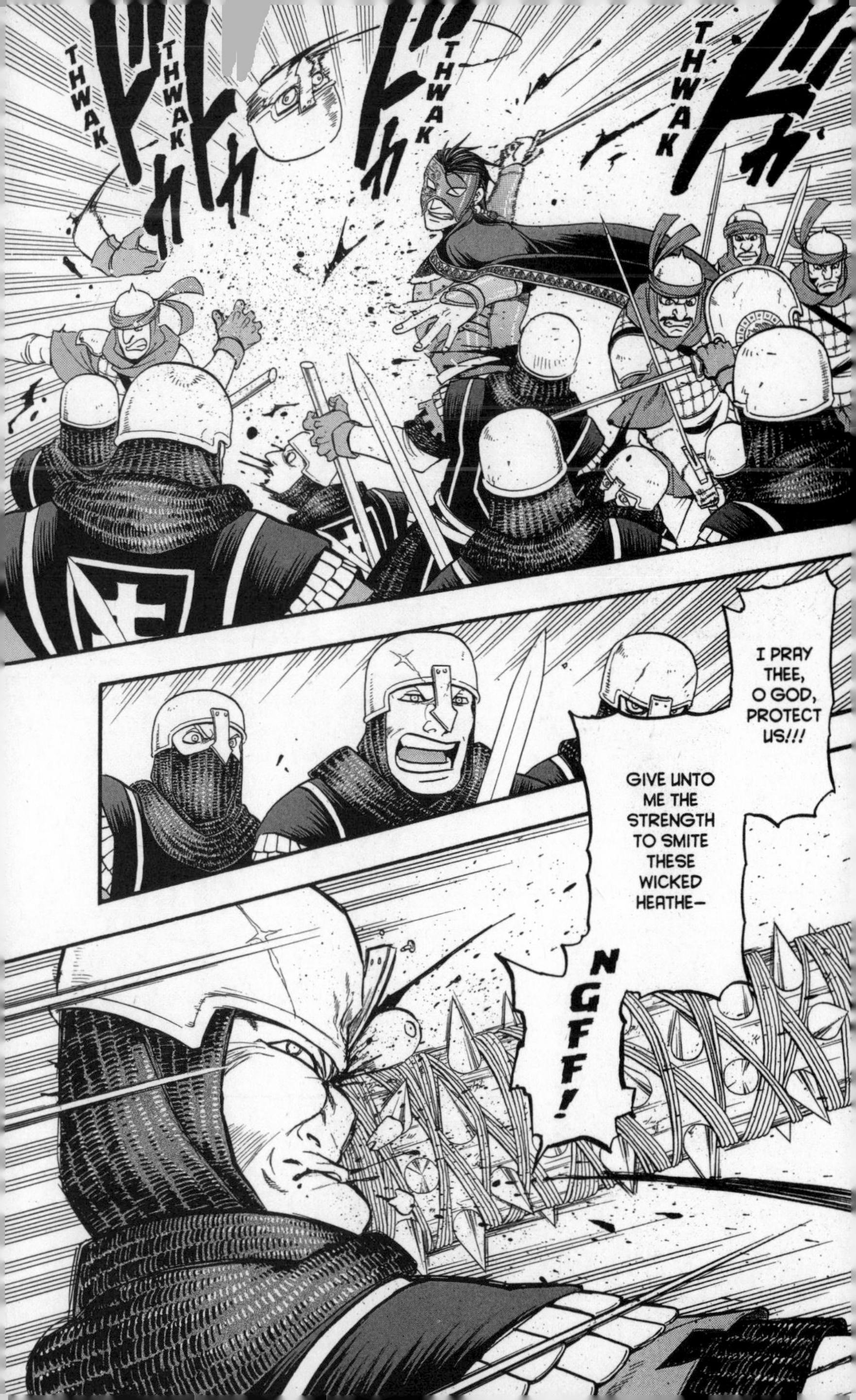
THWAK
THWAK
THWAK
THWAK
I PRAY THEE, O GOD, PROTECT US!!!
GIVE UNTO ME THE STRENGTH TO SMITE THESE WICKED HEATHE–
NGFF!

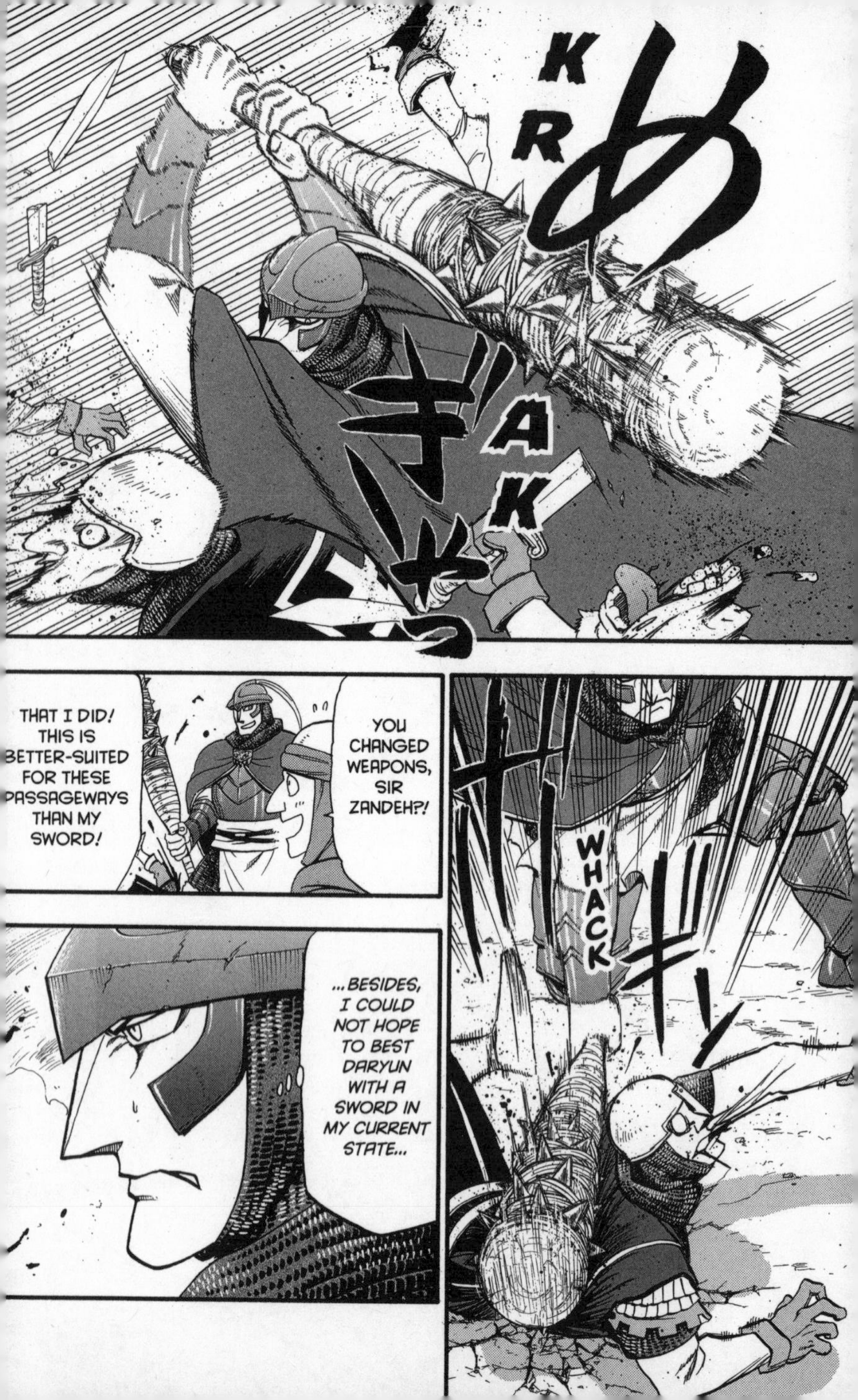
KRAK
WHACK
YOU CHANGED WEAPONS, SIR ZANDEH?!
THAT I DID! THIS IS BETTER-SUITED FOR THESE PASSAGEWAYS THAN MY SWORD!
...BESIDES, I COULD NOT HOPE TO BEST DARYUN WITH A SWORD IN MY CURRENT STATE...

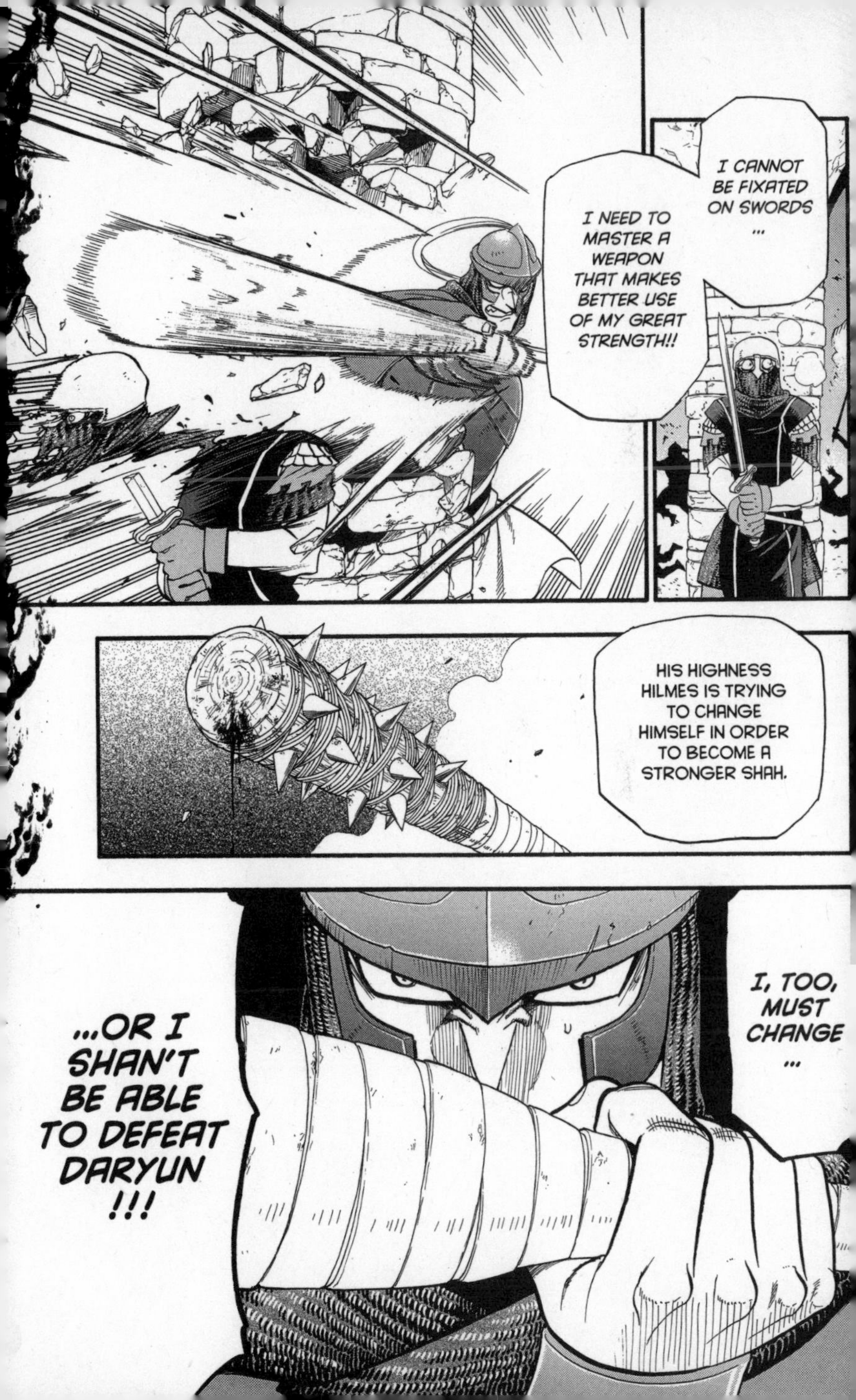
I CANNOT BE FIXATED ON SWORDS ...
I NEED TO MASTER A WEAPON THAT MAKES BETTER USE OF MY GREAT STRENGTH!!
HIS HIGHNESS HILMES IS TRYING TO CHANGE HIMSELF IN ORDER TO BECOME A STRONGER SHAH.
I, TOO, MUST CHANGE ...
...OR I SHAN'T BE ABLE TO DEFEAT DARYUN !!!

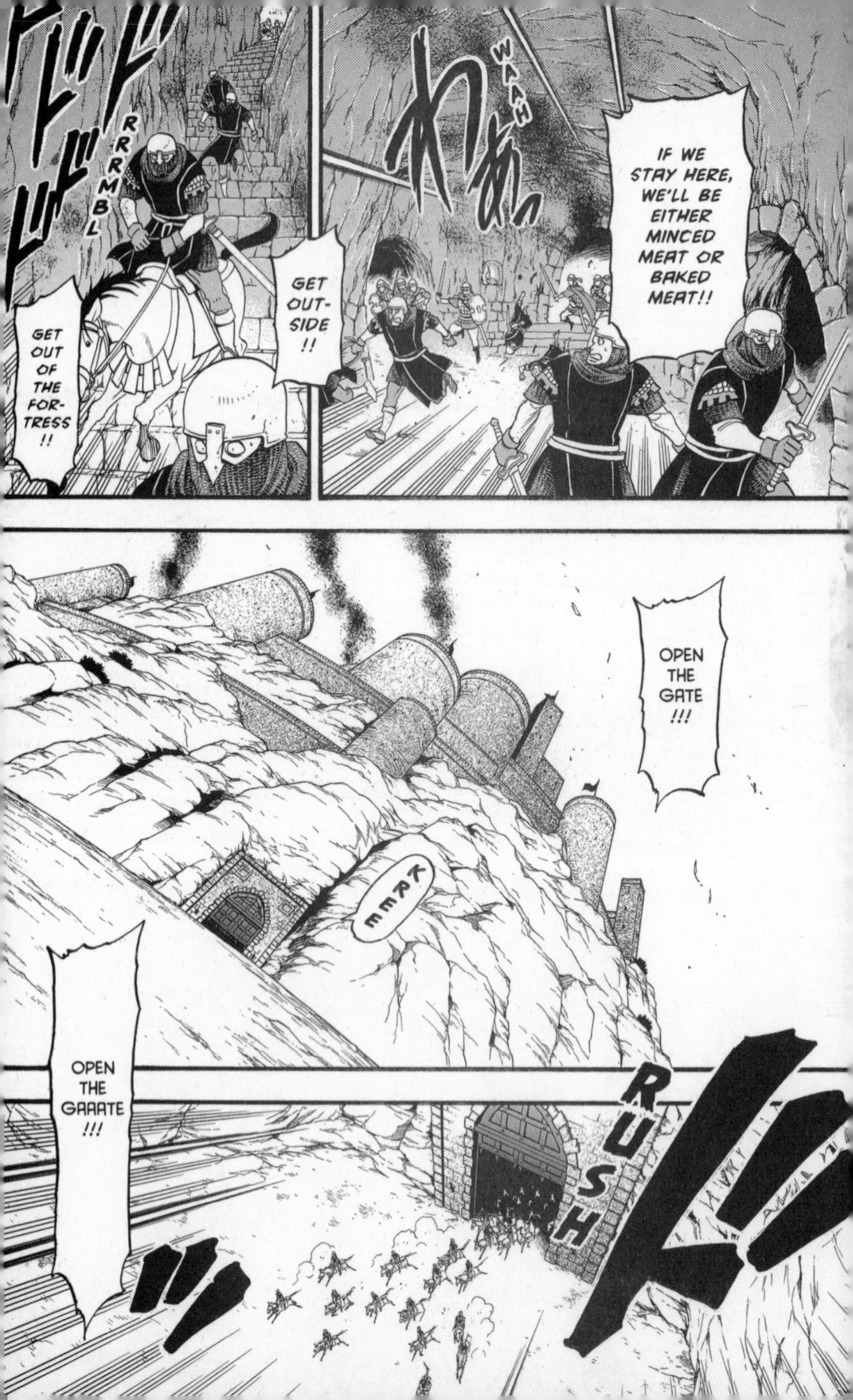
WAAH
IF WE STAY HERE, WE'LL BE EITHER MINCED MEAT OR BAKED MEAT!!
GET OUT-SIDE!!
RRRMBL
GET OUT OF THE FOR-TRESS!!
OPEN THE GATE!!!
KREE
RUSH
OPEN THE GAAATE!!!

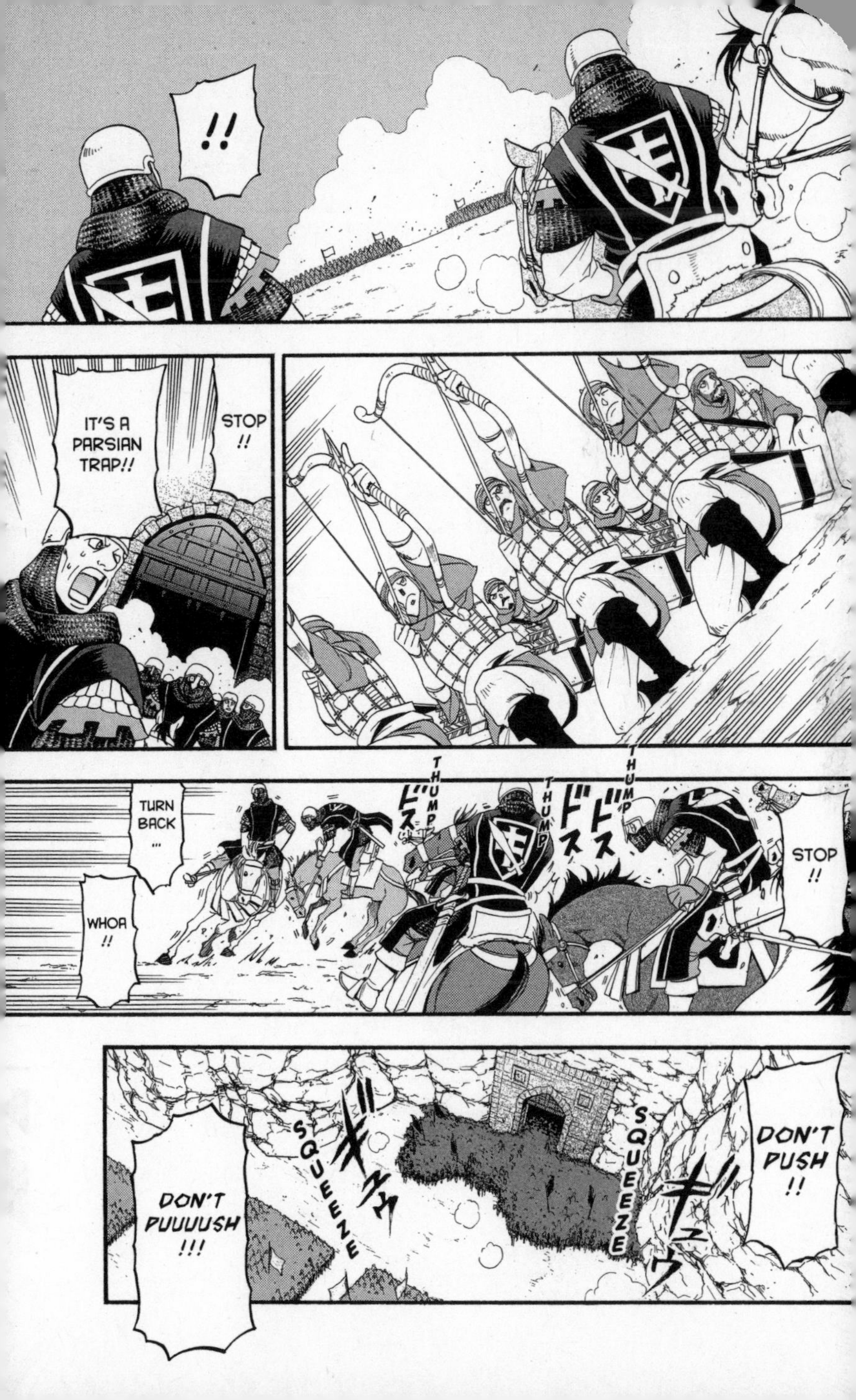
!!
STOP !!
IT'S A PARSIAN TRAP!!
STOP !!
THUMP
ドス
THUMP
ドス
THUMP
ドス
TURN BACK ...
WHOA !!
DON'T PUSH !!
SQUEEZE
SQUEEZE
DON'T PUUUUSH !!!

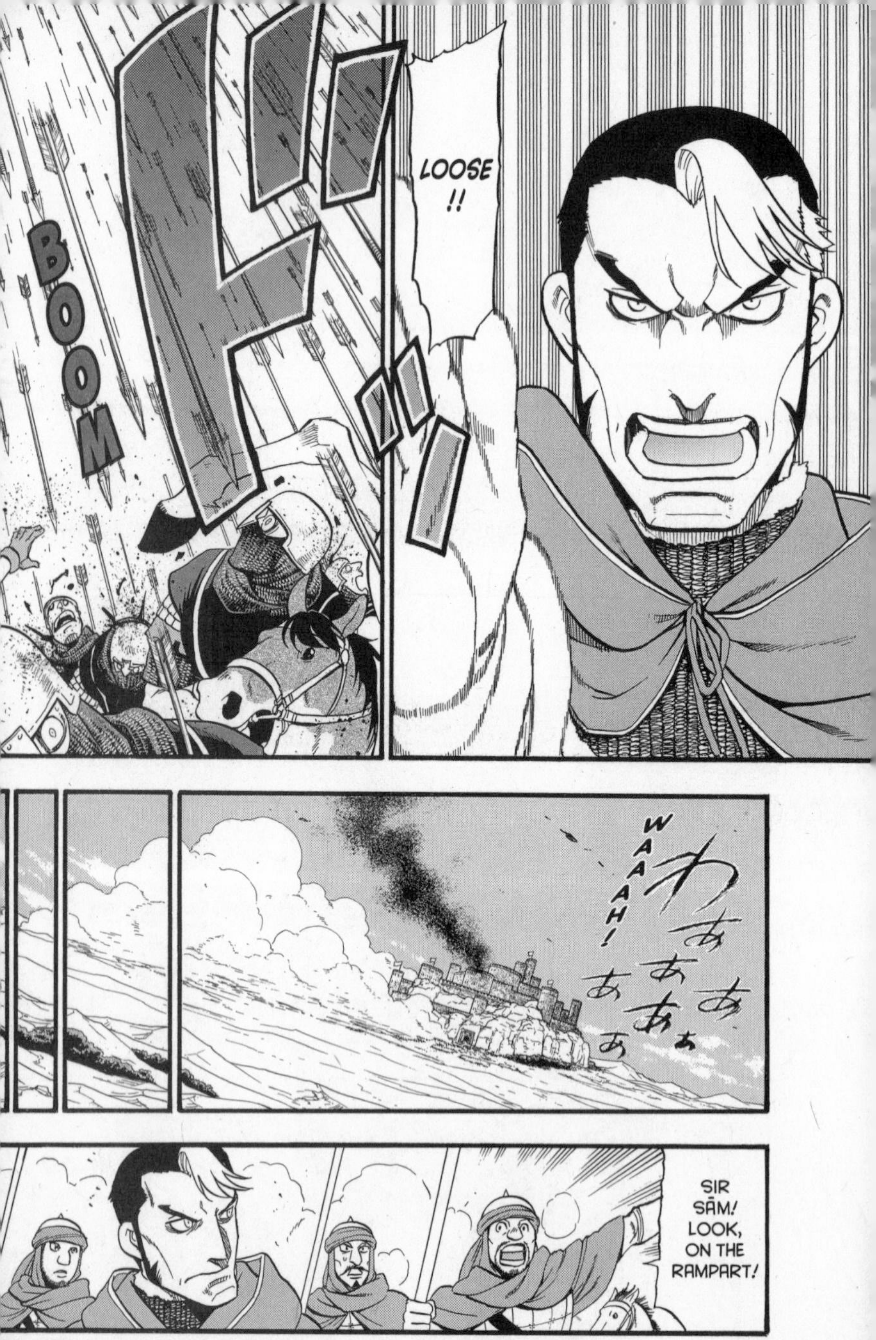
LOOSE !!
BOOM
WAAAAH!
SIR SĀM! LOOK, ON THE RAMPART!

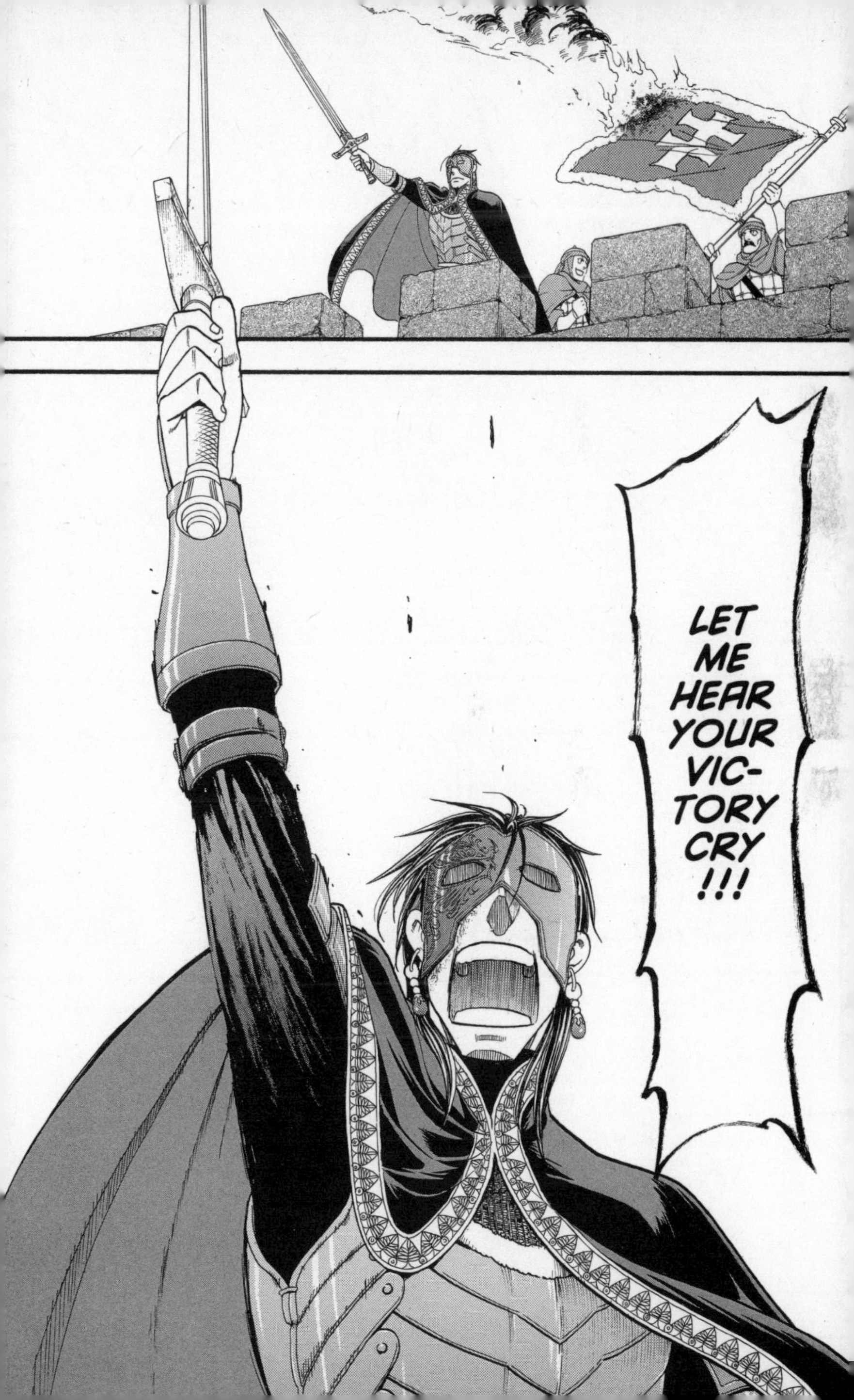
LET ME HEAR YOUR VIC-TORY CRY!!!

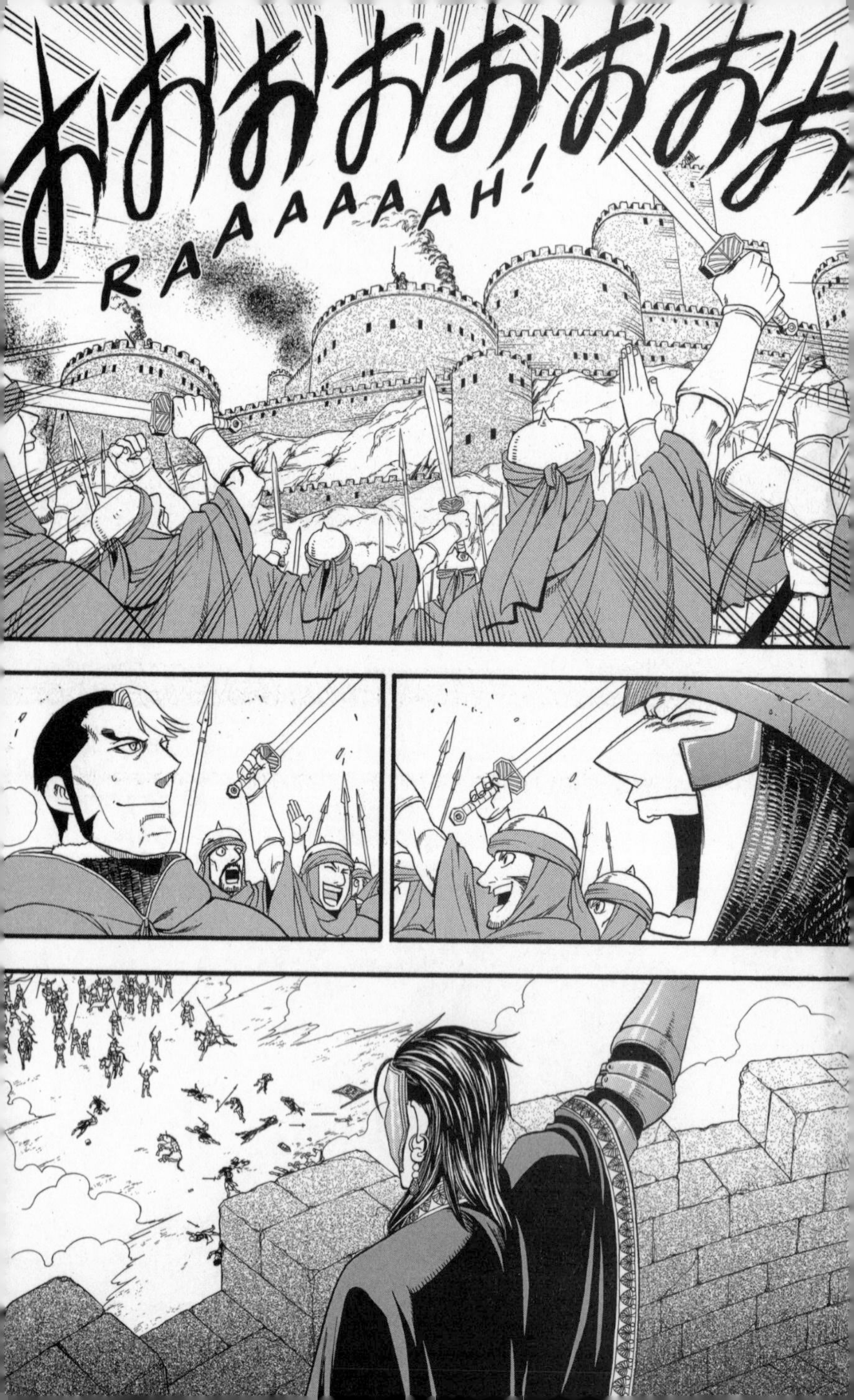
おおおおおおおお
RAAAAAAAH!

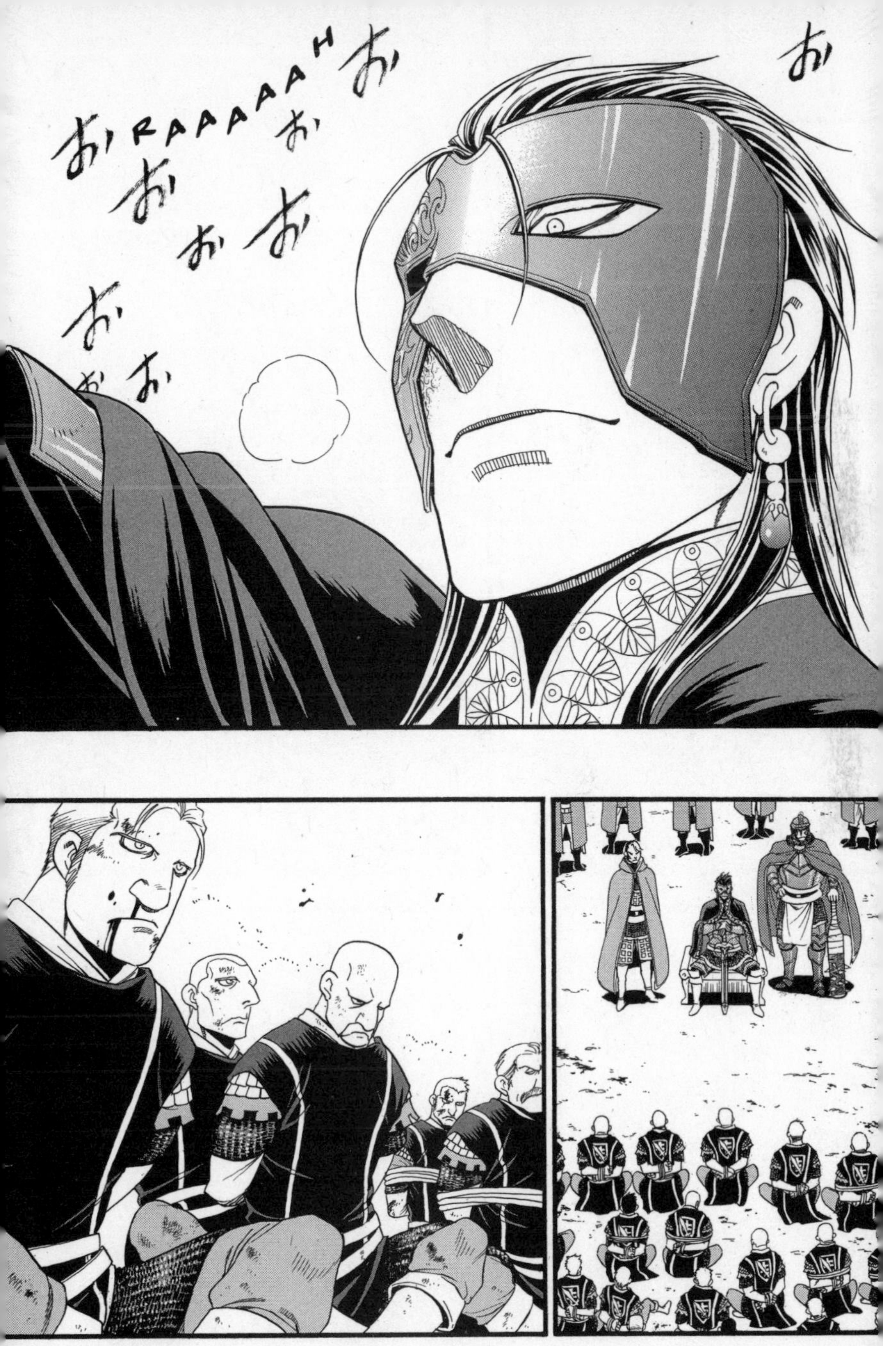
RAAAAAH

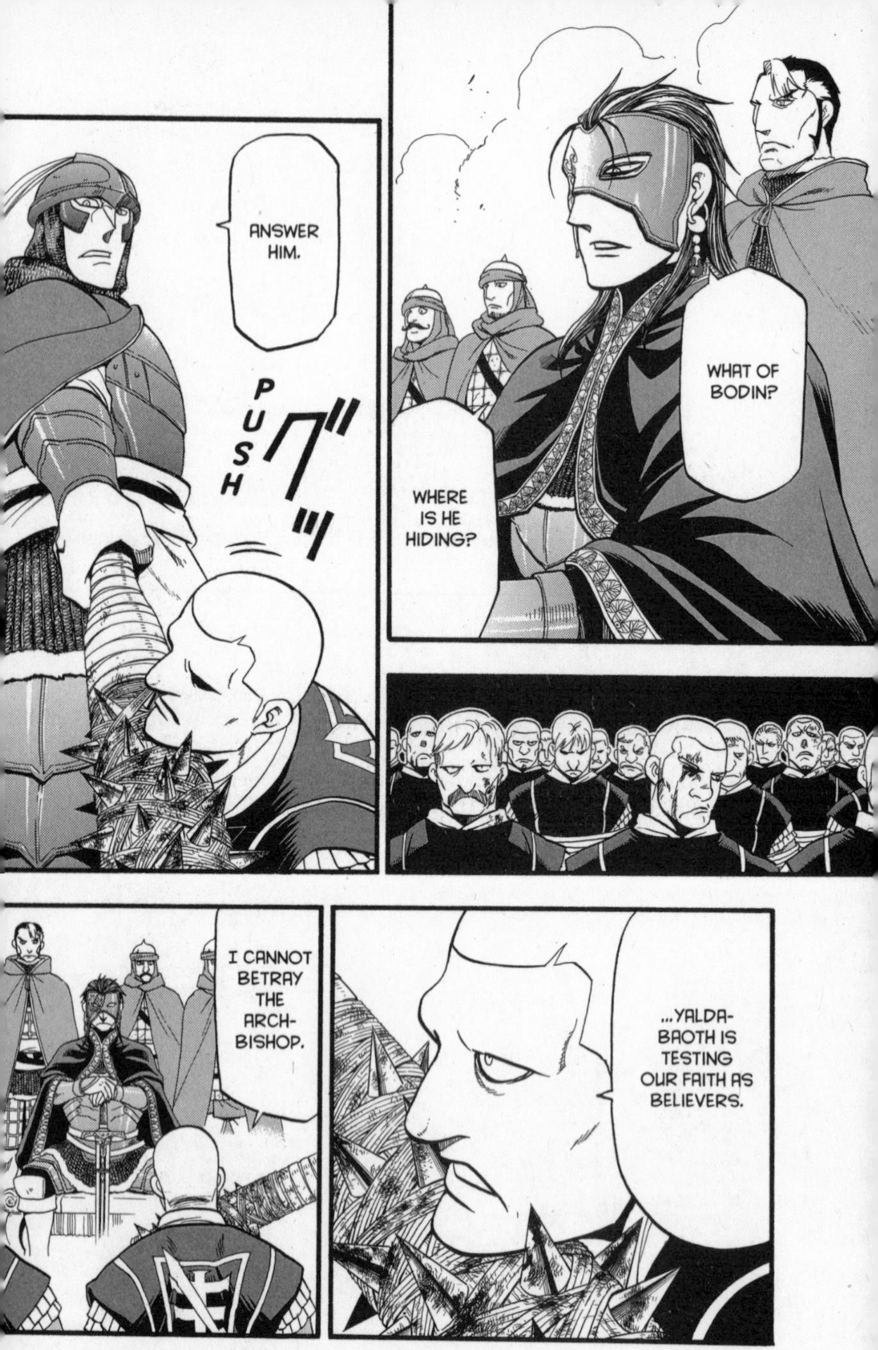
WHAT OF BODIN?
WHERE IS HE HIDING?
ANSWER HIM.
PUSH
...YALDA-BAOTH IS TESTING OUR FAITH AS BELIEVERS.
I CANNOT BETRAY THE ARCH-BISHOP.

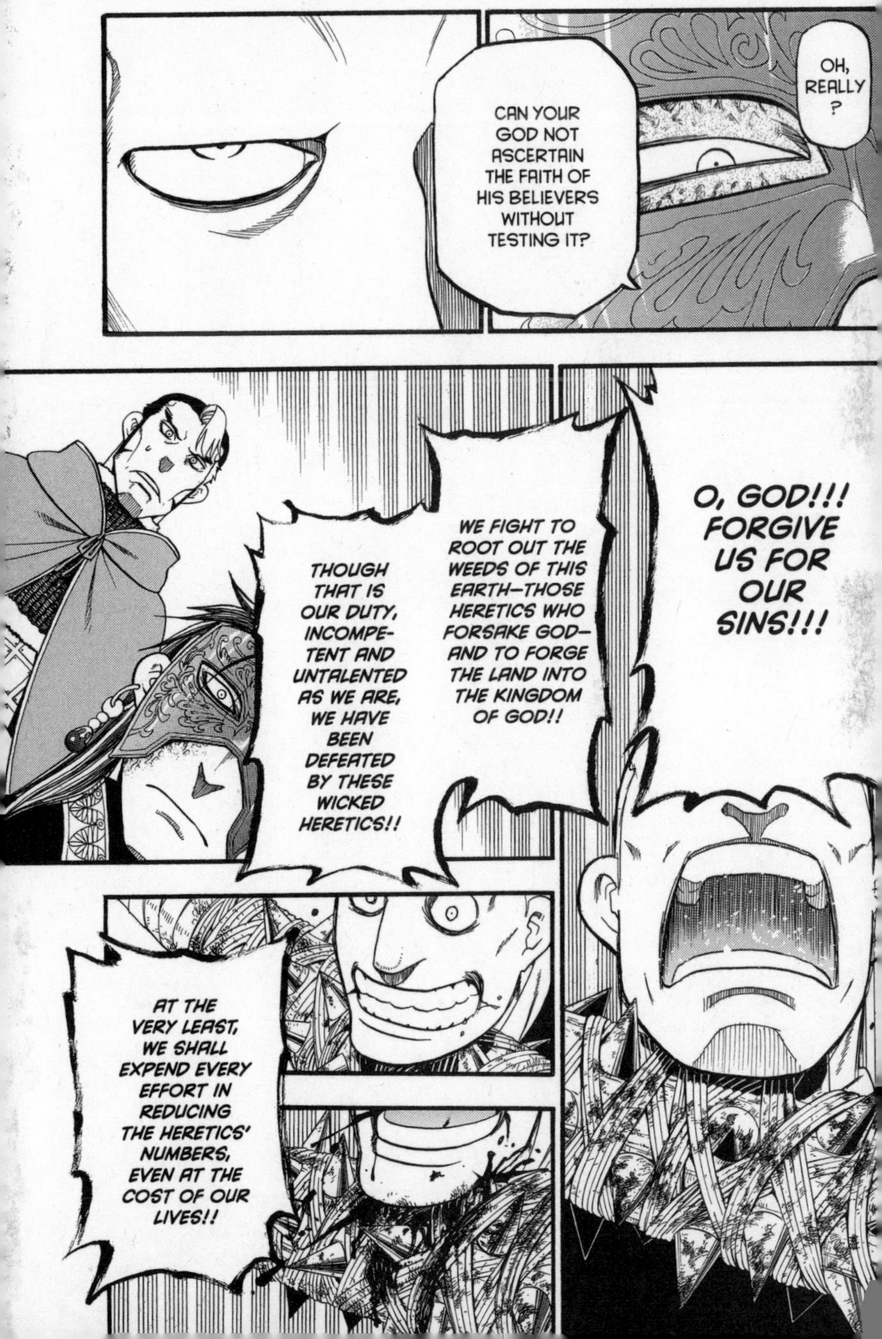

OH, REALLY?
CAN YOUR GOD NOT ASCERTAIN THE FAITH OF HIS BELIEVERS WITHOUT TESTING IT?
O, GOD!!! FORGIVE US FOR OUR SINS!!!
WE FIGHT TO ROOT OUT THE WEEDS OF THIS EARTH—THOSE HERETICS WHO FORSAKE GOD—AND TO FORGE THE LAND INTO THE KINGDOM OF GOD!!
THOUGH THAT IS OUR DUTY, INCOMPETENT AND UNTALENTED AS WE ARE, WE HAVE BEEN DEFEATED BY THESE WICKED HERETICS!!
AT THE VERY LEAST, WE SHALL EXPEND EVERY EFFORT IN REDUCING THE HERETICS' NUMBERS, EVEN AT THE COST OF OUR LIVES!!

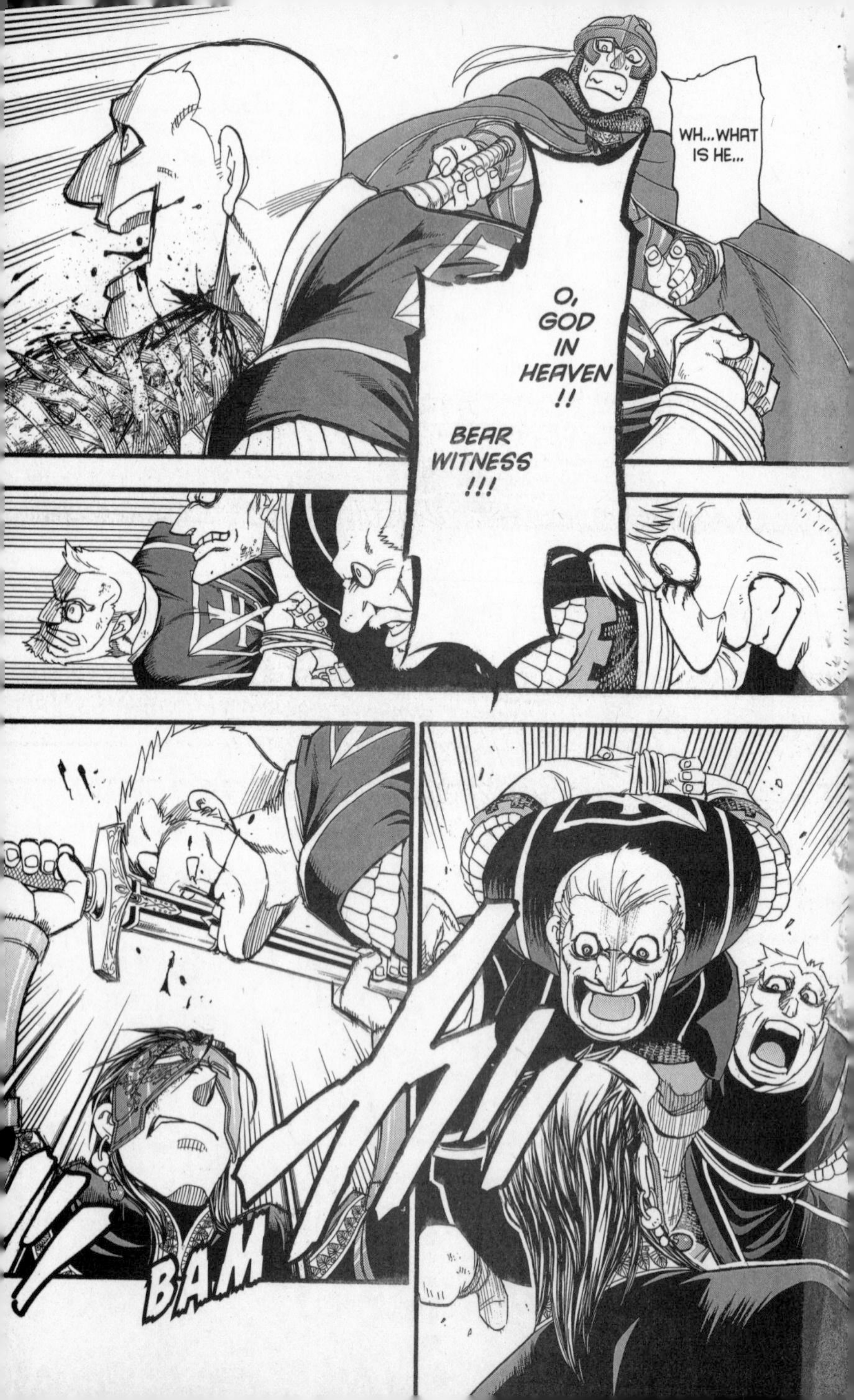
WH...WHAT IS HE...
O, GOD IN HEAVEN !!
BEAR WITNESS !!!
BAM

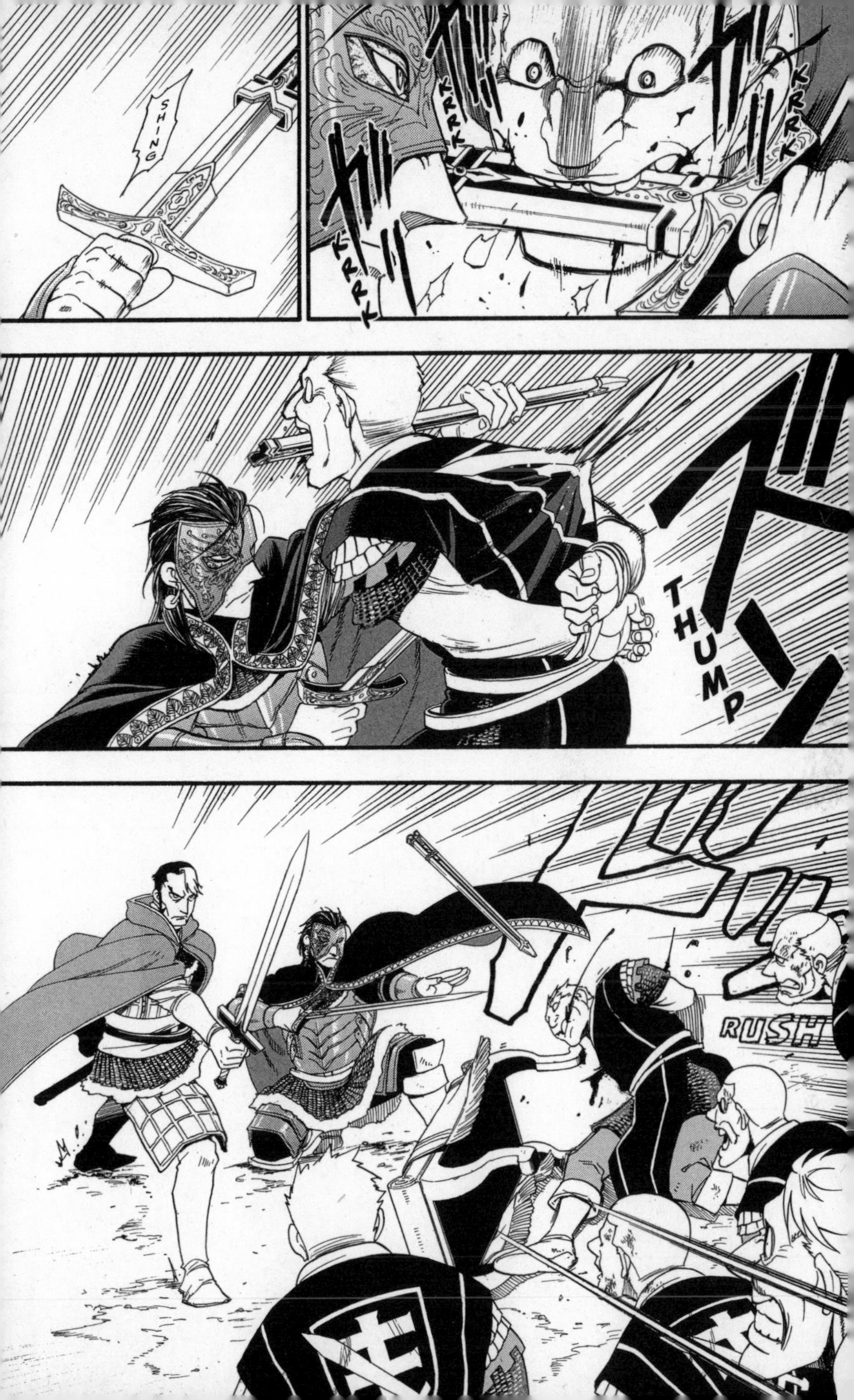
KRRRK
KRRRK
SHING
THUMP
RUSH

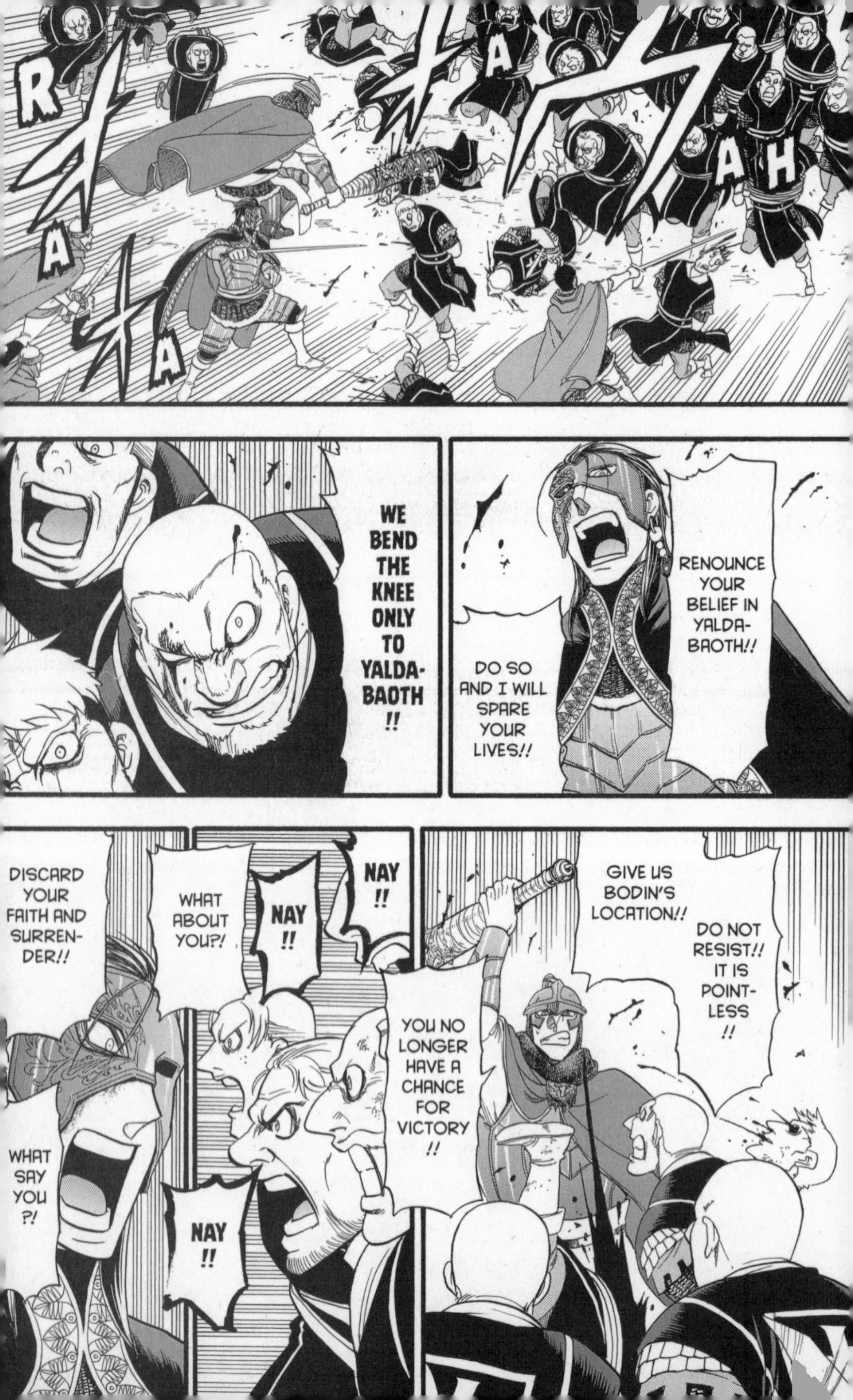

RAAAAH
RENOUNCE YOUR BELIEF IN YALDA-BAOTH!!
DO SO AND I WILL SPARE YOUR LIVES!!
WE BEND THE KNEE ONLY TO YALDA-BAOTH!!
GIVE US BODIN'S LOCATION!!
DO NOT RESIST!! IT IS POINT-LESS!!
YOU NO LONGER HAVE A CHANCE FOR VICTORY!!
NAY!!
WHAT ABOUT YOU?!
NAY!!
DISCARD YOUR FAITH AND SURREN-DER!!
WHAT SAY YOU?!
NAY!!

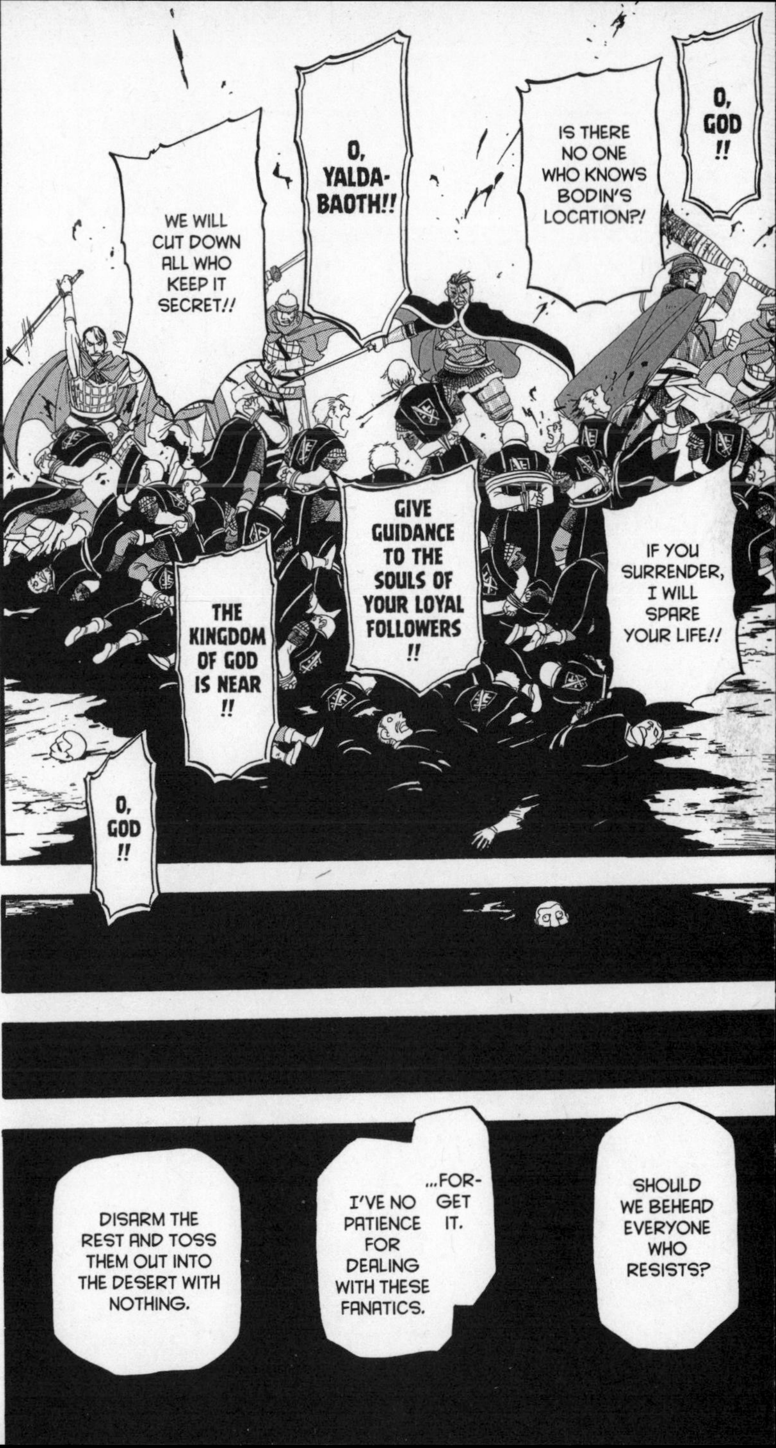
O, GOD!!
IS THERE NO ONE WHO KNOWS BODIN'S LOCATION?!
O, YALDA-BAOTH!!
WE WILL CUT DOWN ALL WHO KEEP IT SECRET!!
IF YOU SURRENDER, I WILL SPARE YOUR LIFE!!
GIVE GUIDANCE TO THE SOULS OF YOUR LOYAL FOLLOWERS!!
THE KINGDOM OF GOD IS NEAR!!
O, GOD!!
SHOULD WE BEHEAD EVERYONE WHO RESISTS?
...FOR-GET IT.
I'VE NO PATIENCE FOR DEALING WITH THESE FANATICS.
DISARM THE REST AND TOSS THEM OUT INTO THE DESERT WITH NOTHING.

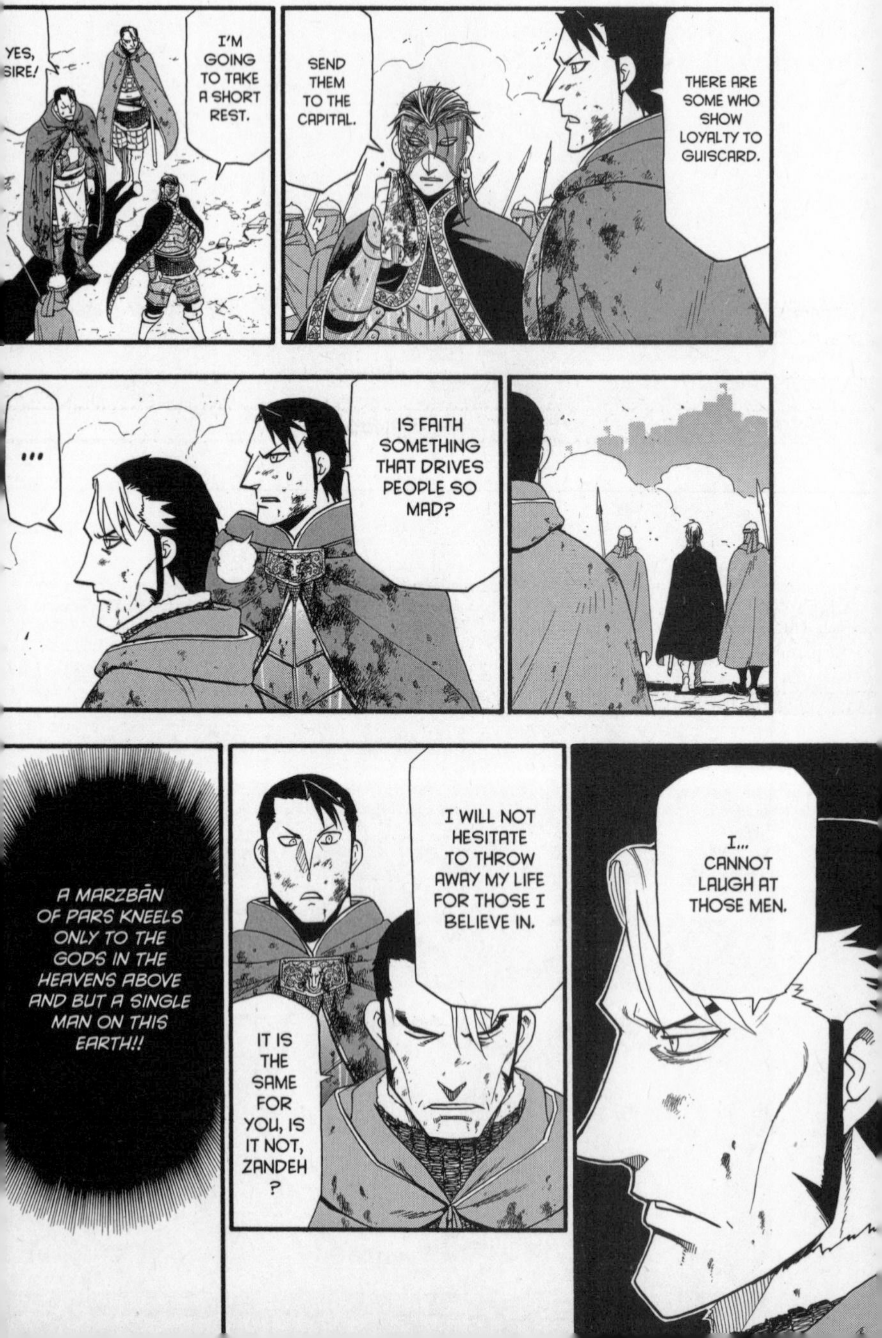
THERE ARE SOME WHO SHOW LOYALTY TO GUISCARD.
SEND THEM TO THE CAPITAL.
I'M GOING TO TAKE A SHORT REST.
YES, SIRE!
IS FAITH SOMETHING THAT DRIVES PEOPLE SO MAD?
...
I... CANNOT LAUGH AT THOSE MEN.
I WILL NOT HESITATE TO THROW AWAY MY LIFE FOR THOSE I BELIEVE IN.
IT IS THE SAME FOR YOU, IS IT NOT, ZANDEH?
A MARZBĀN OF PARS KNEELS ONLY TO THE GODS IN THE HEAVENS ABOVE AND BUT A SINGLE MAN ON THIS EARTH!!

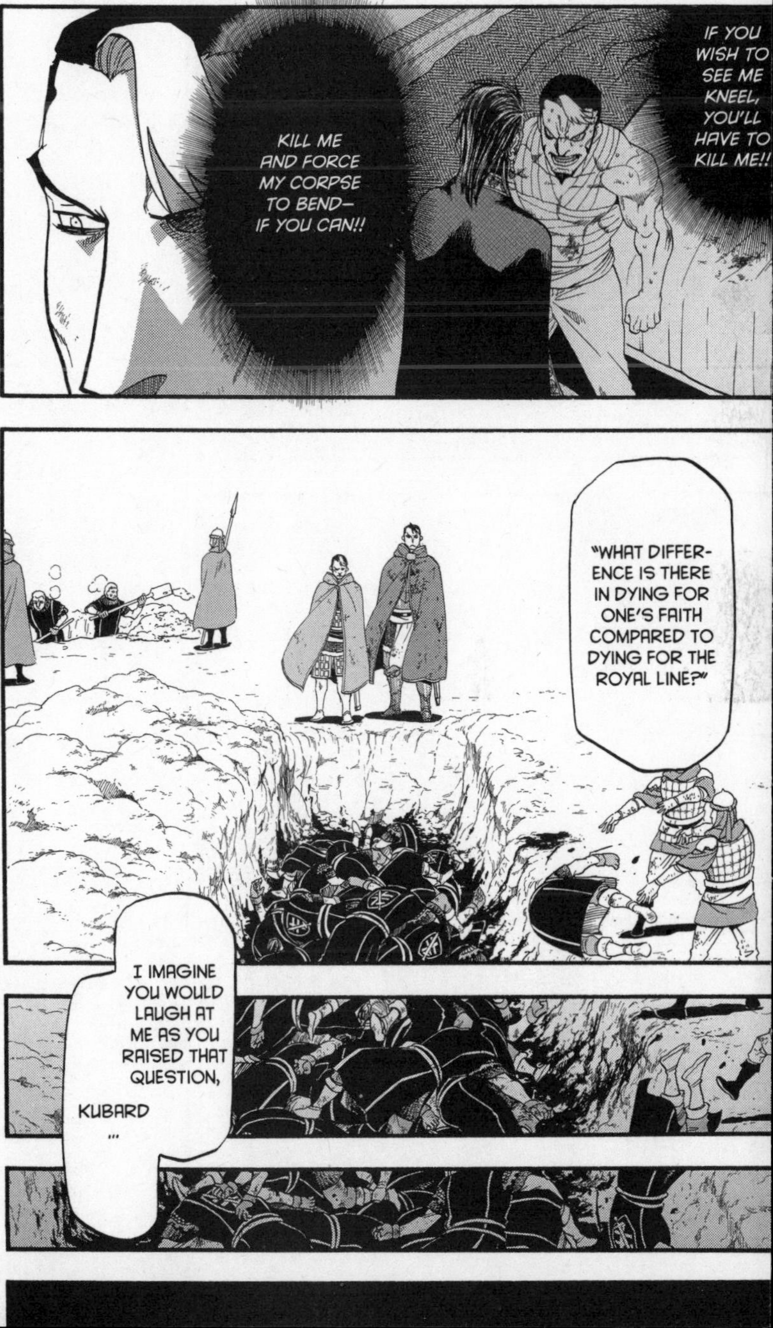
IF YOU WISH TO SEE ME KNEEL, YOU'LL HAVE TO KILL ME!!
KILL ME AND FORCE MY CORPSE TO BEND— IF YOU CAN!!
"WHAT DIFFERENCE IS THERE IN DYING FOR ONE'S FAITH COMPARED TO DYING FOR THE ROYAL LINE?"
I IMAGINE YOU WOULD LAUGH AT ME AS YOU RAISED THAT QUESTION,
KUBARD ...

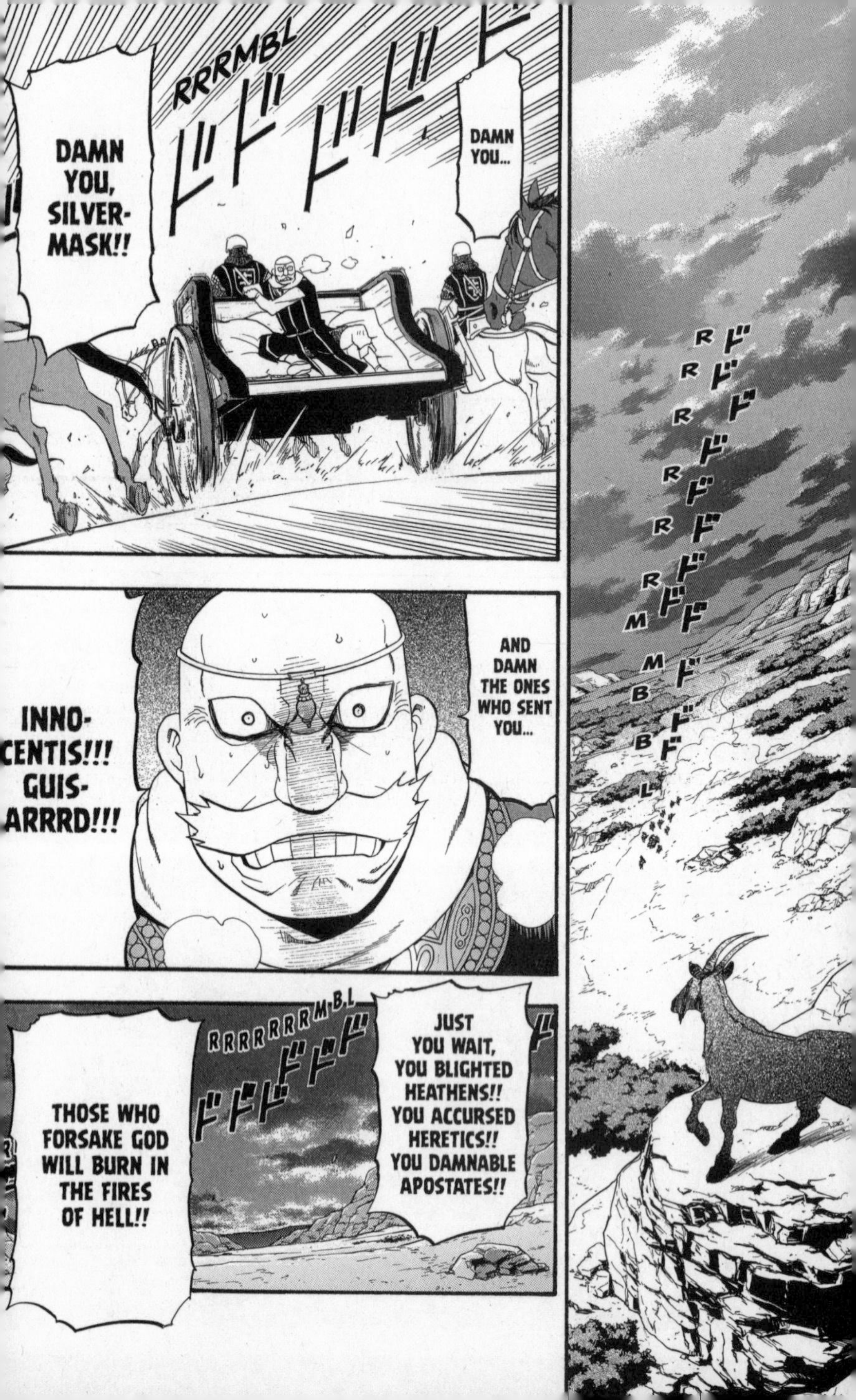

RRRRRRMMBBL
RRRMBL
DAMN YOU...
DAMN YOU, SILVER-MASK!!
AND DAMN THE ONES WHO SENT YOU...
INNO-CENTIS!!! GUIS-ARRRD!!!
JUST YOU WAIT, YOU BLIGHTED HEATHENS!! YOU ACCURSED HERETICS!! YOU DAMNABLE APOSTATES!!
RRRRRRRMBL
THOSE WHO FORSAKE GOD WILL BURN IN THE FIRES OF HELL!!

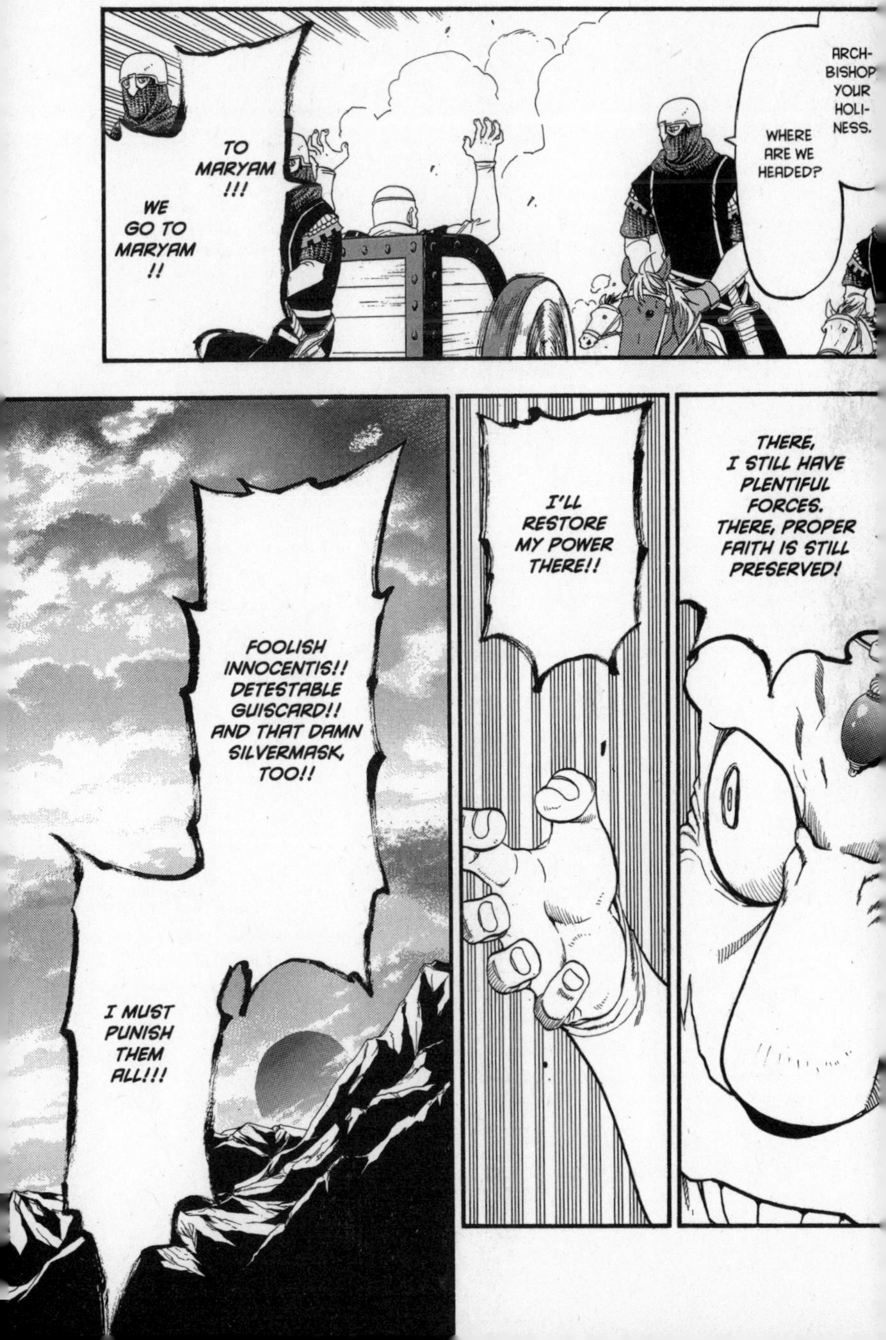
ARCH-BISHOP YOUR HOLI-NESS.
WHERE ARE WE HEADED?
TO MARYAM!!!
WE GO TO MARYAM!!
THERE, I STILL HAVE PLENTIFUL FORCES. THERE, PROPER FAITH IS STILL PRESERVED!
I'LL RESTORE MY POWER THERE!!
FOOLISH INNOCENTIS!! DETESTABLE GUISCARD!! AND THAT DAMN SILVERMASK, TOO!!
I MUST PUNISH THEM ALL!!!

THE HEROIC LEGEND OF
ARSLAN

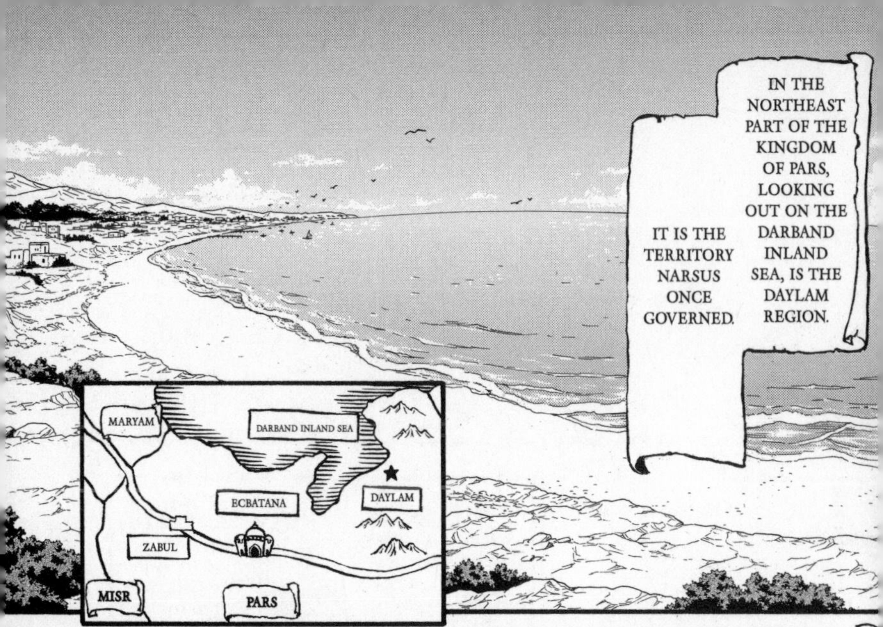
IN THE NORTHEAST PART OF THE KINGDOM OF PARS, LOOKING OUT ON THE DARBAND INLAND SEA, IS THE DAYLAM REGION.
IT IS THE TERRITORY NARSUS ONCE GOVERNED.
MARYAM
DARBAND INLAND SEA
ECBATANA
DAYLAM
ZABUL
MISR
PARS
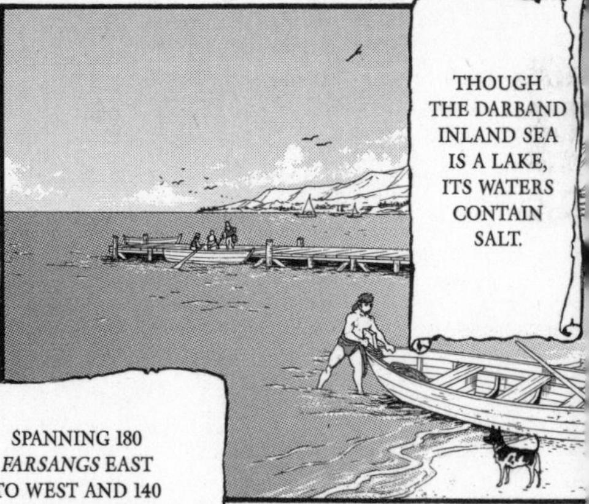
THOUGH THE DARBAND INLAND SEA IS A LAKE, ITS WATERS CONTAIN SALT.
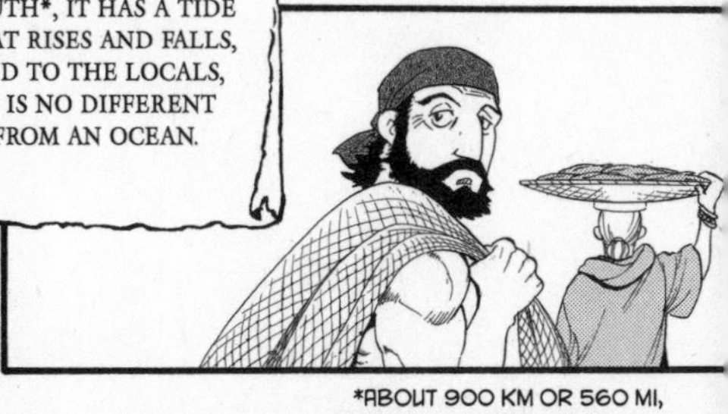
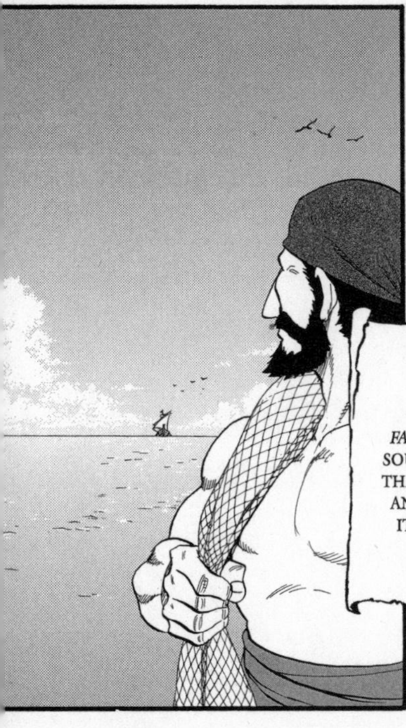
SPANNING 180 *FARSANGS* EAST TO WEST AND 140 *FARSANGS* NORTH TO SOUTH*, IT HAS A TIDE THAT RISES AND FALLS, AND TO THE LOCALS, IT IS NO DIFFERENT FROM AN OCEAN.

*ABOUT 900 KM OR 560 MI, AND 700 KM OR 435 MI

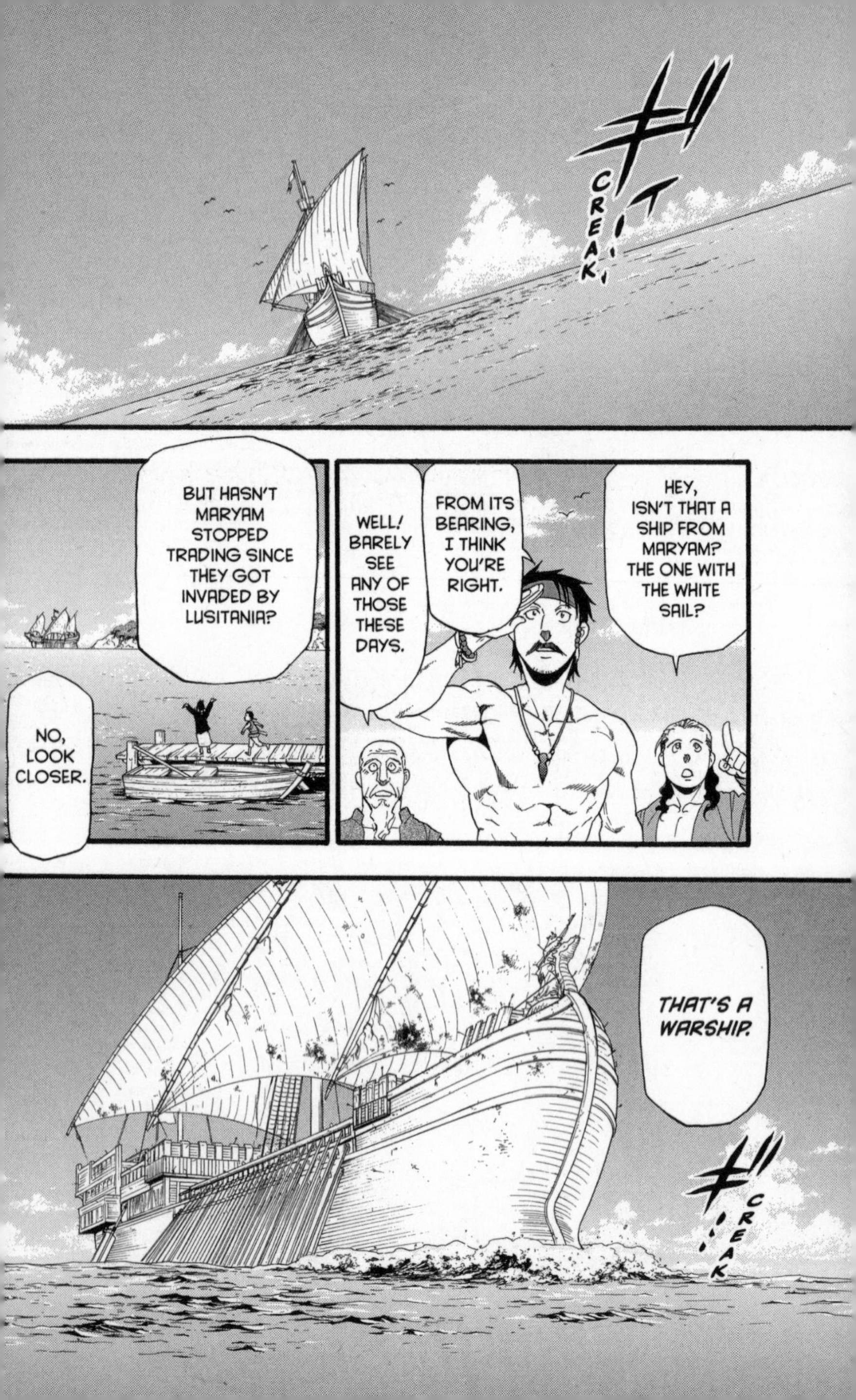
CREAK
HEY, ISN'T THAT A SHIP FROM MARYAM? THE ONE WITH THE WHITE SAIL?
FROM ITS BEARING, I THINK YOU'RE RIGHT.
WELL! BARELY SEE ANY OF THOSE THESE DAYS.
BUT HASN'T MARYAM STOPPED TRADING SINCE THEY GOT INVADED BY LUSITANIA?
NO, LOOK CLOSER.
THAT'S A WARSHIP.
CREAK

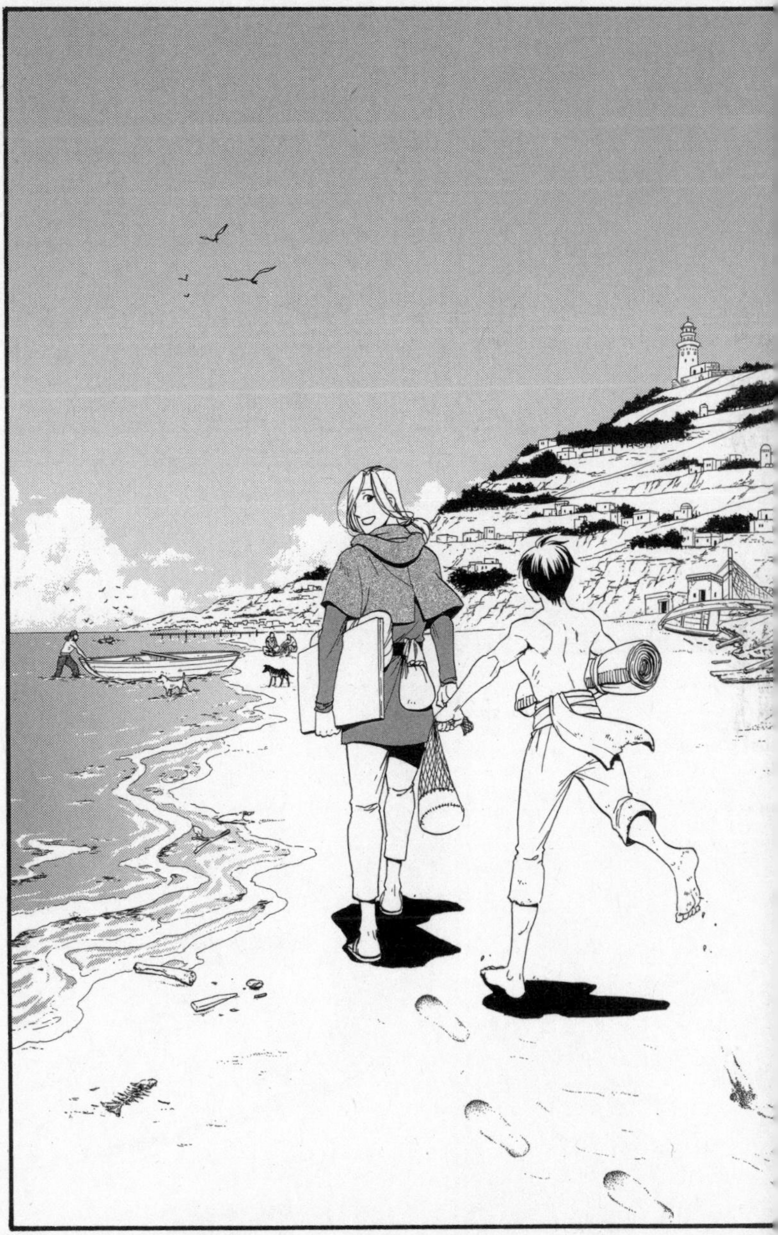

Chapter 61: The Messenger from Maryam

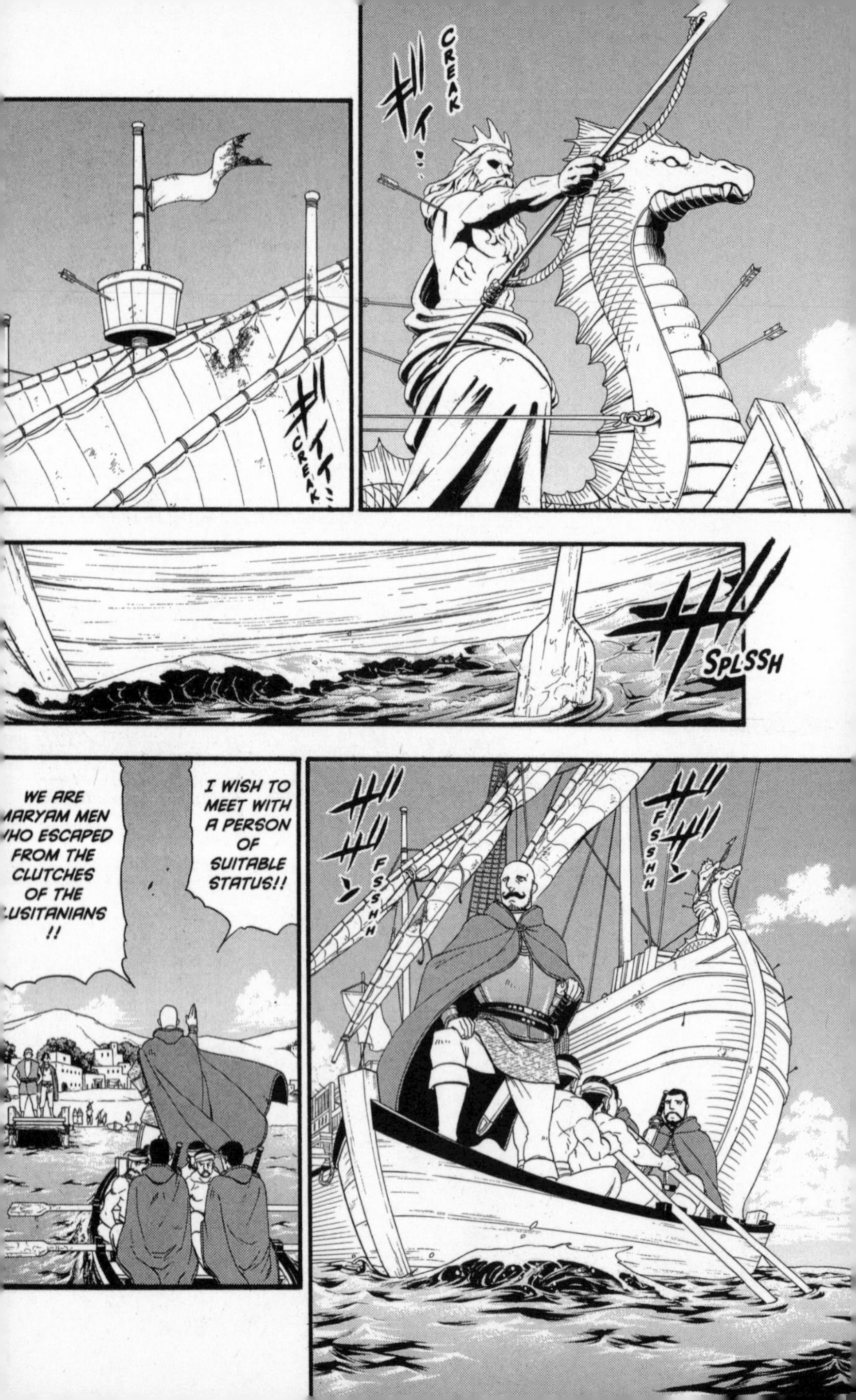
CREAK
CREAK
SPLSSH
FSSHH
FSSHH
I WISH TO MEET WITH A PERSON OF SUITABLE STATUS!!
WE ARE MARYAM MEN WHO ESCAPED FROM THE CLUTCHES OF THE LUSITANIANS !!

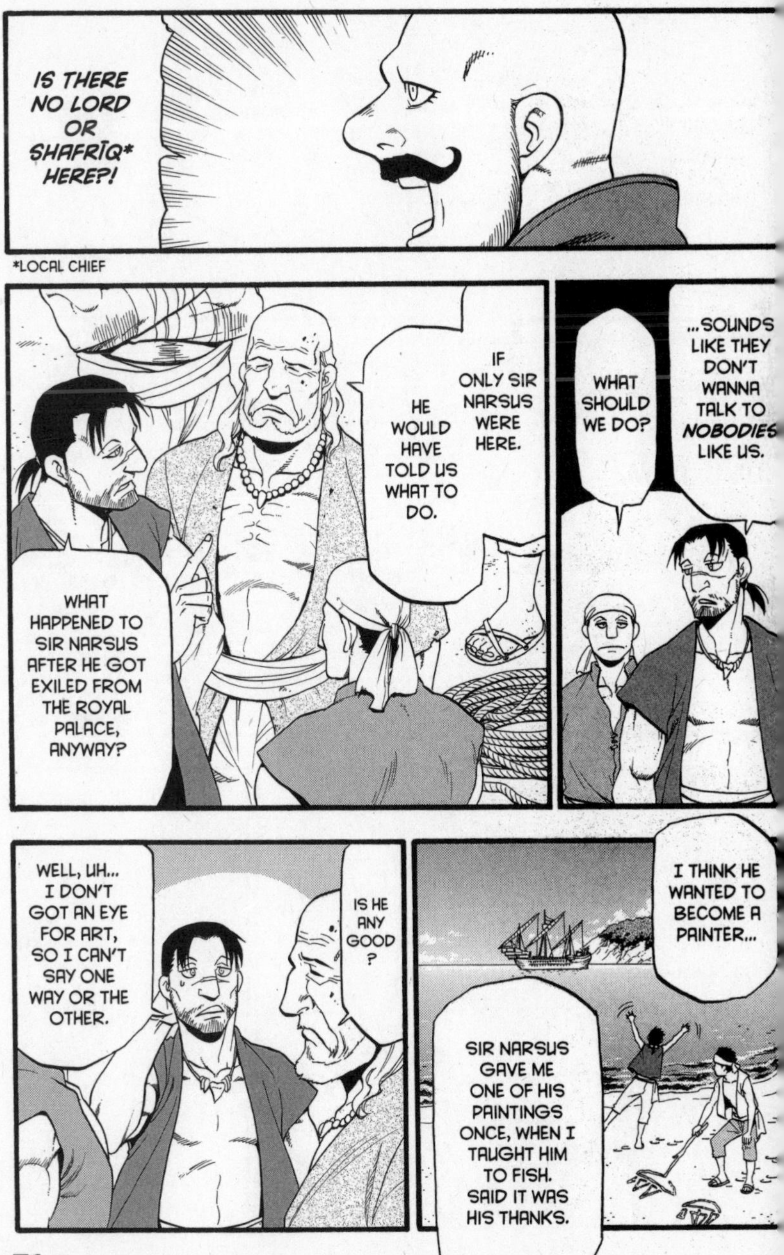
IS THERE NO LORD OR SHAFRĪQ* HERE?!
...SOUNDS LIKE THEY DON'T WANNA TALK TO *NOBODIES* LIKE US.
WHAT SHOULD WE DO?
IF ONLY SIR NARSUS WERE HERE.
HE WOULD HAVE TOLD US WHAT TO DO.
WHAT HAPPENED TO SIR NARSUS AFTER HE GOT EXILED FROM THE ROYAL PALACE, ANYWAY?
I THINK HE WANTED TO BECOME A PAINTER...
SIR NARSUS GAVE ME ONE OF HIS PAINTINGS ONCE, WHEN I TAUGHT HIM TO FISH. SAID IT WAS HIS THANKS.
IS HE ANY GOOD?
WELL, UH... I DON'T GOT AN EYE FOR ART, SO I CAN'T SAY ONE WAY OR THE OTHER.

*LOCAL CHIEF

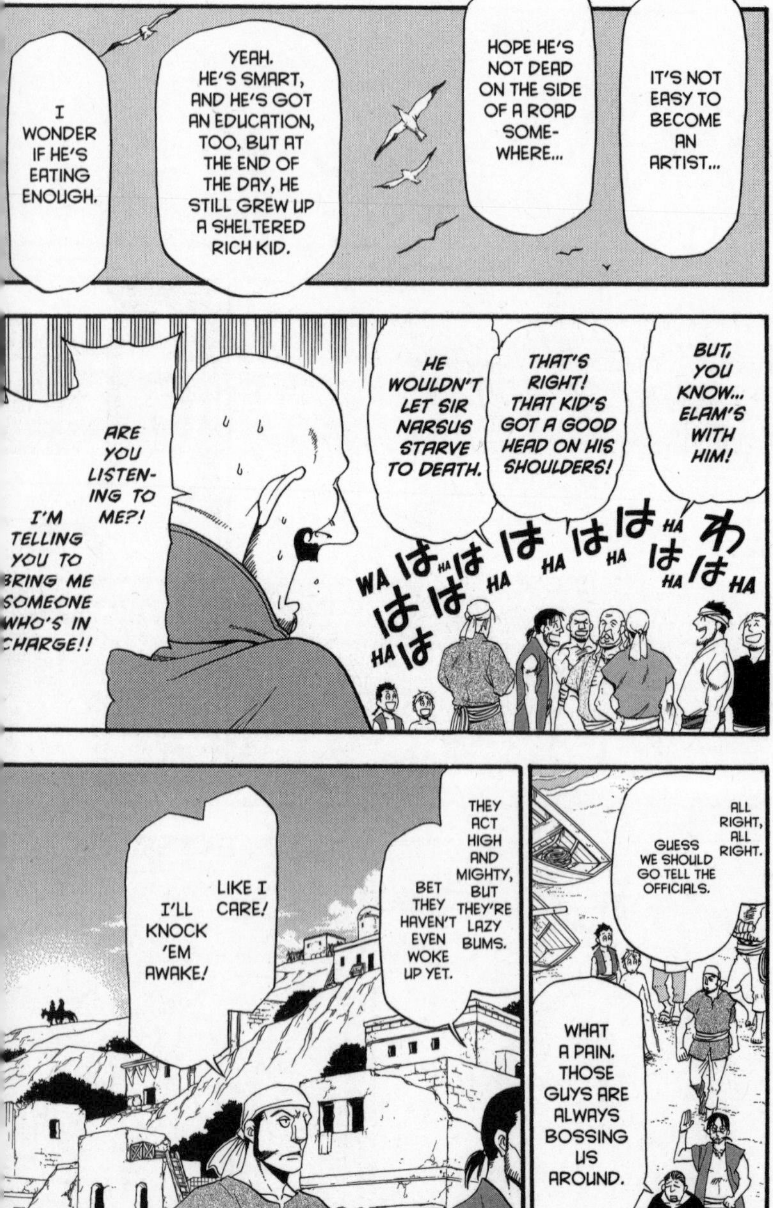

IT'S NOT EASY TO BECOME AN ARTIST...
HOPE HE'S NOT DEAD ON THE SIDE OF A ROAD SOME-WHERE...
YEAH. HE'S SMART, AND HE'S GOT AN EDUCATION, TOO, BUT AT THE END OF THE DAY, HE STILL GREW UP A SHELTERED RICH KID.
I WONDER IF HE'S EATING ENOUGH.
BUT, YOU KNOW... ELAM'S WITH HIM!
THAT'S RIGHT! THAT KID'S GOT A GOOD HEAD ON HIS SHOULDERS!
HE WOULDN'T LET SIR NARSUS STARVE TO DEATH.
WA HA HA HA HA HA HA HA HA
わはははははははははは
ARE YOU LISTEN-ING TO ME?!
I'M TELLING YOU TO BRING ME SOMEONE WHO'S IN CHARGE!!
ALL RIGHT, ALL RIGHT.
GUESS WE SHOULD GO TELL THE OFFICIALS.
WHAT A PAIN. THOSE GUYS ARE ALWAYS BOSSING US AROUND.
THEY ACT HIGH AND MIGHTY, BUT THEY'RE LAZY BUMS.
BET THEY HAVEN'T EVEN WOKE UP YET.
LIKE I CARE!
I'LL KNOCK 'EM AWAKE!

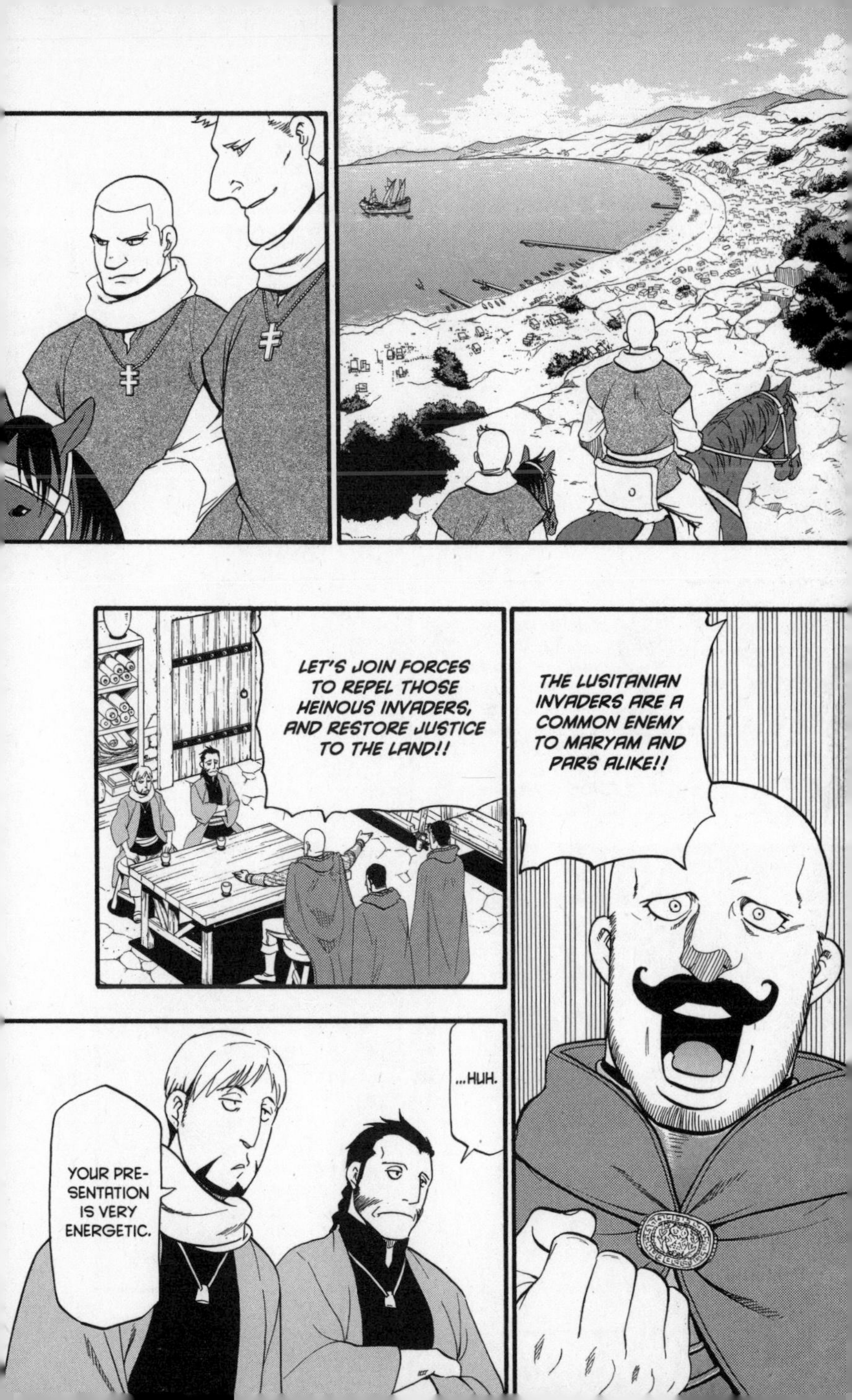
THE LUSITANIAN INVADERS ARE A COMMON ENEMY TO MARYAM AND PARS ALIKE!!
LET'S JOIN FORCES TO REPEL THOSE HEINOUS INVADERS, AND RESTORE JUSTICE TO THE LAND!!
...HUH.
YOUR PRE-SENTATION IS VERY ENERGETIC.

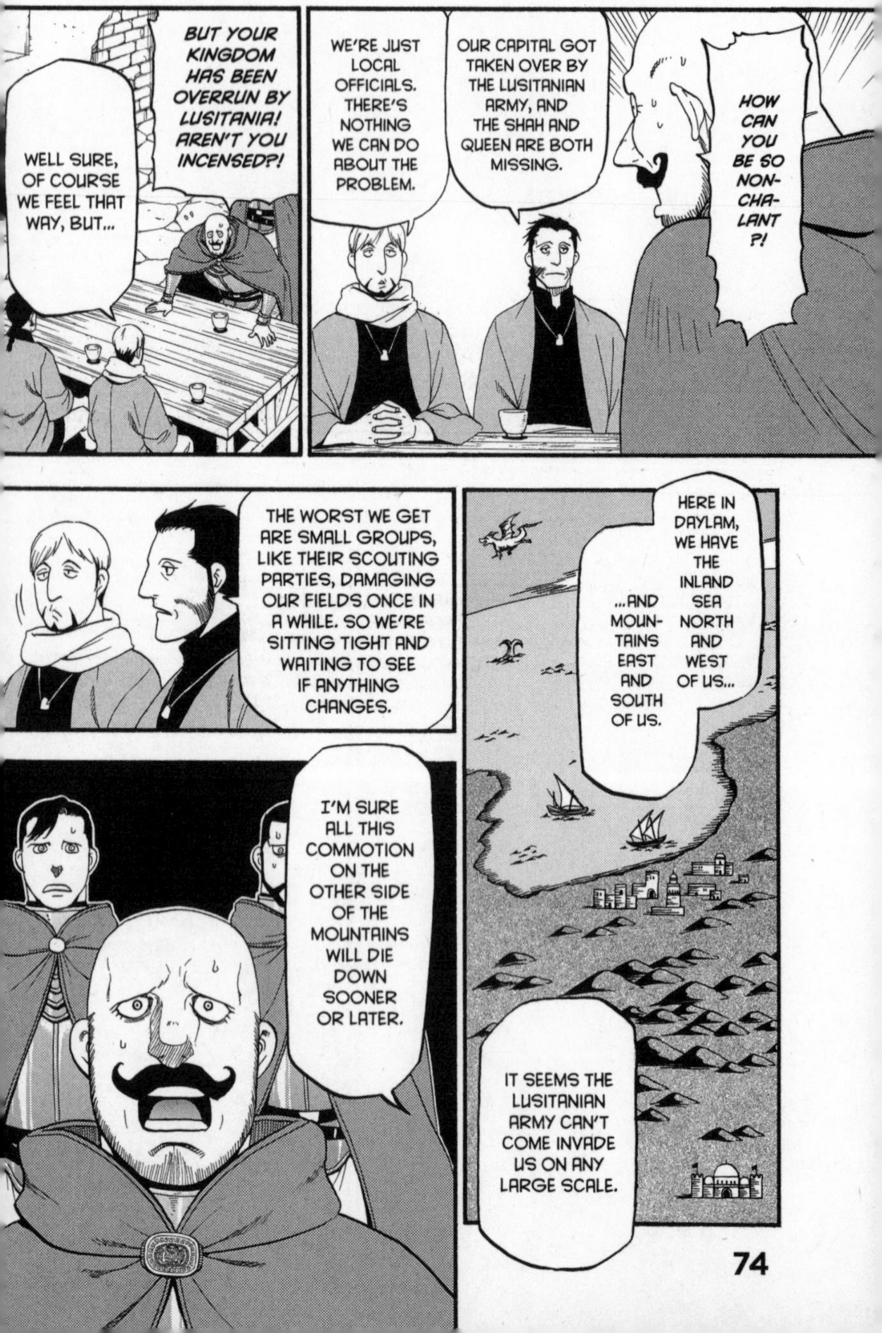
HOW CAN YOU BE SO NONCHALANT?!
OUR CAPITAL GOT TAKEN OVER BY THE LUSITANIAN ARMY, AND THE SHAH AND QUEEN ARE BOTH MISSING.
WE'RE JUST LOCAL OFFICIALS. THERE'S NOTHING WE CAN DO ABOUT THE PROBLEM.
BUT YOUR KINGDOM HAS BEEN OVERRUN BY LUSITANIA! AREN'T YOU INCENSED?!
WELL SURE, OF COURSE WE FEEL THAT WAY, BUT...
HERE IN DAYLAM, WE HAVE THE INLAND SEA NORTH AND WEST OF US...
...AND MOUNTAINS EAST AND SOUTH OF US.
IT SEEMS THE LUSITANIAN ARMY CAN'T COME INVADE US ON ANY LARGE SCALE.
THE WORST WE GET ARE SMALL GROUPS, LIKE THEIR SCOUTING PARTIES, DAMAGING OUR FIELDS ONCE IN A WHILE. SO WE'RE SITTING TIGHT AND WAITING TO SEE IF ANYTHING CHANGES.
I'M SURE ALL THIS COMMOTION ON THE OTHER SIDE OF THE MOUNTAINS WILL DIE DOWN SOONER OR LATER.

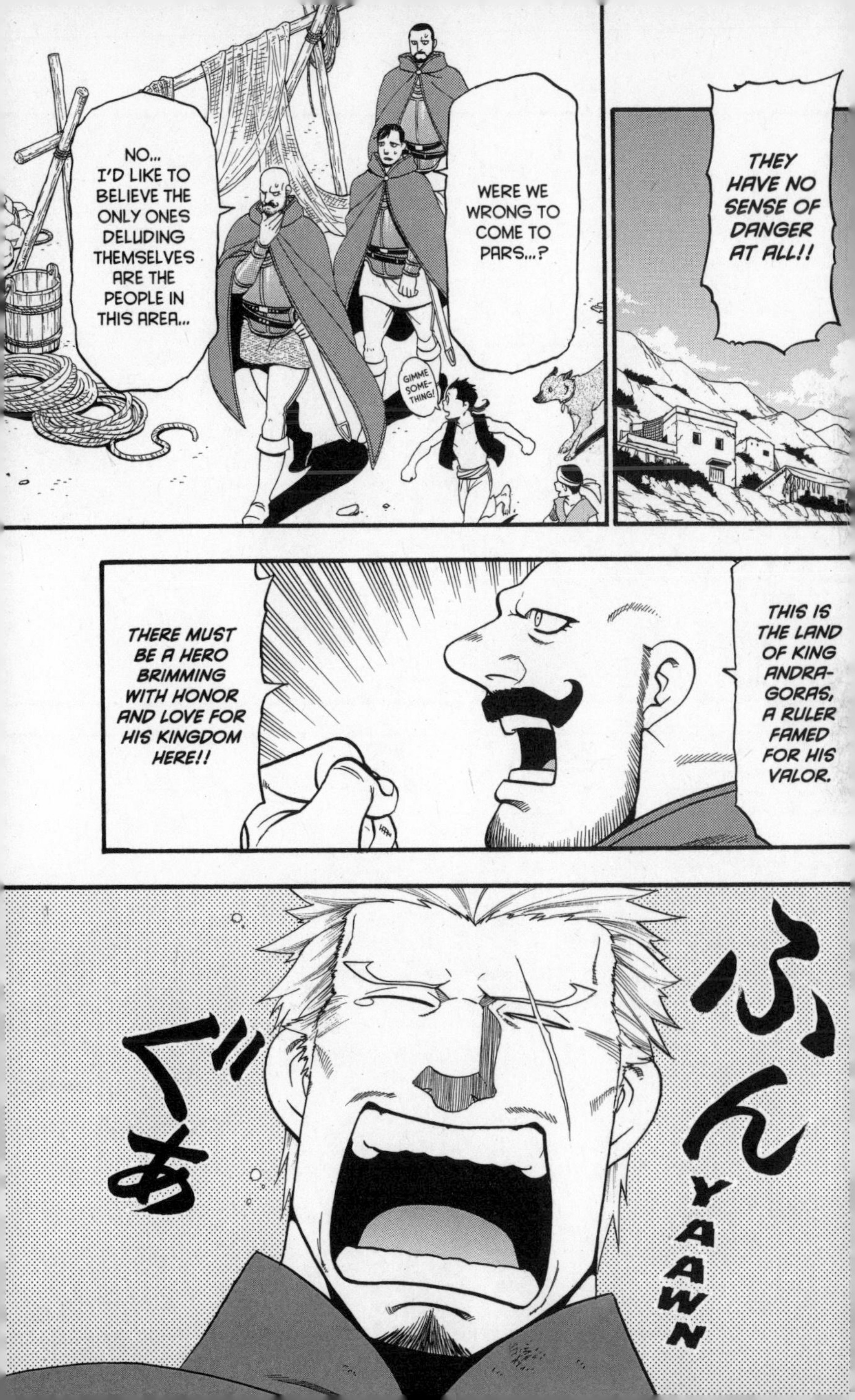
THEY HAVE NO SENSE OF DANGER AT ALL!!
WERE WE WRONG TO COME TO PARS...?
NO... I'D LIKE TO BELIEVE THE ONLY ONES DELUDING THEMSELVES ARE THE PEOPLE IN THIS AREA...
GIMME SOMETHING!
THIS IS THE LAND OF KING ANDRAGORAS, A RULER FAMED FOR HIS VALOR.
THERE MUST BE A HERO BRIMMING WITH HONOR AND LOVE FOR HIS KINGDOM HERE!!
ふん
YAAWN
ぐあ

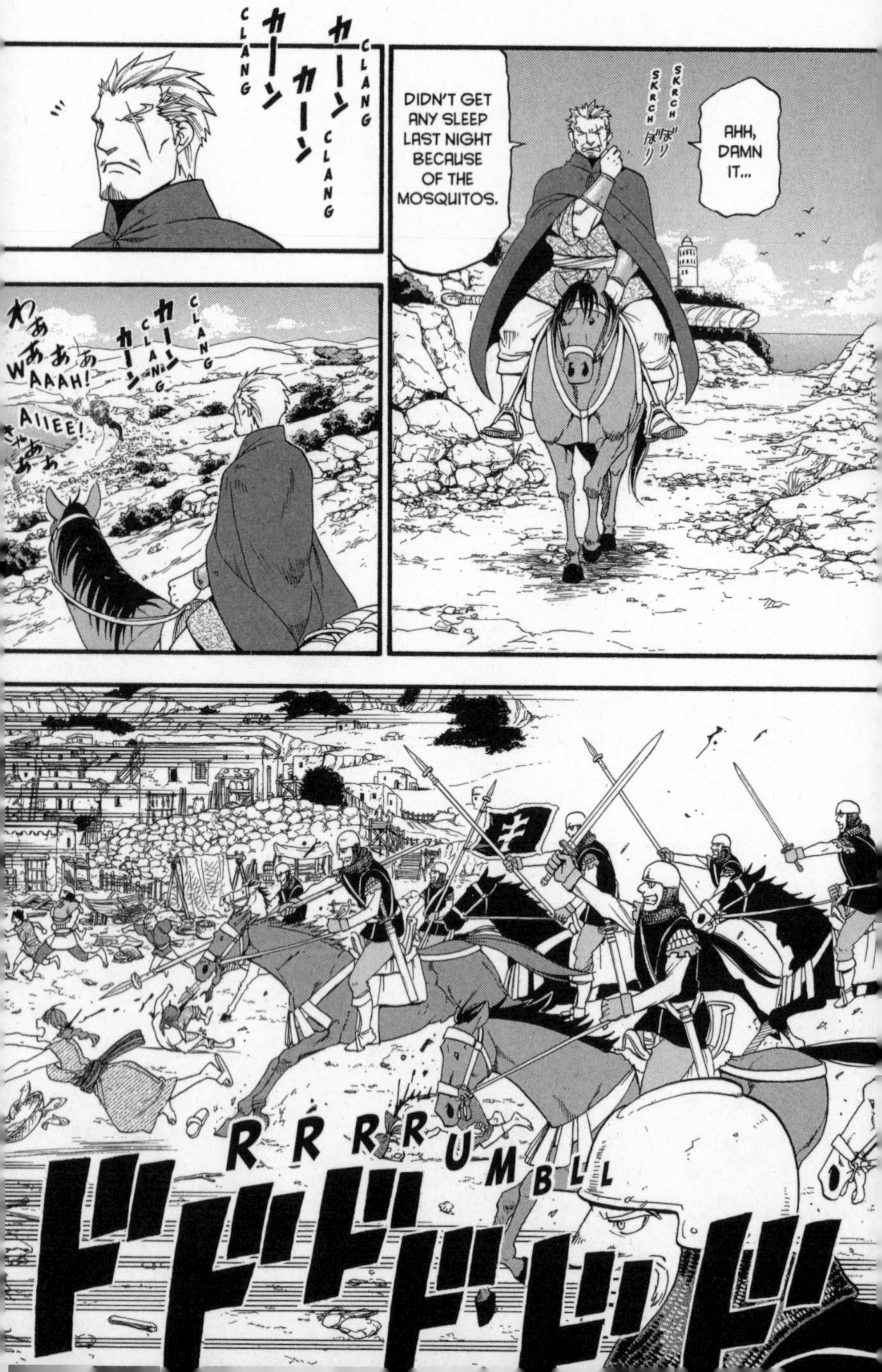

SKRCH SKRCH
ばり ばり
AHH, DAMN IT...
DIDN'T GET ANY SLEEP LAST NIGHT BECAUSE OF THE MOSQUITOS.
カーン カーン カーン
CLANG CLANG CLANG
...
わあ あ あ あ
WAAAH!
きゃあ あ
AIIEE!
カーン カーン
CLANG CLANG
RRRRUMBLL
ドドドドドド

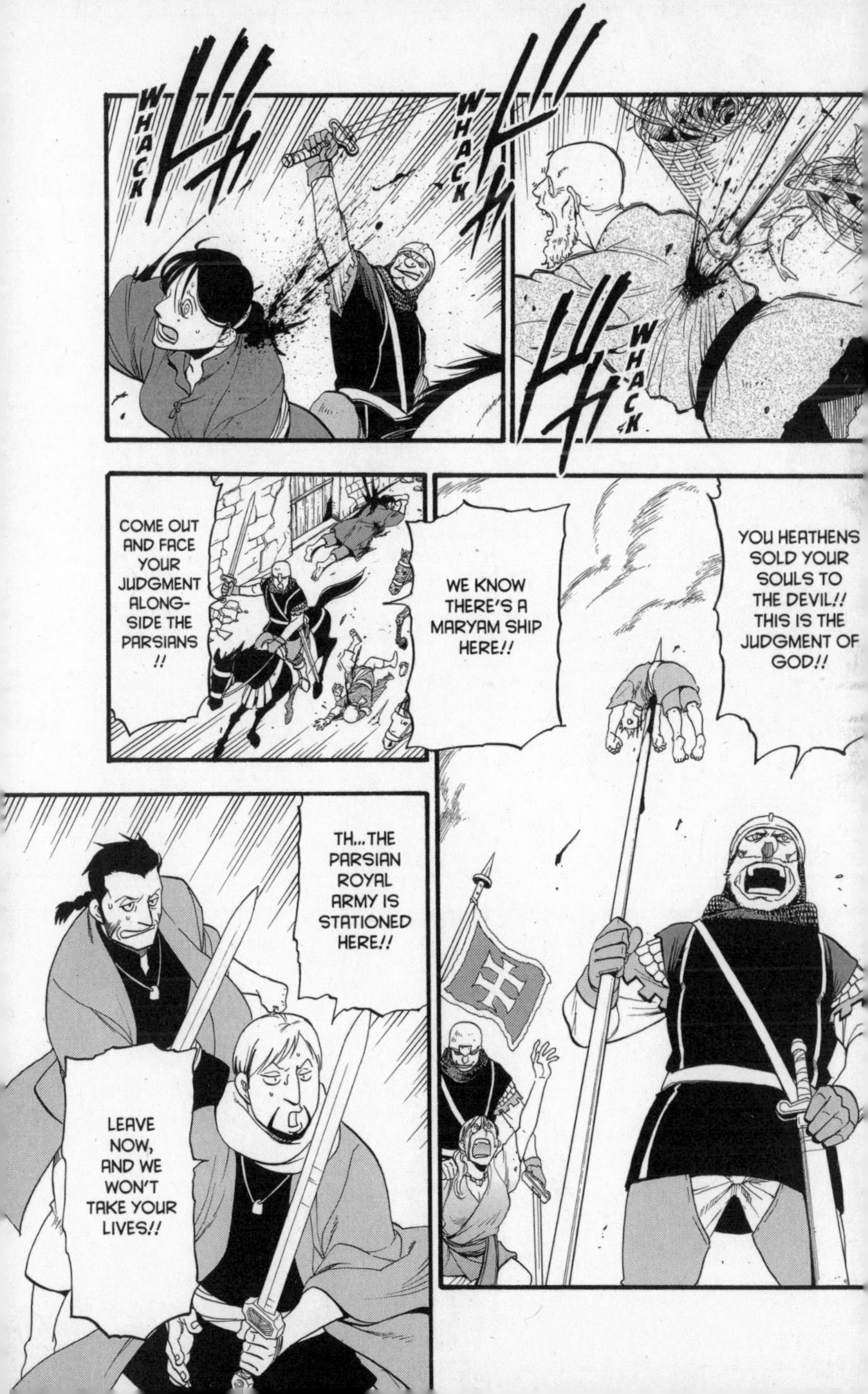
WHACK
WHACK
WHACK
YOU HEATHENS SOLD YOUR SOULS TO THE DEVIL!! THIS IS THE JUDGMENT OF GOD!!
WE KNOW THERE'S A MARYAM SHIP HERE!!
COME OUT AND FACE YOUR JUDGMENT ALONG-SIDE THE PARSIANS!!
TH...THE PARSIAN ROYAL ARMY IS STATIONED HERE!!
LEAVE NOW, AND WE WON'T TAKE YOUR LIVES!!

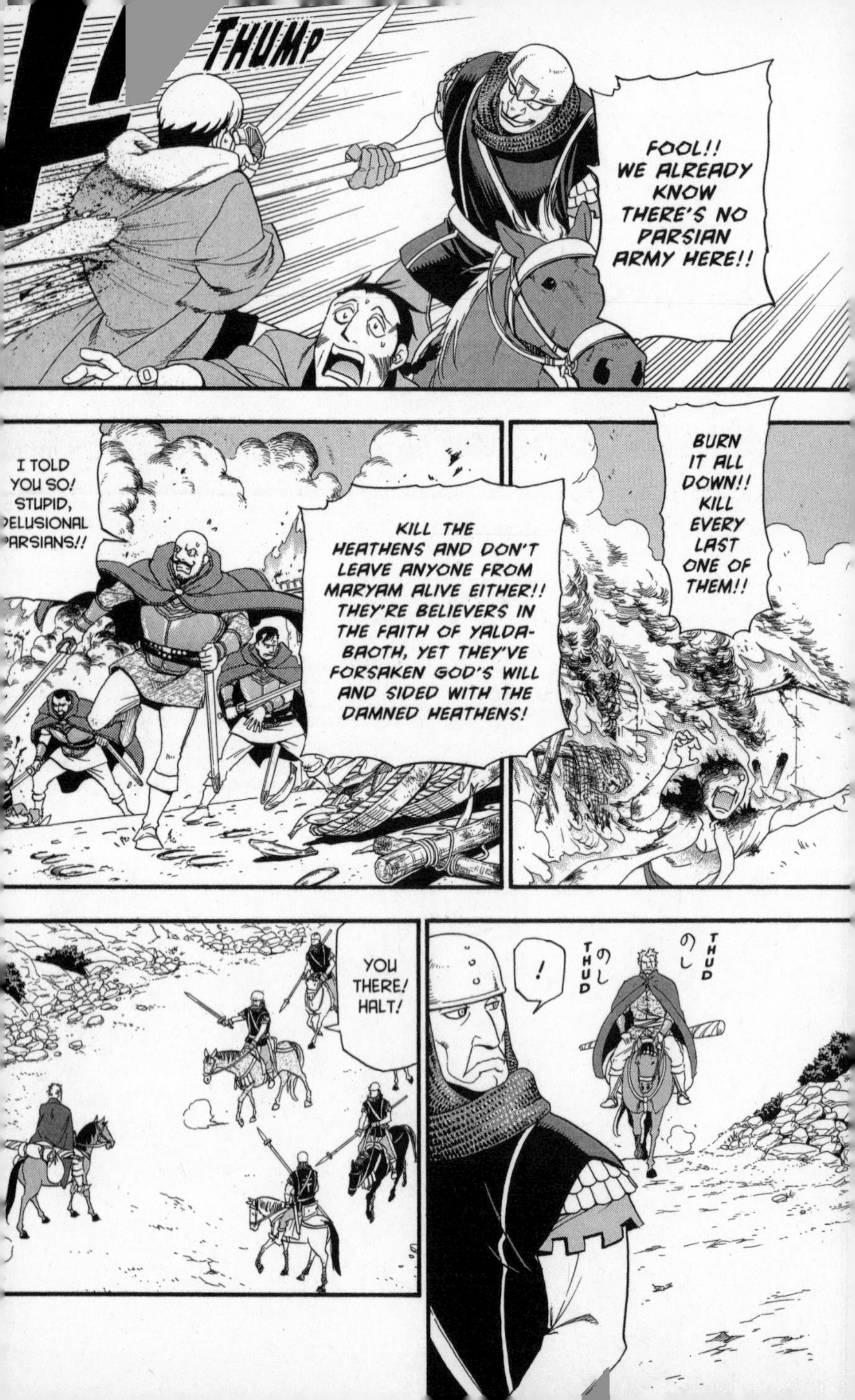
THUMP
FOOL!! WE ALREADY KNOW THERE'S NO PARSIAN ARMY HERE!!
BURN IT ALL DOWN!! KILL EVERY LAST ONE OF THEM!!
KILL THE HEATHENS AND DON'T LEAVE ANYONE FROM MARYAM ALIVE EITHER!! THEY'RE BELIEVERS IN THE FAITH OF YALDA-BAOTH, YET THEY'VE FORSAKEN GOD'S WILL AND SIDED WITH THE DAMNED HEATHENS!
I TOLD YOU SO! STUPID, DELUSIONAL PARSIANS!!
THUD のし
THUD のし
!
YOU THERE! HALT!

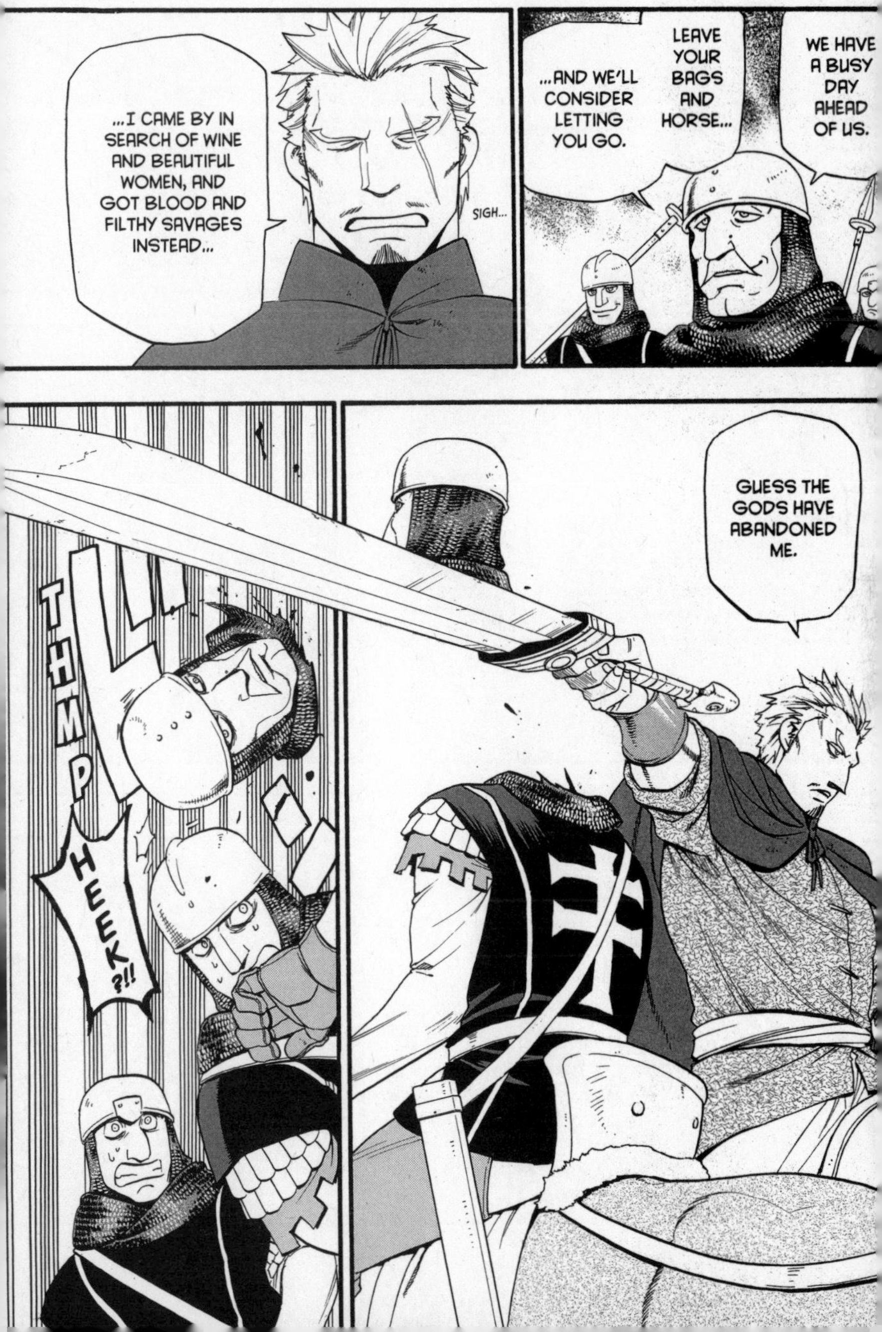
WE HAVE A BUSY DAY AHEAD OF US.
LEAVE YOUR BAGS AND HORSE...
...AND WE'LL CONSIDER LETTING YOU GO.
SIGH...
...I CAME BY IN SEARCH OF WINE AND BEAUTIFUL WOMEN, AND GOT BLOOD AND FILTHY SAVAGES INSTEAD...
GUESS THE GODS HAVE ABANDONED ME.
THMP
HEEK?!!

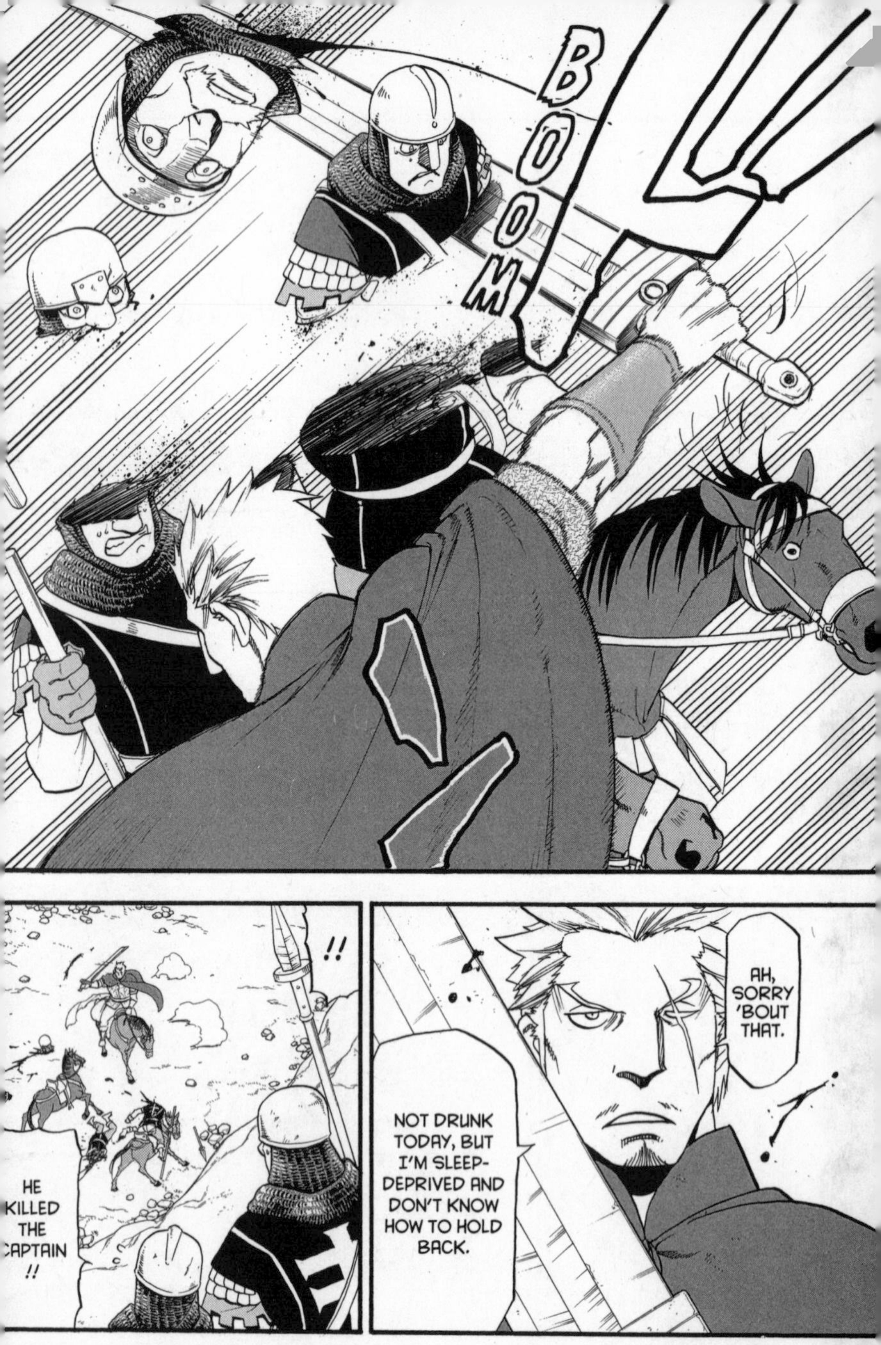
BOOM
AH, SORRY 'BOUT THAT.
NOT DRUNK TODAY, BUT I'M SLEEP-DEPRIVED AND DON'T KNOW HOW TO HOLD BACK.
!!
HE KILLED THE CAPTAIN !!

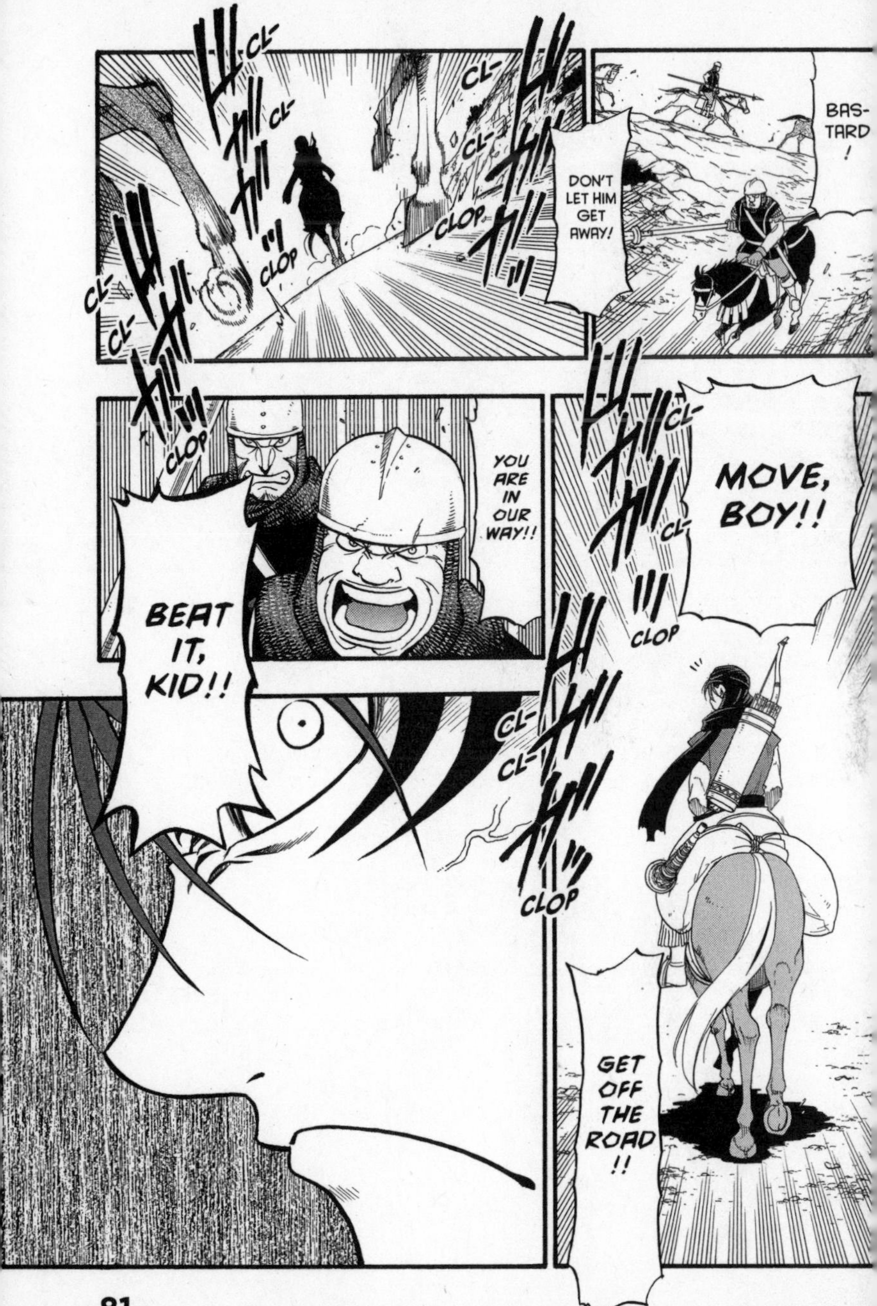
BAS-TARD!
DON'T LET HIM GET AWAY!
CL- CL- CLOP
CL- CL- CLOP
CL- CL- CLOP
MOVE, BOY!!
CL- CL- CLOP
CL- CL- CLOP
GET OFF THE ROAD!!
YOU ARE IN OUR WAY!!
BEAT IT, KID!!

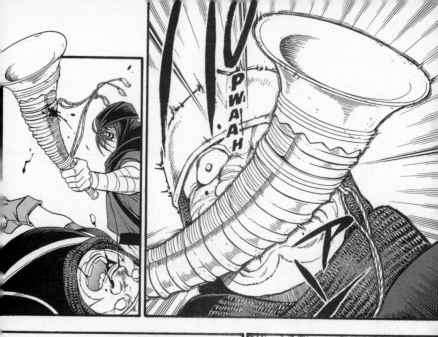

PWAAH

?!

PLOP

82

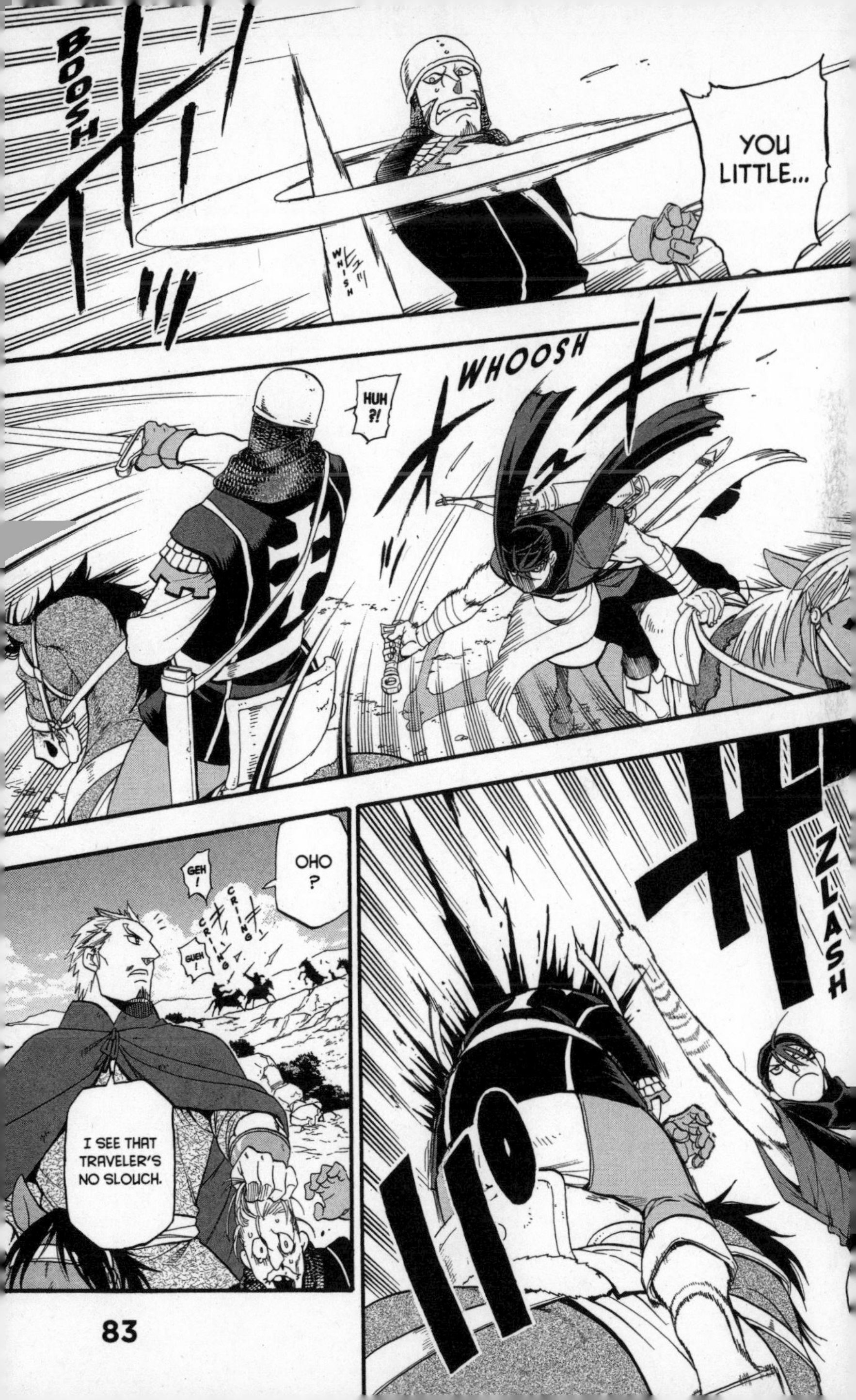

YOU LITTLE...
WHISH
BOOSH
WHOOSH
HUH?!
ZLASH
OHO?
GEH!
CRING CRING
GUEH!
I SEE THAT TRAVELER'S NO SLOUCH.

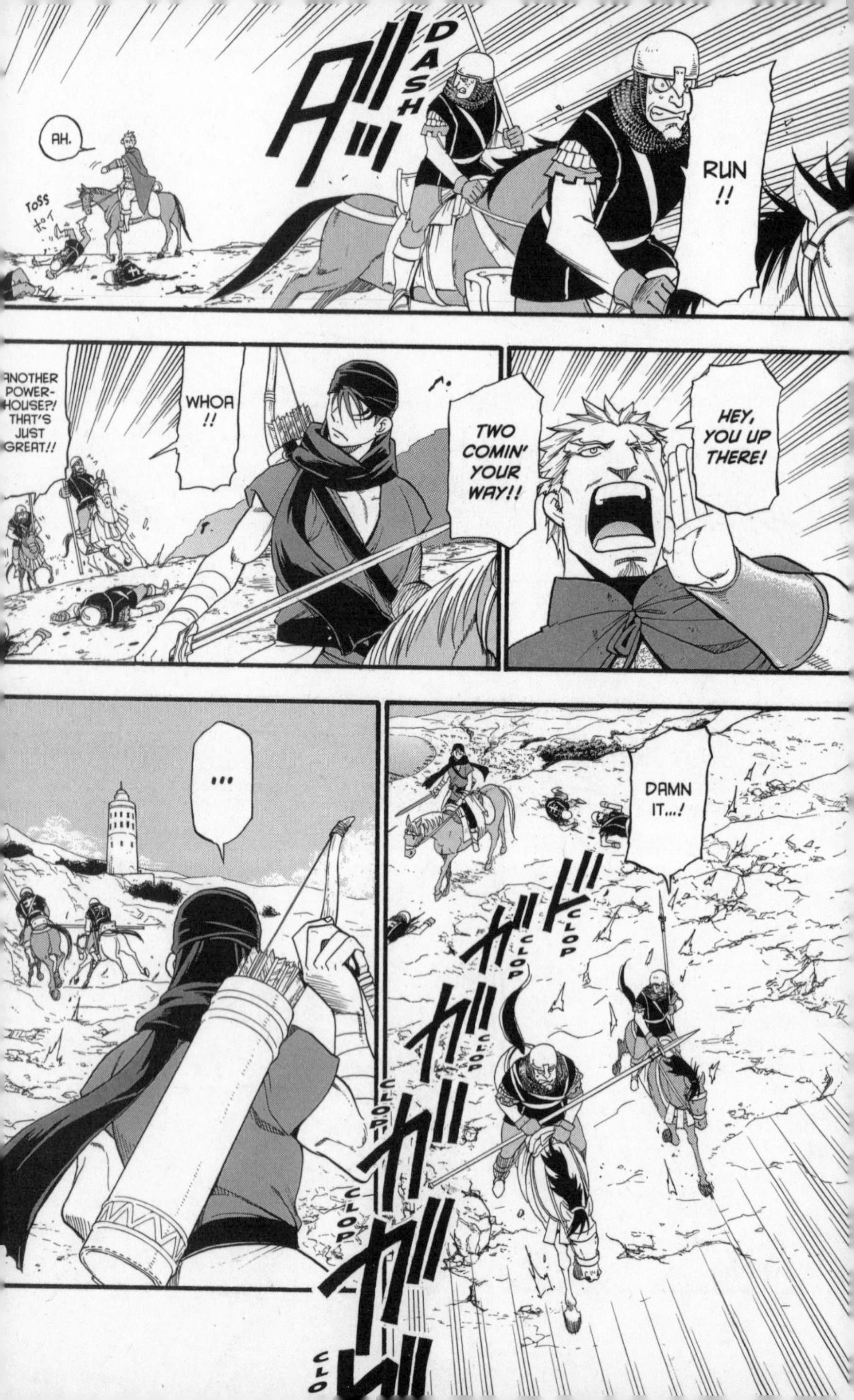
RUN !!
DASH
AH.
TOSS
HEY, YOU UP THERE!
TWO COMIN' YOUR WAY!!
WHOA !!
ANOTHER POWER-HOUSE?! THAT'S JUST GREAT!!
DAMN IT...!
CLOP CLOP
CLOP CLOP
CLOP CLOP
CLO
...

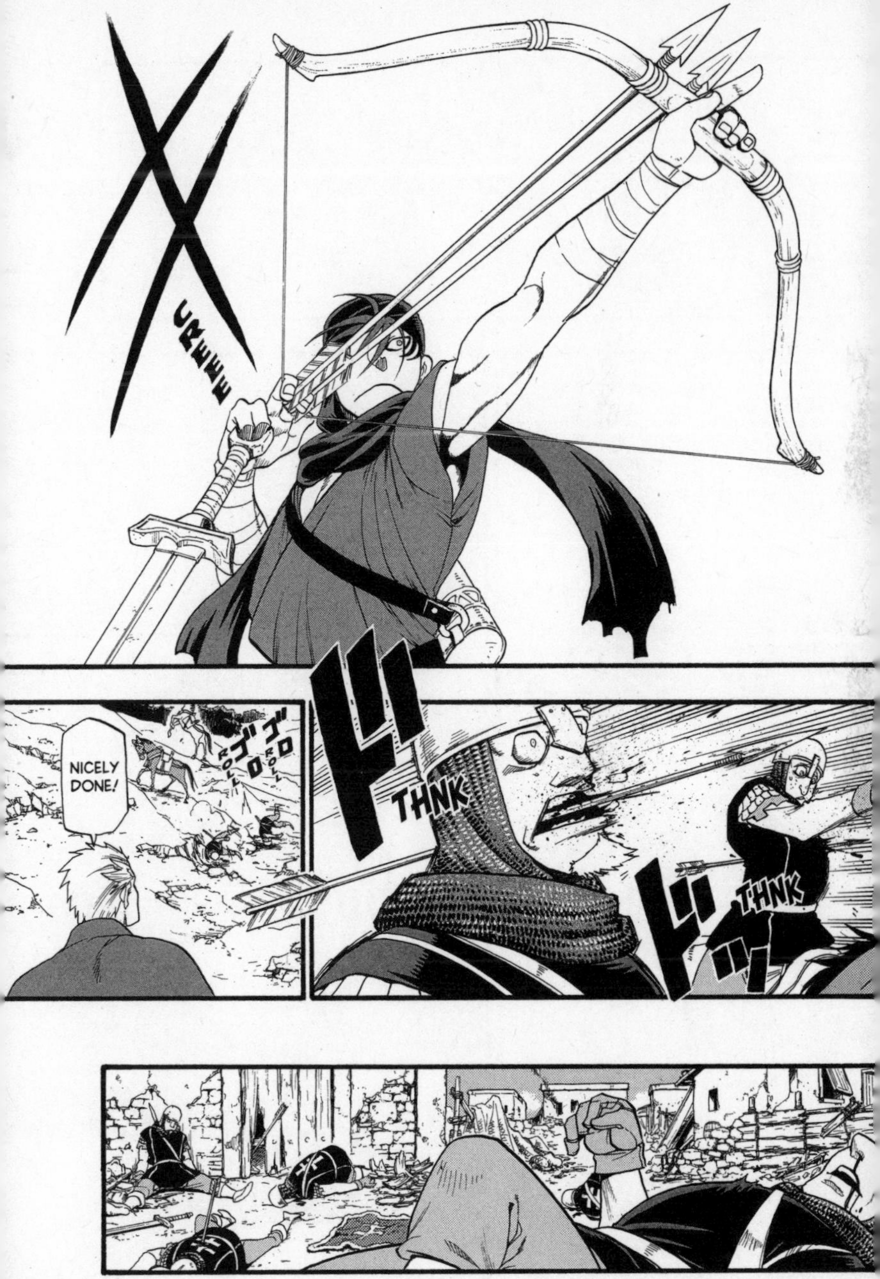
CREEE
THNK
THNK
ROLL ROLL
NICELY DONE!

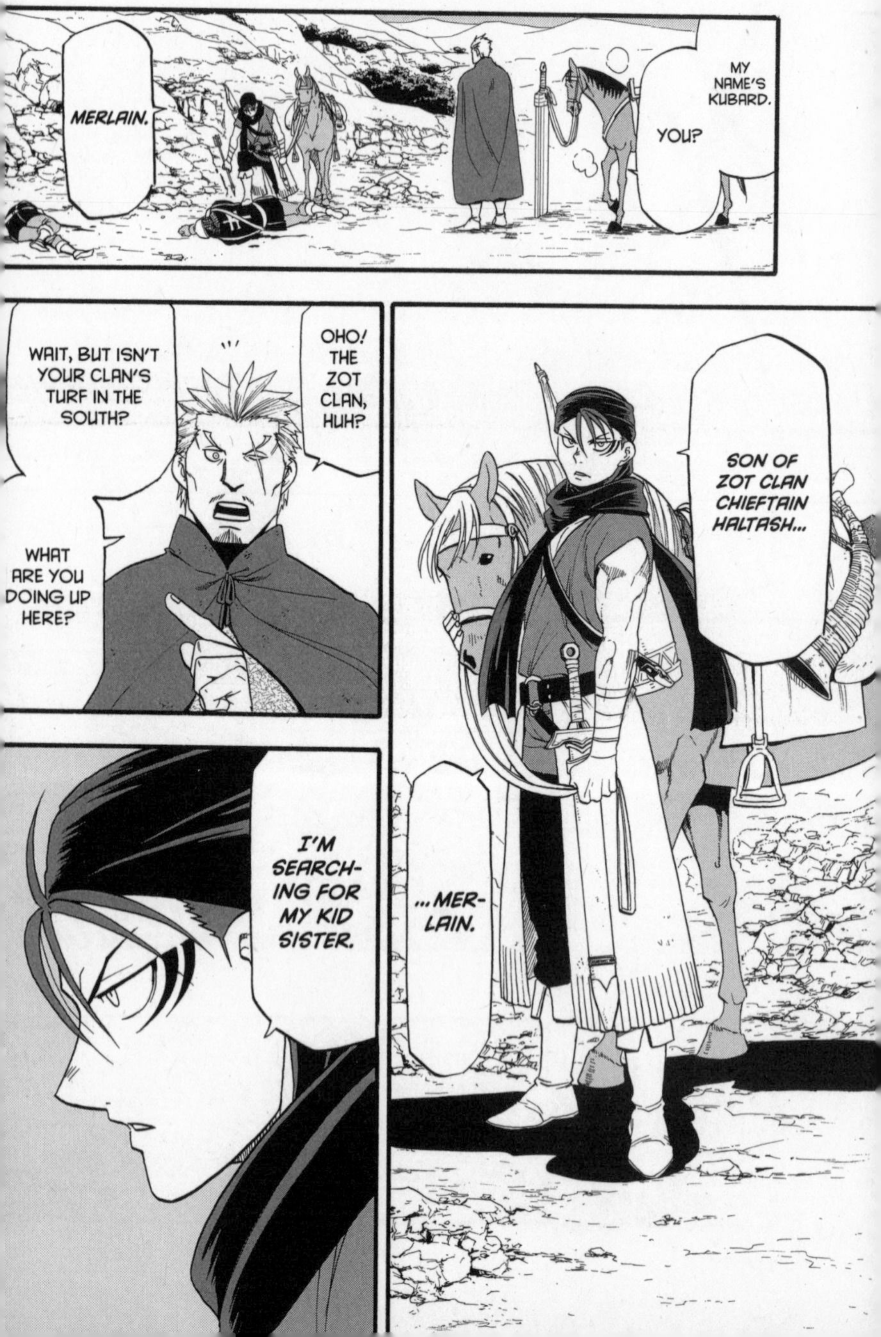
MY NAME'S KUBARD.
YOU?
MERLAIN.
SON OF ZOT CLAN CHIEFTAIN HALTASH...
...MER-LAIN.
OHO! THE ZOT CLAN, HUH?
WAIT, BUT ISN'T YOUR CLAN'S TURF IN THE SOUTH?
WHAT ARE YOU DOING UP HERE?
I'M SEARCHING FOR MY KID SISTER.

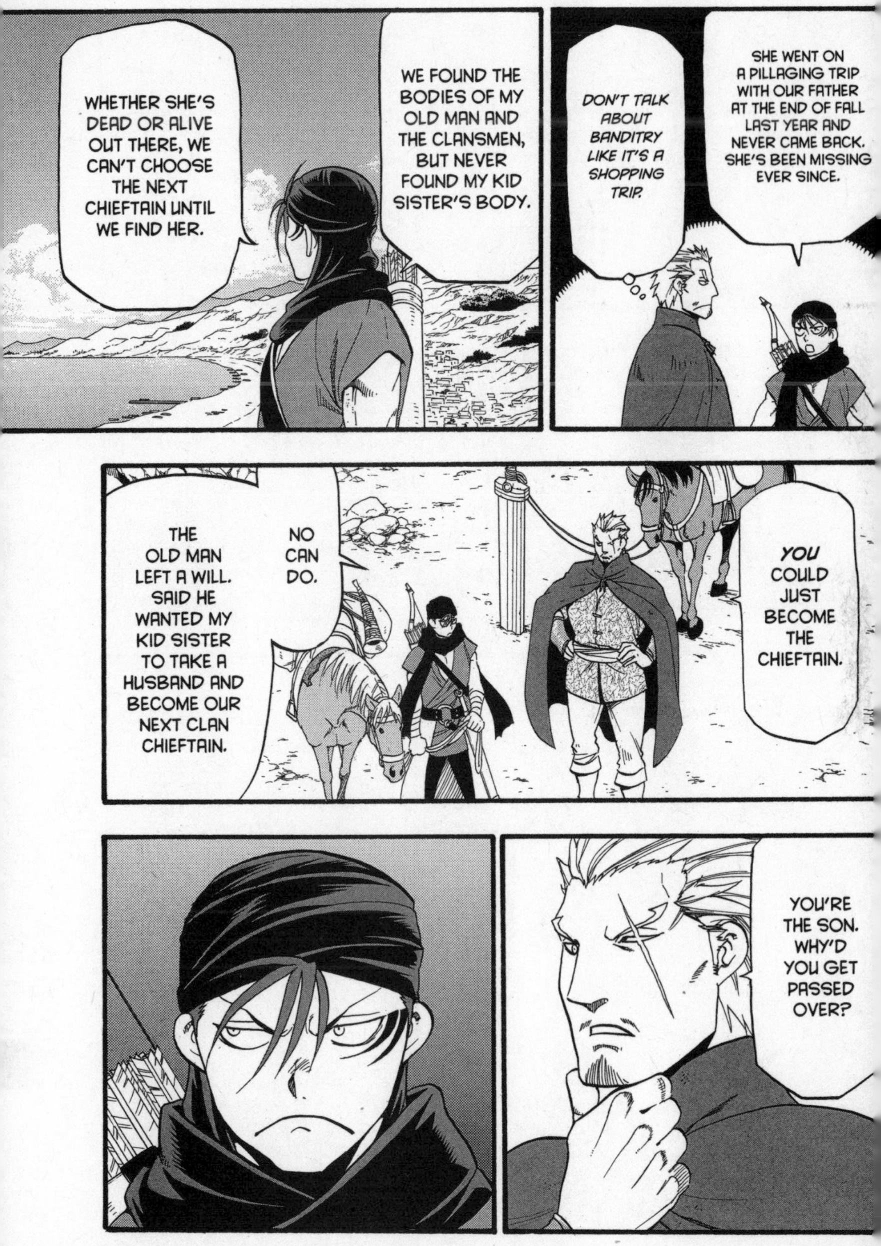
SHE WENT ON A PILLAGING TRIP WITH OUR FATHER AT THE END OF FALL LAST YEAR AND NEVER CAME BACK. SHE'S BEEN MISSING EVER SINCE.
DON'T TALK ABOUT BANDITRY LIKE IT'S A SHOPPING TRIP.
WE FOUND THE BODIES OF MY OLD MAN AND THE CLANSMEN, BUT NEVER FOUND MY KID SISTER'S BODY.
WHETHER SHE'S DEAD OR ALIVE OUT THERE, WE CAN'T CHOOSE THE NEXT CHIEFTAIN UNTIL WE FIND HER.
YOU COULD JUST BECOME THE CHIEFTAIN.
NO CAN DO.
THE OLD MAN LEFT A WILL. SAID HE WANTED MY KID SISTER TO TAKE A HUSBAND AND BECOME OUR NEXT CLAN CHIEFTAIN.
YOU'RE THE SON. WHY'D YOU GET PASSED OVER?

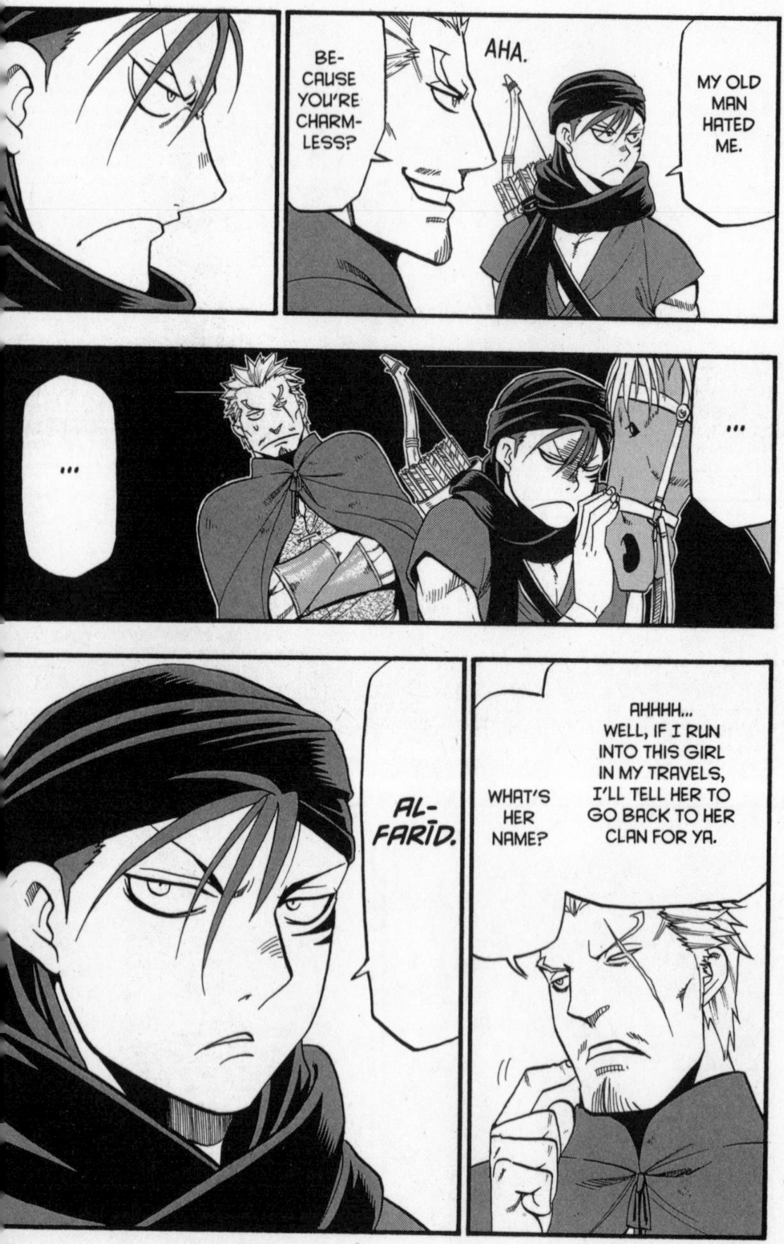
MY OLD MAN HATED ME.
AHA.
BE-CAUSE YOU'RE CHARM-LESS?
...
...
AHHHH... WELL, IF I RUN INTO THIS GIRL IN MY TRAVELS, I'LL TELL HER TO GO BACK TO HER CLAN FOR YA.
WHAT'S HER NAME?
AL-FARĪD.

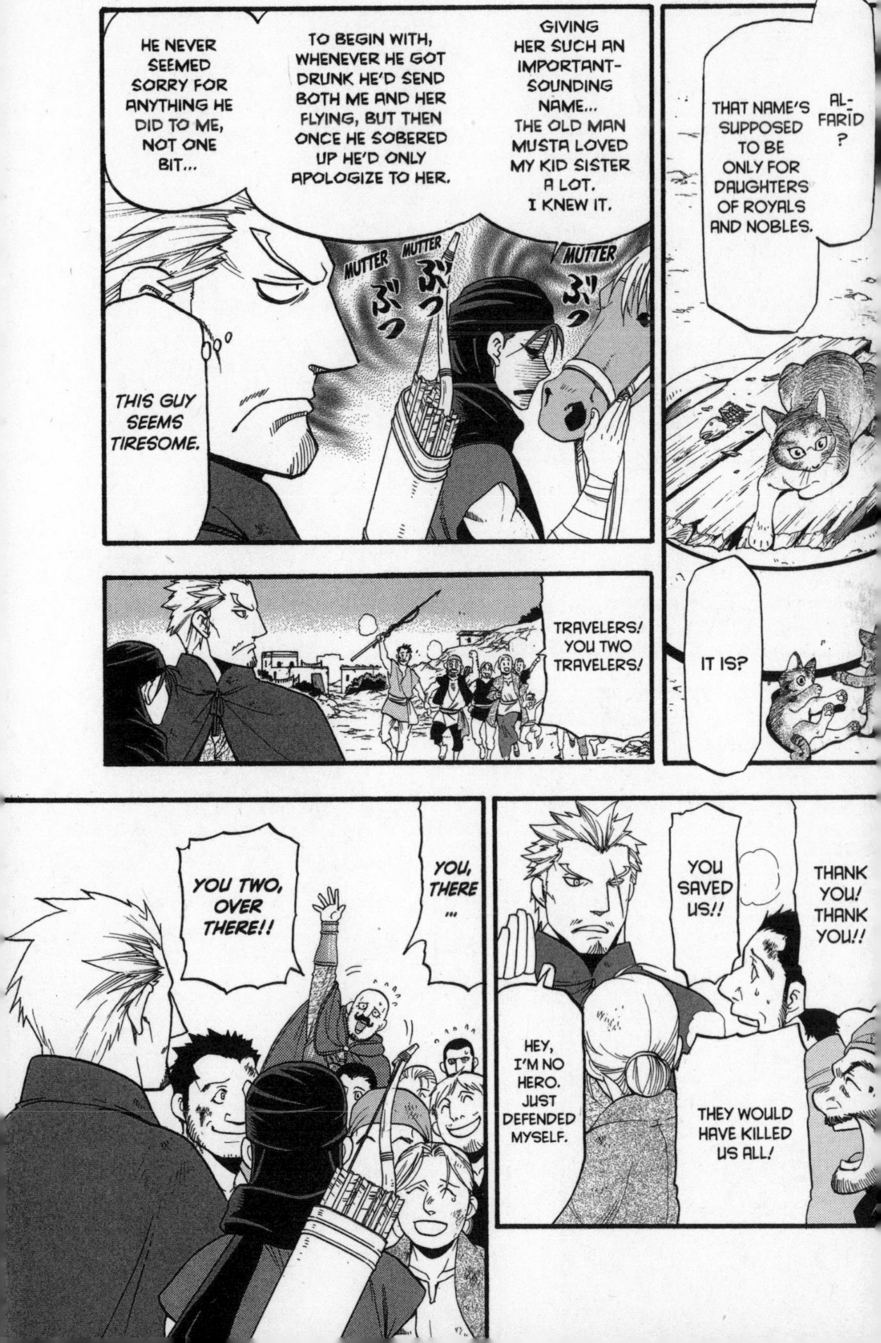
AL-FARID?
THAT NAME'S SUPPOSED TO BE ONLY FOR DAUGHTERS OF ROYALS AND NOBLES.
GIVING HER SUCH AN IMPORTANT-SOUNDING NAME... THE OLD MAN MUSTA LOVED MY KID SISTER A LOT. I KNEW IT.
TO BEGIN WITH, WHENEVER HE GOT DRUNK HE'D SEND BOTH ME AND HER FLYING, BUT THEN ONCE HE SOBERED UP HE'D ONLY APOLOGIZE TO HER.
HE NEVER SEEMED SORRY FOR ANYTHING HE DID TO ME, NOT ONE BIT...
MUTTER ぶつ
MUTTER ぶつ
MUTTER ぶつ
THIS GUY SEEMS TIRESOME.
IT IS?
TRAVELERS! YOU TWO TRAVELERS!
THANK YOU! THANK YOU!!
YOU SAVED US!!
THEY WOULD HAVE KILLED US ALL!
HEY, I'M NO HERO. JUST DEFENDED MYSELF.
YOU, THERE...
YOU TWO, OVER THERE!!

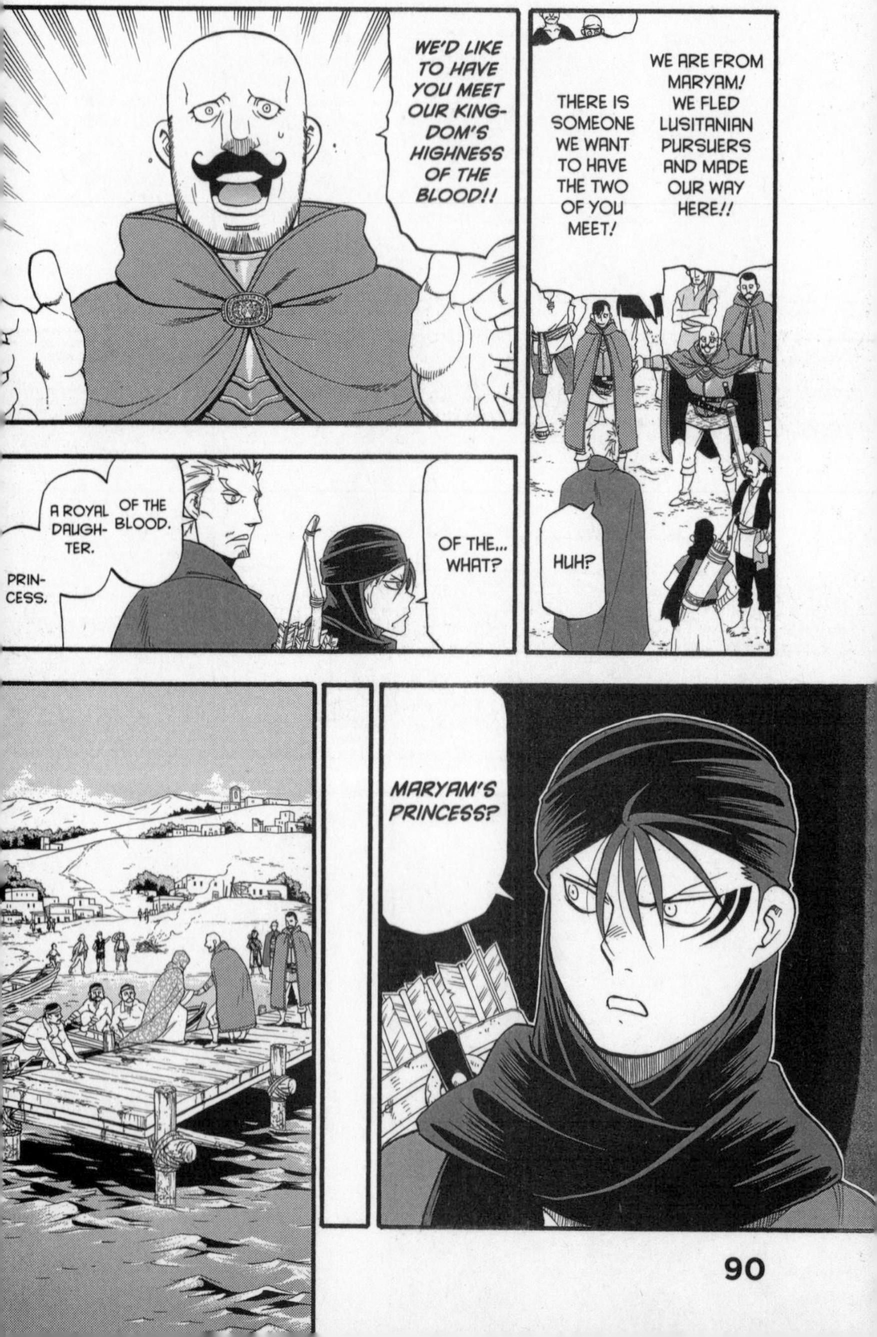
WE ARE FROM MARYAM! WE FLED LUSITANIAN PURSUERS AND MADE OUR WAY HERE!!
THERE IS SOMEONE WE WANT TO HAVE THE TWO OF YOU MEET!
HUH?
WE'D LIKE TO HAVE YOU MEET OUR KING-DOM'S HIGHNESS OF THE BLOOD!!
OF THE... WHAT?
OF THE BLOOD.
A ROYAL DAUGH-TER.
PRIN-CESS.
MARYAM'S PRINCESS?

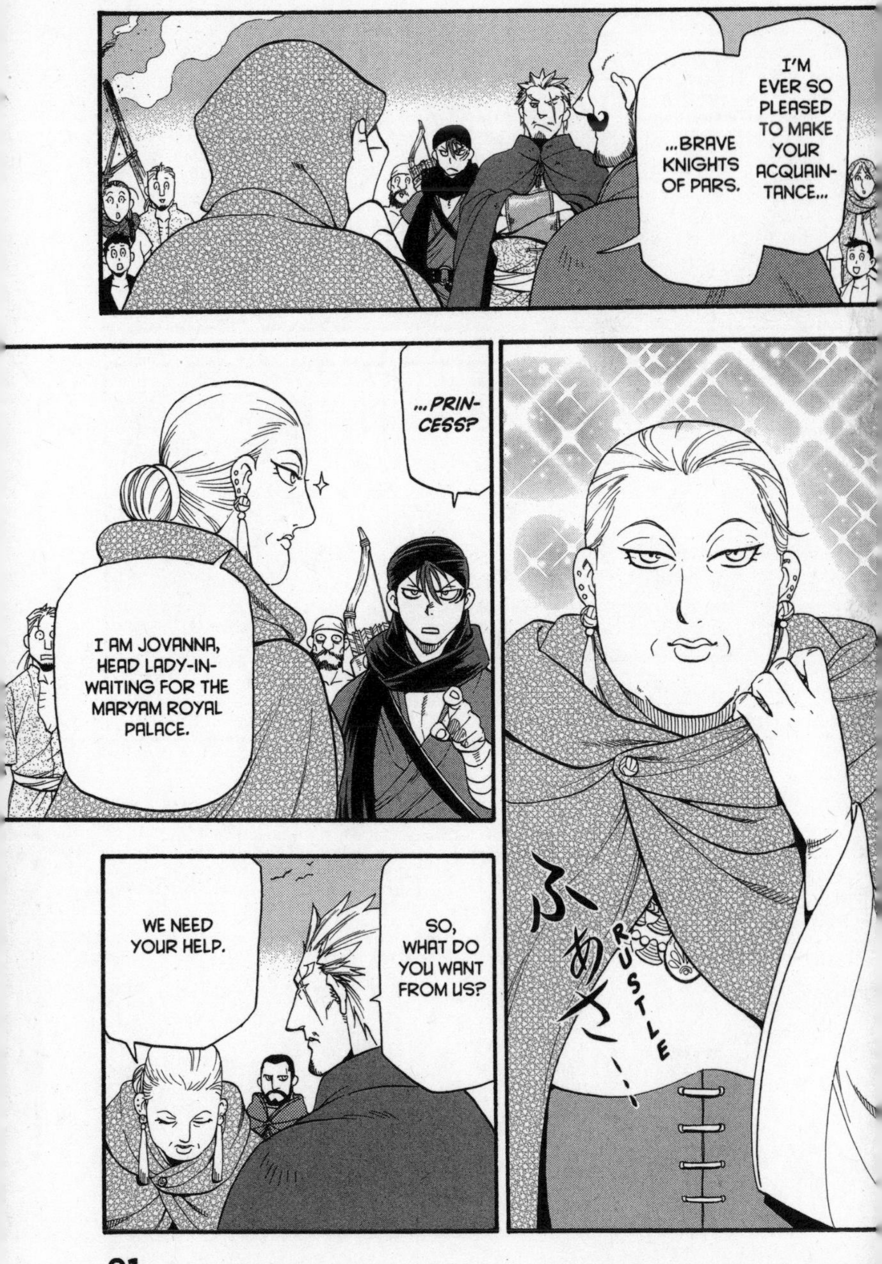
I'M EVER SO PLEASED TO MAKE YOUR ACQUAINTANCE...
...BRAVE KNIGHTS OF PARS.
ふぁさ…
RUSTLE
...PRINCESS?
I AM JOVANNA, HEAD LADY-IN-WAITING FOR THE MARYAM ROYAL PALACE.
SO, WHAT DO YOU WANT FROM US?
WE NEED YOUR HELP.

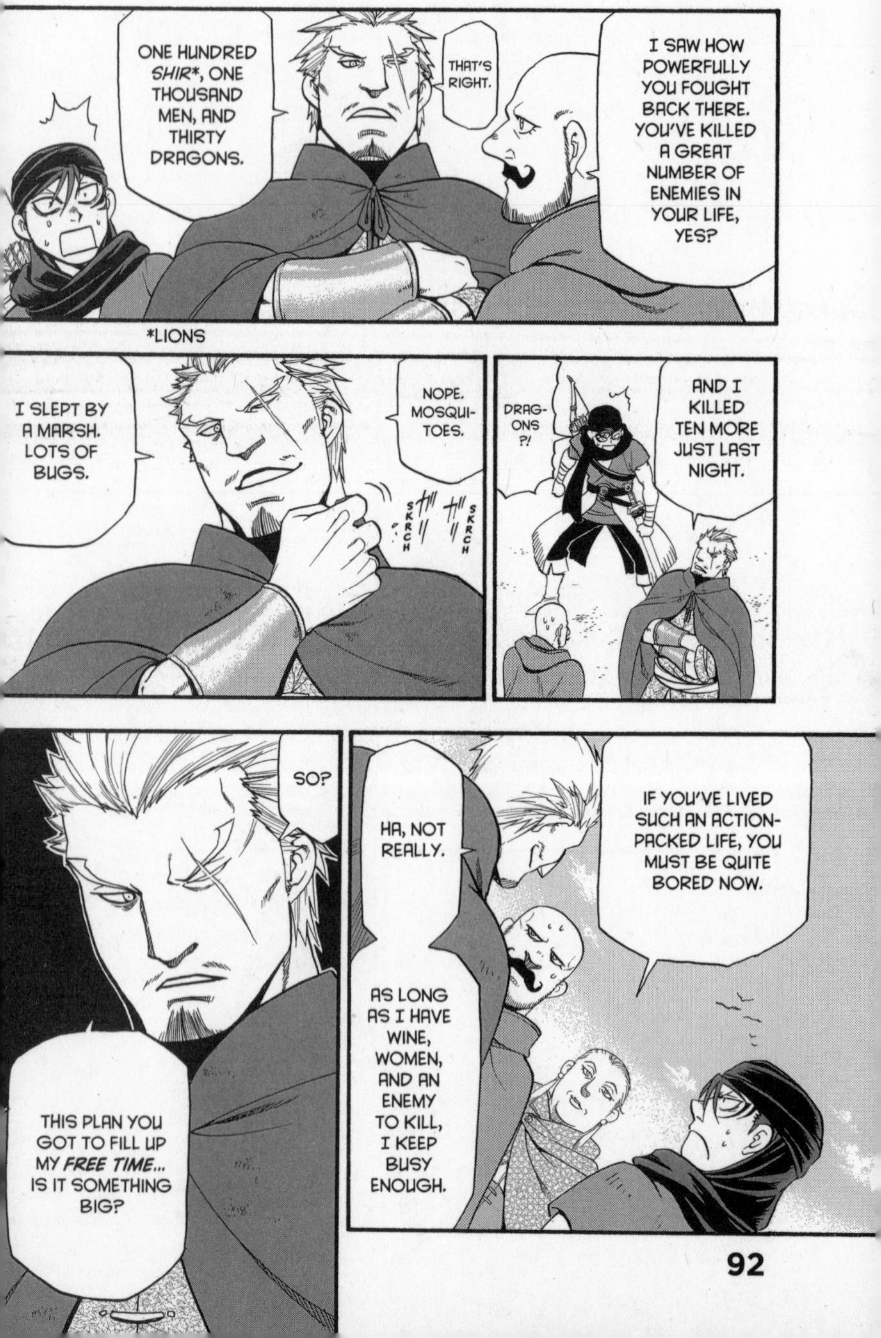
I SAW HOW POWERFULLY YOU FOUGHT BACK THERE. YOU'VE KILLED A GREAT NUMBER OF ENEMIES IN YOUR LIFE, YES?
THAT'S RIGHT.
ONE HUNDRED *SHIR**, ONE THOUSAND MEN, AND THIRTY DRAGONS.
*LIONS
AND I KILLED TEN MORE JUST LAST NIGHT.
DRAG-ONS?!
NOPE. MOSQUI-TOES.
SKRCH
SKRCH
I SLEPT BY A MARSH. LOTS OF BUGS.
IF YOU'VE LIVED SUCH AN ACTION-PACKED LIFE, YOU MUST BE QUITE BORED NOW.
HA, NOT REALLY.
AS LONG AS I HAVE WINE, WOMEN, AND AN ENEMY TO KILL, I KEEP BUSY ENOUGH.
SO?
THIS PLAN YOU GOT TO FILL UP MY ***FREE TIME***... IS IT SOMETHING BIG?

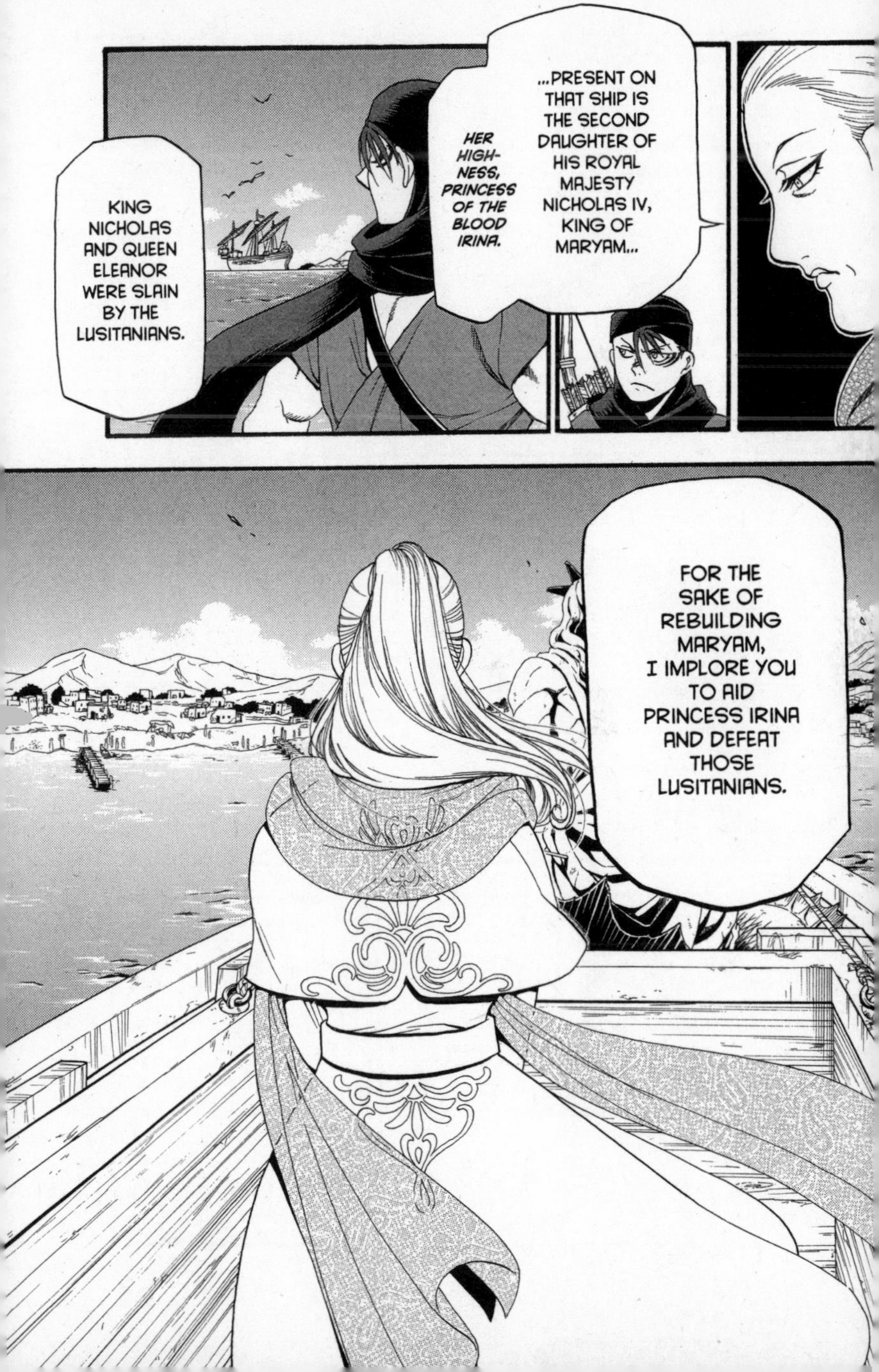
...PRESENT ON THAT SHIP IS THE SECOND DAUGHTER OF HIS ROYAL MAJESTY NICHOLAS IV, KING OF MARYAM...
HER HIGHNESS, PRINCESS OF THE BLOOD IRINA.
KING NICHOLAS AND QUEEN ELEANOR WERE SLAIN BY THE LUSITANIANS.
FOR THE SAKE OF REBUILDING MARYAM, I IMPLORE YOU TO AID PRINCESS IRINA AND DEFEAT THOSE LUSITANIANS.

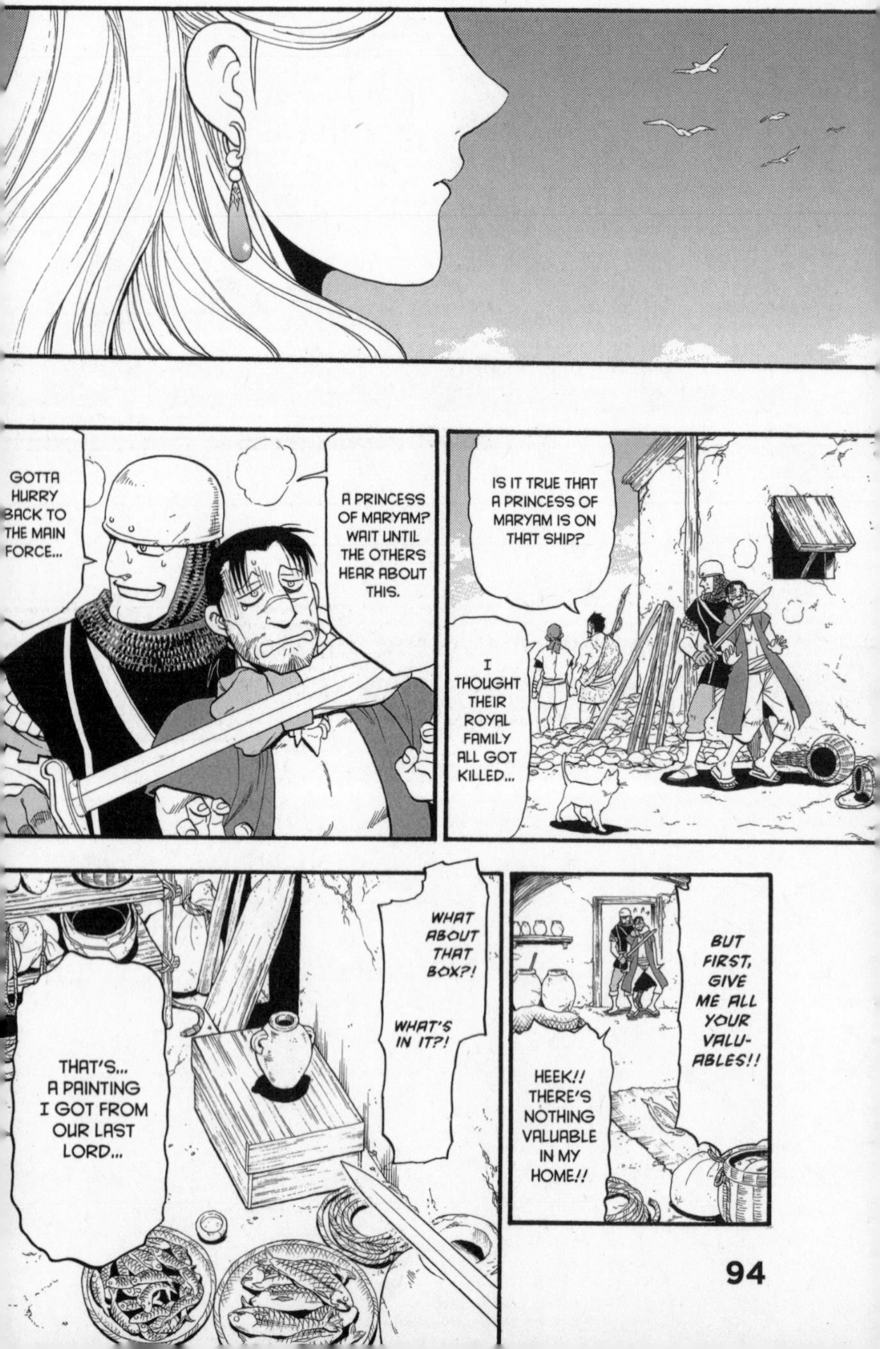
IS IT TRUE THAT A PRINCESS OF MARYAM IS ON THAT SHIP?
I THOUGHT THEIR ROYAL FAMILY ALL GOT KILLED...
A PRINCESS OF MARYAM? WAIT UNTIL THE OTHERS HEAR ABOUT THIS.
GOTTA HURRY BACK TO THE MAIN FORCE...
BUT FIRST, GIVE ME ALL YOUR VALUABLES!!
HEEK!! THERE'S NOTHING VALUABLE IN MY HOME!!
WHAT ABOUT THAT BOX?!
WHAT'S IN IT?!
THAT'S... A PAINTING I GOT FROM OUR LAST LORD...

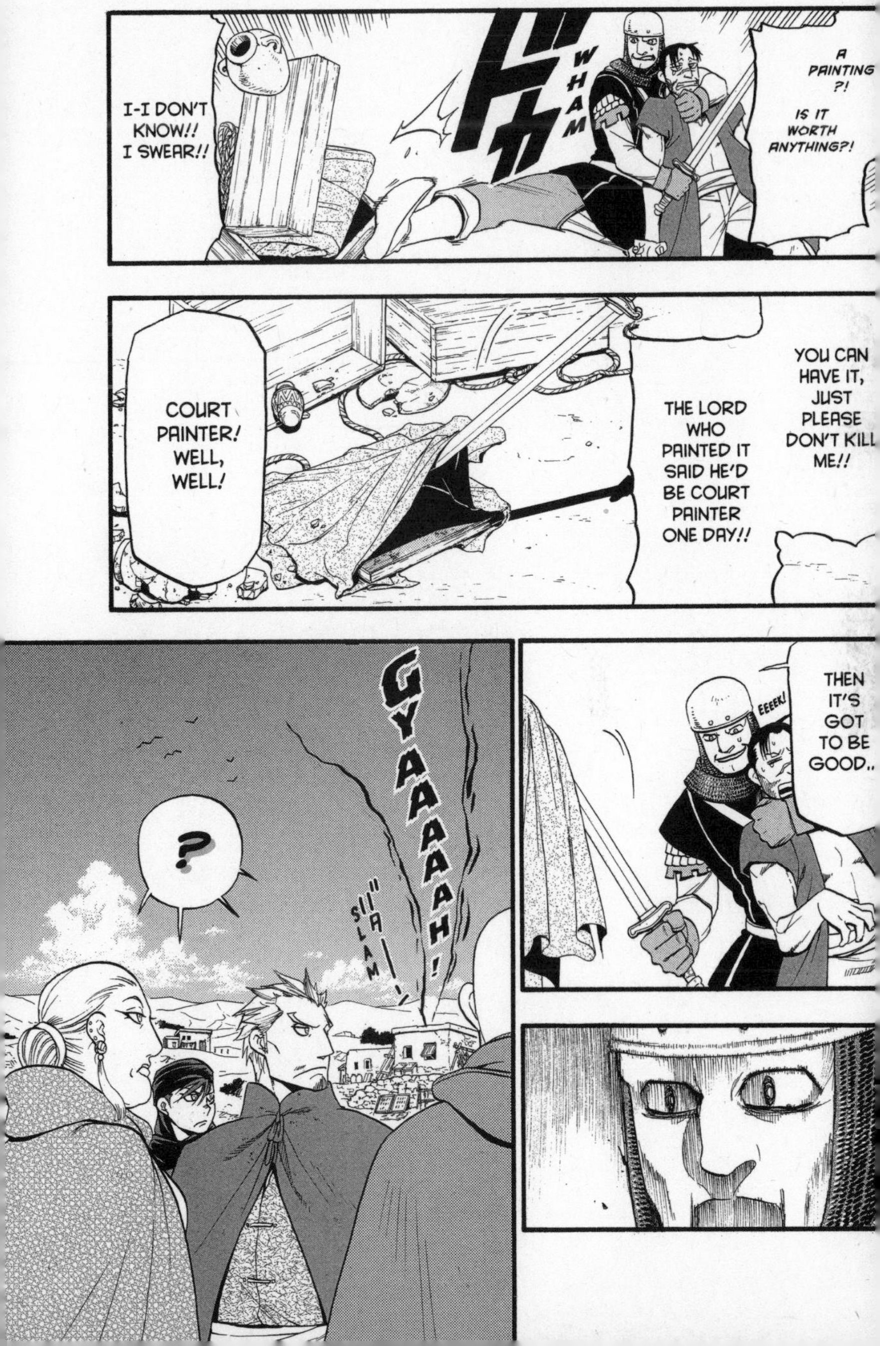
A PAINTING ?!
IS IT WORTH ANYTHING?!
WHAM
I-I DON'T KNOW!! I SWEAR!!
YOU CAN HAVE IT, JUST PLEASE DON'T KILL ME!!
THE LORD WHO PAINTED IT SAID HE'D BE COURT PAINTER ONE DAY!!
COURT PAINTER! WELL, WELL!
THEN IT'S GOT TO BE GOOD..
EEEEK!
GYAAAAAH!
SLAM
?

THE HEROIC LEGEND OF
ARSLAN

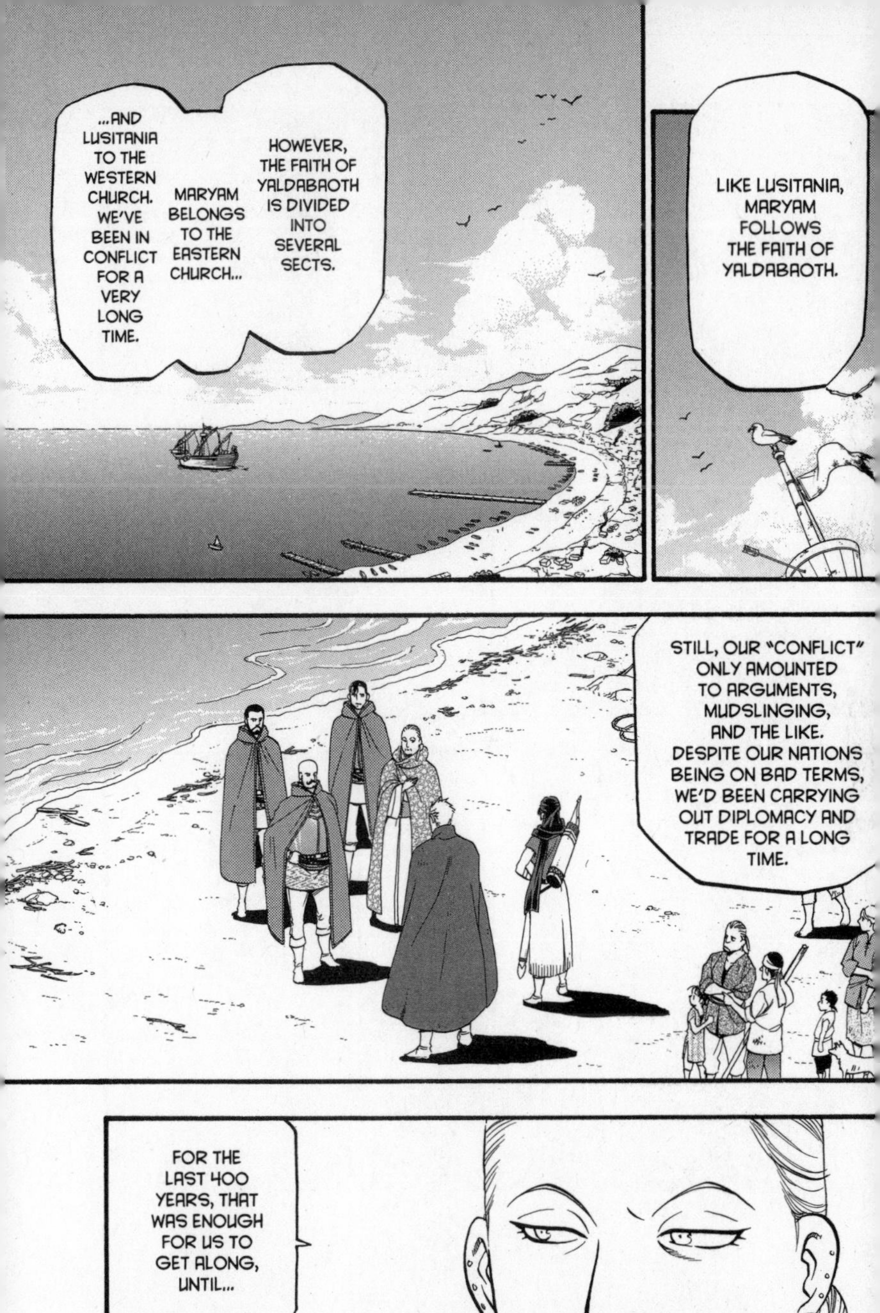
LIKE LUSITANIA, MARYAM FOLLOWS THE FAITH OF YALDABAOTH.
HOWEVER, THE FAITH OF YALDABAOTH IS DIVIDED INTO SEVERAL SECTS.
MARYAM BELONGS TO THE EASTERN CHURCH...
...AND LUSITANIA TO THE WESTERN CHURCH. WE'VE BEEN IN CONFLICT FOR A VERY LONG TIME.
STILL, OUR "CONFLICT" ONLY AMOUNTED TO ARGUMENTS, MUDSLINGING, AND THE LIKE. DESPITE OUR NATIONS BEING ON BAD TERMS, WE'D BEEN CARRYING OUT DIPLOMACY AND TRADE FOR A LONG TIME.
FOR THE LAST 400 YEARS, THAT WAS ENOUGH FOR US TO GET ALONG, UNTIL...

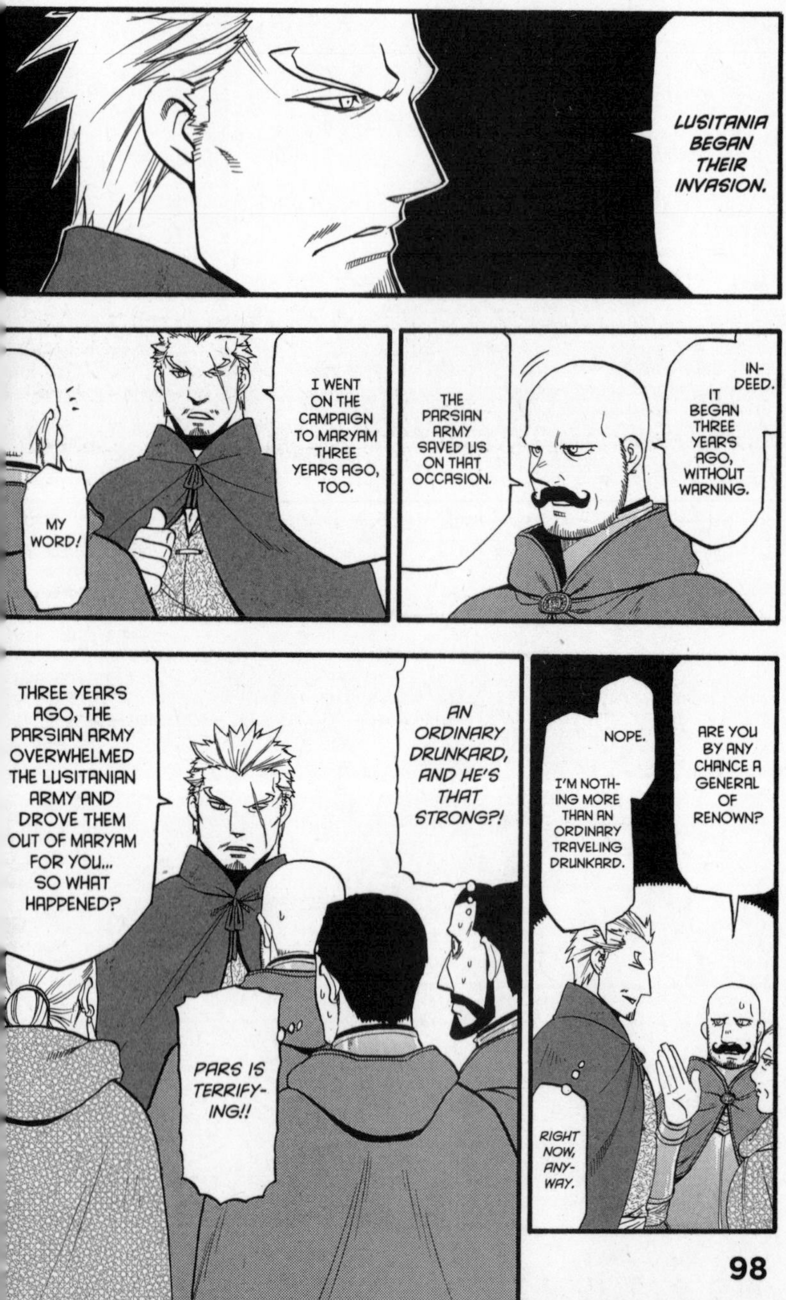
LUSITANIA BEGAN THEIR INVASION.
IN-DEED.
IT BEGAN THREE YEARS AGO, WITHOUT WARNING.
THE PARSIAN ARMY SAVED US ON THAT OCCASION.
I WENT ON THE CAMPAIGN TO MARYAM THREE YEARS AGO, TOO.
MY WORD!
ARE YOU BY ANY CHANCE A GENERAL OF RENOWN?
NOPE.
I'M NOTH-ING MORE THAN AN ORDINARY TRAVELING DRUNKARD.
RIGHT NOW, ANY-WAY.
AN ORDINARY DRUNKARD, AND HE'S THAT STRONG?!
THREE YEARS AGO, THE PARSIAN ARMY OVERWHELMED THE LUSITANIAN ARMY AND DROVE THEM OUT OF MARYAM FOR YOU... SO WHAT HAPPENED?
PARS IS TERRIFY-ING!!

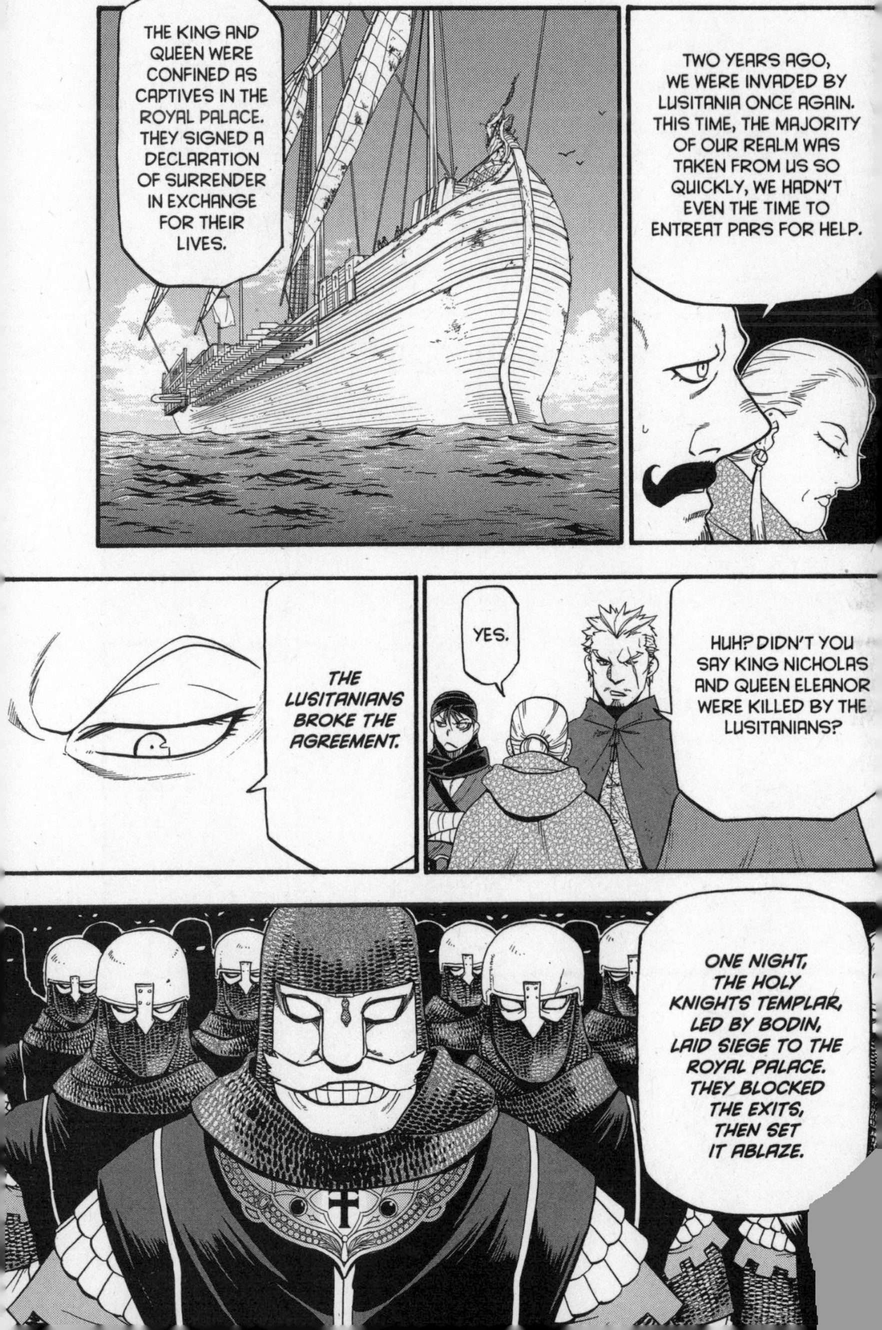
TWO YEARS AGO, WE WERE INVADED BY LUSITANIA ONCE AGAIN. THIS TIME, THE MAJORITY OF OUR REALM WAS TAKEN FROM US SO QUICKLY, WE HADN'T EVEN THE TIME TO ENTREAT PARS FOR HELP.
THE KING AND QUEEN WERE CONFINED AS CAPTIVES IN THE ROYAL PALACE. THEY SIGNED A DECLARATION OF SURRENDER IN EXCHANGE FOR THEIR LIVES.
HUH? DIDN'T YOU SAY KING NICHOLAS AND QUEEN ELEANOR WERE KILLED BY THE LUSITANIANS?
YES.
THE LUSITANIANS BROKE THE AGREEMENT.
ONE NIGHT, THE HOLY KNIGHTS TEMPLAR, LED BY BODIN, LAID SIEGE TO THE ROYAL PALACE. THEY BLOCKED THE EXITS, THEN SET IT ABLAZE.

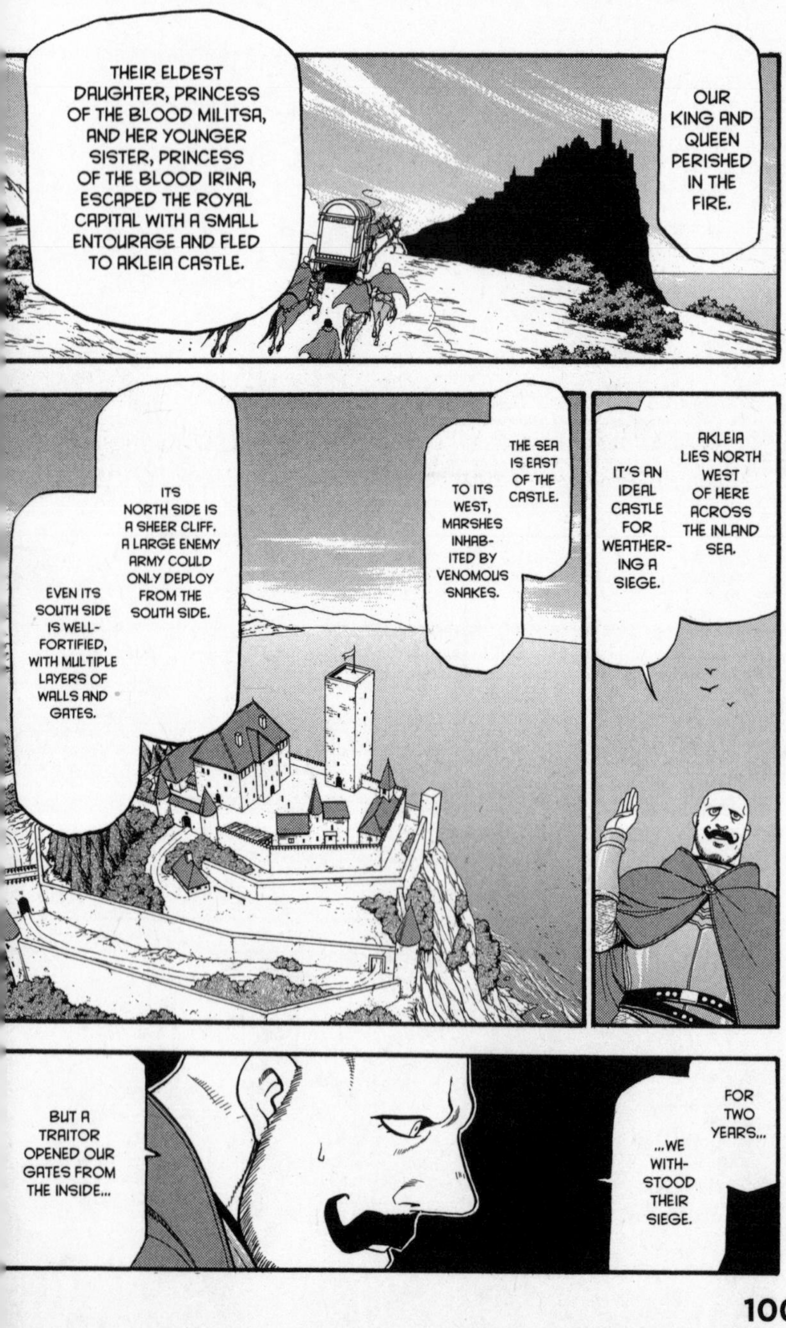
OUR KING AND QUEEN PERISHED IN THE FIRE.
THEIR ELDEST DAUGHTER, PRINCESS OF THE BLOOD MILITSA, AND HER YOUNGER SISTER, PRINCESS OF THE BLOOD IRINA, ESCAPED THE ROYAL CAPITAL WITH A SMALL ENTOURAGE AND FLED TO AKLEIA CASTLE.
AKLEIA LIES NORTH WEST OF HERE ACROSS THE INLAND SEA.
IT'S AN IDEAL CASTLE FOR WEATHERING A SIEGE.
THE SEA IS EAST OF THE CASTLE.
TO ITS WEST, MARSHES INHABITED BY VENOMOUS SNAKES.
ITS NORTH SIDE IS A SHEER CLIFF. A LARGE ENEMY ARMY COULD ONLY DEPLOY FROM THE SOUTH SIDE.
EVEN ITS SOUTH SIDE IS WELL-FORTIFIED, WITH MULTIPLE LAYERS OF WALLS AND GATES.
FOR TWO YEARS...
...WE WITHSTOOD THEIR SIEGE.
BUT A TRAITOR OPENED OUR GATES FROM THE INSIDE...

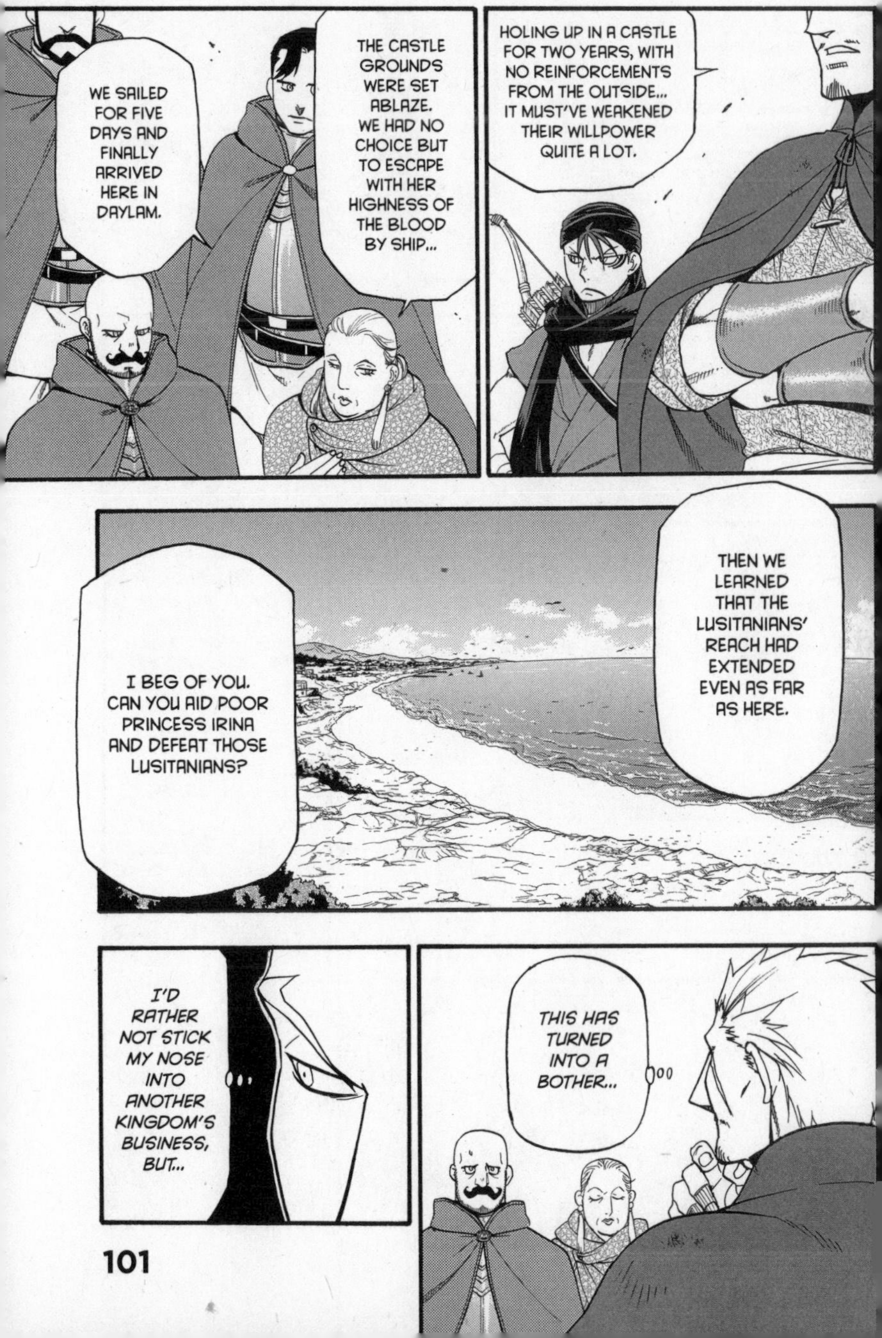
HOLING UP IN A CASTLE FOR TWO YEARS, WITH NO REINFORCEMENTS FROM THE OUTSIDE... IT MUST'VE WEAKENED THEIR WILLPOWER QUITE A LOT.
THE CASTLE GROUNDS WERE SET ABLAZE. WE HAD NO CHOICE BUT TO ESCAPE WITH HER HIGHNESS OF THE BLOOD BY SHIP...
WE SAILED FOR FIVE DAYS AND FINALLY ARRIVED HERE IN DAYLAM.
THEN WE LEARNED THAT THE LUSITANIANS' REACH HAD EXTENDED EVEN AS FAR AS HERE.
I BEG OF YOU. CAN YOU AID POOR PRINCESS IRINA AND DEFEAT THOSE LUSITANIANS?
THIS HAS TURNED INTO A BOTHER...
I'D RATHER NOT STICK MY NOSE INTO ANOTHER KINGDOM'S BUSINESS, BUT...

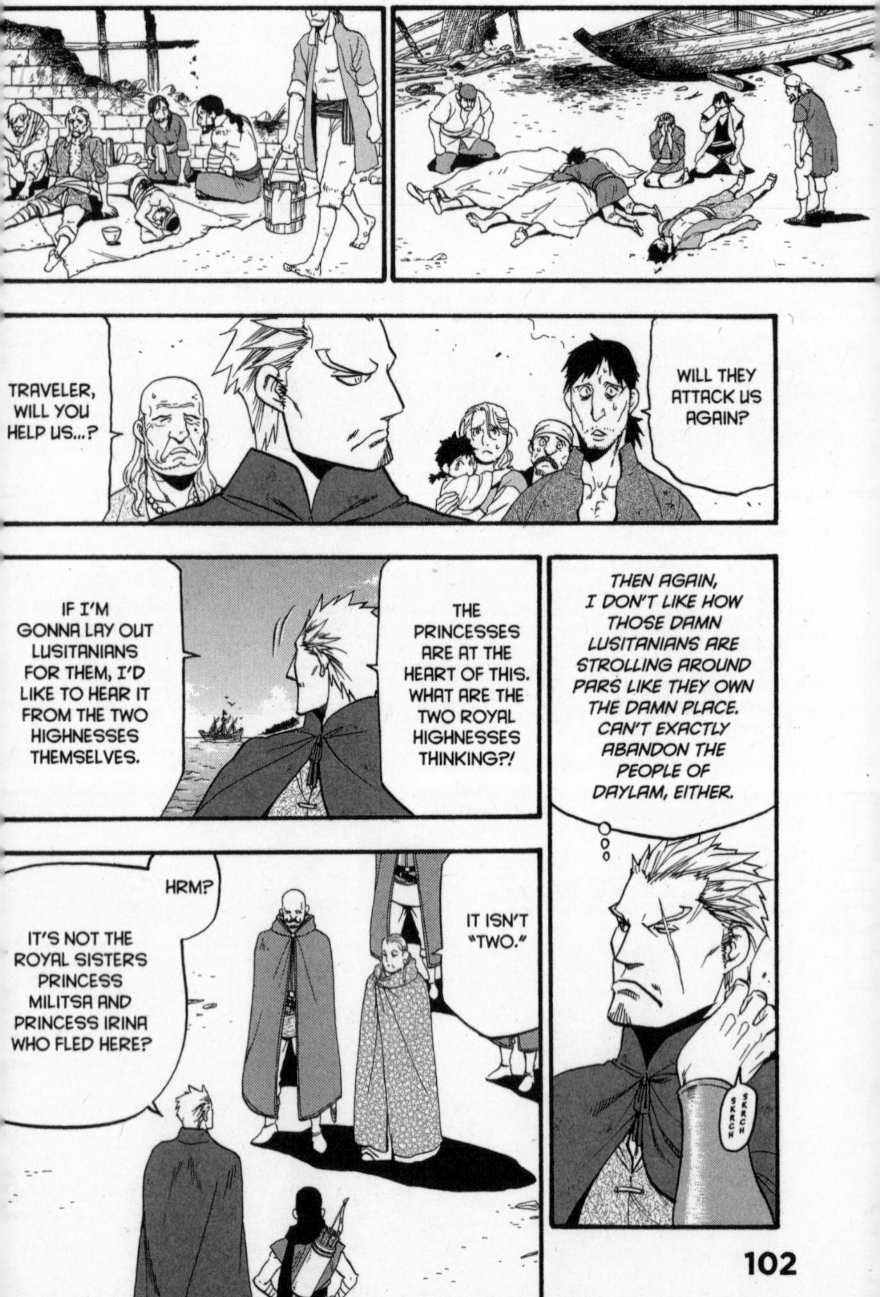
WILL THEY ATTACK US AGAIN?
TRAVELER, WILL YOU HELP US...?
THEN AGAIN, I DON'T LIKE HOW THOSE DAMN LUSITANIANS ARE STROLLING AROUND PARS LIKE THEY OWN THE DAMN PLACE. CAN'T EXACTLY ABANDON THE PEOPLE OF DAYLAM, EITHER.
SKRCH SKRCH
THE PRINCESSES ARE AT THE HEART OF THIS. WHAT ARE THE TWO ROYAL HIGHNESSES THINKING?!
IF I'M GONNA LAY OUT LUSITANIANS FOR THEM, I'D LIKE TO HEAR IT FROM THE TWO HIGHNESSES THEMSELVES.
IT ISN'T "TWO."
HRM?
IT'S NOT THE ROYAL SISTERS PRINCESS MILITSA AND PRINCESS IRINA WHO FLED HERE?

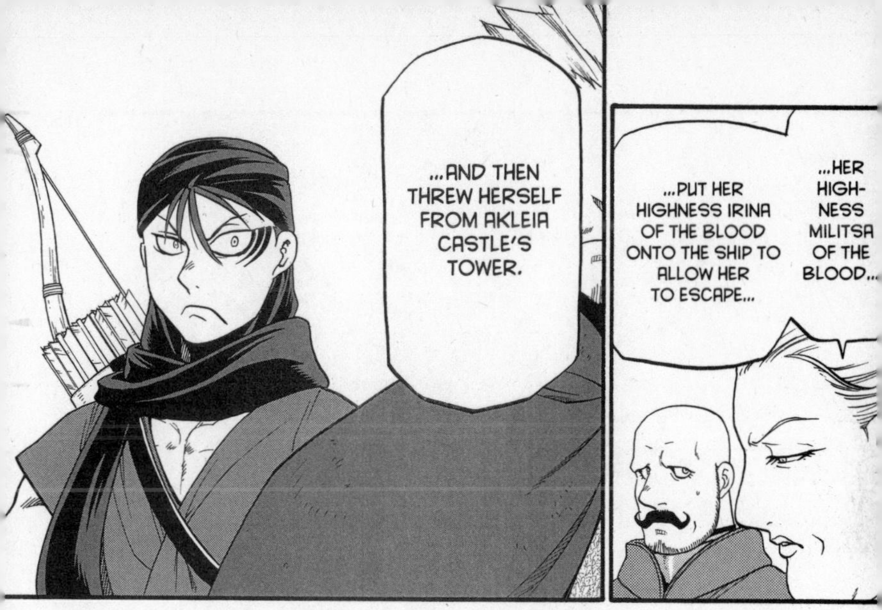
...HER HIGHNESS MILITSA OF THE BLOOD...
...PUT HER HIGHNESS IRINA OF THE BLOOD ONTO THE SHIP TO ALLOW HER TO ESCAPE...
...AND THEN THREW HERSELF FROM AKLEIA CASTLE'S TOWER.

Chapter 62: The Queen of a Ruined Kingdom

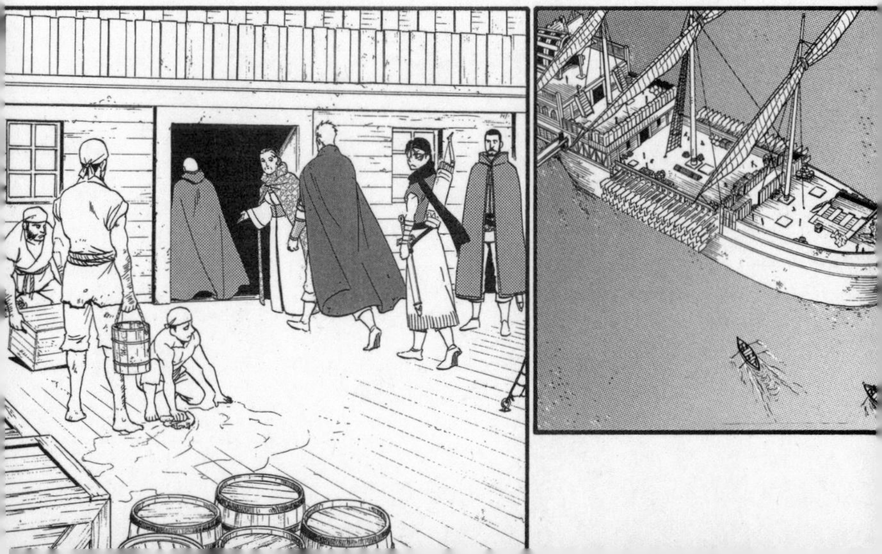

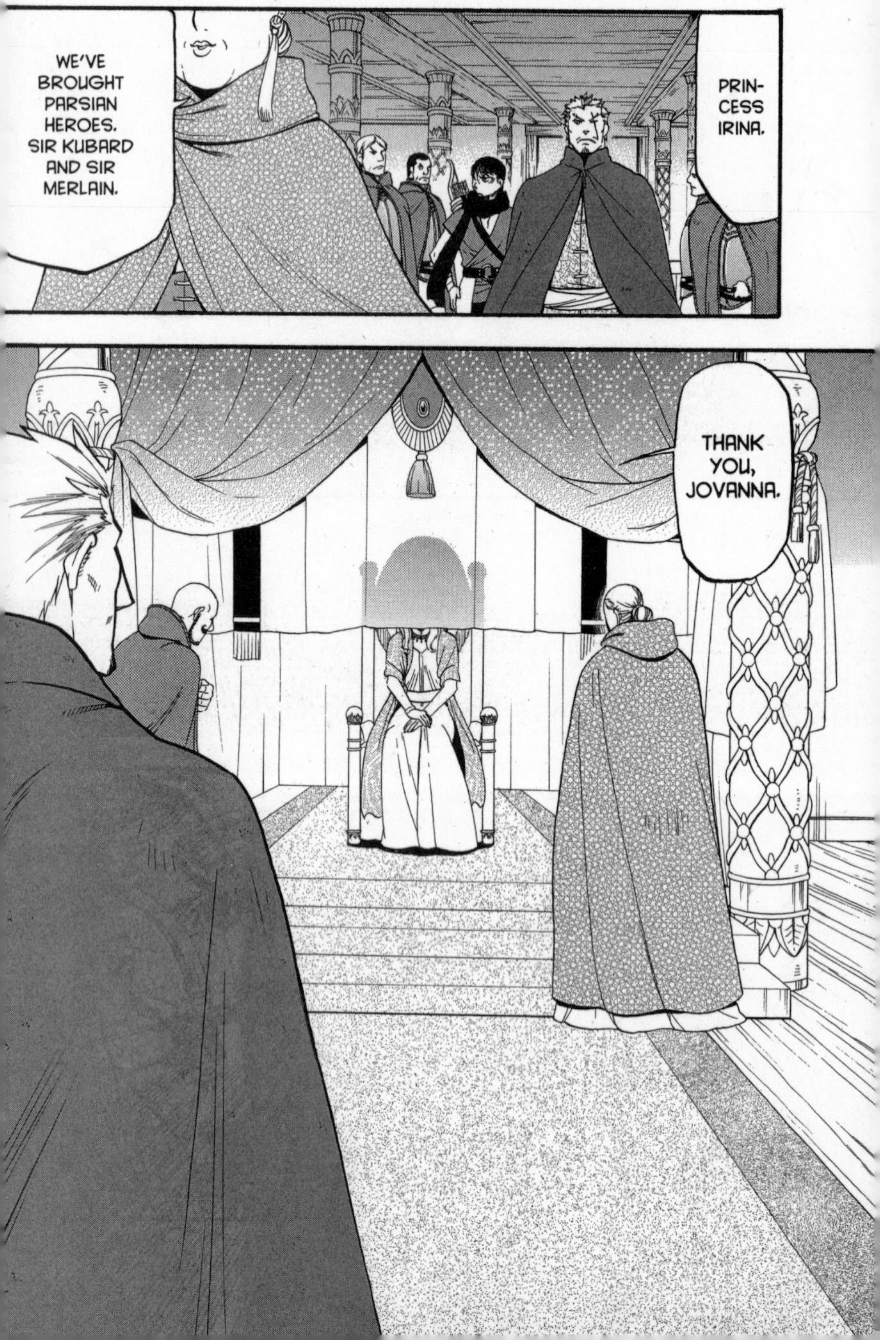
PRIN-
CESS
IRINA.
WE'VE BROUGHT PARSIAN HEROES. SIR KUBARD AND SIR MERLAIN.
THANK YOU, JOVANNA.

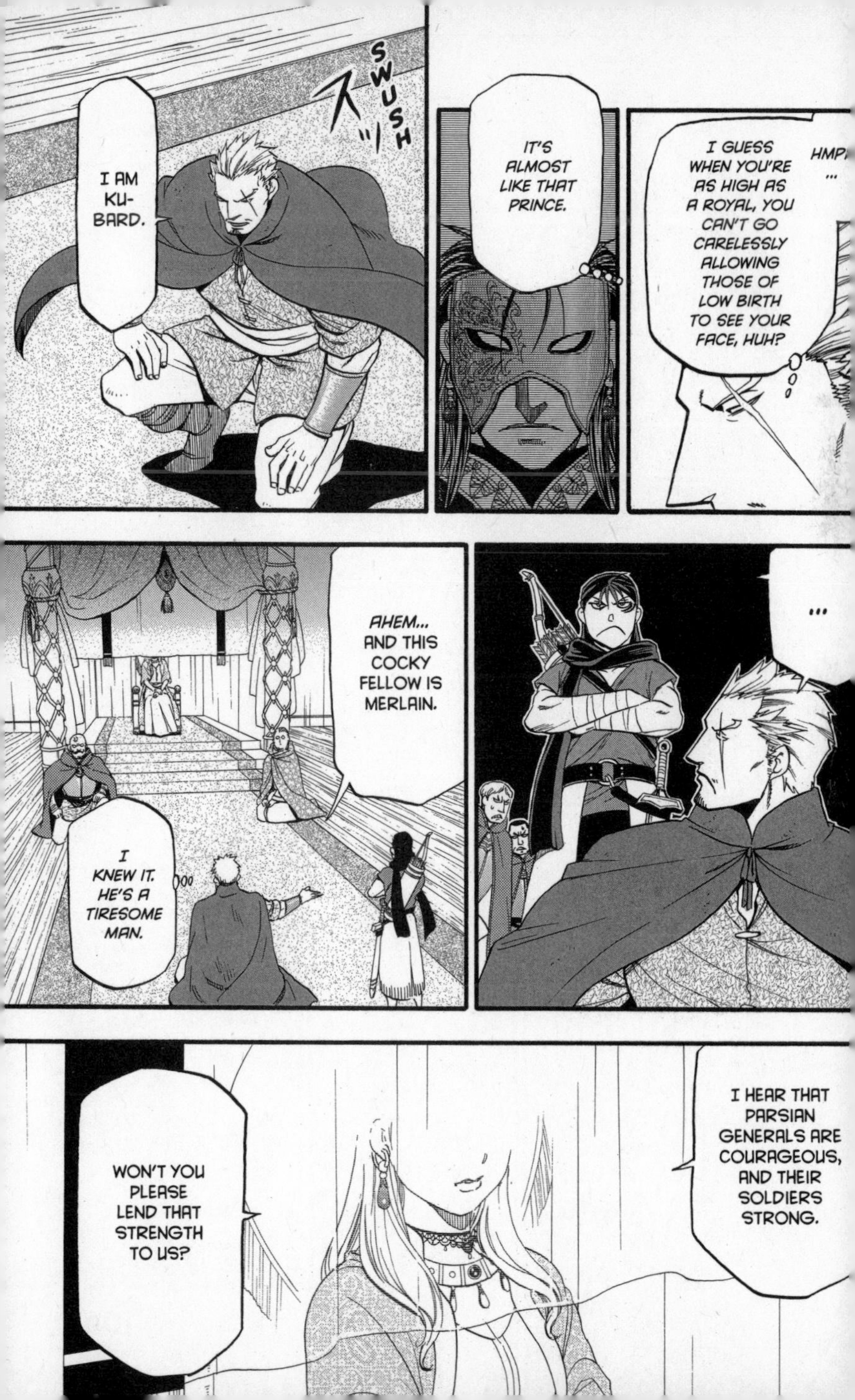
HMP ...
I GUESS WHEN YOU'RE AS HIGH AS A ROYAL, YOU CAN'T GO CARELESSLY ALLOWING THOSE OF LOW BIRTH TO SEE YOUR FACE, HUH?
IT'S ALMOST LIKE THAT PRINCE.
SWUSH
I AM KU-BARD.
...
AHEM... AND THIS COCKY FELLOW IS MERLAIN.
I KNEW IT. HE'S A TIRESOME MAN.
I HEAR THAT PARSIAN GENERALS ARE COURAGEOUS, AND THEIR SOLDIERS STRONG.
WON'T YOU PLEASE LEND THAT STRENGTH TO US?

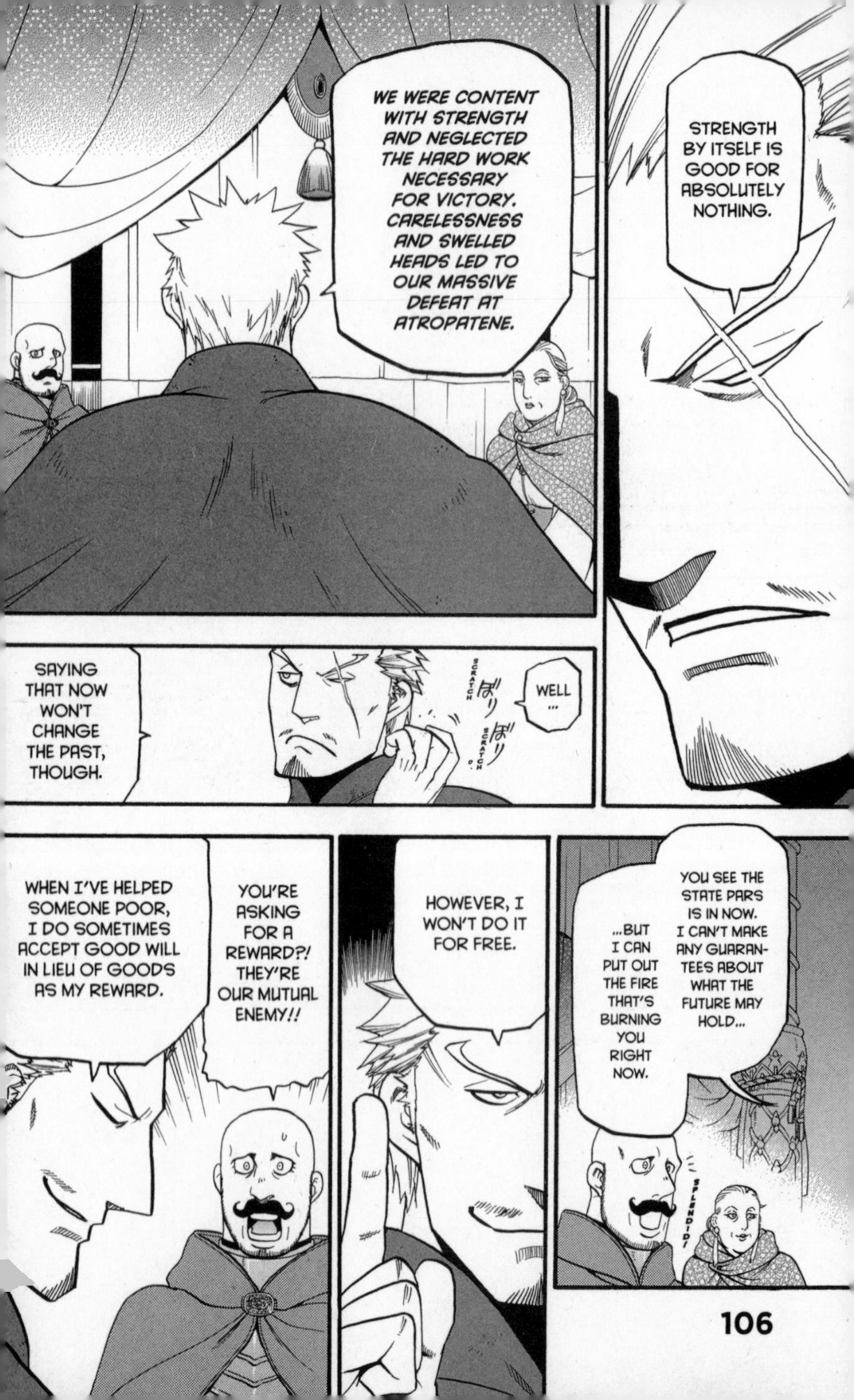
STRENGTH BY ITSELF IS GOOD FOR ABSOLUTELY NOTHING.
WE WERE CONTENT WITH STRENGTH AND NEGLECTED THE HARD WORK NECESSARY FOR VICTORY. CARELESSNESS AND SWELLED HEADS LED TO OUR MASSIVE DEFEAT AT ATROPATENE.
WELL ...
SCRATCH
SCRATCH
SAYING THAT NOW WON'T CHANGE THE PAST, THOUGH.
YOU SEE THE STATE PARS IS IN NOW. I CAN'T MAKE ANY GUARANTEES ABOUT WHAT THE FUTURE MAY HOLD...
...BUT I CAN PUT OUT THE FIRE THAT'S BURNING YOU RIGHT NOW.
SPLENDID!
HOWEVER, I WON'T DO IT FOR FREE.
YOU'RE ASKING FOR A REWARD?! THEY'RE OUR MUTUAL ENEMY!!
WHEN I'VE HELPED SOMEONE POOR, I DO SOMETIMES ACCEPT GOOD WILL IN LIEU OF GOODS AS MY REWARD.

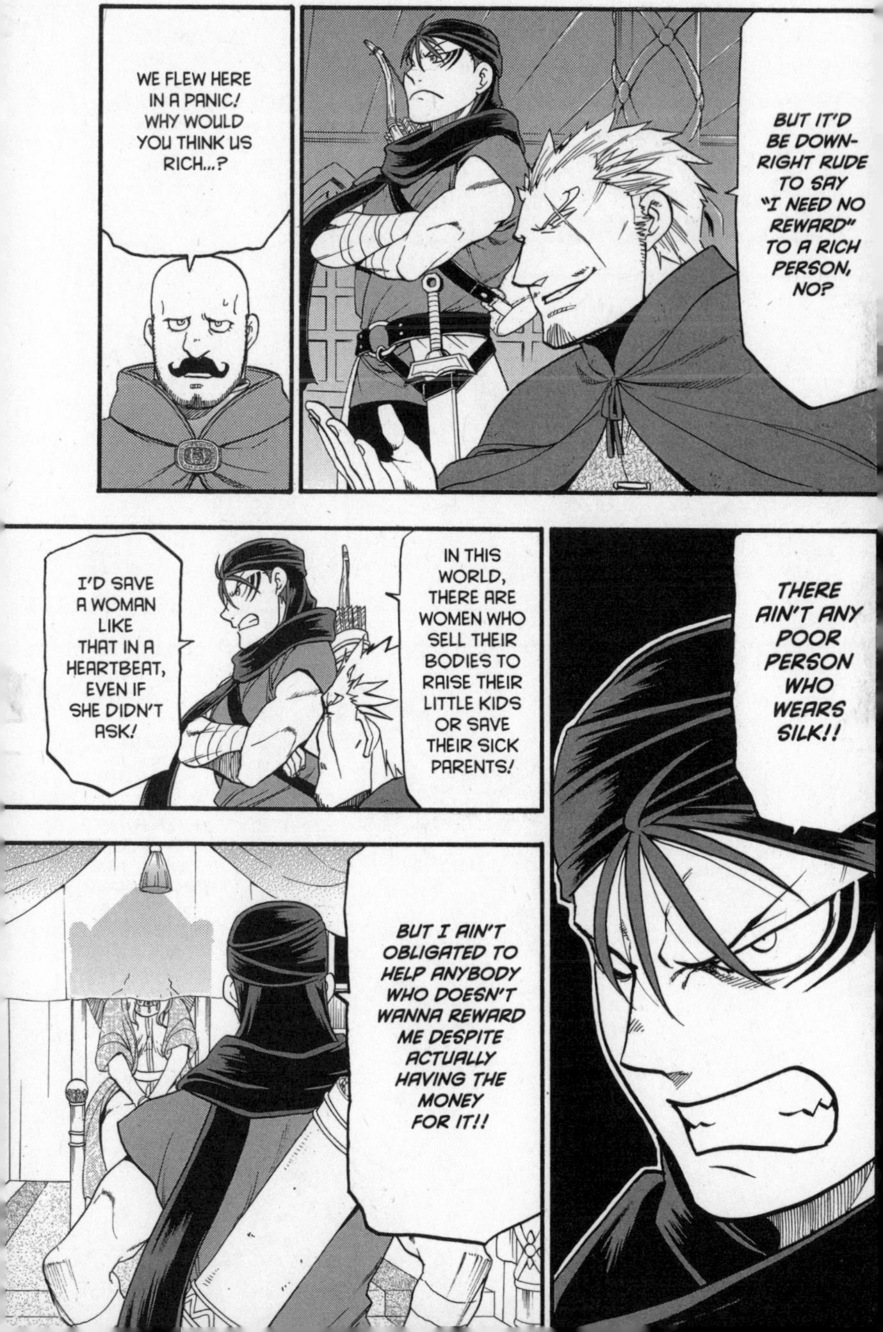
BUT IT'D BE DOWN-RIGHT RUDE TO SAY "I NEED NO REWARD" TO A RICH PERSON, NO?
WE FLEW HERE IN A PANIC! WHY WOULD YOU THINK US RICH...?
THERE AIN'T ANY POOR PERSON WHO WEARS SILK!!
IN THIS WORLD, THERE ARE WOMEN WHO SELL THEIR BODIES TO RAISE THEIR LITTLE KIDS OR SAVE THEIR SICK PARENTS!
I'D SAVE A WOMAN LIKE THAT IN A HEARTBEAT, EVEN IF SHE DIDN'T ASK!
BUT I AIN'T OBLIGATED TO HELP ANYBODY WHO DOESN'T WANNA REWARD ME DESPITE ACTUALLY HAVING THE MONEY FOR IT!!

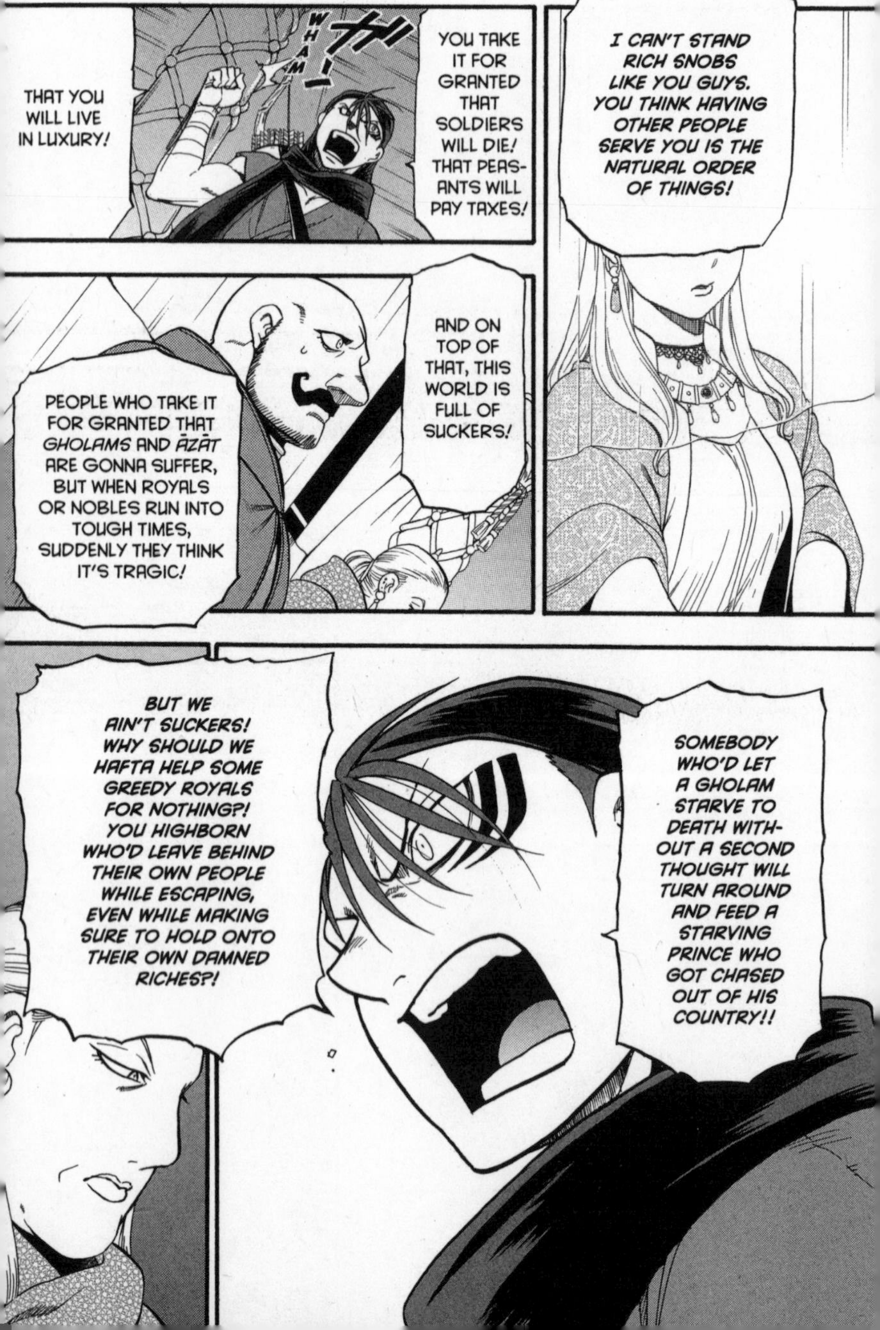

I CAN'T STAND RICH SNOBS LIKE YOU GUYS. YOU THINK HAVING OTHER PEOPLE SERVE YOU IS THE NATURAL ORDER OF THINGS!
YOU TAKE IT FOR GRANTED THAT SOLDIERS WILL DIE! THAT PEAS-ANTS WILL PAY TAXES!
WHAM
THAT YOU WILL LIVE IN LUXURY!
AND ON TOP OF THAT, THIS WORLD IS FULL OF SUCKERS!
PEOPLE WHO TAKE IT FOR GRANTED THAT GHOLAMS AND ĀZĀT ARE GONNA SUFFER, BUT WHEN ROYALS OR NOBLES RUN INTO TOUGH TIMES, SUDDENLY THEY THINK IT'S TRAGIC!
SOMEBODY WHO'D LET A GHOLAM STARVE TO DEATH WITH-OUT A SECOND THOUGHT WILL TURN AROUND AND FEED A STARVING PRINCE WHO GOT CHASED OUT OF HIS COUNTRY!!
BUT WE AIN'T SUCKERS! WHY SHOULD WE HAFTA HELP SOME GREEDY ROYALS FOR NOTHING?! YOU HIGHBORN WHO'D LEAVE BEHIND THEIR OWN PEOPLE WHILE ESCAPING, EVEN WHILE MAKING SURE TO HOLD ONTO THEIR OWN DAMNED RICHES?!

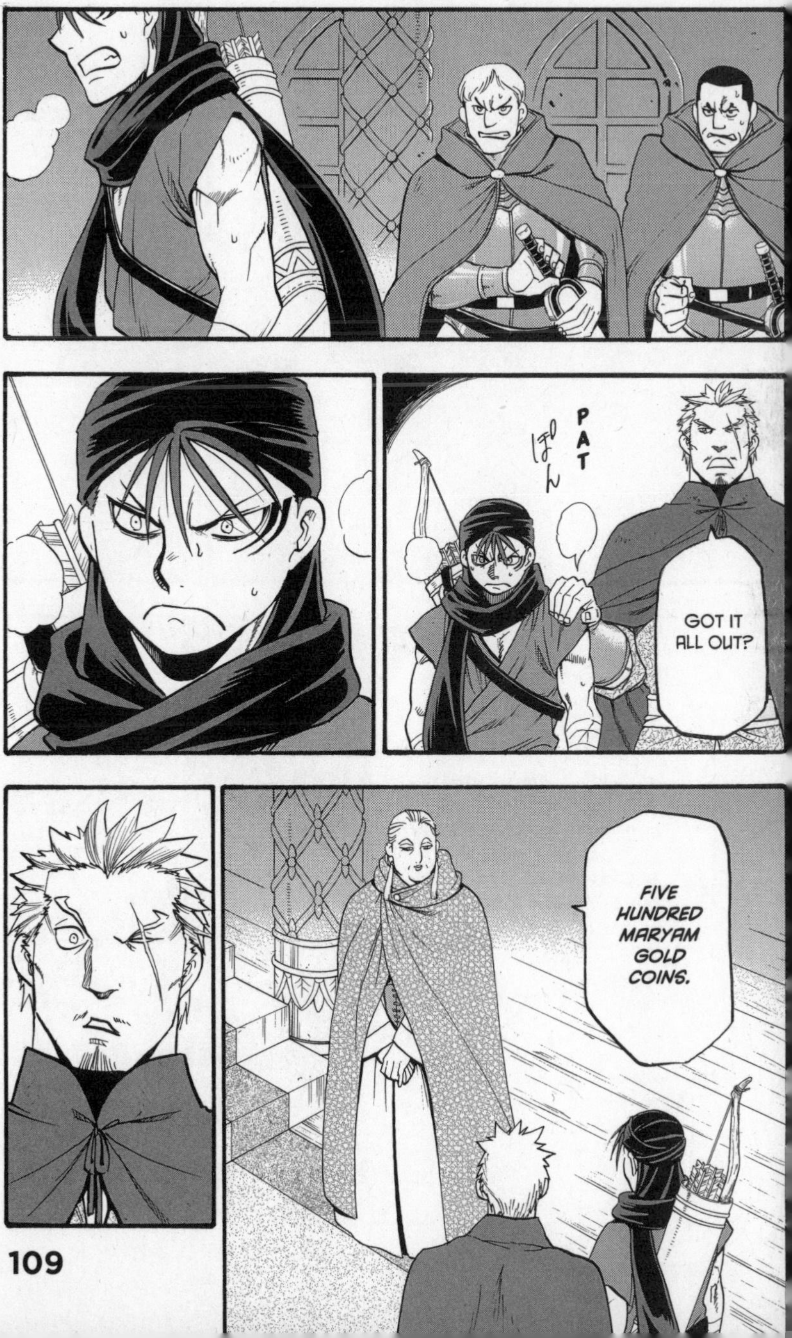
PAT
ぽん
GOT IT ALL OUT?
FIVE HUNDRED MARYAM GOLD COINS.

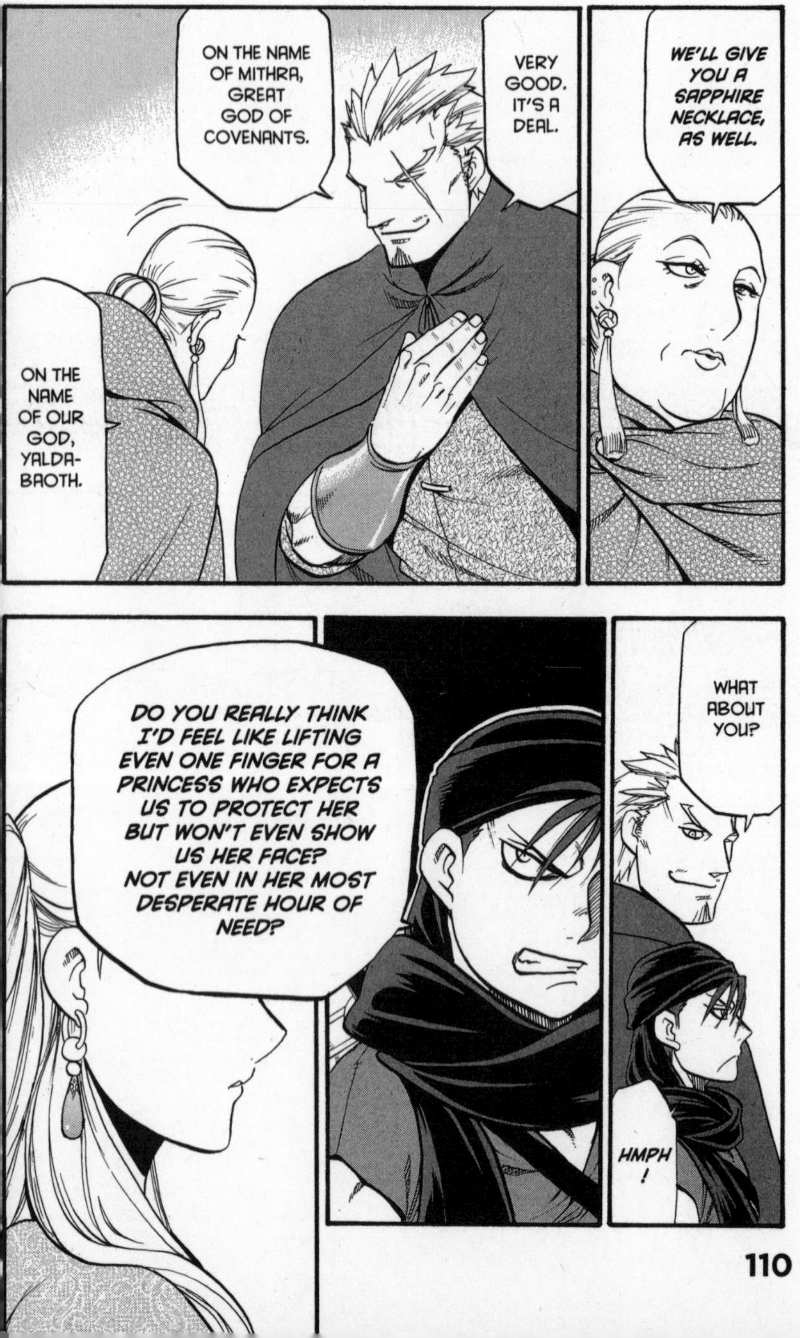
WE'LL GIVE YOU A SAPPHIRE NECKLACE, AS WELL.
VERY GOOD. IT'S A DEAL.
ON THE NAME OF MITHRA, GREAT GOD OF COVENANTS.
ON THE NAME OF OUR GOD, YALDA-BAOTH.
WHAT ABOUT YOU?
HMPH!
DO YOU REALLY THINK I'D FEEL LIKE LIFTING EVEN ONE FINGER FOR A PRINCESS WHO EXPECTS US TO PROTECT HER BUT WON'T EVEN SHOW US HER FACE? NOT EVEN IN HER MOST DESPERATE HOUR OF NEED?

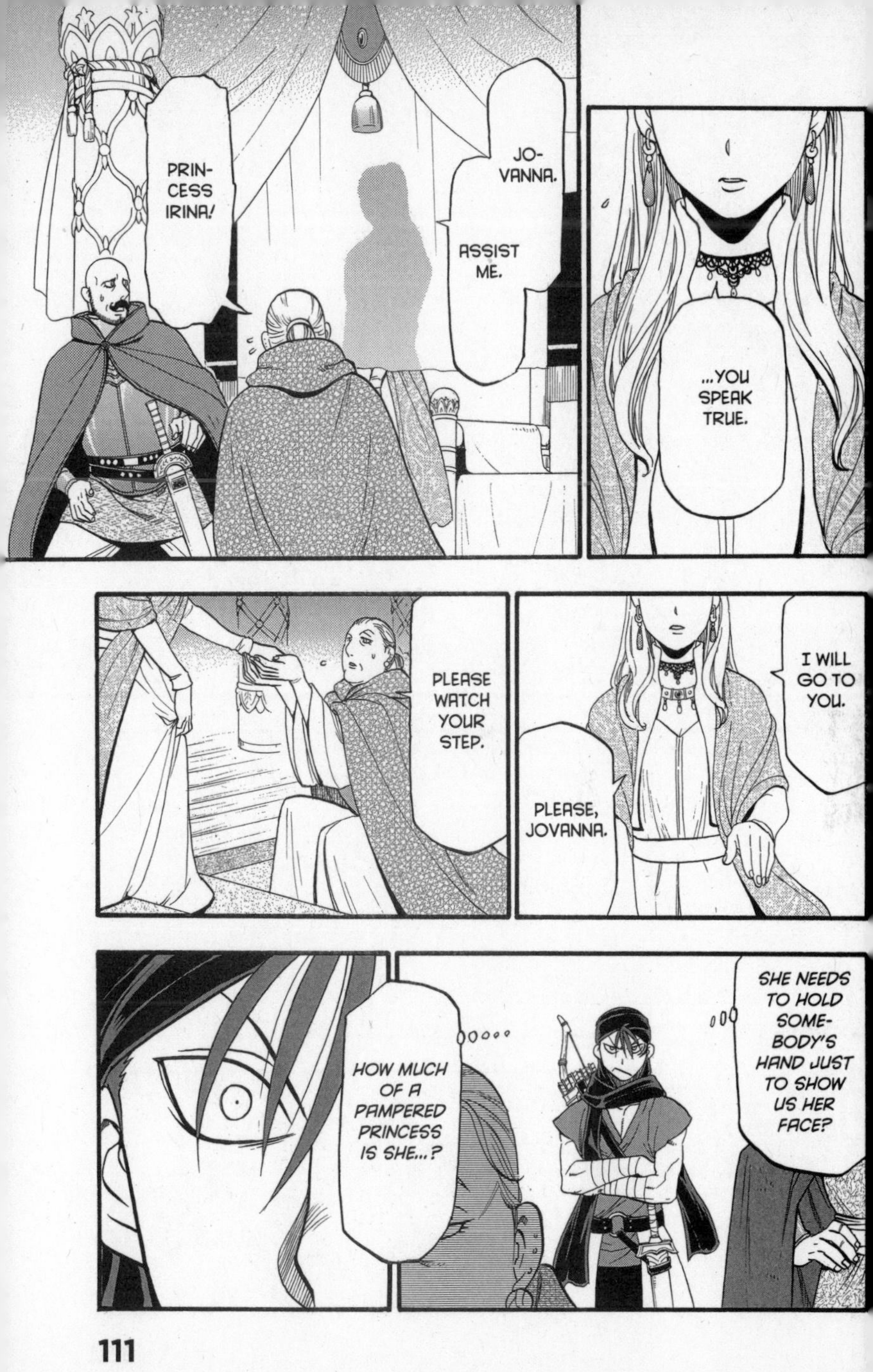
...YOU SPEAK TRUE.
JO-VANNA.
ASSIST ME.
PRIN-CESS IRINA!
I WILL GO TO YOU.
PLEASE, JOVANNA.
PLEASE WATCH YOUR STEP.
SHE NEEDS TO HOLD SOME-BODY'S HAND JUST TO SHOW US HER FACE?
HOW MUCH OF A PAMPERED PRINCESS IS SHE...?

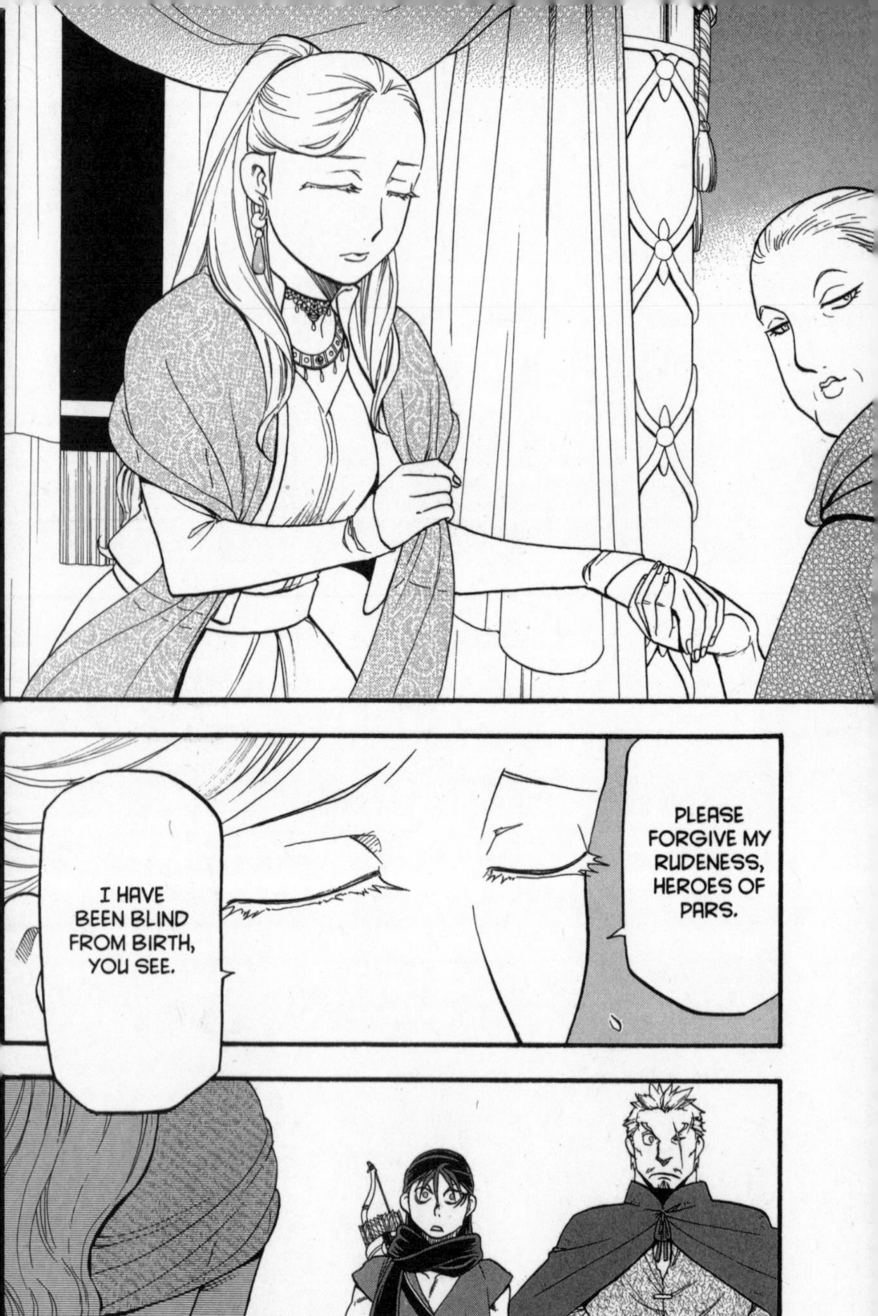
PLEASE FORGIVE MY RUDENESS, HEROES OF PARS.
I HAVE BEEN BLIND FROM BIRTH, YOU SEE.

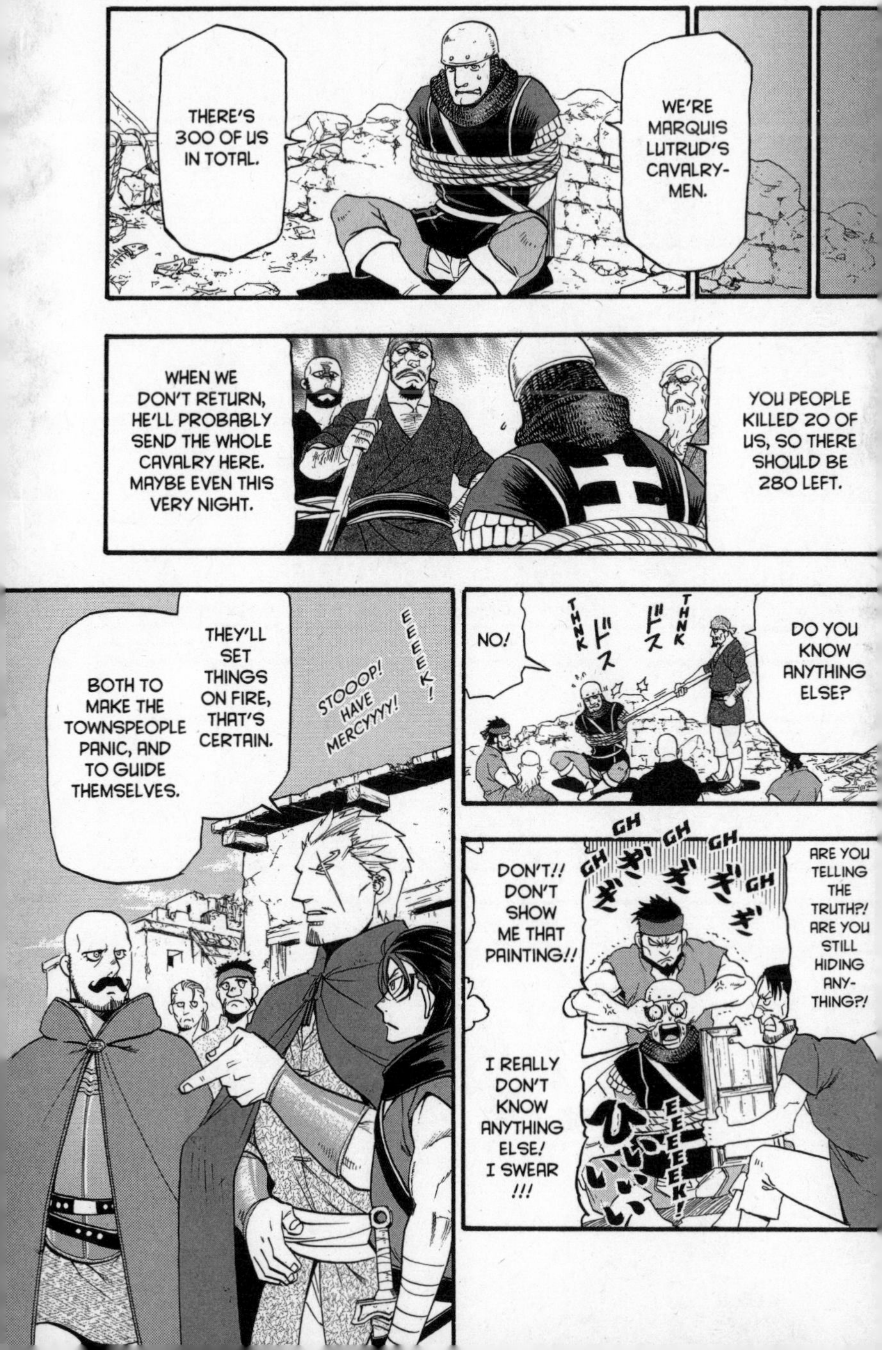
WE'RE MARQUIS LUTRUD'S CAVALRY-MEN.
THERE'S 300 OF US IN TOTAL.
YOU PEOPLE KILLED 20 OF US, SO THERE SHOULD BE 280 LEFT.
WHEN WE DON'T RETURN, HE'LL PROBABLY SEND THE WHOLE CAVALRY HERE. MAYBE EVEN THIS VERY NIGHT.
DO YOU KNOW ANYTHING ELSE?
THNK ドス
THNK ドス
NO!
ARE YOU TELLING THE TRUTH?! ARE YOU STILL HIDING ANYTHING?!
GH ぎ GH ぎ GH ぎ GH ぎ GH
DON'T!! DON'T SHOW ME THAT PAINTING!!
I REALLY DON'T KNOW ANYTHING ELSE! I SWEAR!!!
EEEEEEK!
EEEEEK!
STOOOP! HAVE MERCYYYY!
THEY'LL SET THINGS ON FIRE, THAT'S CERTAIN.
BOTH TO MAKE THE TOWNSPEOPLE PANIC, AND TO GUIDE THEMSELVES.

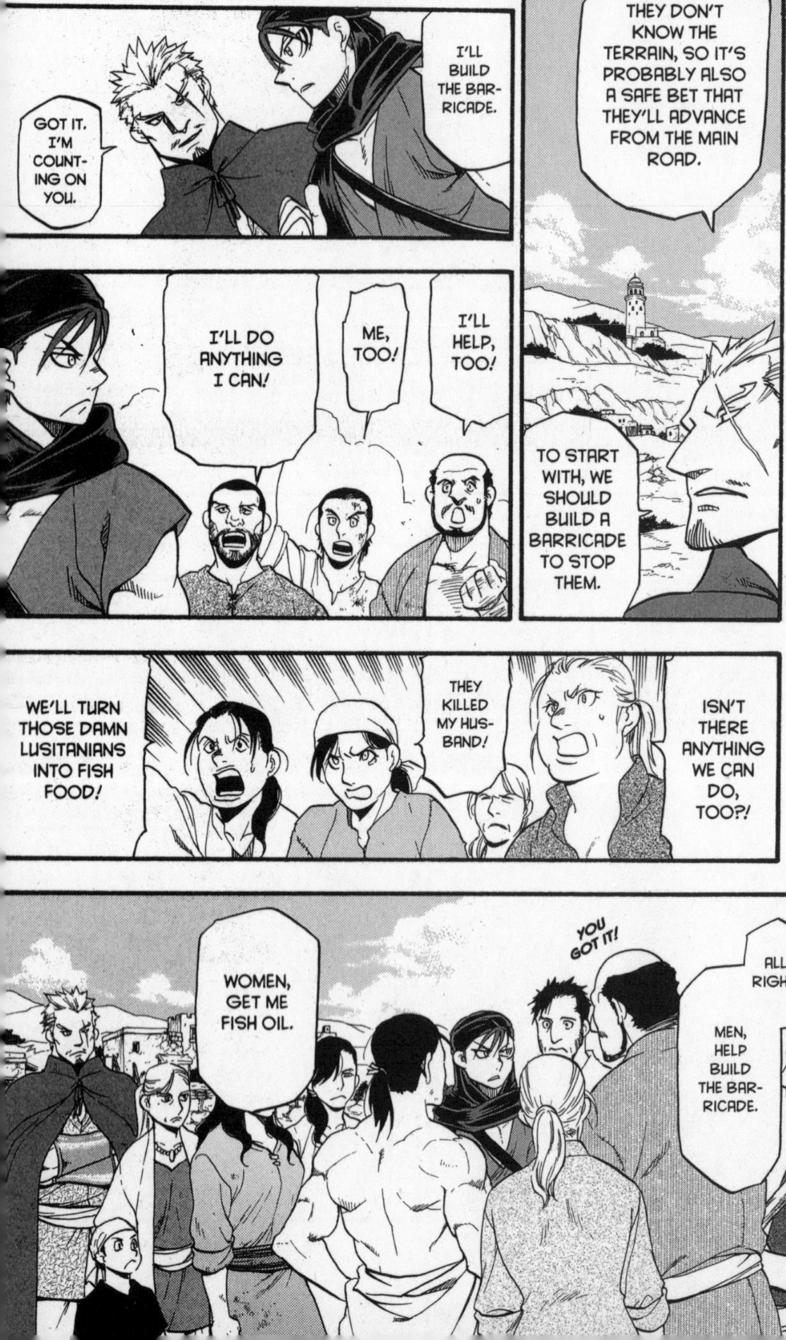
THEY DON'T KNOW THE TERRAIN, SO IT'S PROBABLY ALSO A SAFE BET THAT THEY'LL ADVANCE FROM THE MAIN ROAD.
TO START WITH, WE SHOULD BUILD A BARRICADE TO STOP THEM.
I'LL BUILD THE BARRICADE.
GOT IT. I'M COUNTING ON YOU.
I'LL HELP, TOO!
ME, TOO!
I'LL DO ANYTHING I CAN!
ISN'T THERE ANYTHING WE CAN DO, TOO?!
THEY KILLED MY HUSBAND!
WE'LL TURN THOSE DAMN LUSITANIANS INTO FISH FOOD!
ALL RIGHT.
MEN, HELP BUILD THE BARRICADE.
YOU GOT IT!
WOMEN, GET ME FISH OIL.

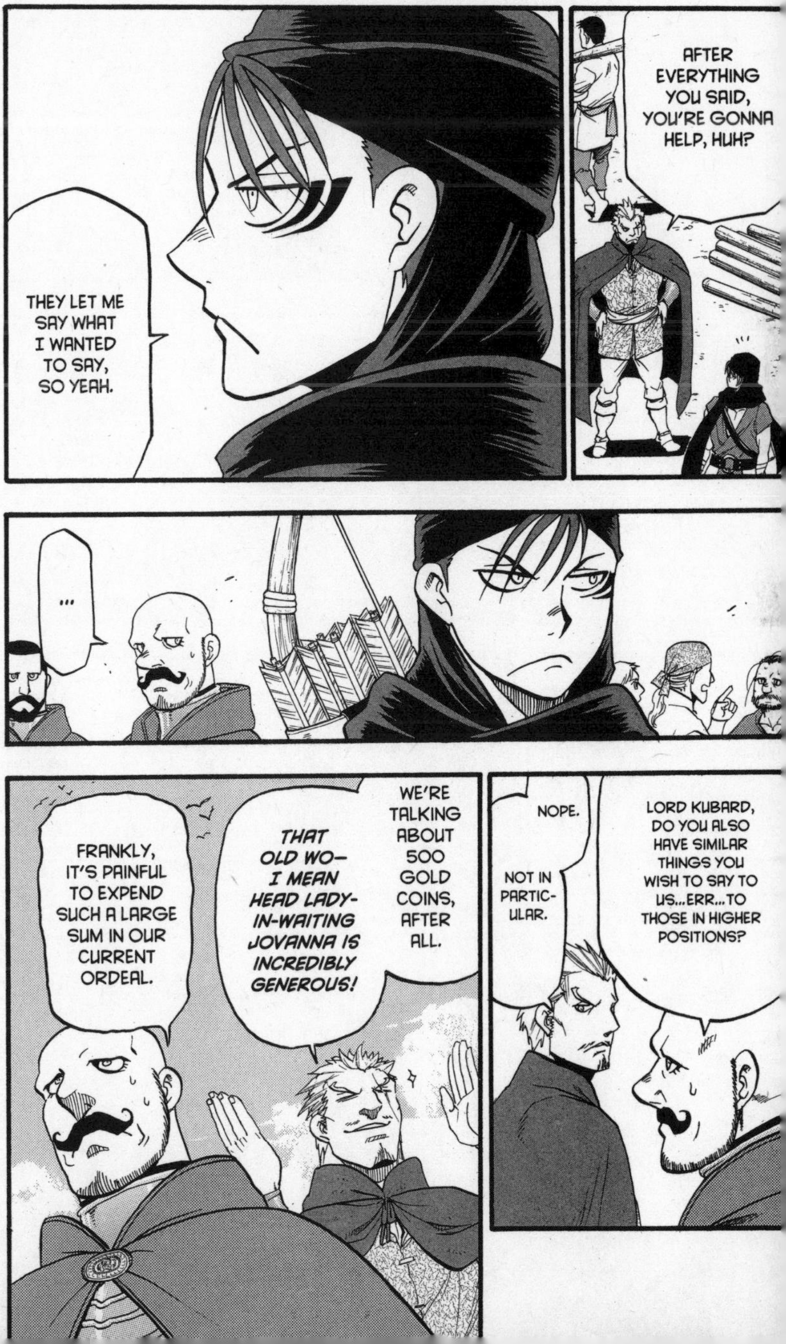
AFTER EVERYTHING YOU SAID, YOU'RE GONNA HELP, HUH?
THEY LET ME SAY WHAT I WANTED TO SAY, SO YEAH.
...
LORD KUBARD, DO YOU ALSO HAVE SIMILAR THINGS YOU WISH TO SAY TO US...ERR...TO THOSE IN HIGHER POSITIONS?
NOPE.
NOT IN PARTIC-ULAR.
FRANKLY, IT'S PAINFUL TO EXPEND SUCH A LARGE SUM IN OUR CURRENT ORDEAL.
WE'RE TALKING ABOUT 500 GOLD COINS, AFTER ALL.
THAT OLD WO— I MEAN HEAD LADY-IN-WAITING JOVANNA IS INCREDIBLY GENEROUS!

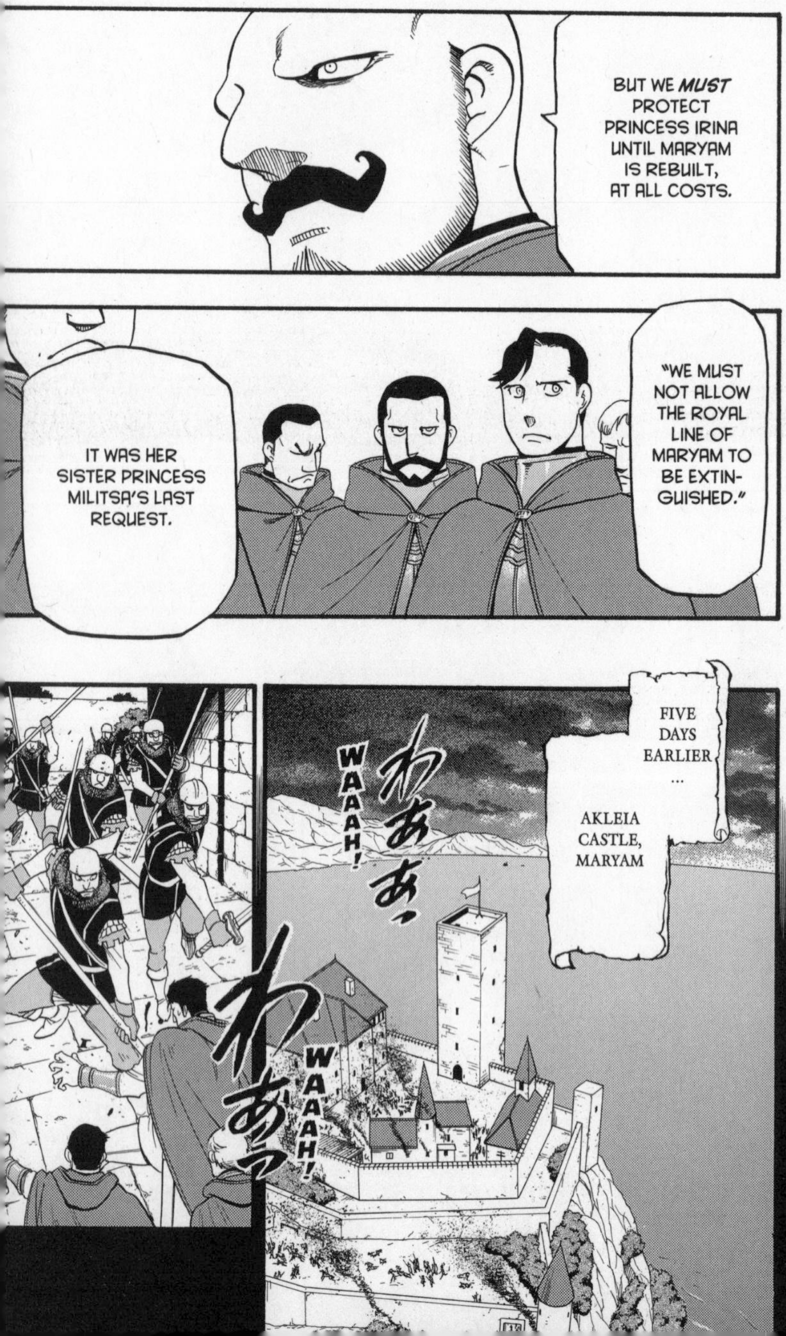
BUT WE *MUST* PROTECT PRINCESS IRINA UNTIL MARYAM IS REBUILT, AT ALL COSTS.
"WE MUST NOT ALLOW THE ROYAL LINE OF MARYAM TO BE EXTIN-GUISHED."
IT WAS HER SISTER PRINCESS MILITSA'S LAST REQUEST.
FIVE DAYS EARLIER ...
AKLEIA CASTLE, MARYAM
WAAAH!
WAAAH!

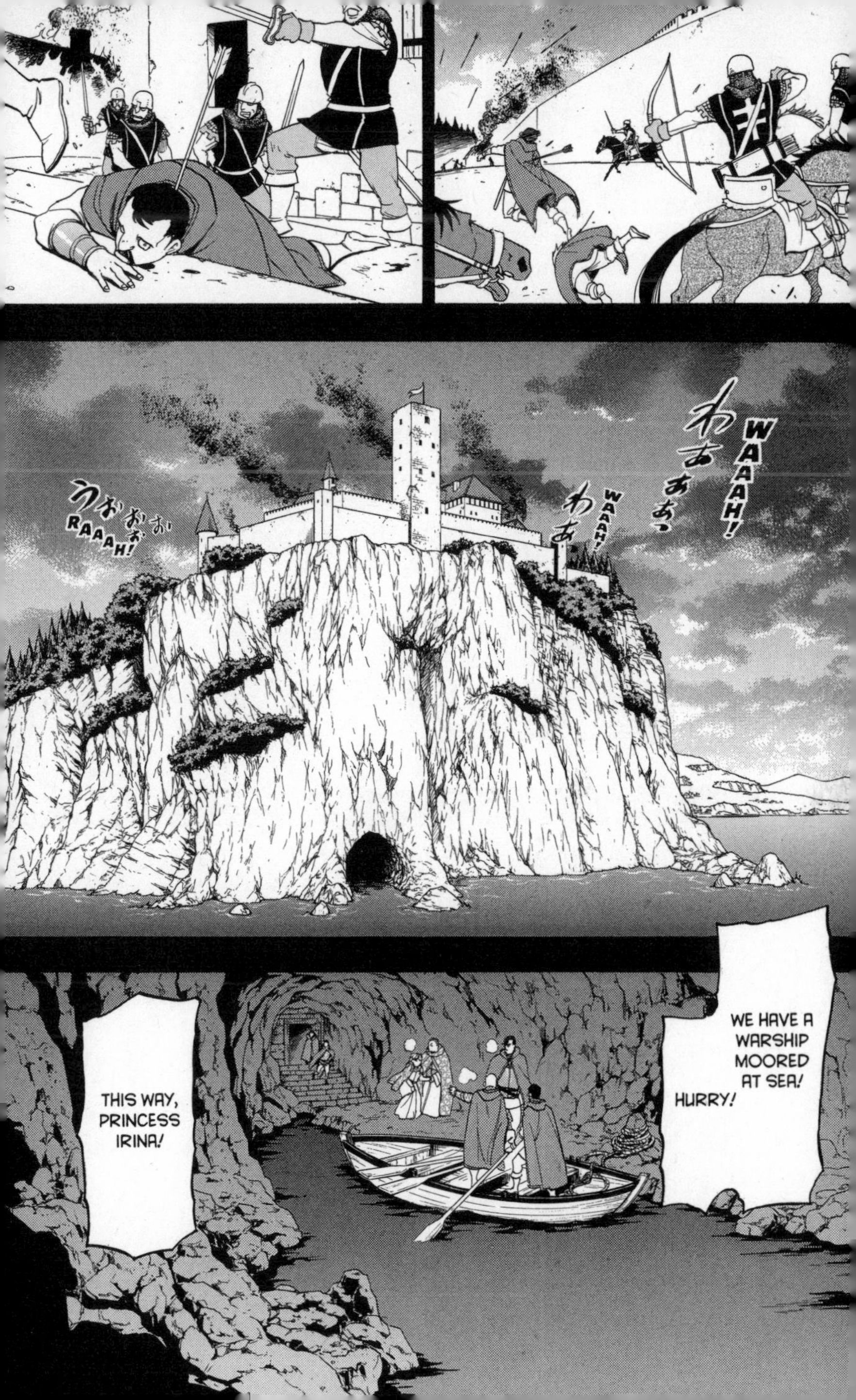
わあああっ
WAAAAH!
わあ
WAAAH!
うおおおお
RAAAH!
WE HAVE A WARSHIP MOORED AT SEA!
HURRY!
THIS WAY, PRINCESS IRINA!

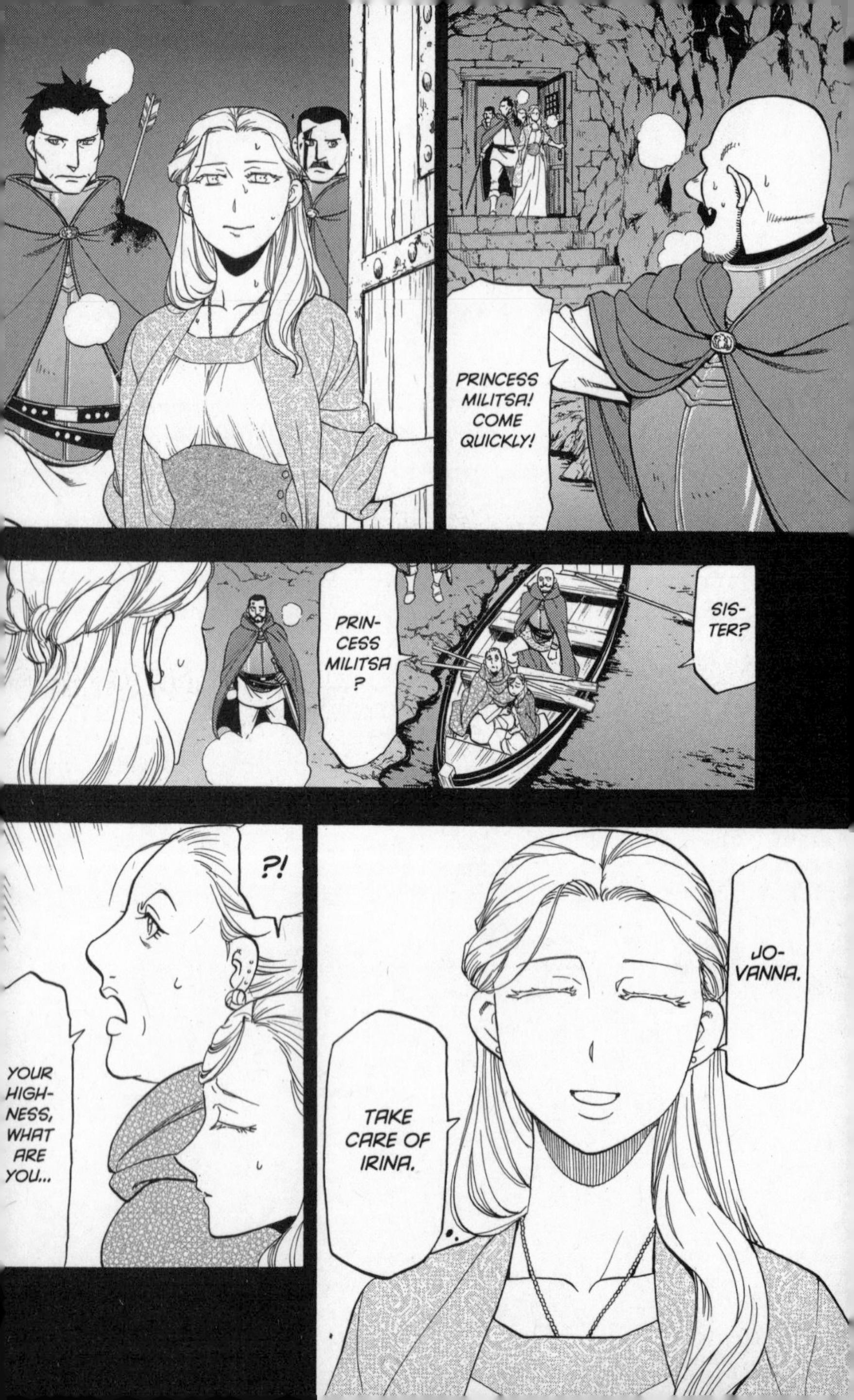
PRINCESS MILITSA! COME QUICKLY!
SIS-TER?
PRIN-CESS MILITSA?
JO-VANNA.
TAKE CARE OF IRINA.
?!
YOUR HIGH-NESS, WHAT ARE YOU...

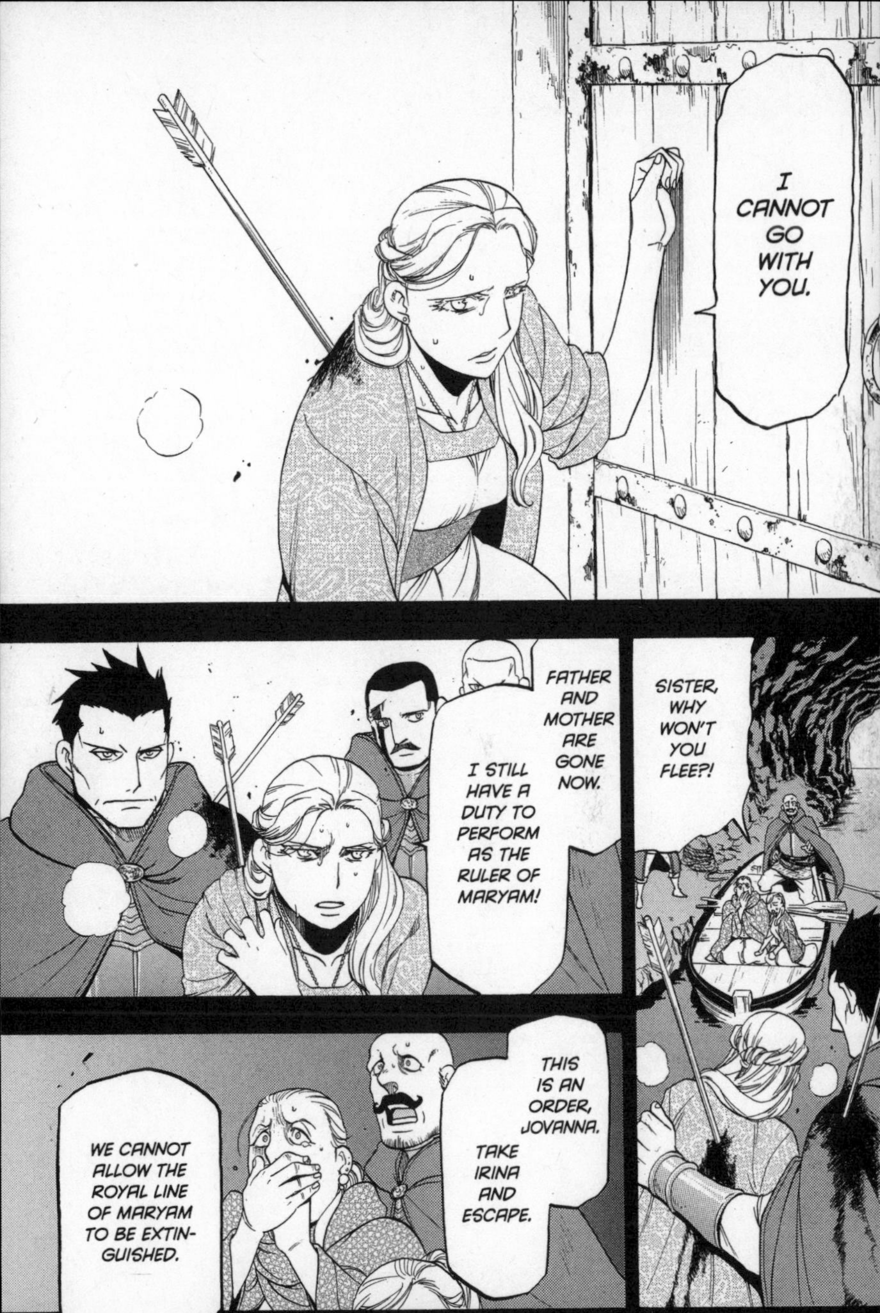
I CANNOT GO WITH YOU.
SISTER, WHY WON'T YOU FLEE?!
FATHER AND MOTHER ARE GONE NOW.
I STILL HAVE A DUTY TO PERFORM AS THE RULER OF MARYAM!
THIS IS AN ORDER, JOVANNA.
TAKE IRINA AND ESCAPE.
WE CANNOT ALLOW THE ROYAL LINE OF MARYAM TO BE EXTIN-GUISHED.

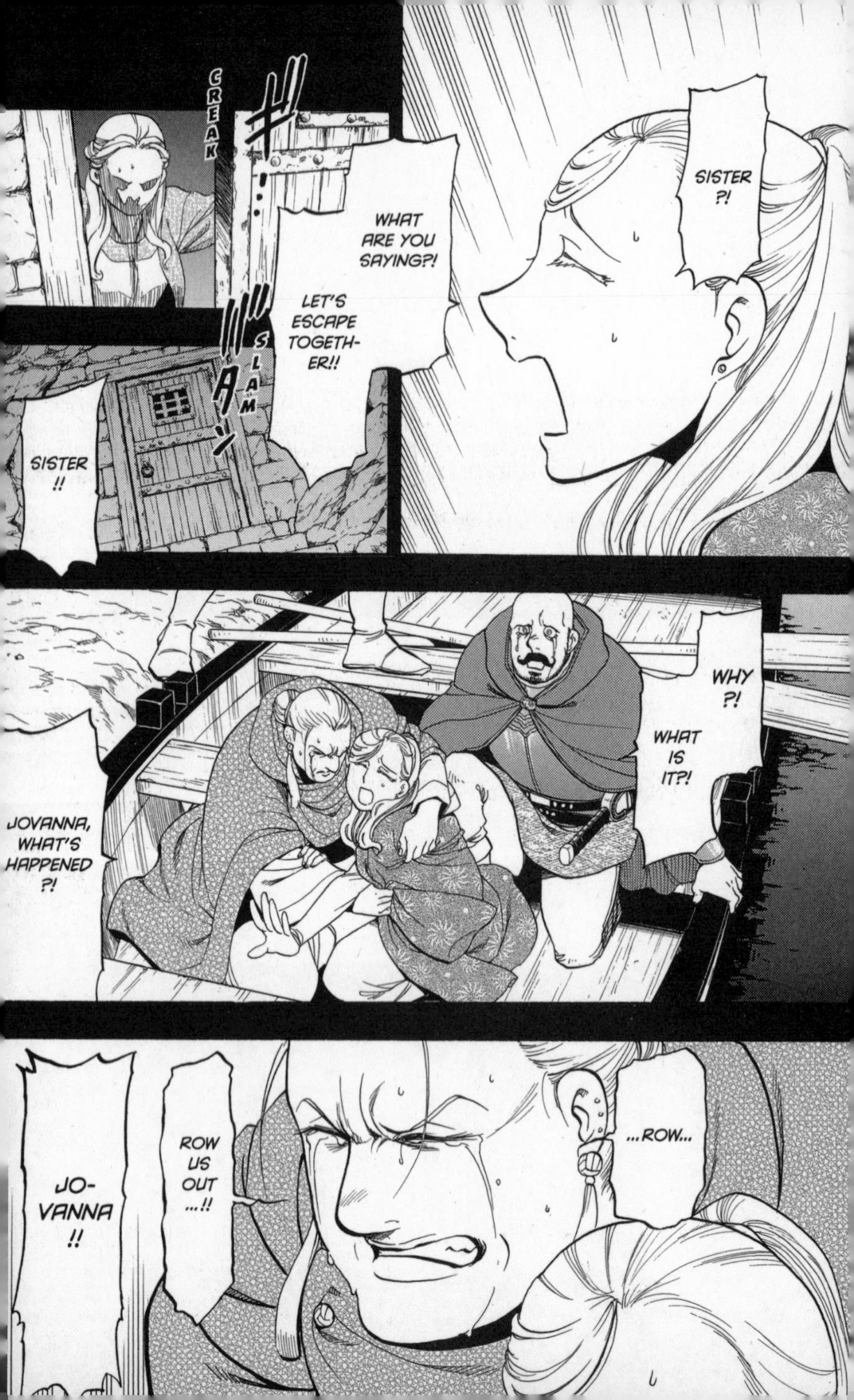
SISTER?!
WHAT ARE YOU SAYING?!
LET'S ESCAPE TOGETHER!!
CREAK
SLAM
SISTER!!
WHY?!
WHAT IS IT?!
JOVANNA, WHAT'S HAPPENED?!
...ROW...
ROW US OUT...!!
JO-VANNA!!

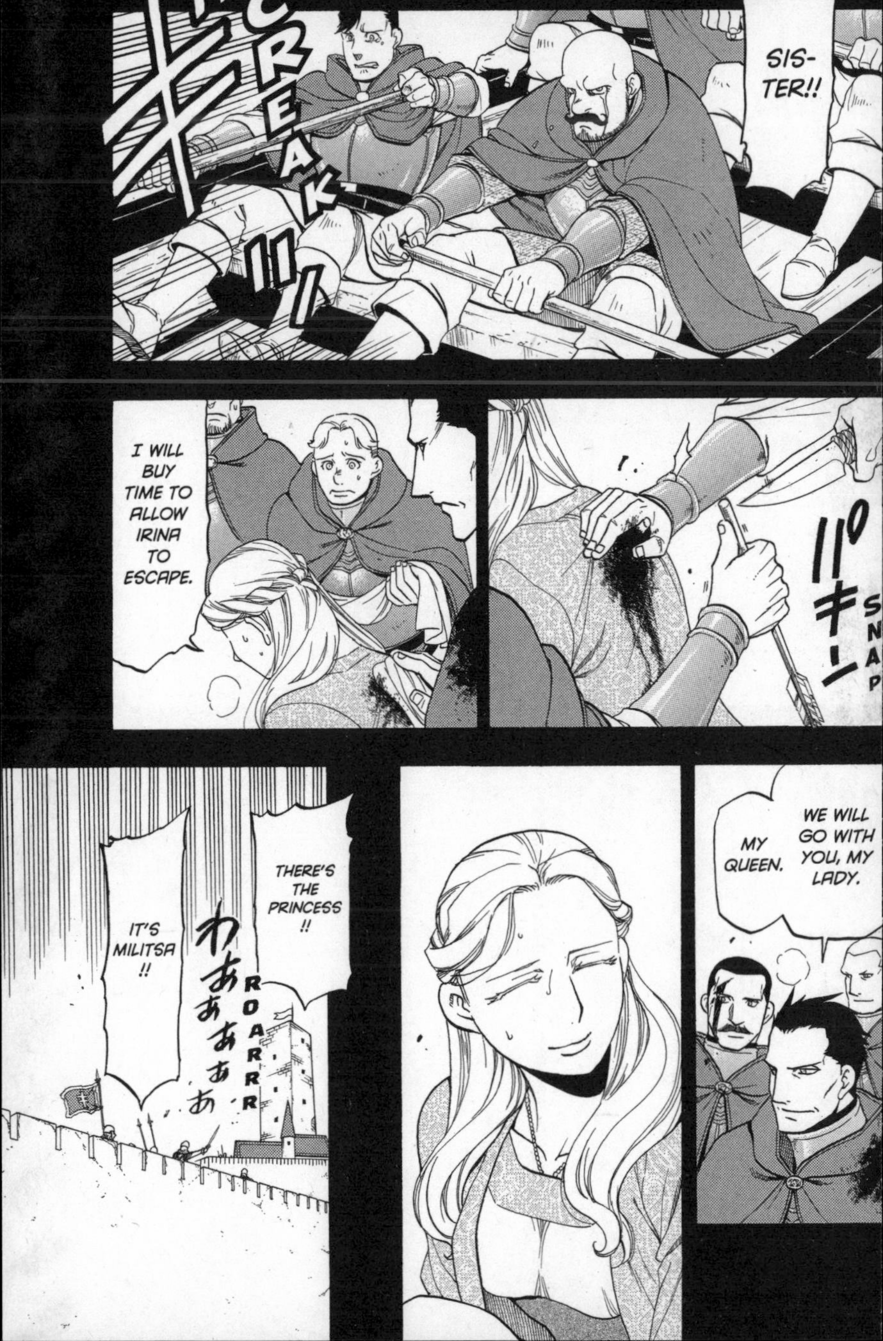
SIS-TER!!
CREAK
SNAP
I WILL BUY TIME TO ALLOW IRINA TO ESCAPE.
WE WILL GO WITH YOU, MY LADY.
MY QUEEN.
THERE'S THE PRINCESS!!
ROARRR
IT'S MILITSA!!

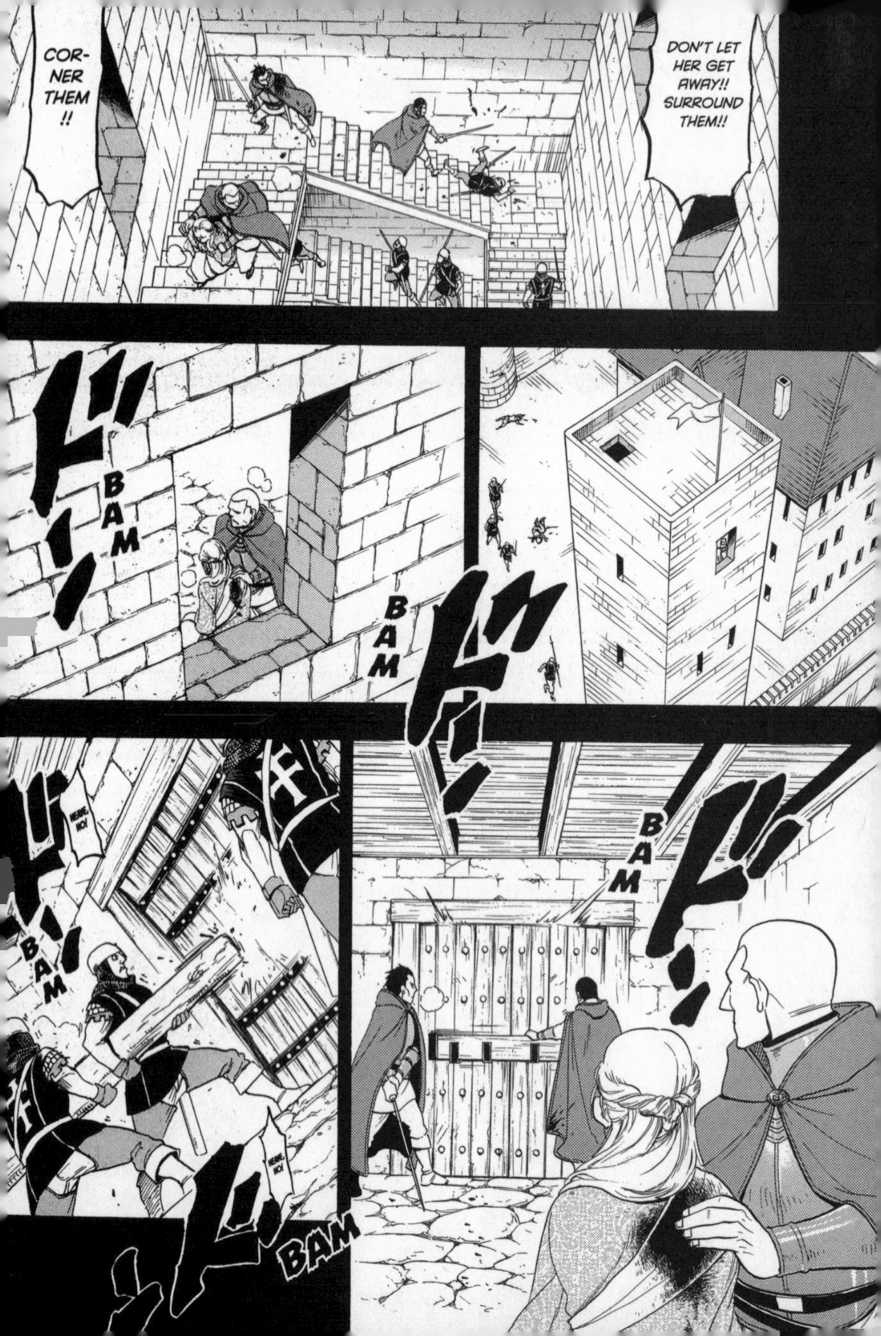
DON'T LET HER GET AWAY!! SURROUND THEM!!
COR-NER THEM!!
BAM
BAM
BAM
HEAVE, HO!
BAM
HEAVE, HO!
BAM

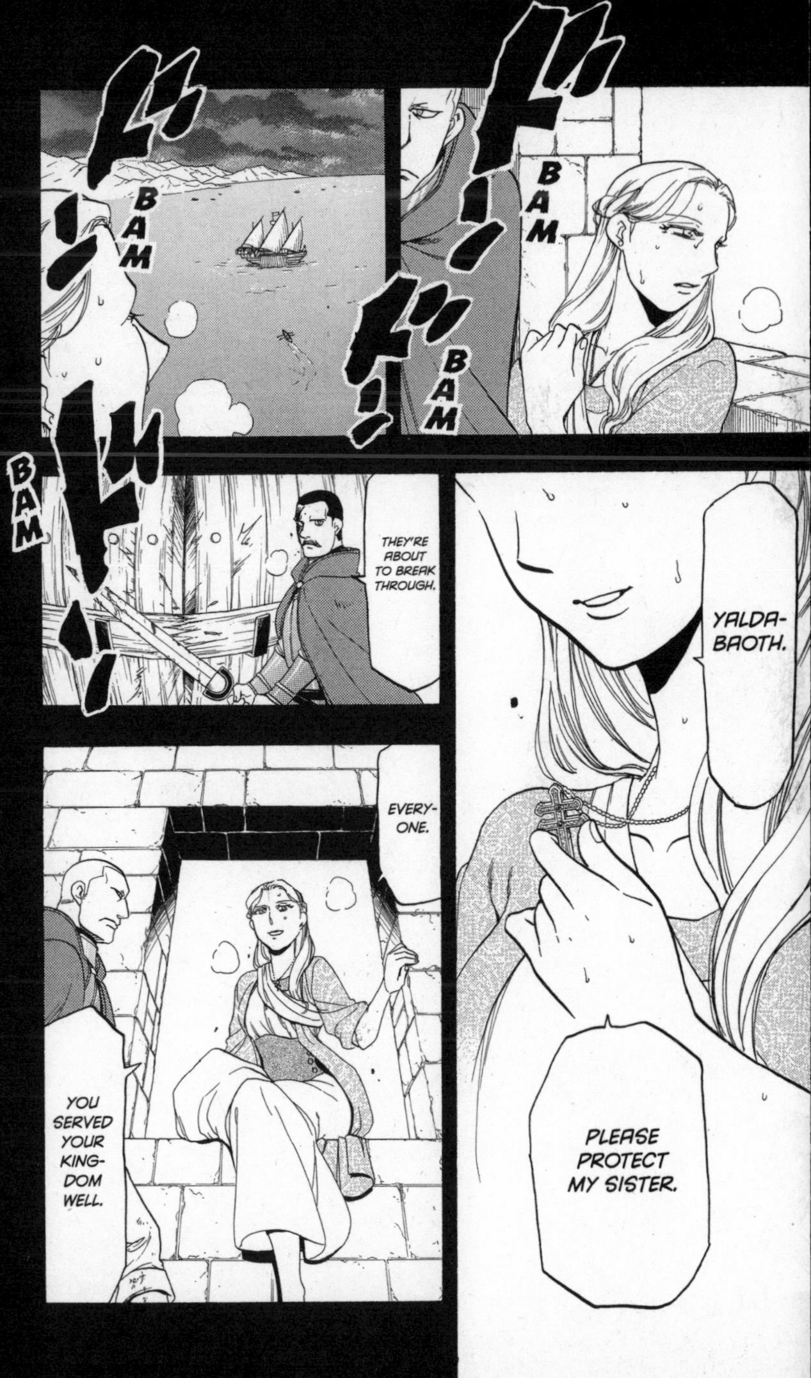
BAM
BAM
BAM
BAM
YALDA-BAOTH.
PLEASE PROTECT MY SISTER.
THEY'RE ABOUT TO BREAK THROUGH.
EVERY-ONE.
YOU SERVED YOUR KING-DOM WELL.

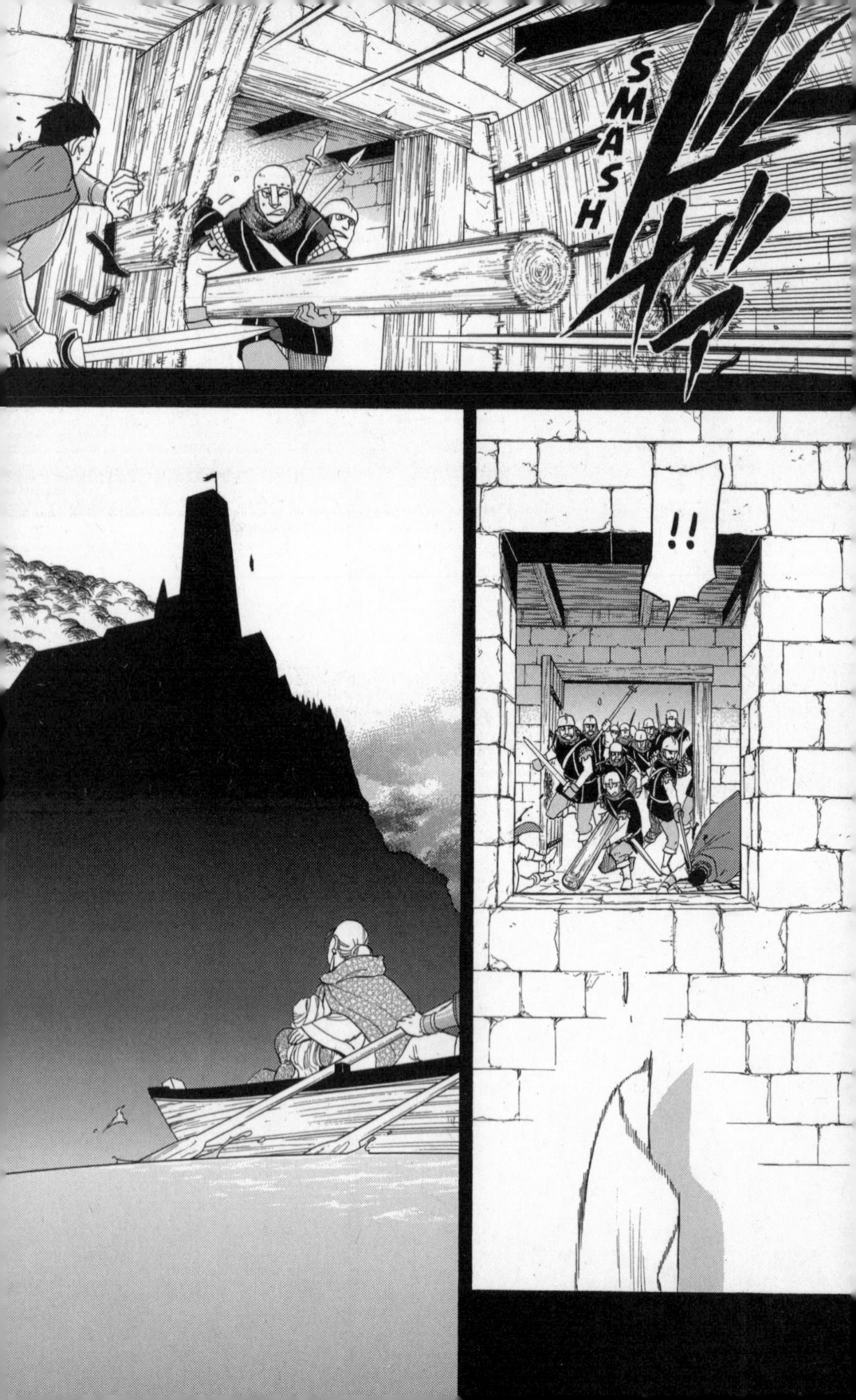
SMASH
!!

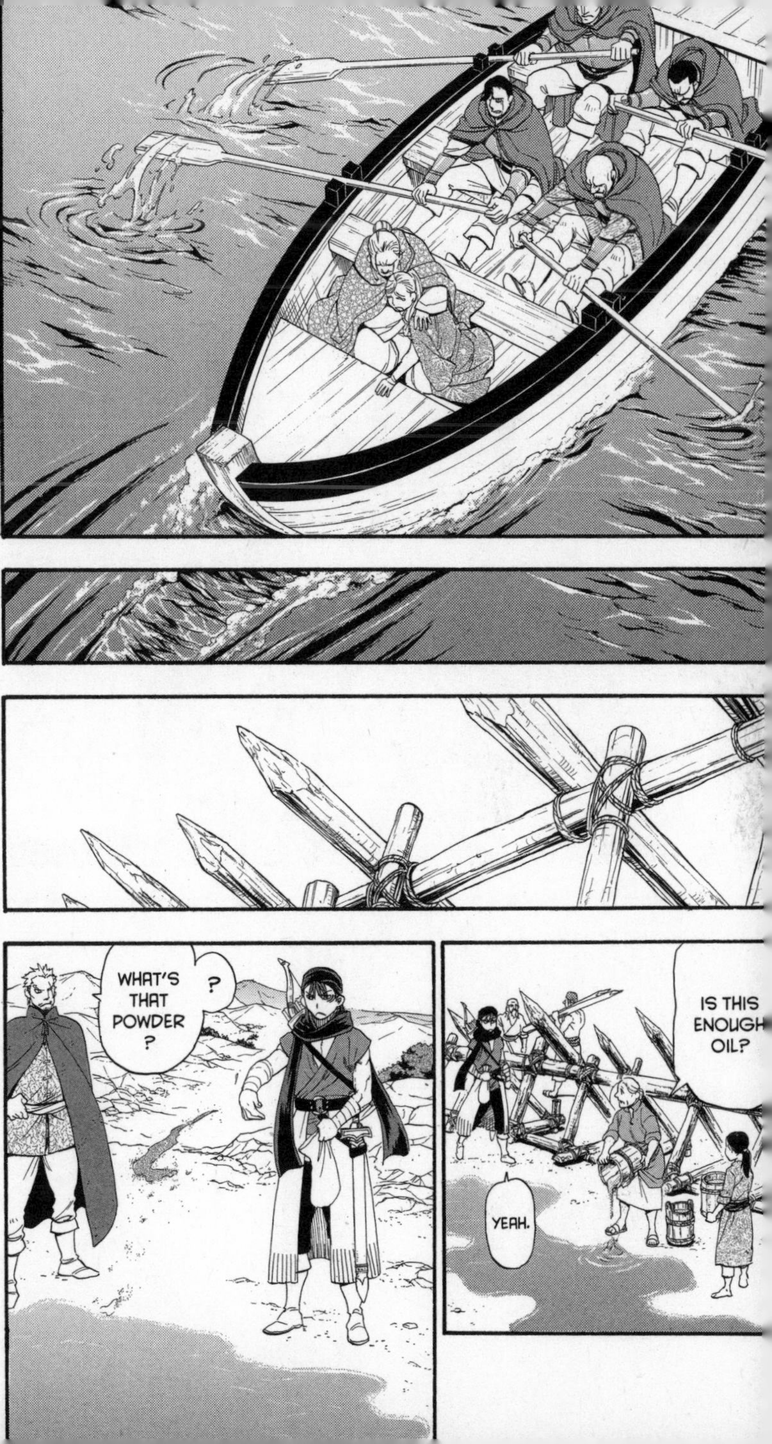
IS THIS ENOUGH OIL?
YEAH.
WHAT'S THAT POWDER?
?

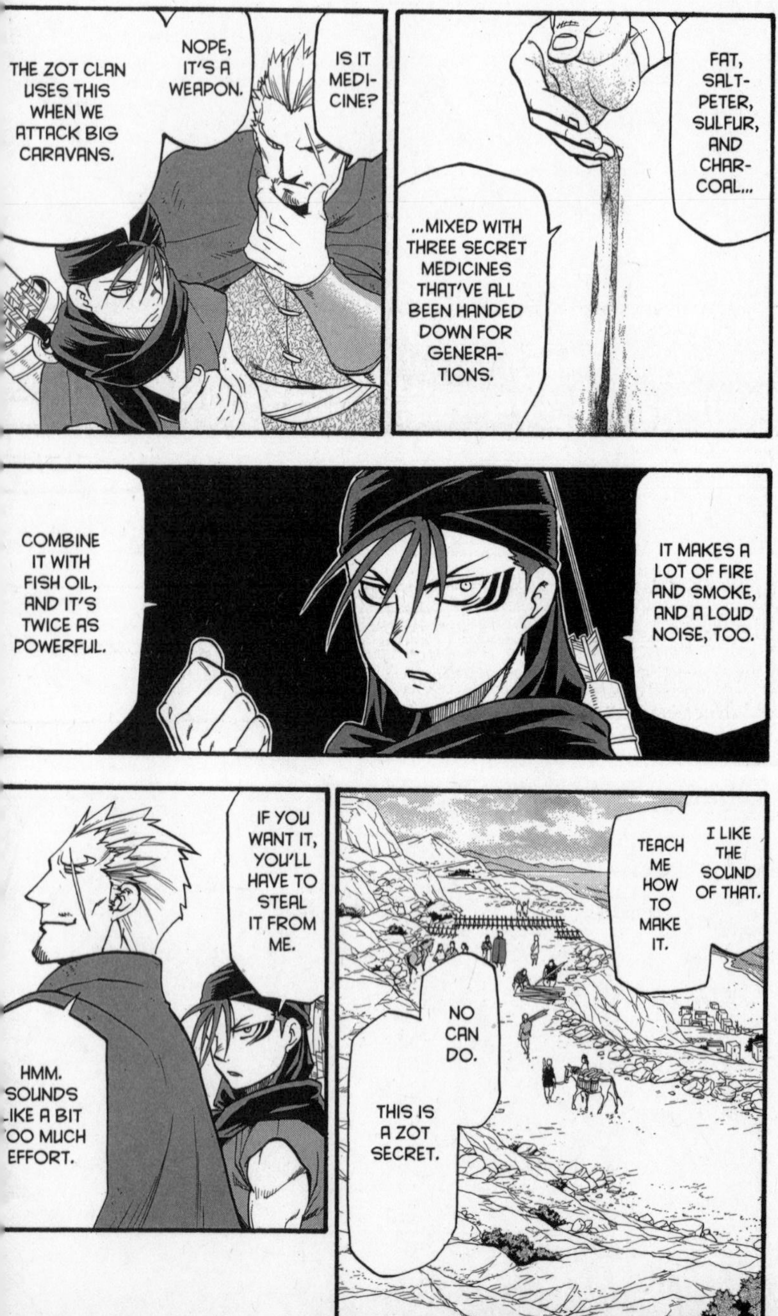
FAT, SALT-PETER, SULFUR, AND CHAR-COAL...
...MIXED WITH THREE SECRET MEDICINES THAT'VE ALL BEEN HANDED DOWN FOR GENERA-TIONS.
IS IT MEDI-CINE?
NOPE, IT'S A WEAPON.
THE ZOT CLAN USES THIS WHEN WE ATTACK BIG CARAVANS.
IT MAKES A LOT OF FIRE AND SMOKE, AND A LOUD NOISE, TOO.
COMBINE IT WITH FISH OIL, AND IT'S TWICE AS POWERFUL.
I LIKE THE SOUND OF THAT.
TEACH ME HOW TO MAKE IT.
NO CAN DO.
THIS IS A ZOT SECRET.
IF YOU WANT IT, YOU'LL HAVE TO STEAL IT FROM ME.
HMM. SOUNDS IKE A BIT OO MUCH EFFORT.

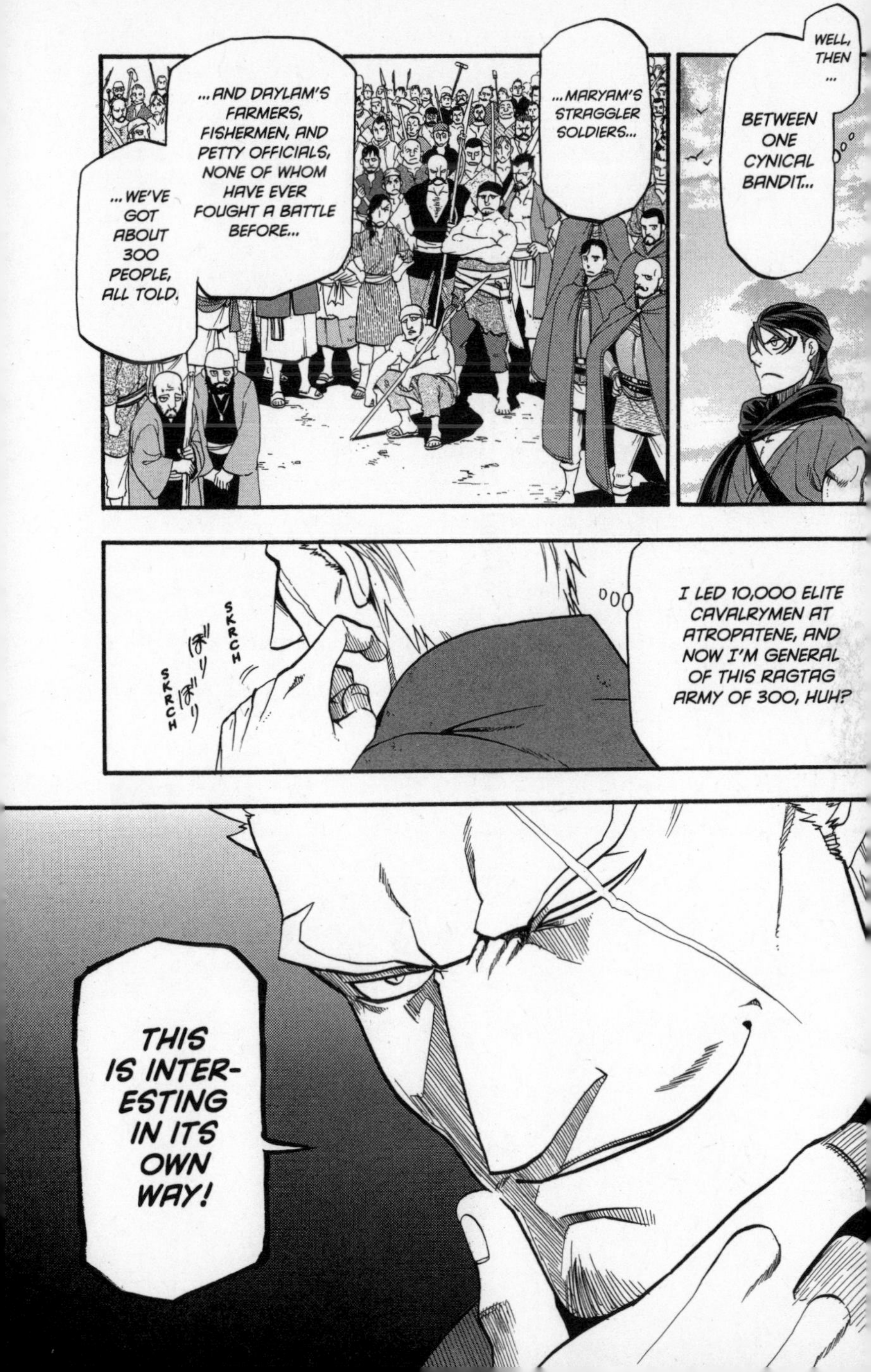
WELL, THEN ...
BETWEEN ONE CYNICAL BANDIT...
...MARYAM'S STRAGGLER SOLDIERS...
...AND DAYLAM'S FARMERS, FISHERMEN, AND PETTY OFFICIALS, NONE OF WHOM HAVE EVER FOUGHT A BATTLE BEFORE...
...WE'VE GOT ABOUT 300 PEOPLE, ALL TOLD.
I LED 10,000 ELITE CAVALRYMEN AT ATROPATENE, AND NOW I'M GENERAL OF THIS RAGTAG ARMY OF 300, HUH?
SKRCH
ぼり
ぼり
SKRCH
THIS IS INTER-ESTING IN ITS OWN WAY!

THE HEROIC LEGEND OF
ARSLAN

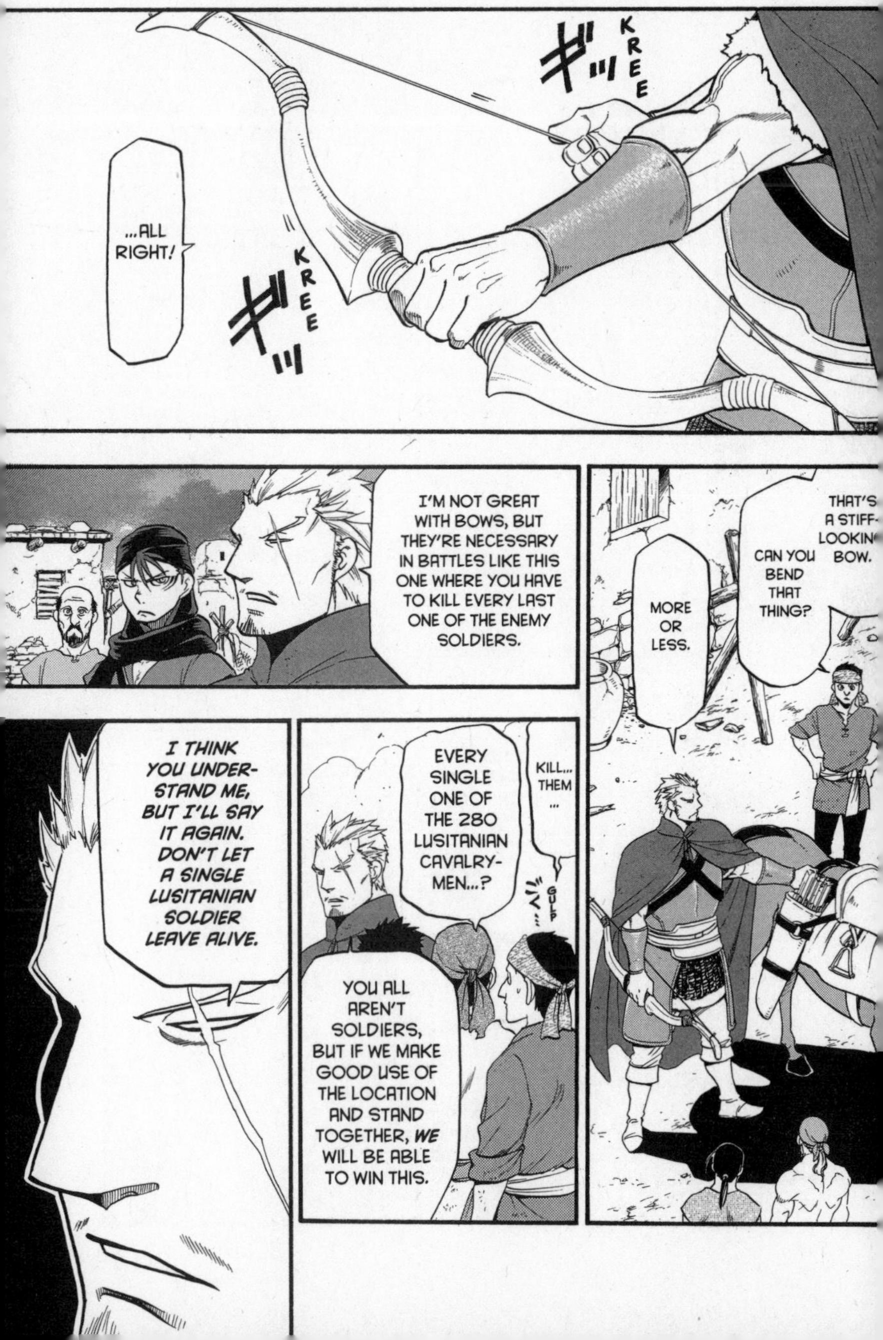
KREE
...ALL RIGHT!
KREE
THAT'S A STIFF-LOOKIN BOW.
CAN YOU BEND THAT THING?
MORE OR LESS.
I'M NOT GREAT WITH BOWS, BUT THEY'RE NECESSARY IN BATTLES LIKE THIS ONE WHERE YOU HAVE TO KILL EVERY LAST ONE OF THE ENEMY SOLDIERS.
KILL... THEM ...
EVERY SINGLE ONE OF THE 280 LUSITANIAN CAVALRYMEN...?
GULP
YOU ALL AREN'T SOLDIERS, BUT IF WE MAKE GOOD USE OF THE LOCATION AND STAND TOGETHER, *WE* WILL BE ABLE TO WIN THIS.
I THINK YOU UNDERSTAND ME, BUT I'LL SAY IT AGAIN. DON'T LET A SINGLE LUSITANIAN SOLDIER LEAVE ALIVE.

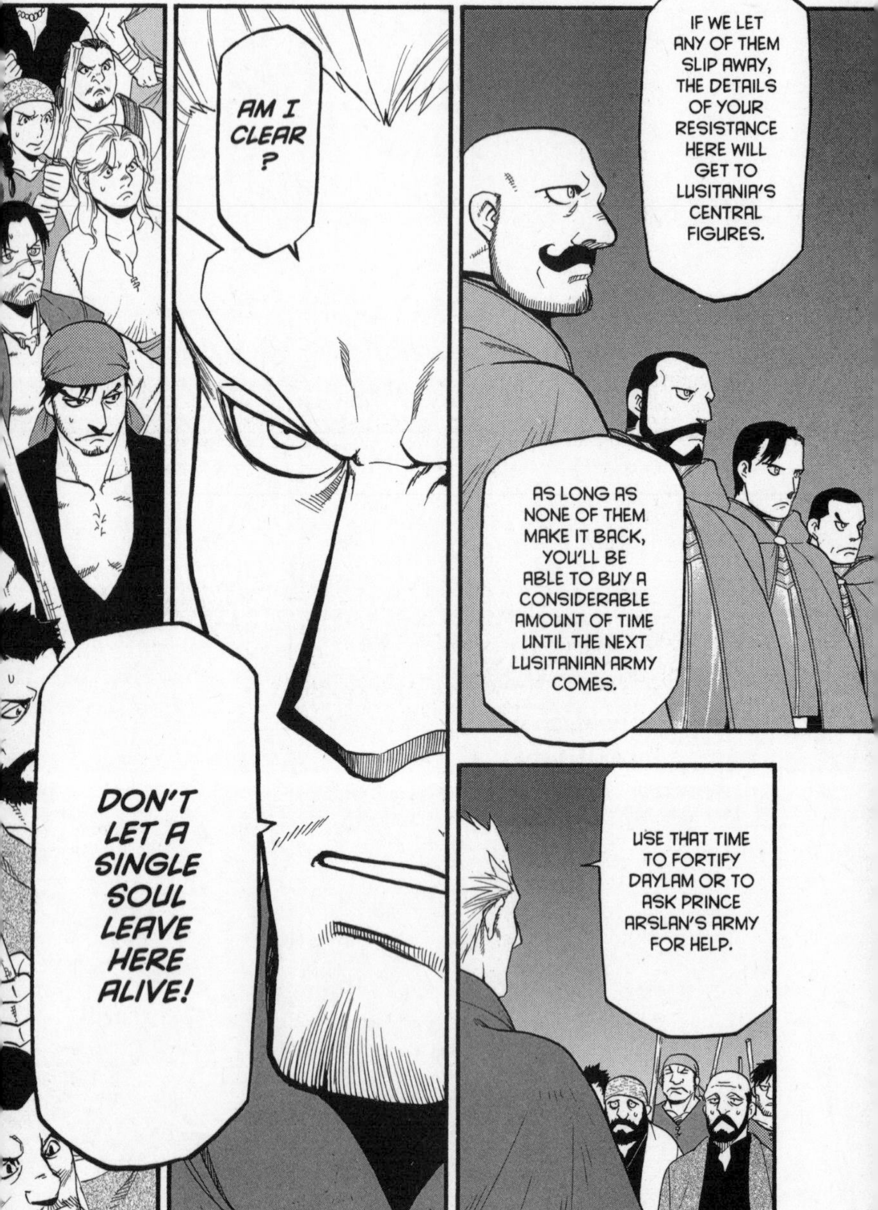
IF WE LET ANY OF THEM SLIP AWAY, THE DETAILS OF YOUR RESISTANCE HERE WILL GET TO LUSITANIA'S CENTRAL FIGURES.
AS LONG AS NONE OF THEM MAKE IT BACK, YOU'LL BE ABLE TO BUY A CONSIDERABLE AMOUNT OF TIME UNTIL THE NEXT LUSITANIAN ARMY COMES.
USE THAT TIME TO FORTIFY DAYLAM OR TO ASK PRINCE ARSLAN'S ARMY FOR HELP.
AM I CLEAR?
DON'T LET A SINGLE SOUL LEAVE HERE ALIVE!

Chapter 63: The Job of a Bandit

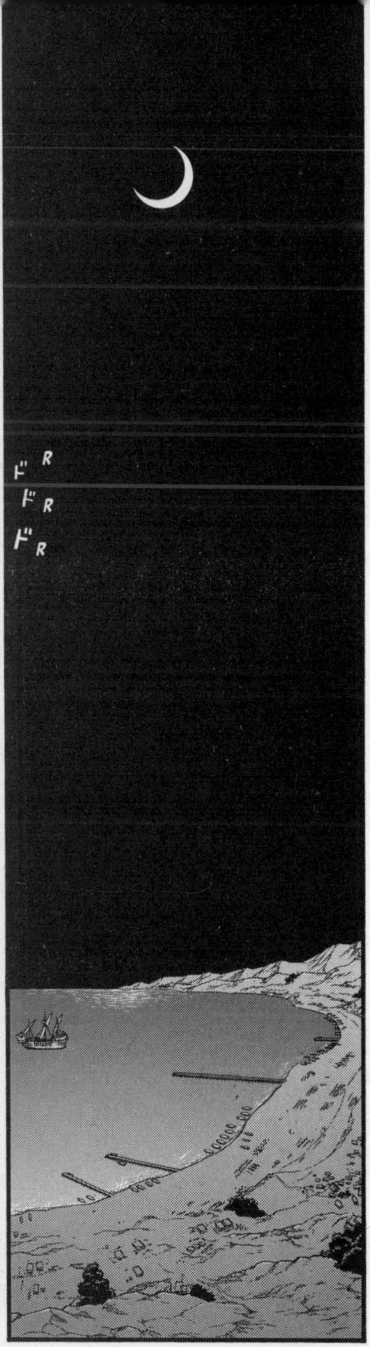
ド R
ド R
ド R

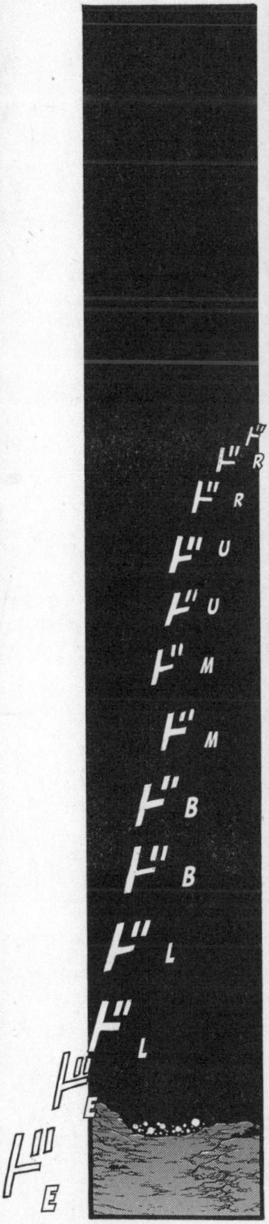
ド R
ド R
ド U
ド U
ド M
ド M
ド B
ド B
ド L
ド L
ド E
ド E

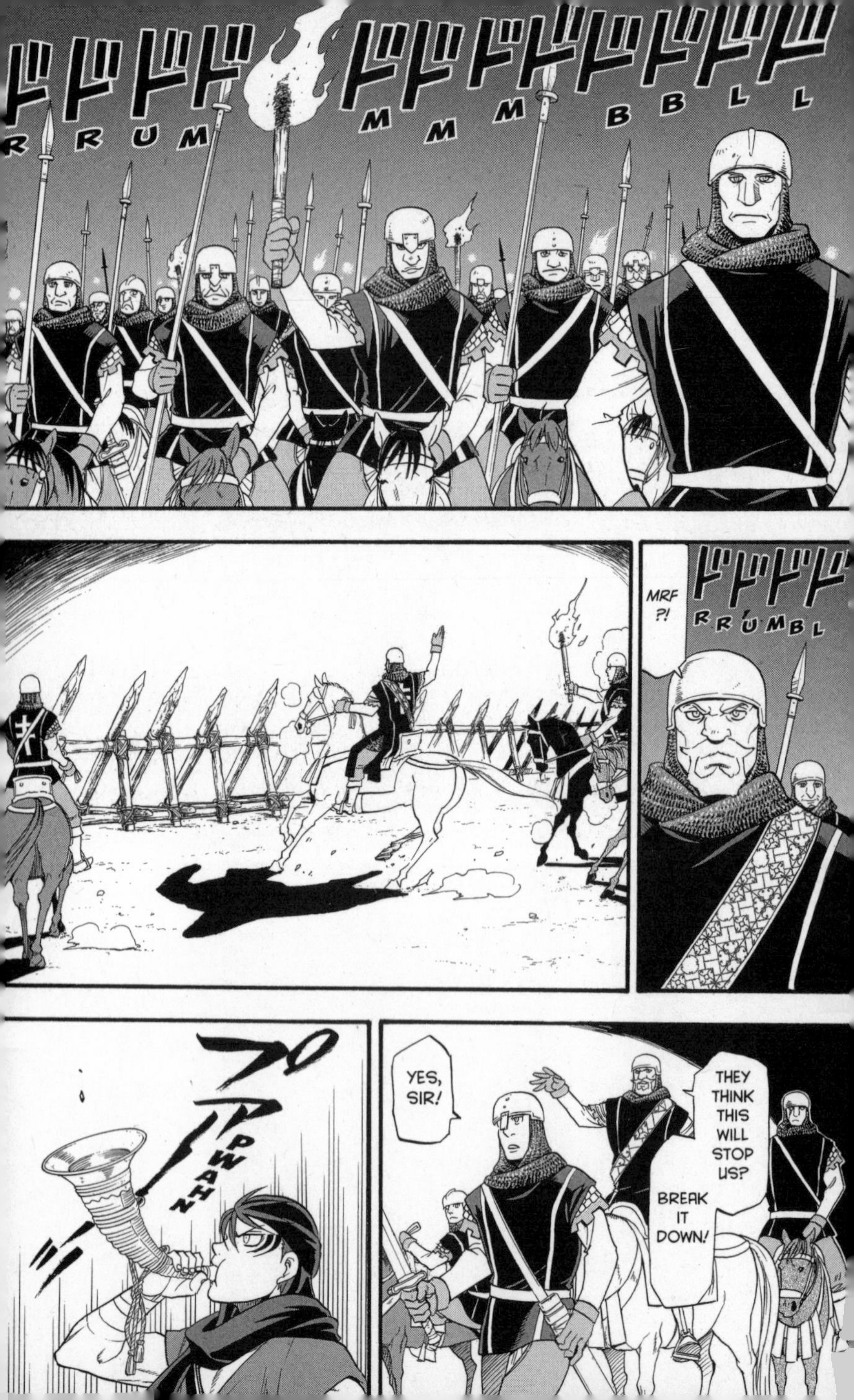
ドドドド ドドドドドドド
RRUMMMBBLL
MRF?!
ドドドド
RRUMBL
THEY THINK THIS WILL STOP US?
BREAK IT DOWN!
YES, SIR!
PWAHN

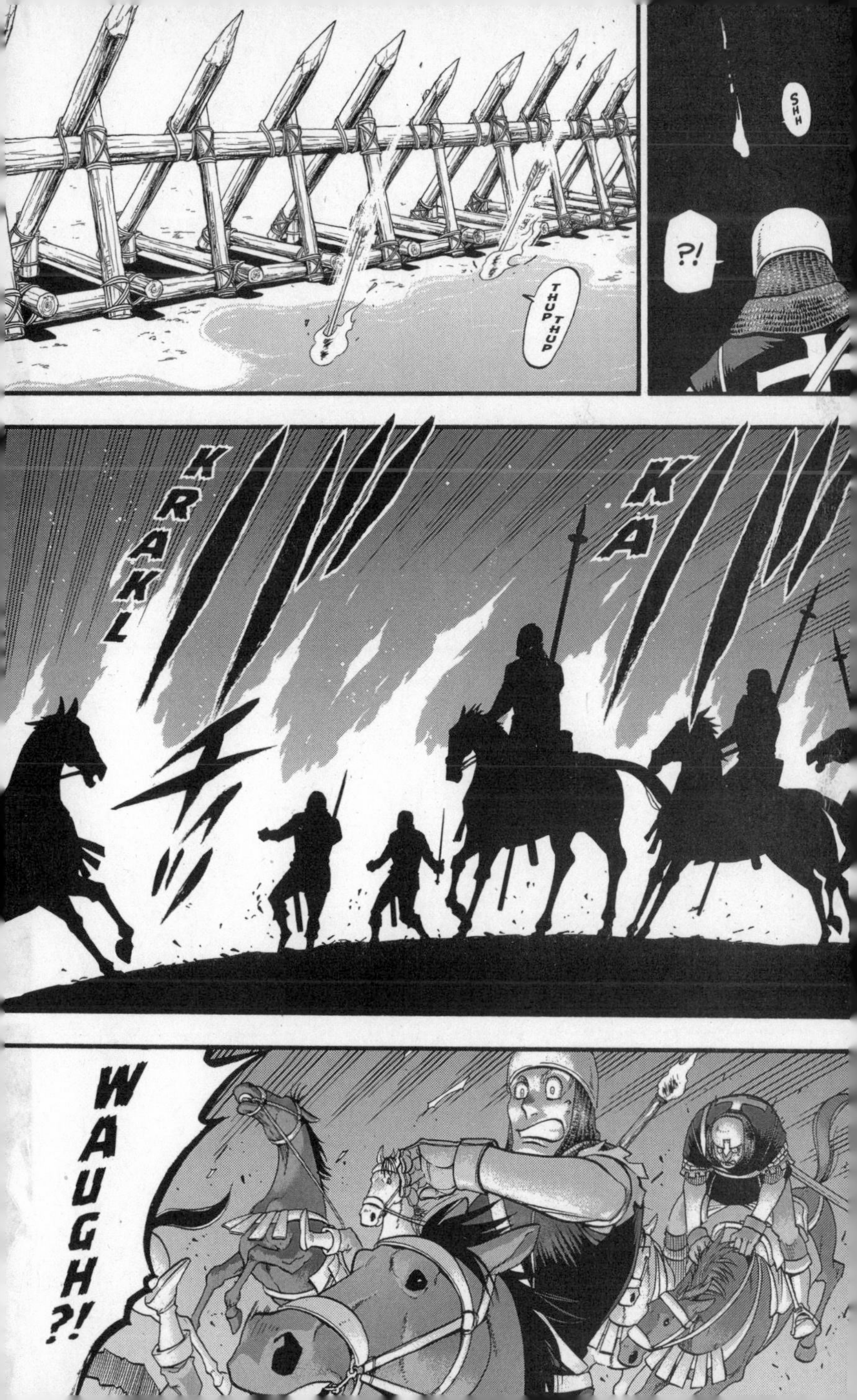
SHH
?!
THUP THUP
KA
KRAKL
WAUGH?!

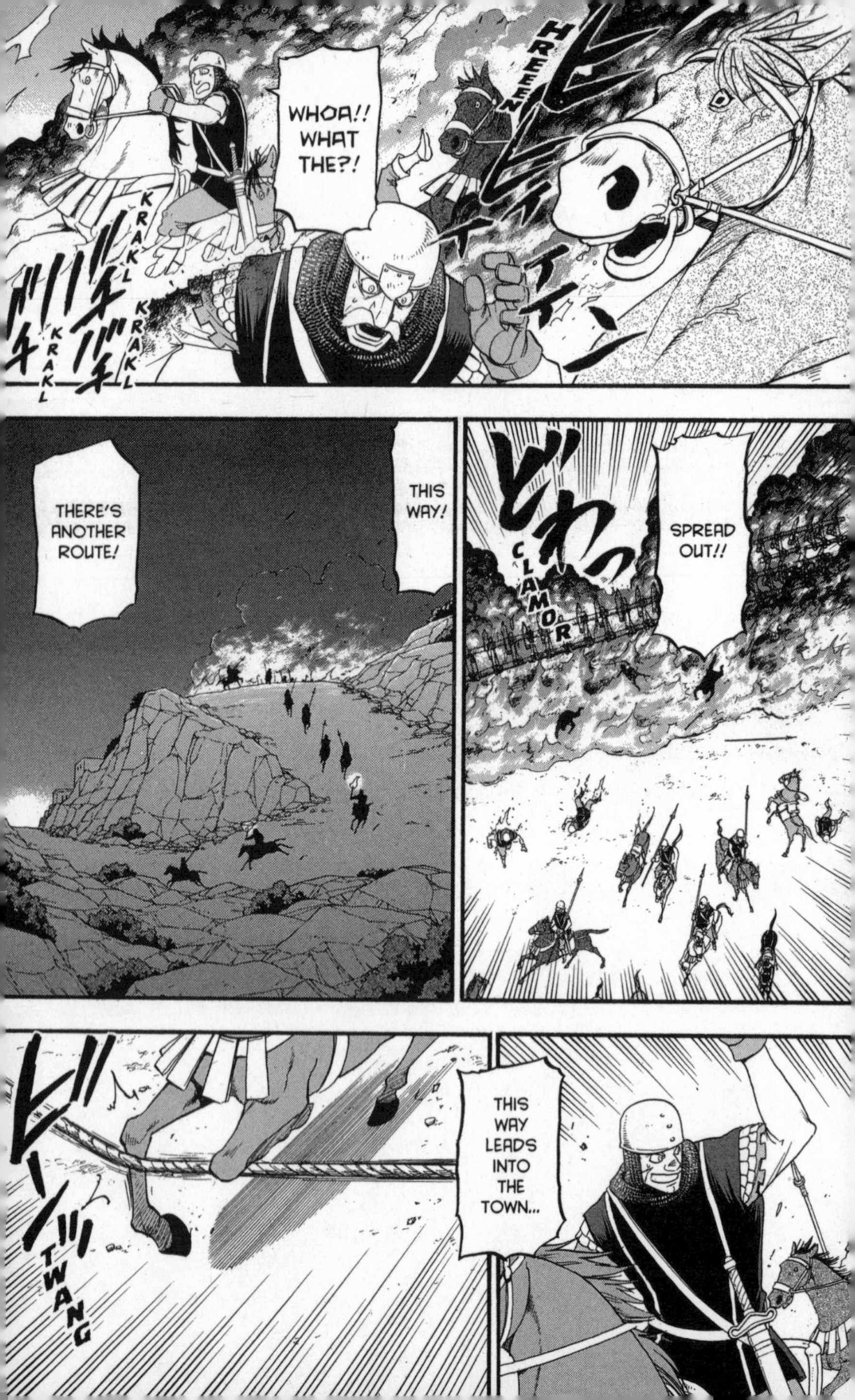
HREEEEN
WHOA!! WHAT THE?!
KRAKL KRAKL KRAKL
CLAMOR
SPREAD OUT!!
THIS WAY!
THERE'S ANOTHER ROUTE!
THIS WAY LEADS INTO THE TOWN...
TWANG

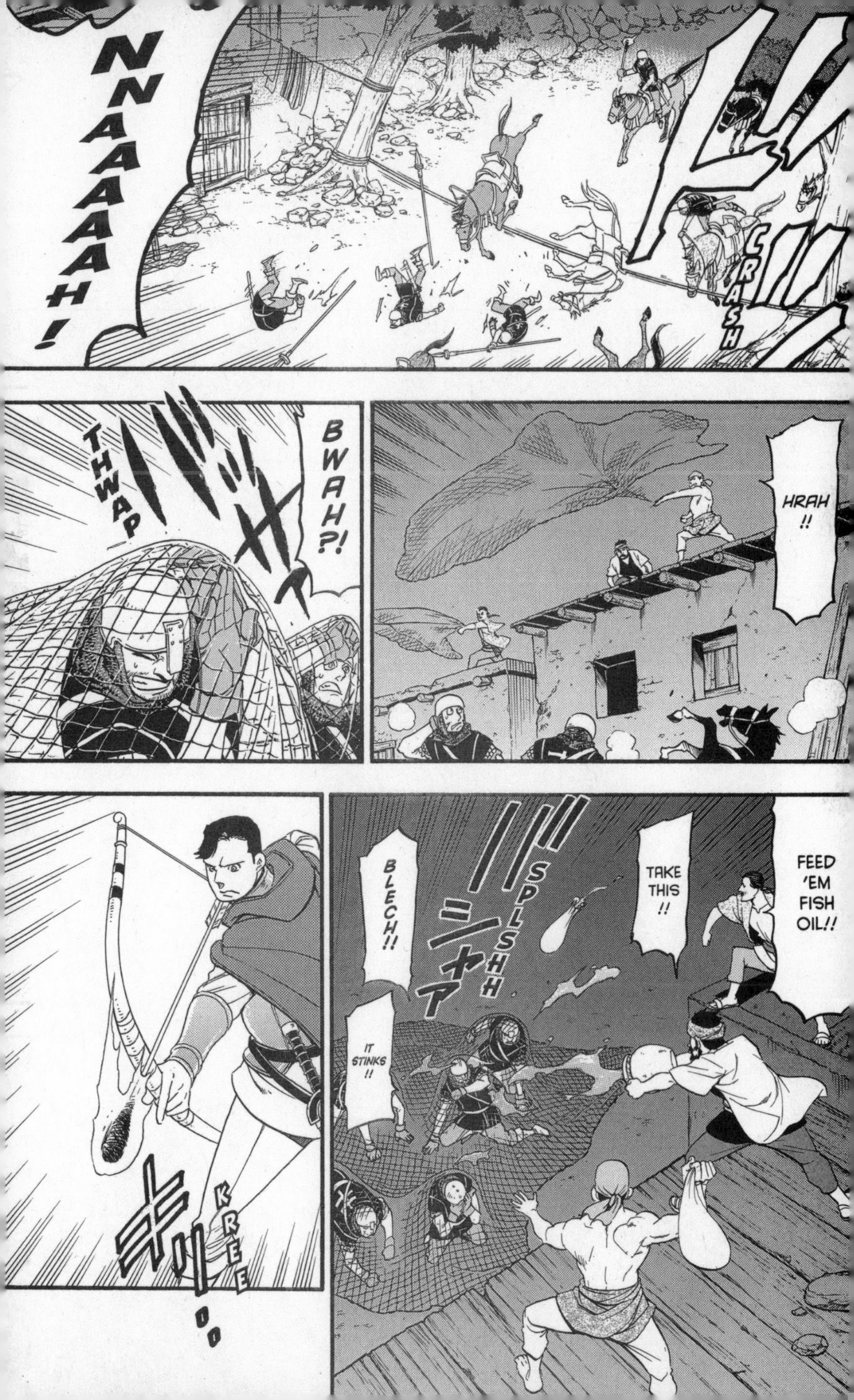
CRASH
NNAAAAAAH!
HRAH!!
BWAH?!
THWAP
FEED 'EM FISH OIL!!
TAKE THIS!!
SPLSHH
BLECH!!
IT STINKS!!
KREE

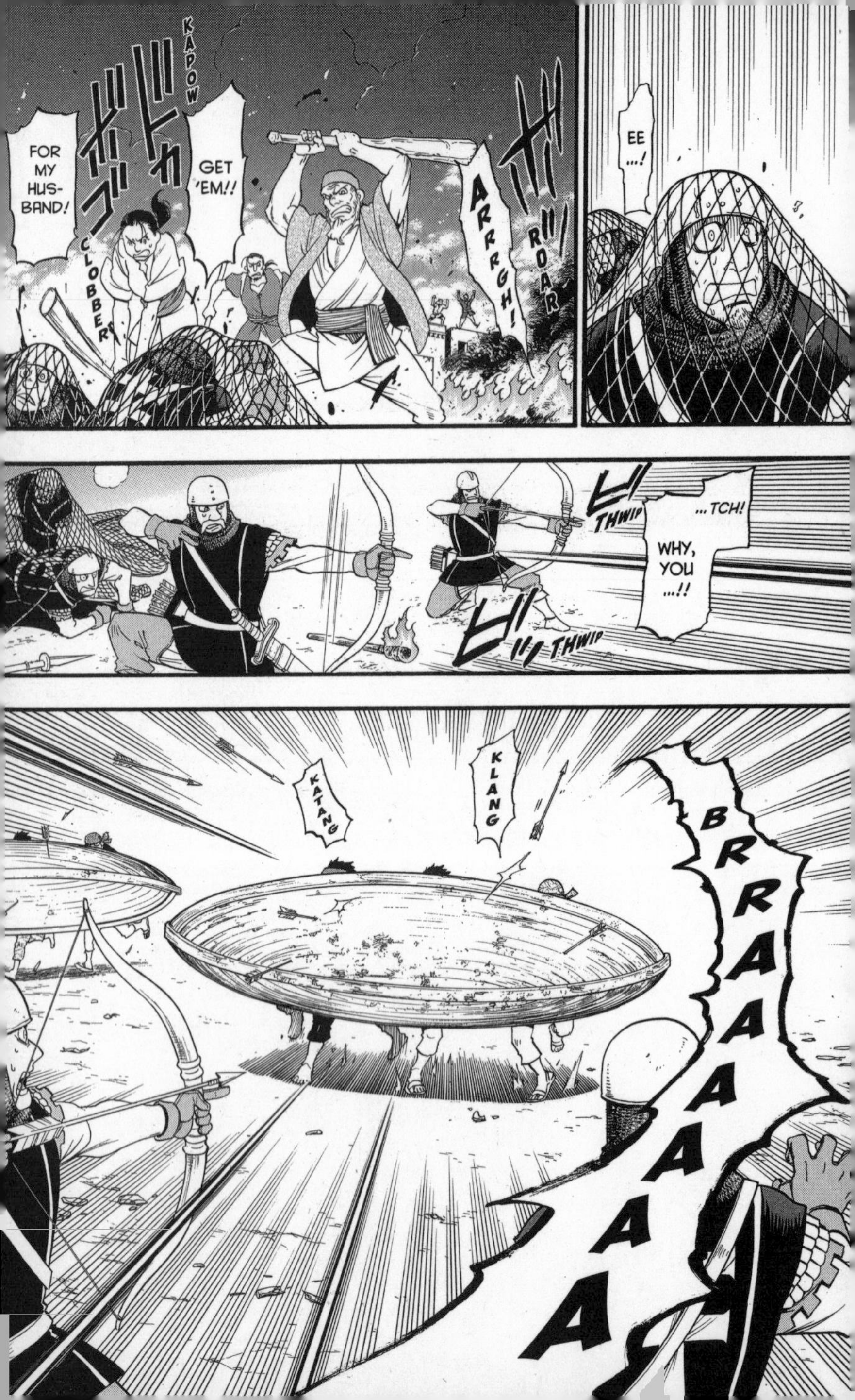
EE ...!
ARRRGH!
ROAR
GET 'EM!!
KAPOW
FOR MY HUS-BAND!
CLOBBER
...TCH!
WHY, YOU ...!!
THWIP
THWIP
BRRAAAAAA
KLANG
KATANG

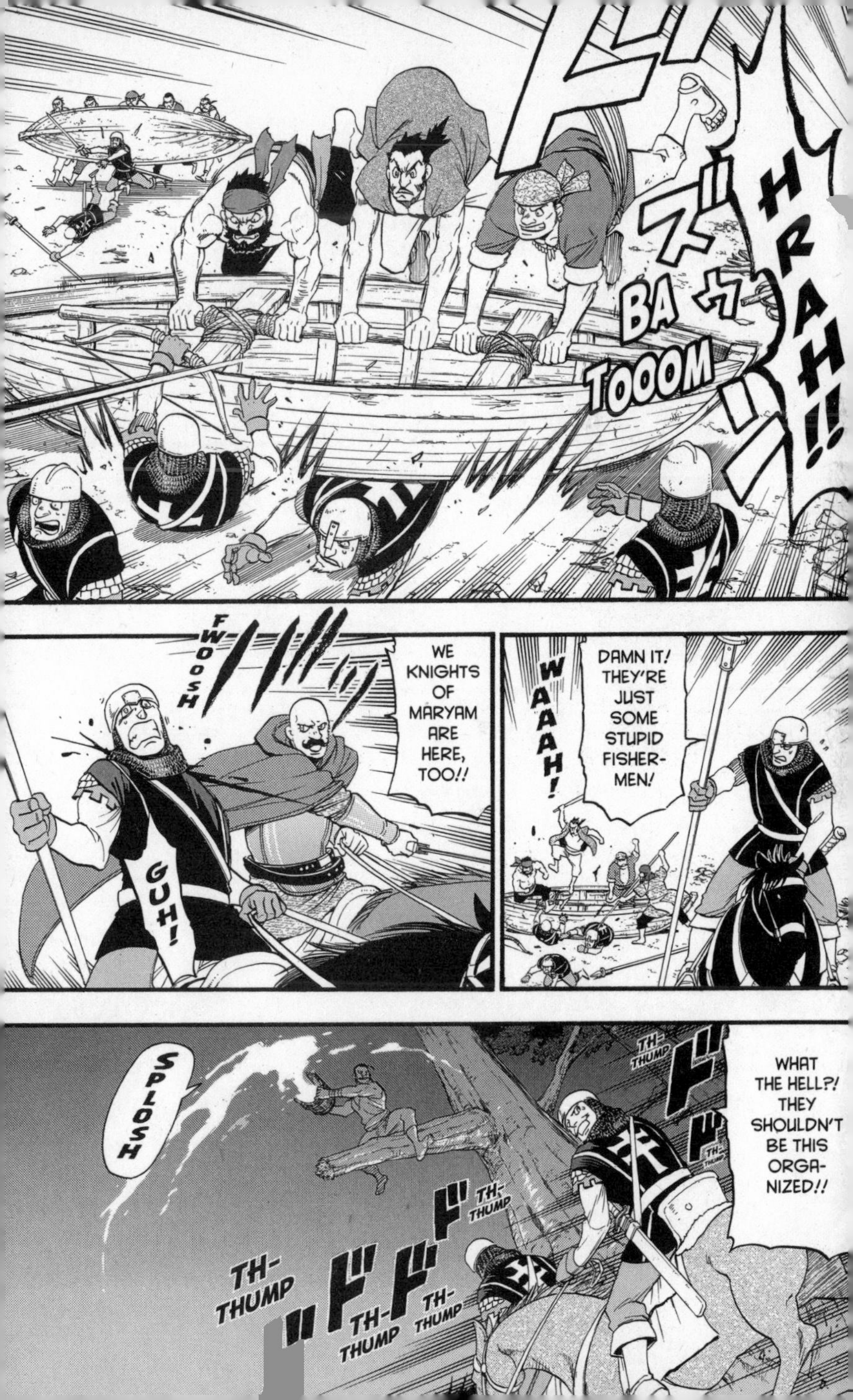
HRAH!!
BA TOOOM
WAAAH!
DAMN IT! THEY'RE JUST SOME STUPID FISHER-MEN!
FWOOSH
WE KNIGHTS OF MARYAM ARE HERE, TOO!!
GUH!
WHAT THE HELL?! THEY SHOULDN'T BE THIS ORGA-NIZED!!
TH-THUMP
TH-THUMP
TH-THUMP
TH-THUMP
TH-THUMP
SPLOSH

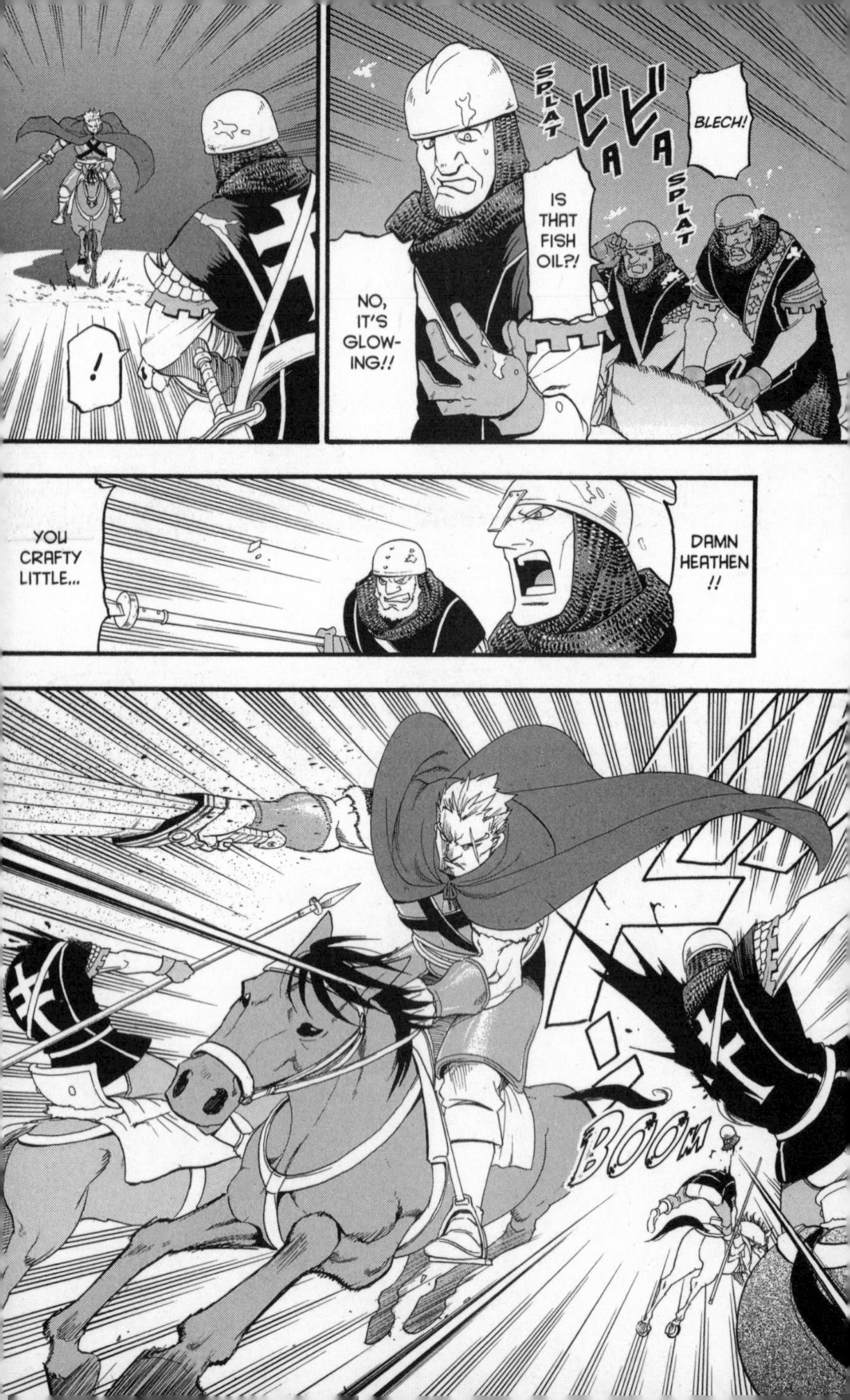
BLECH!
SPLAT
SPLAT
IS THAT FISH OIL?!
NO, IT'S GLOWING!!
!
DAMN HEATHEN!!
YOU CRAFTY LITTLE...
BOOM

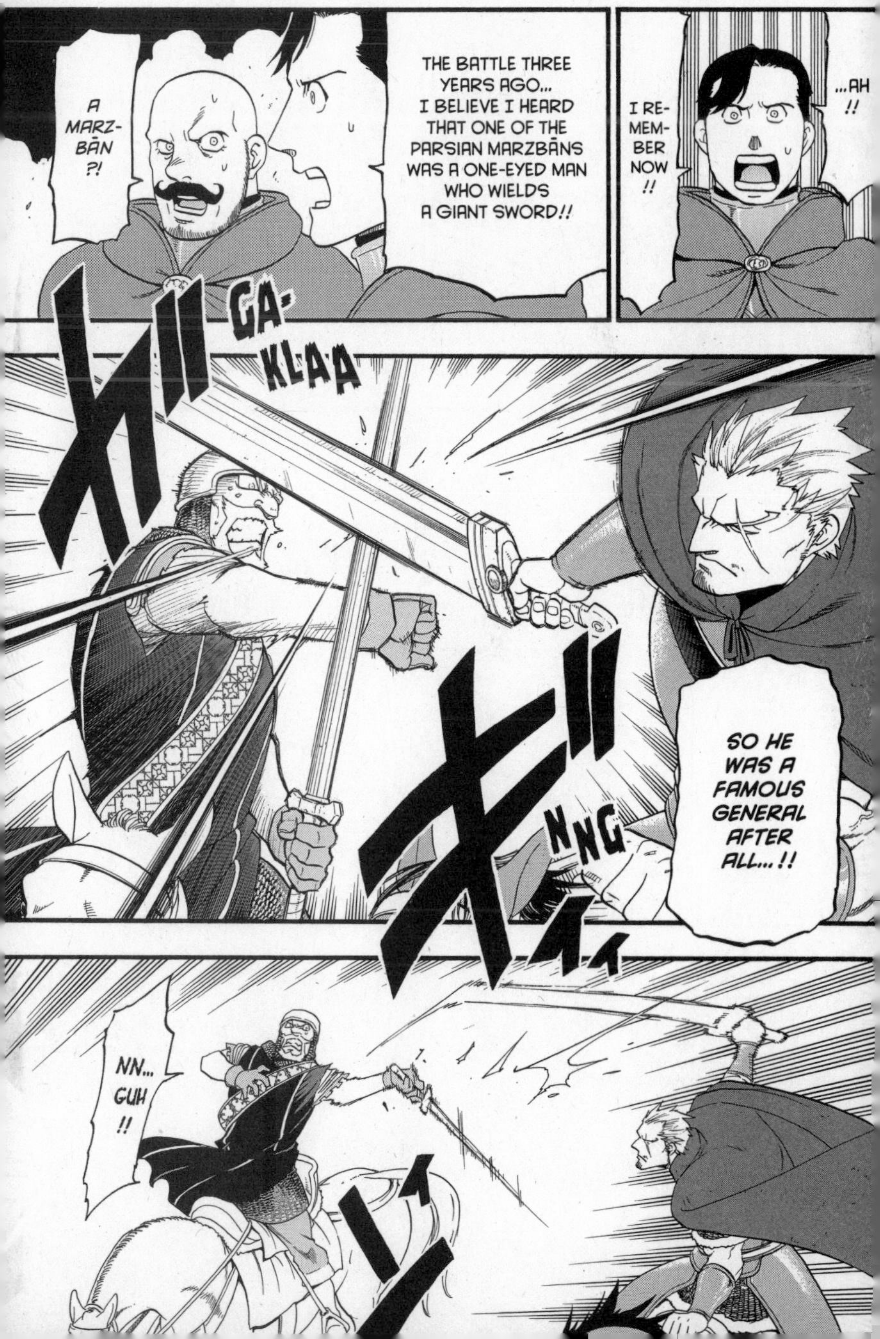
...AH!!
I RE-MEM-BER NOW!!
THE BATTLE THREE YEARS AGO... I BELIEVE I HEARD THAT ONE OF THE PARSIAN MARZBĀNS WAS A ONE-EYED MAN WHO WIELDS A GIANT SWORD!!
A MARZ-BĀN?!
GA-KLAA
NNG
SO HE WAS A FAMOUS GENERAL AFTER ALL...!!
NN... GUH!!

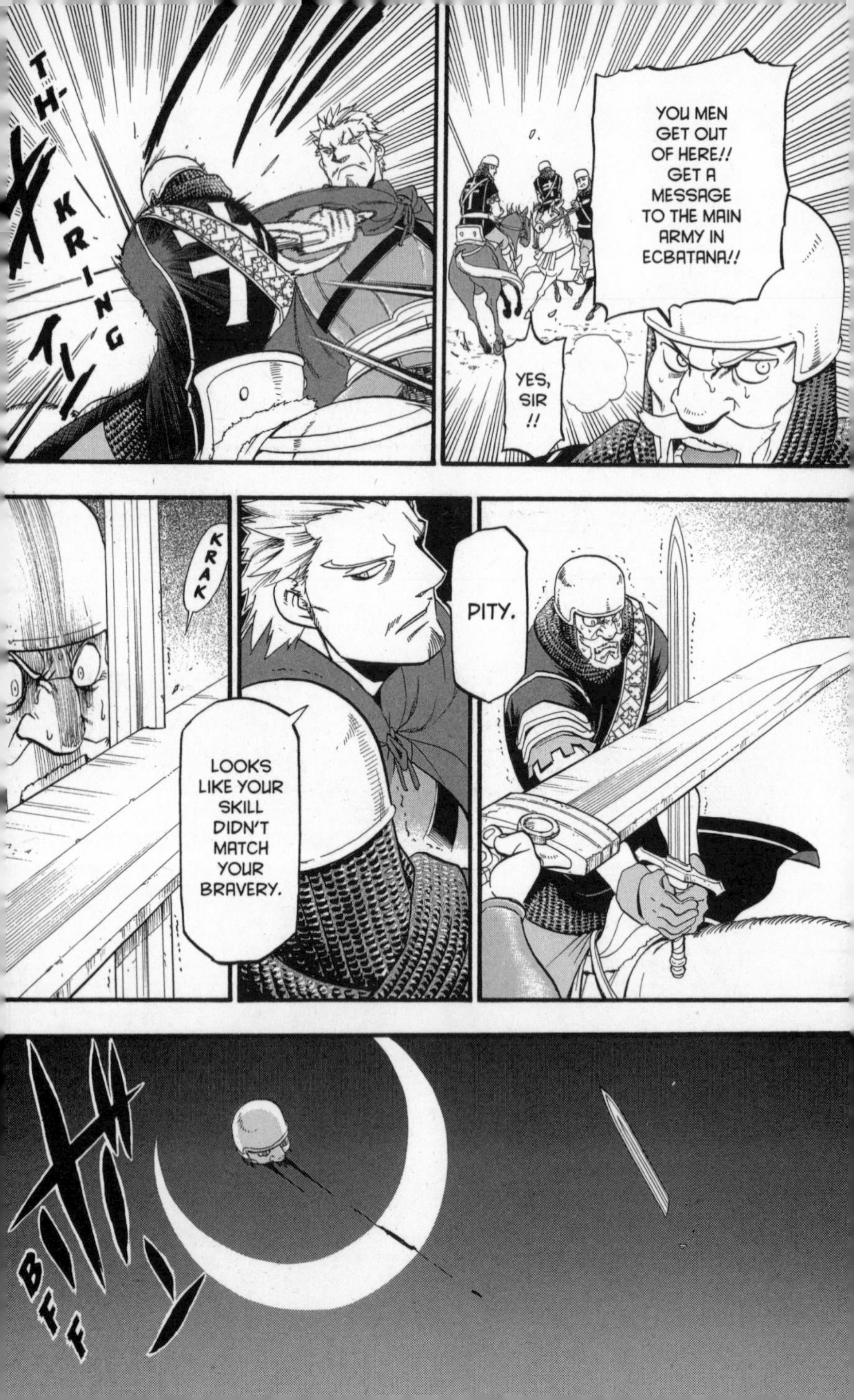
YOU MEN GET OUT OF HERE!! GET A MESSAGE TO THE MAIN ARMY IN ECBATANA!!
YES, SIR!!
TH-KRING
PITY.
LOOKS LIKE YOUR SKILL DIDN'T MATCH YOUR BRAVERY.
KRAK
BFFF

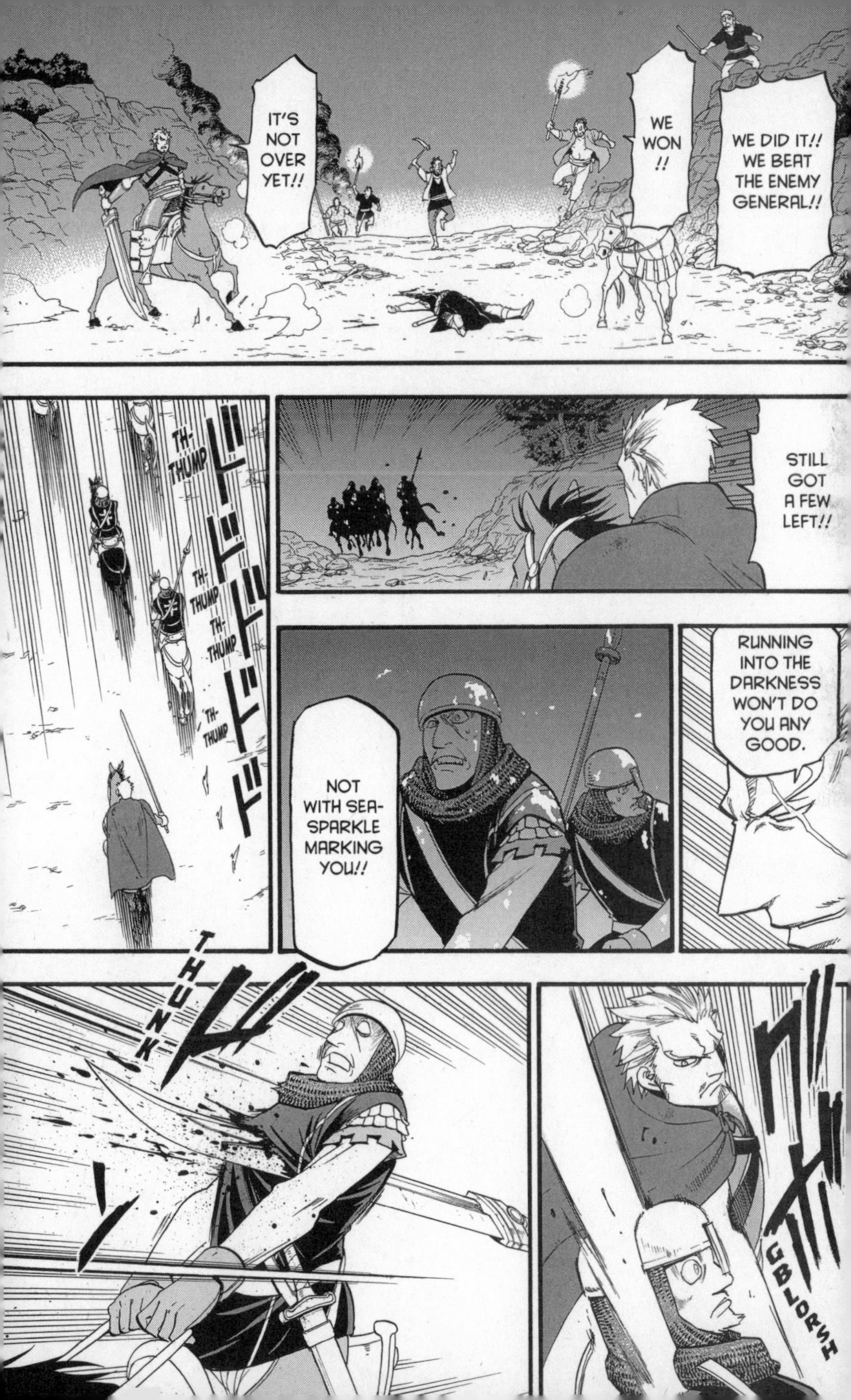
WE DID IT!! WE BEAT THE ENEMY GENERAL!!
WE WON!!
IT'S NOT OVER YET!!
STILL GOT A FEW LEFT!!
RUNNING INTO THE DARKNESS WON'T DO YOU ANY GOOD.
NOT WITH SEA-SPARKLE MARKING YOU!!
TH-THUMP
TH-THUMP
TH-THUMP
TH-THUMP
GBLORSH
THUNK

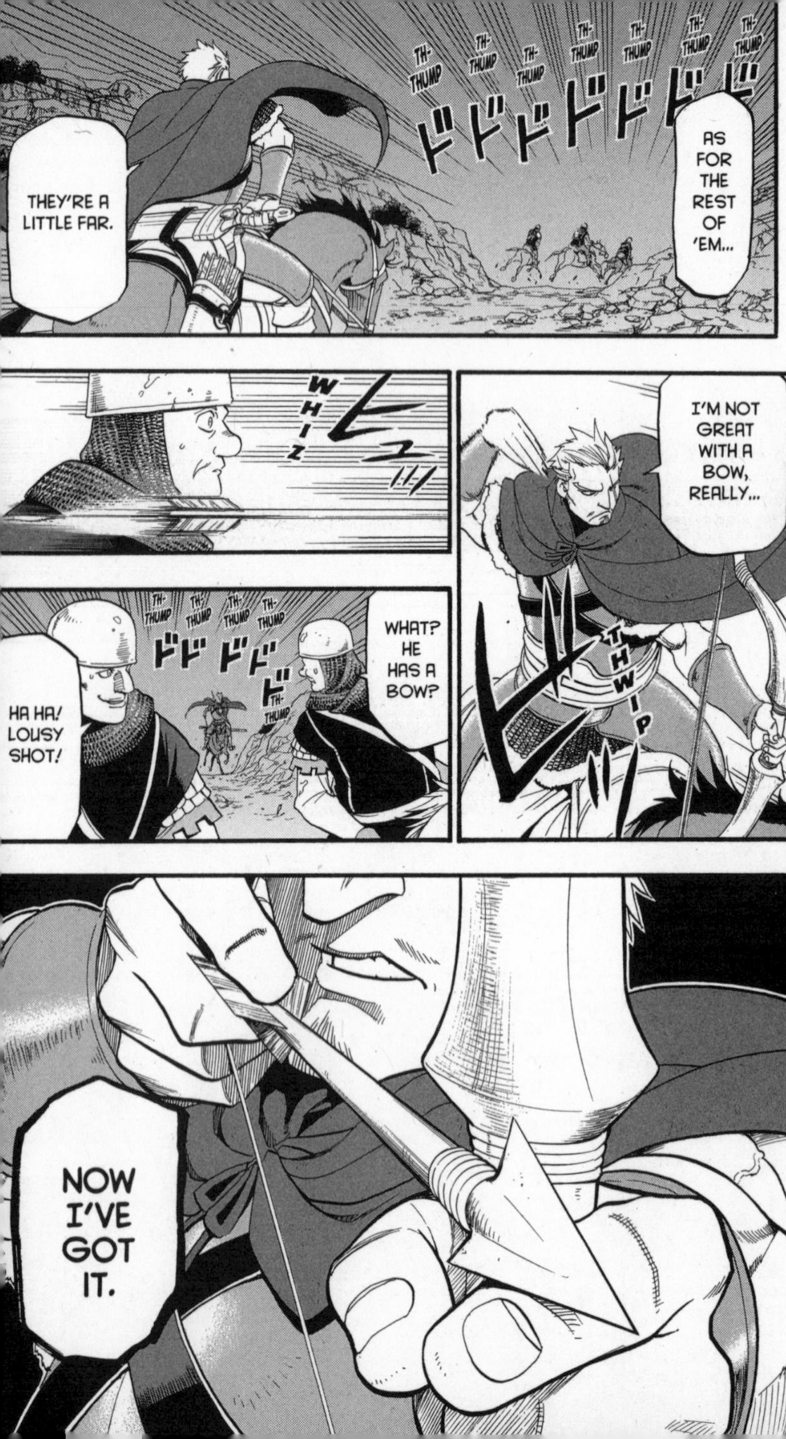
TH-THUMP TH-THUMP TH-THUMP TH-THUMP TH-THUMP TH-THUMP TH-THUMP
ドドドドドドド
AS FOR THE REST OF 'EM...
THEY'RE A LITTLE FAR.
I'M NOT GREAT WITH A BOW, REALLY...
ド
THWIP
WHIZ
ヒュ
TH-THUMP TH-THUMP TH-THUMP TH-THUMP
ドド ドド ド
TH-THUMP
WHAT? HE HAS A BOW?
HA HA! LOUSY SHOT!
NOW I'VE GOT IT.

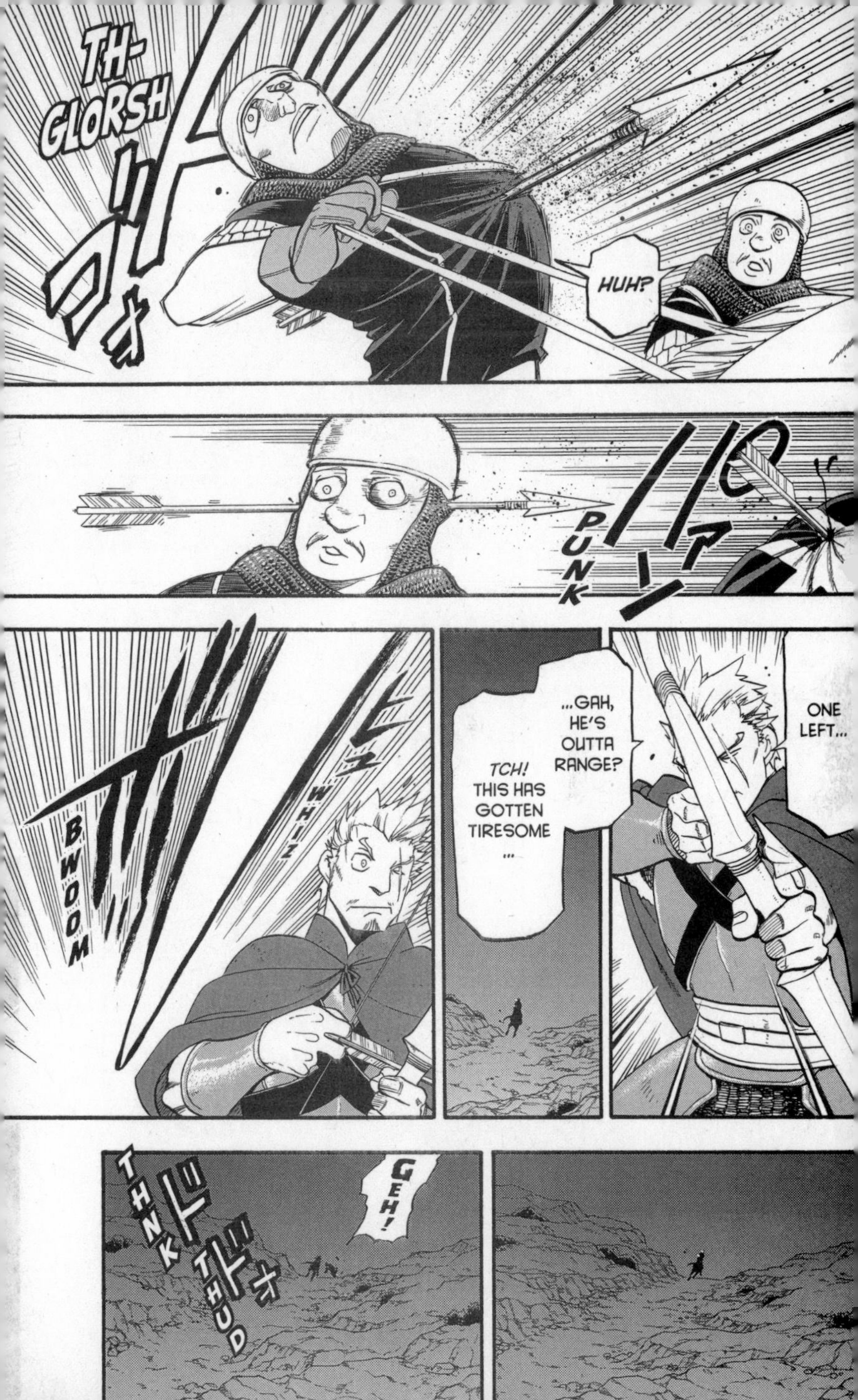
TH-GLORSH
HUH?
PUNK
ONE LEFT...
...GAH, HE'S OUTTA RANGE?
TCH! THIS HAS GOTTEN TIRESOME ...
WHIZ
BWOOM
GEH!
THNK
THUD

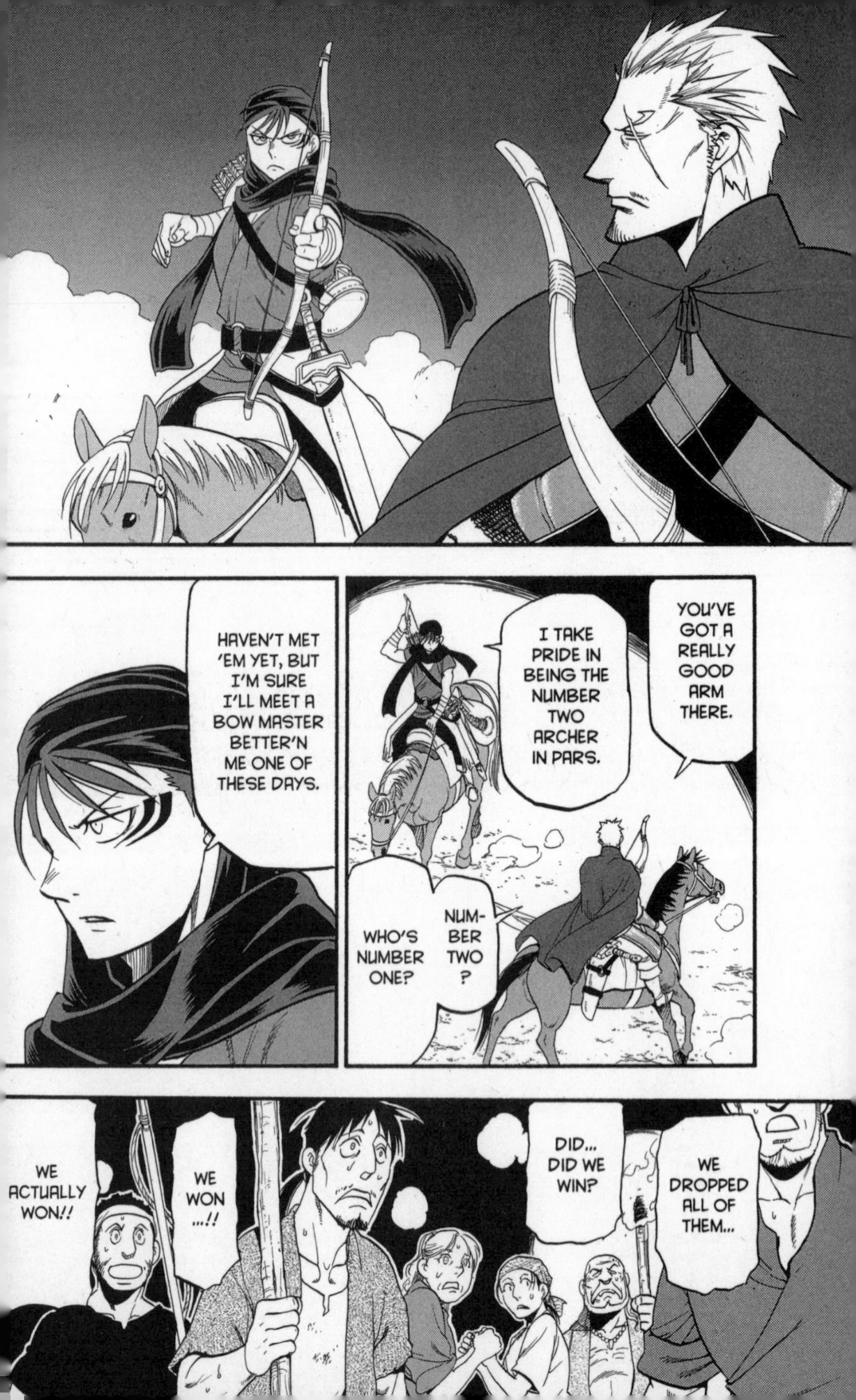
YOU'VE GOT A REALLY GOOD ARM THERE.
I TAKE PRIDE IN BEING THE NUMBER TWO ARCHER IN PARS.
NUMBER TWO ?
WHO'S NUMBER ONE?
HAVEN'T MET 'EM YET, BUT I'M SURE I'LL MEET A BOW MASTER BETTER'N ME ONE OF THESE DAYS.
WE DROPPED ALL OF THEM...
DID... DID WE WIN?
WE WON ...!!
WE ACTUALLY WON!!

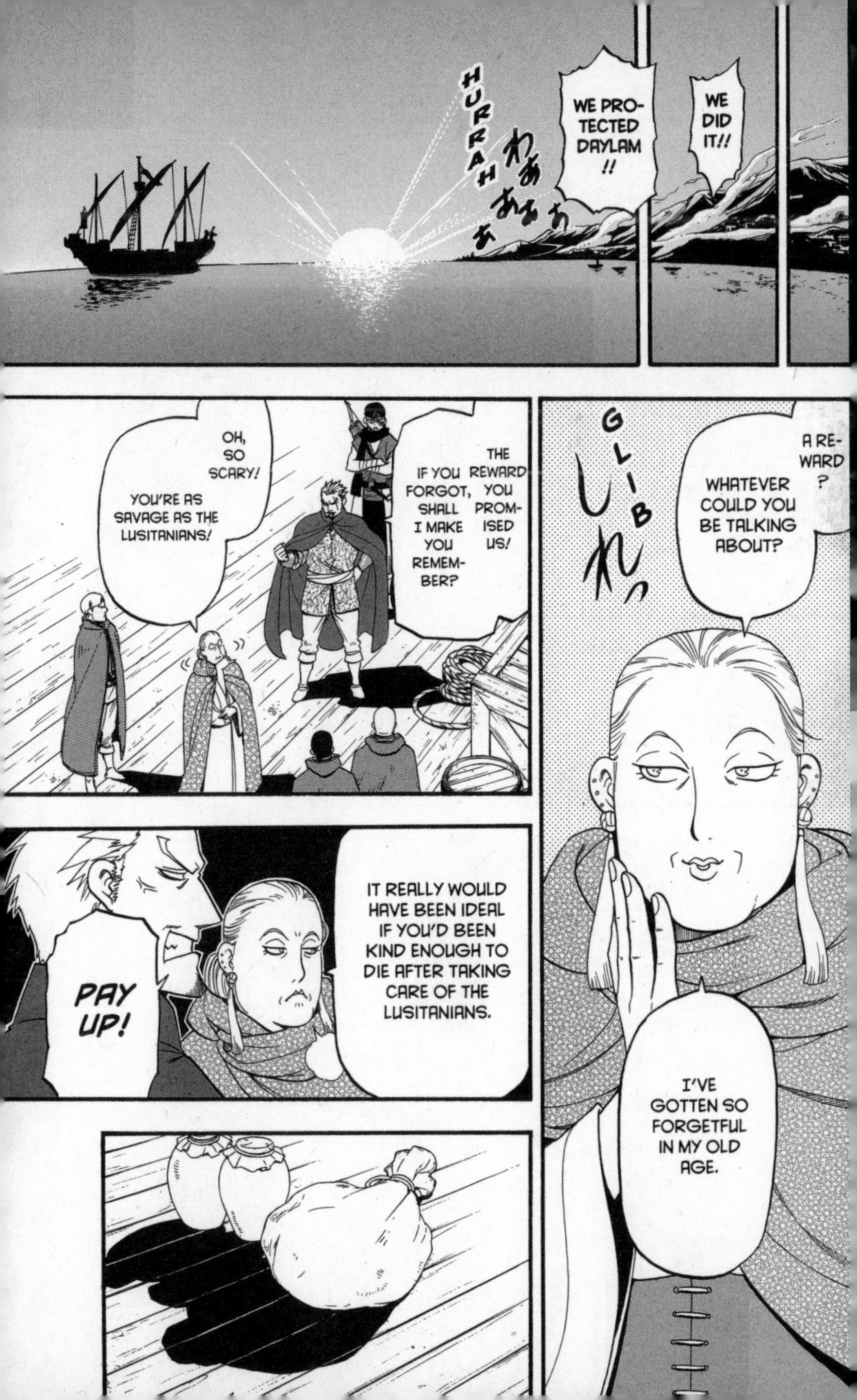
WE DID IT!!
WE PROTECTED DAYLAM!!
HURRAH
わあああああ
GLIB
しれっ
A REWARD?
WHATEVER COULD YOU BE TALKING ABOUT?
I'VE GOTTEN SO FORGETFUL IN MY OLD AGE.
THE REWARD YOU PROMISED US!
IF YOU FORGOT, SHALL I MAKE YOU REMEMBER?
OH, SO SCARY!
YOU'RE AS SAVAGE AS THE LUSITANIANS!
IT REALLY WOULD HAVE BEEN IDEAL IF YOU'D BEEN KIND ENOUGH TO DIE AFTER TAKING CARE OF THE LUSITANIANS.
PAY UP!

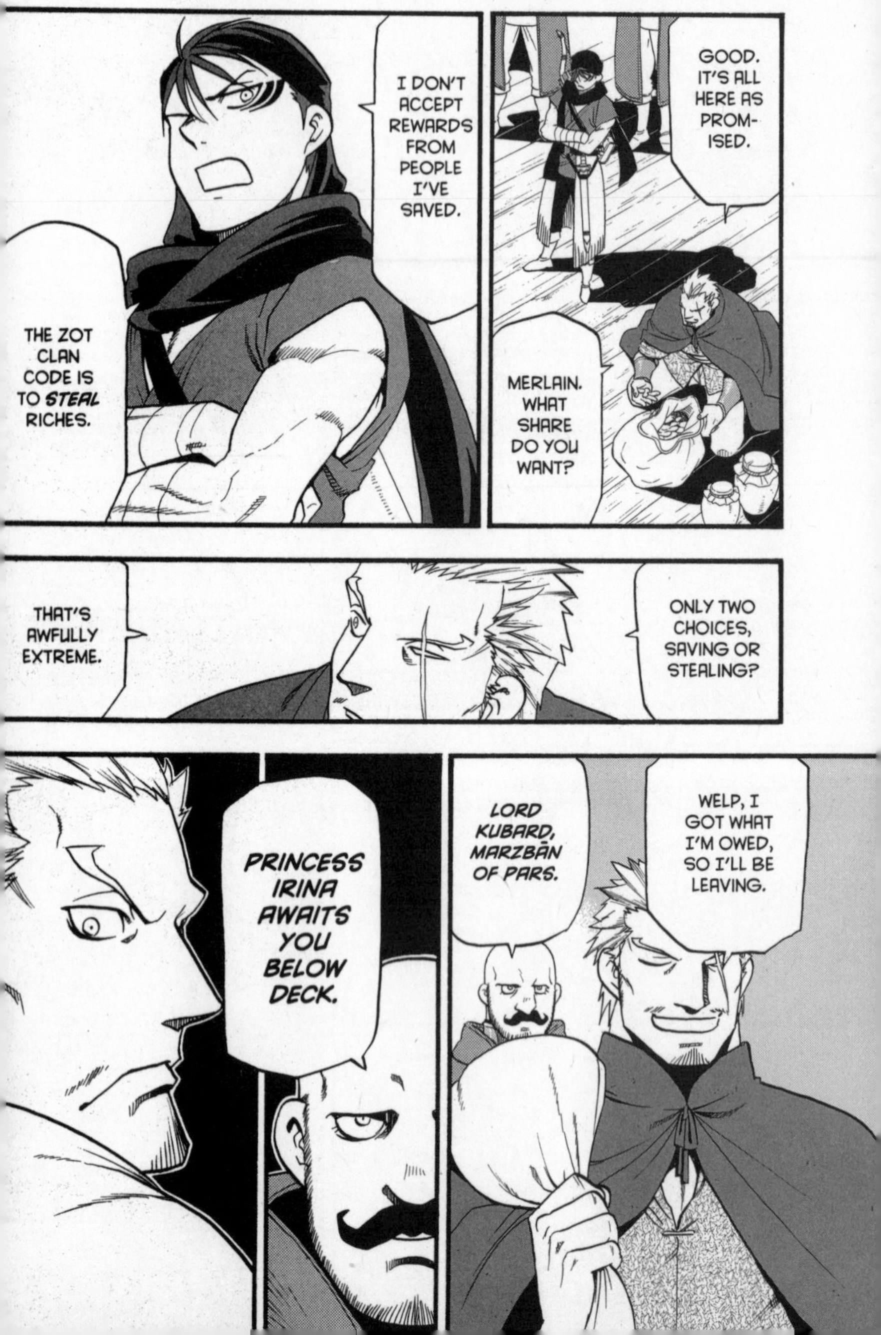
GOOD. IT'S ALL HERE AS PROM-ISED.
MERLAIN. WHAT SHARE DO YOU WANT?
I DON'T ACCEPT REWARDS FROM PEOPLE I'VE SAVED.
THE ZOT CLAN CODE IS TO *STEAL* RICHES.
ONLY TWO CHOICES, SAVING OR STEALING?
THAT'S AWFULLY EXTREME.
WELP, I GOT WHAT I'M OWED, SO I'LL BE LEAVING.
LORD KUBARD, MARZBĀN OF PARS.
PRINCESS IRINA AWAITS YOU BELOW DECK.

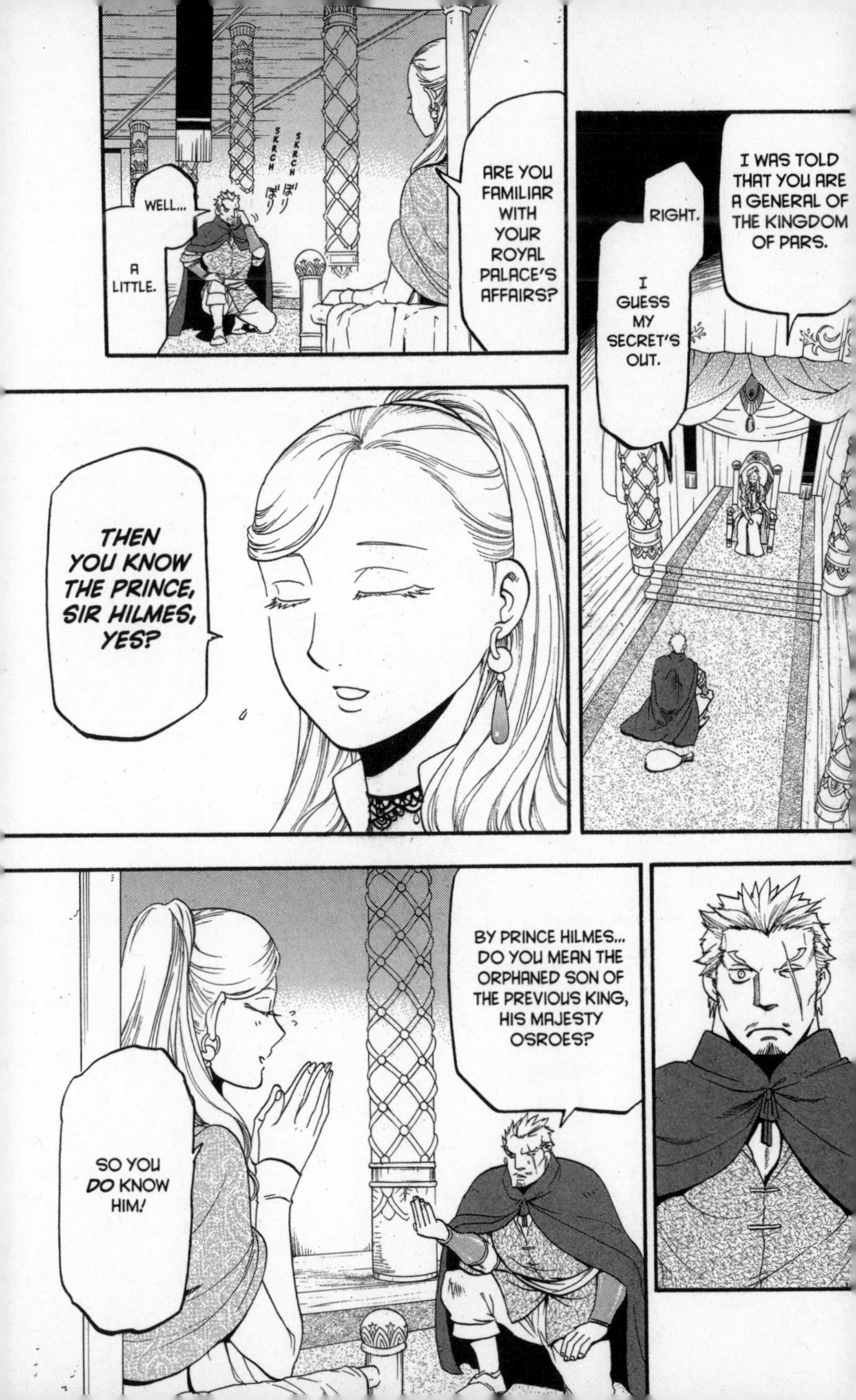
I WAS TOLD THAT YOU ARE A GENERAL OF THE KINGDOM OF PARS.
RIGHT.
I GUESS MY SECRET'S OUT.
ARE YOU FAMILIAR WITH YOUR ROYAL PALACE'S AFFAIRS?
SKRCH SKRCH
WELL...
A LITTLE.
THEN YOU KNOW THE PRINCE, SIR HILMES, YES?
BY PRINCE HILMES... DO YOU MEAN THE ORPHANED SON OF THE PREVIOUS KING, HIS MAJESTY OSROES?
SO YOU DO KNOW HIM!

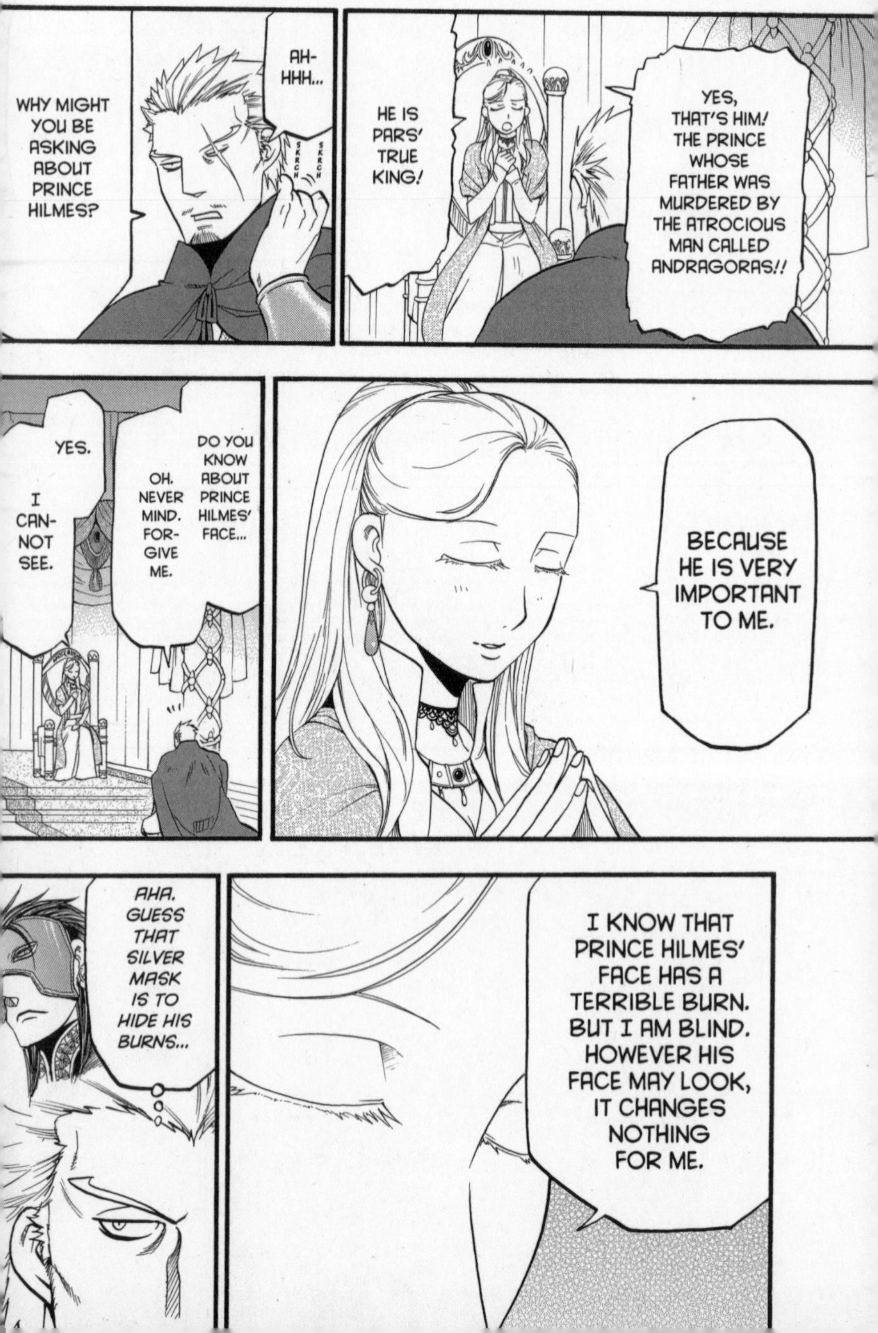
YES, THAT'S HIM! THE PRINCE WHOSE FATHER WAS MURDERED BY THE ATROCIOUS MAN CALLED ANDRAGORAS!!
HE IS PARS' TRUE KING!
AH-HHH...
SKRCH SKRCH
WHY MIGHT YOU BE ASKING ABOUT PRINCE HILMES?
BECAUSE HE IS VERY IMPORTANT TO ME.
DO YOU KNOW ABOUT PRINCE HILMES' FACE...
OH. NEVER MIND. FOR-GIVE ME.
YES.
I CAN-NOT SEE.
I KNOW THAT PRINCE HILMES' FACE HAS A TERRIBLE BURN. BUT I AM BLIND. HOWEVER HIS FACE MAY LOOK, IT CHANGES NOTHING FOR ME.
AHA. GUESS THAT SILVER MASK IS TO HIDE HIS BURNS...

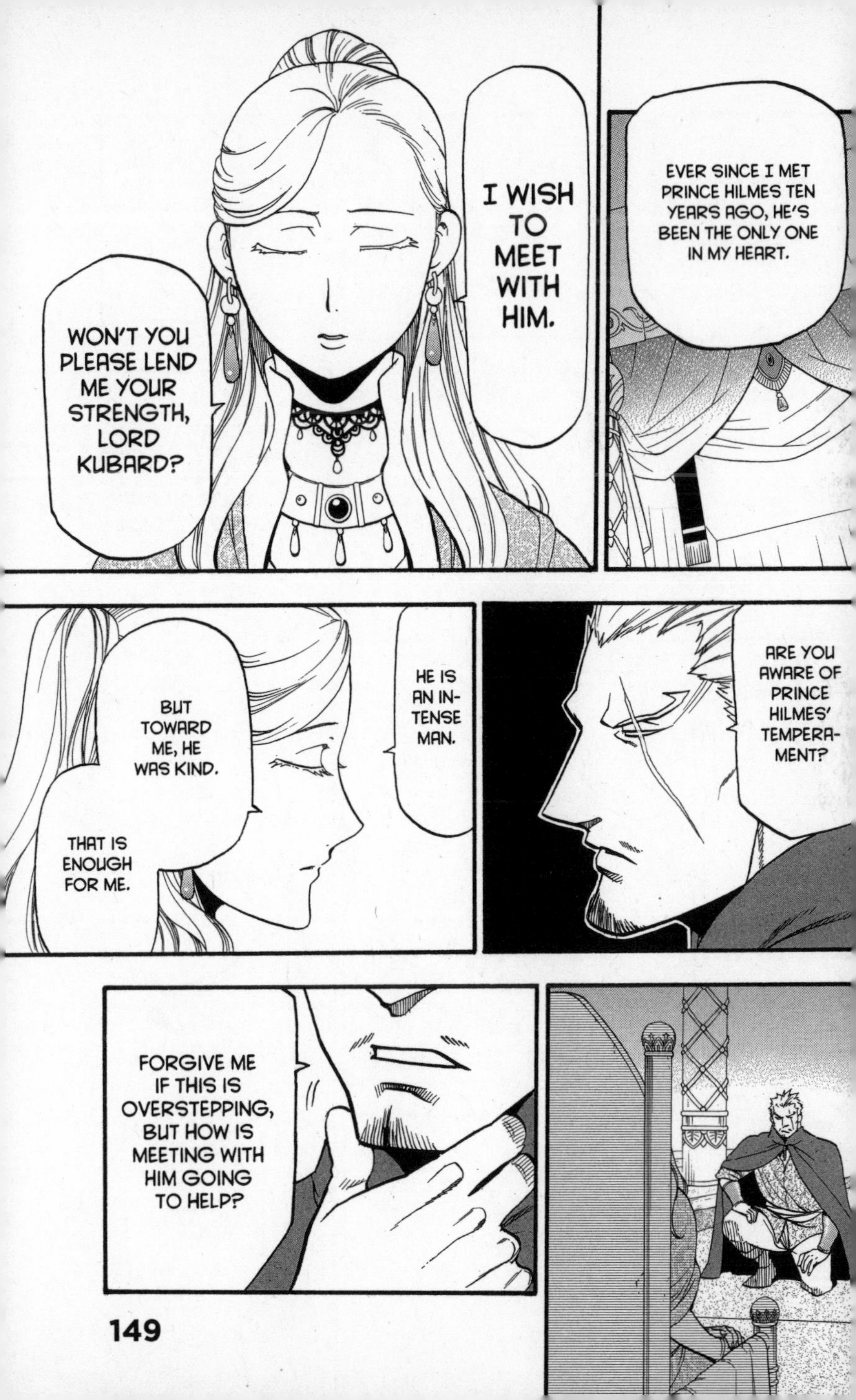

EVER SINCE I MET PRINCE HILMES TEN YEARS AGO, HE'S BEEN THE ONLY ONE IN MY HEART.
I WISH TO MEET WITH HIM.
WON'T YOU PLEASE LEND ME YOUR STRENGTH, LORD KUBARD?
ARE YOU AWARE OF PRINCE HILMES' TEMPERA-MENT?
HE IS AN IN-TENSE MAN.
BUT TOWARD ME, HE WAS KIND.
THAT IS ENOUGH FOR ME.
FORGIVE ME IF THIS IS OVERSTEPPING, BUT HOW IS MEETING WITH HIM GOING TO HELP?

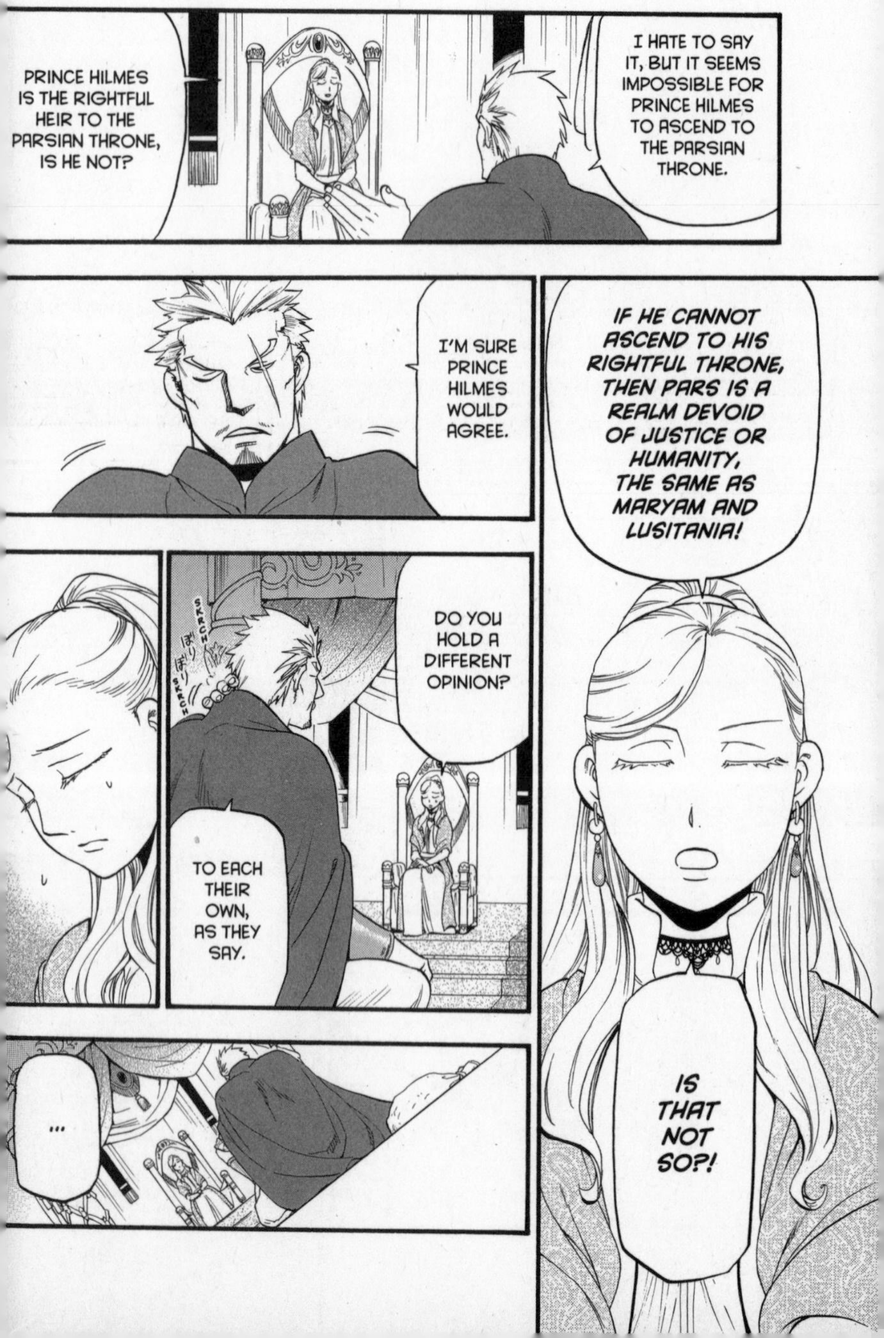
I HATE TO SAY IT, BUT IT SEEMS IMPOSSIBLE FOR PRINCE HILMES TO ASCEND TO THE PARSIAN THRONE.
PRINCE HILMES IS THE RIGHTFUL HEIR TO THE PARSIAN THRONE, IS HE NOT?
IF HE CANNOT ASCEND TO HIS RIGHTFUL THRONE, THEN PARS IS A REALM DEVOID OF JUSTICE OR HUMANITY, THE SAME AS MARYAM AND LUSITANIA!
IS THAT NOT SO?!
I'M SURE PRINCE HILMES WOULD AGREE.
DO YOU HOLD A DIFFERENT OPINION?
SKRCH ぼり
SKRCH ぼり
TO EACH THEIR OWN, AS THEY SAY.
...

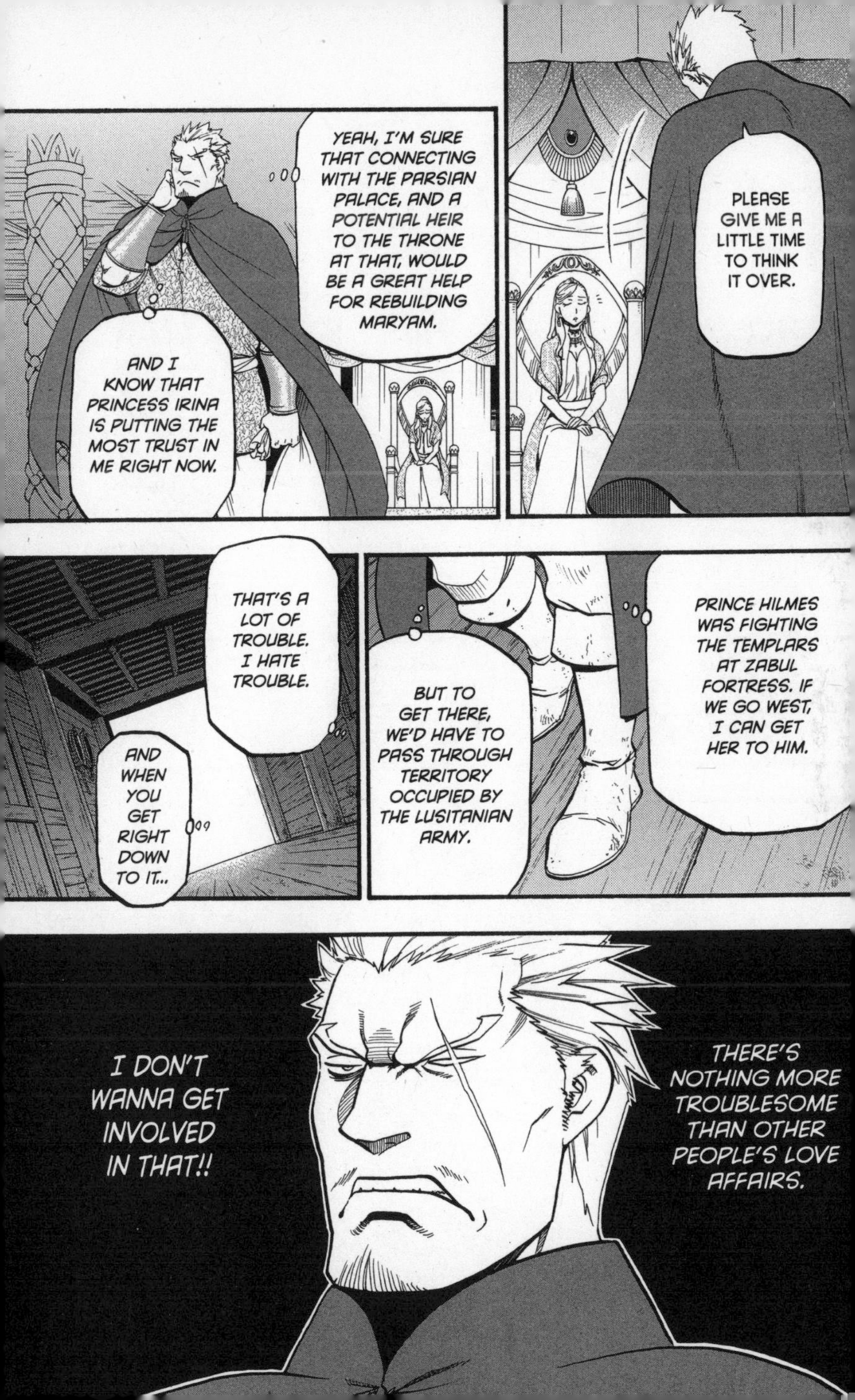
PLEASE GIVE ME A LITTLE TIME TO THINK IT OVER.
YEAH, I'M SURE THAT CONNECTING WITH THE PARSIAN PALACE, AND A POTENTIAL HEIR TO THE THRONE AT THAT, WOULD BE A GREAT HELP FOR REBUILDING MARYAM.
AND I KNOW THAT PRINCESS IRINA IS PUTTING THE MOST TRUST IN ME RIGHT NOW.
PRINCE HILMES WAS FIGHTING THE TEMPLARS AT ZABUL FORTRESS. IF WE GO WEST, I CAN GET HER TO HIM.
BUT TO GET THERE, WE'D HAVE TO PASS THROUGH TERRITORY OCCUPIED BY THE LUSITANIAN ARMY.
THAT'S A LOT OF TROUBLE. I HATE TROUBLE.
AND WHEN YOU GET RIGHT DOWN TO IT...
THERE'S NOTHING MORE TROUBLESOME THAN OTHER PEOPLE'S LOVE AFFAIRS.
I DON'T WANNA GET INVOLVED IN THAT!!

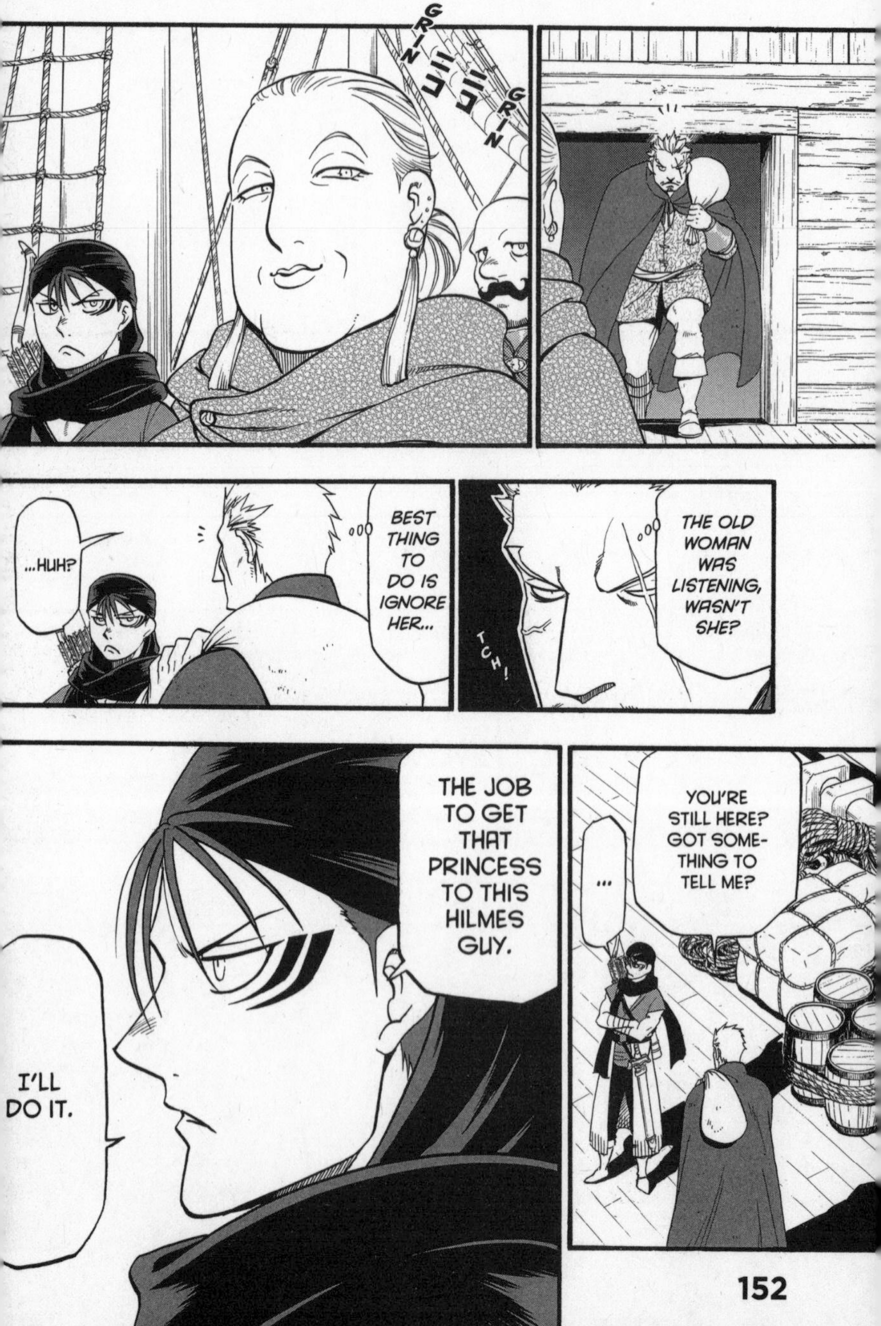
GRIN ニコ
ニコ GRIN
THE OLD WOMAN WAS LISTENING, WASN'T SHE?
TCH!
BEST THING TO DO IS IGNORE HER...
...HUH?
YOU'RE STILL HERE? GOT SOME-THING TO TELL ME?
...
THE JOB TO GET THAT PRINCESS TO THIS HILMES GUY.
I'LL DO IT.

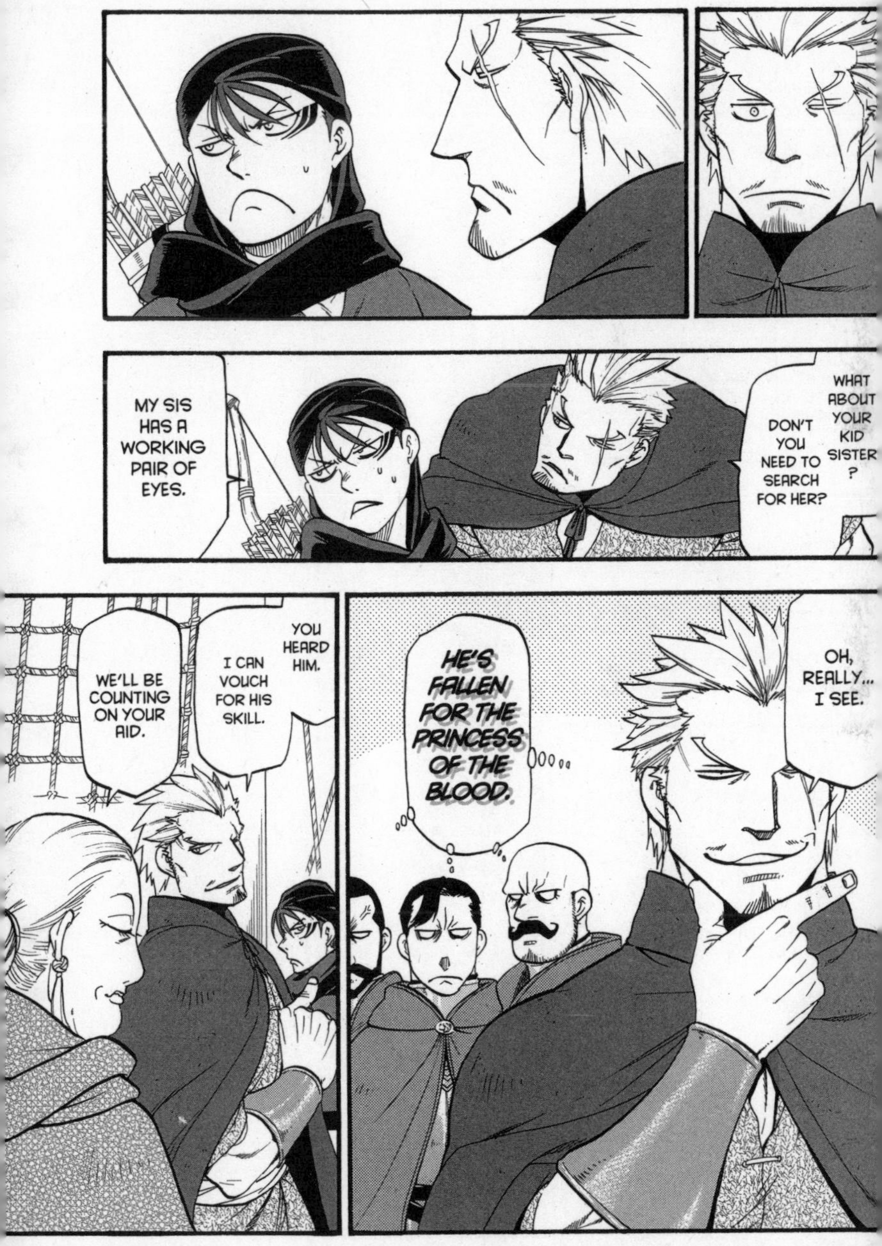
WHAT ABOUT YOUR KID SISTER?
DON'T YOU NEED TO SEARCH FOR HER?
MY SIS HAS A WORKING PAIR OF EYES.
OH, REALLY... I SEE.
HE'S FALLEN FOR THE PRINCESS OF THE BLOOD.
YOU HEARD HIM.
I CAN VOUCH FOR HIS SKILL.
WE'LL BE COUNTING ON YOUR AID.

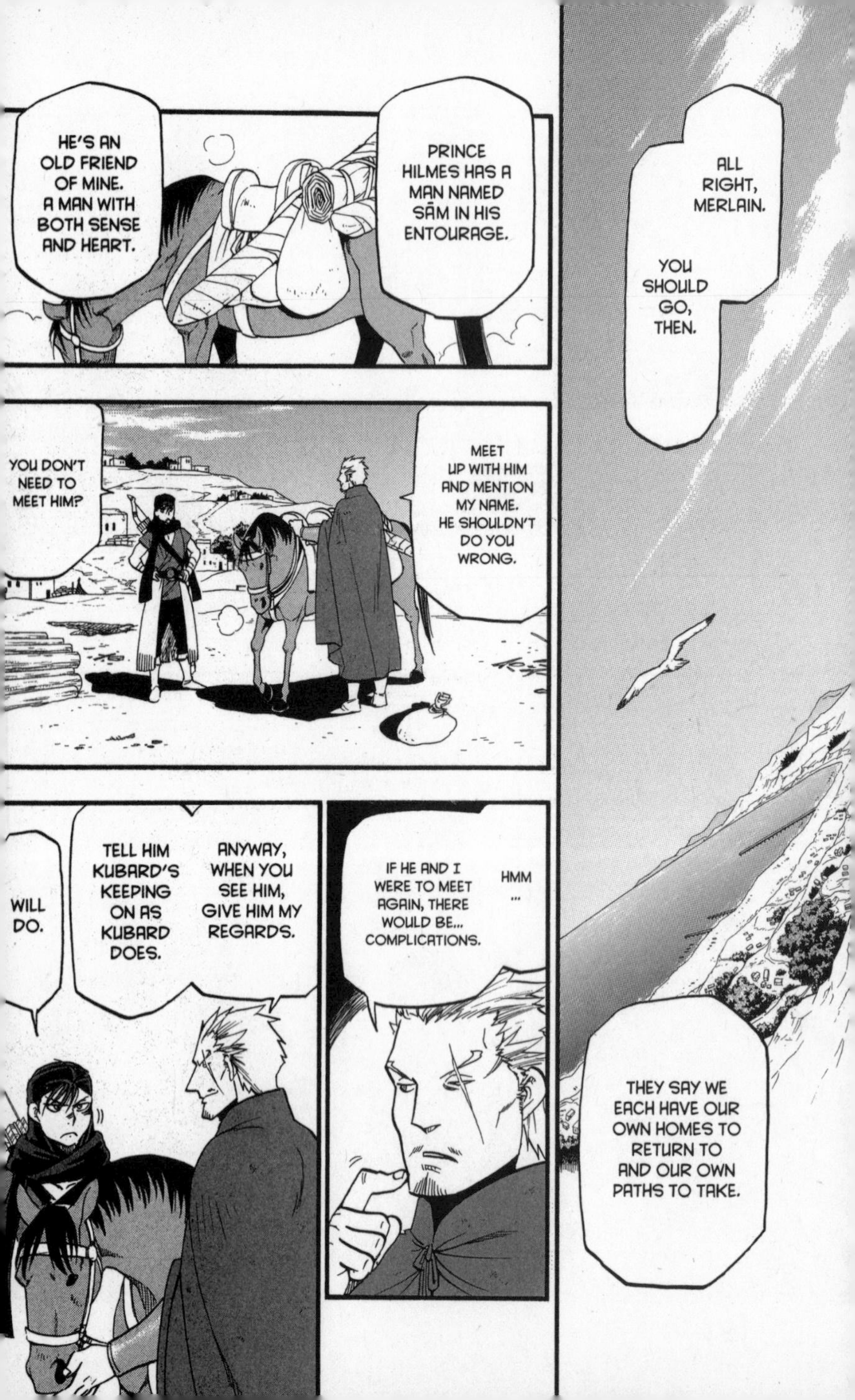
ALL RIGHT, MERLAIN.
YOU SHOULD GO, THEN.
THEY SAY WE EACH HAVE OUR OWN HOMES TO RETURN TO AND OUR OWN PATHS TO TAKE.
PRINCE HILMES HAS A MAN NAMED SĀM IN HIS ENTOURAGE.
HE'S AN OLD FRIEND OF MINE. A MAN WITH BOTH SENSE AND HEART.
MEET UP WITH HIM AND MENTION MY NAME. HE SHOULDN'T DO YOU WRONG.
YOU DON'T NEED TO MEET HIM?
HMM...
IF HE AND I WERE TO MEET AGAIN, THERE WOULD BE... COMPLICATIONS.
ANYWAY, WHEN YOU SEE HIM, GIVE HIM MY REGARDS.
TELL HIM KUBARD'S KEEPING ON AS KUBARD DOES.
WILL DO.

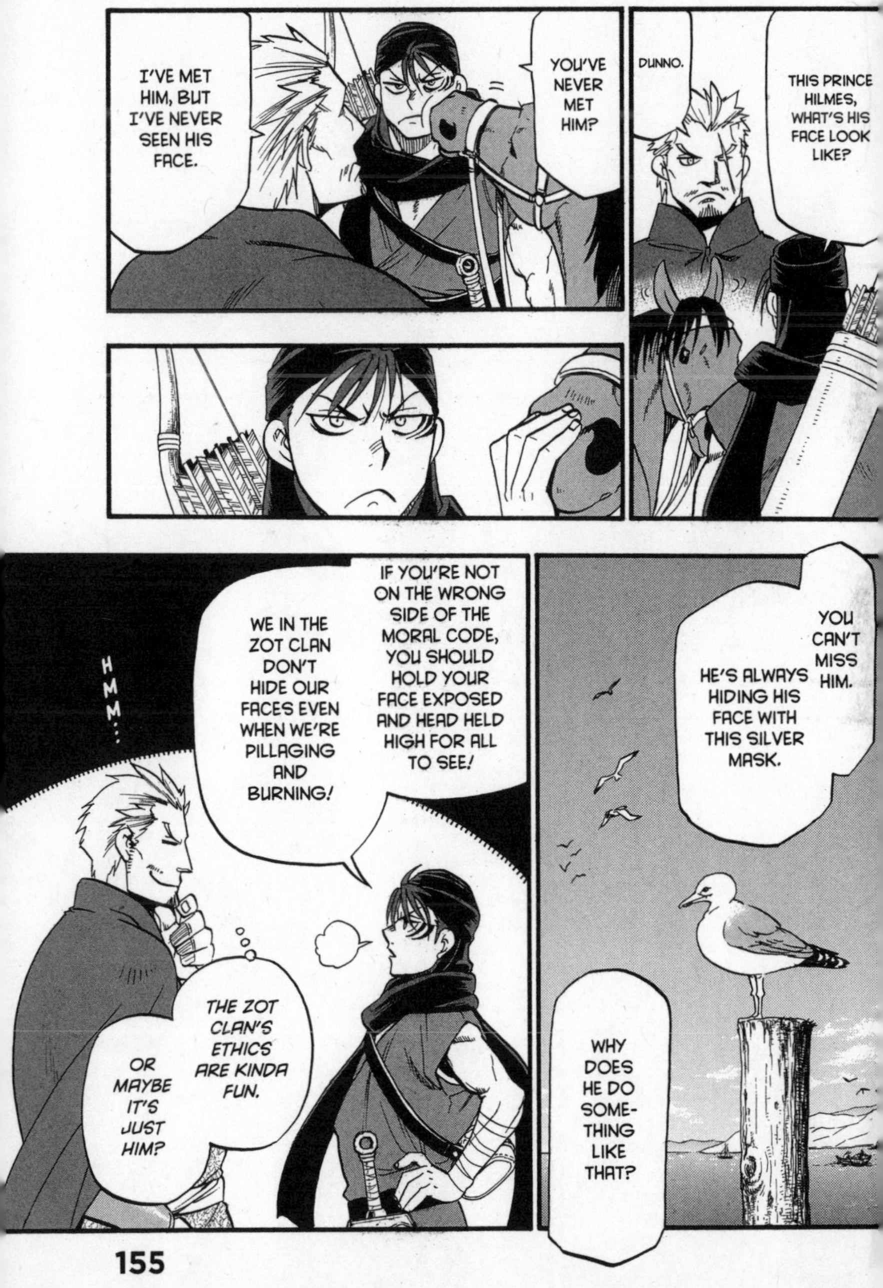
THIS PRINCE HILMES, WHAT'S HIS FACE LOOK LIKE?
DUNNO.
YOU'VE NEVER MET HIM?
I'VE MET HIM, BUT I'VE NEVER SEEN HIS FACE.
YOU CAN'T MISS HIM.
HE'S ALWAYS HIDING HIS FACE WITH THIS SILVER MASK.
WHY DOES HE DO SOME-THING LIKE THAT?
IF YOU'RE NOT ON THE WRONG SIDE OF THE MORAL CODE, YOU SHOULD HOLD YOUR FACE EXPOSED AND HEAD HELD HIGH FOR ALL TO SEE!
WE IN THE ZOT CLAN DON'T HIDE OUR FACES EVEN WHEN WE'RE PILLAGING AND BURNING!
HMM...
THE ZOT CLAN'S ETHICS ARE KINDA FUN.
OR MAYBE IT'S JUST HIM?

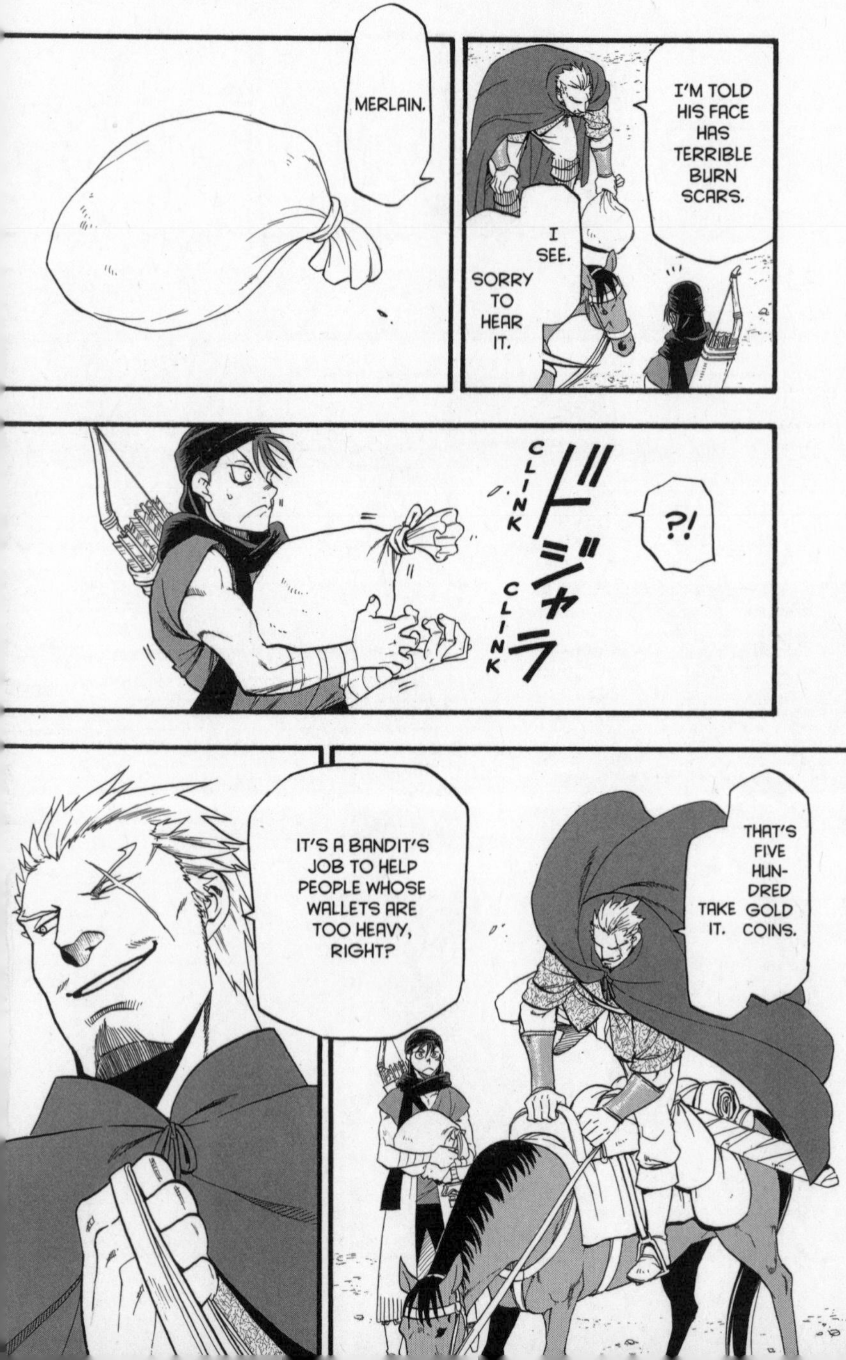
I'M TOLD HIS FACE HAS TERRIBLE BURN SCARS.
I SEE.
SORRY TO HEAR IT.
MERLAIN.
?!
ドジャラ
CLINK CLINK
THAT'S FIVE HUNDRED GOLD COINS.
TAKE IT.
IT'S A BANDIT'S JOB TO HELP PEOPLE WHOSE WALLETS ARE TOO HEAVY, RIGHT?

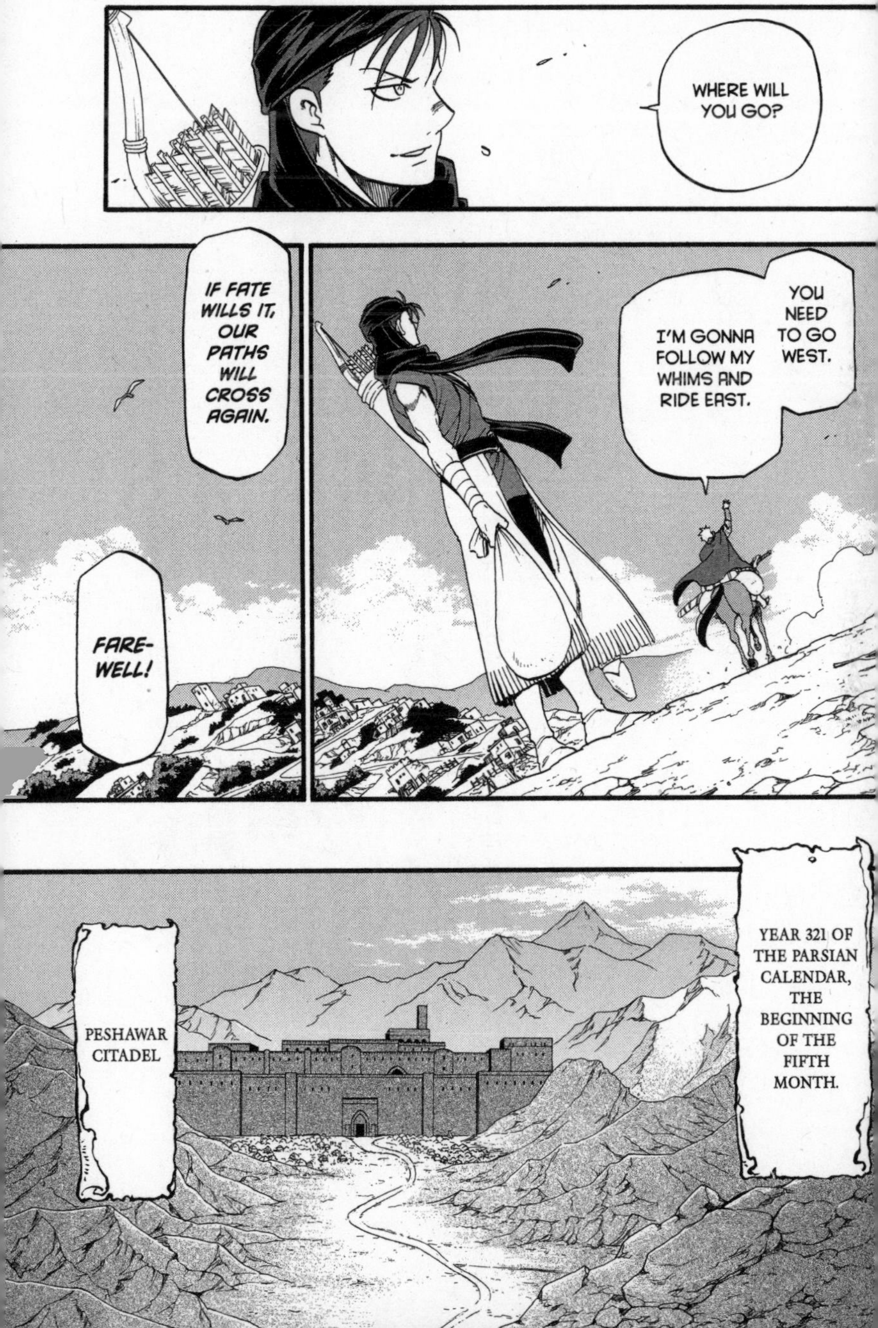
WHERE WILL YOU GO?
YOU NEED TO GO WEST.
I'M GONNA FOLLOW MY WHIMS AND RIDE EAST.
IF FATE WILLS IT, OUR PATHS WILL CROSS AGAIN.
FARE-WELL!
YEAR 321 OF THE PARSIAN CALENDAR, THE BEGINNING OF THE FIFTH MONTH.
PESHAWAR CITADEL

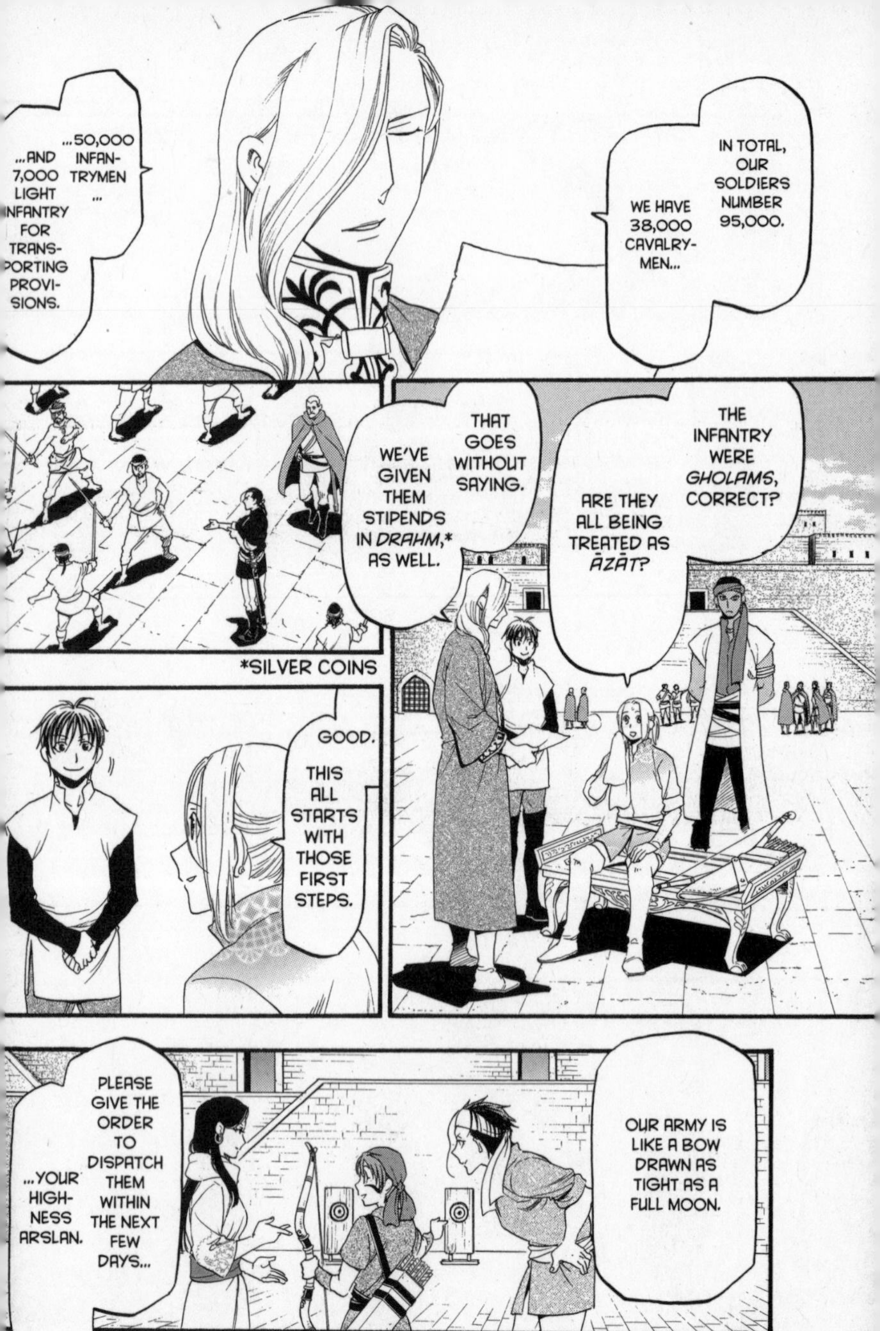
IN TOTAL, OUR SOLDIERS NUMBER 95,000.
WE HAVE 38,000 CAVALRYMEN...
...50,000 INFANTRYMEN...
...AND 7,000 LIGHT INFANTRY FOR TRANSPORTING PROVISIONS.
THE INFANTRY WERE *GHOLAMS*, CORRECT?
ARE THEY ALL BEING TREATED AS *ĀZĀT*?
THAT GOES WITHOUT SAYING.
WE'VE GIVEN THEM STIPENDS IN *DRAHM*,* AS WELL.
*SILVER COINS
GOOD.
THIS ALL STARTS WITH THOSE FIRST STEPS.
OUR ARMY IS LIKE A BOW DRAWN AS TIGHT AS A FULL MOON.
PLEASE GIVE THE ORDER TO DISPATCH THEM WITHIN THE NEXT FEW DAYS...
...YOUR HIGHNESS ARSLAN.

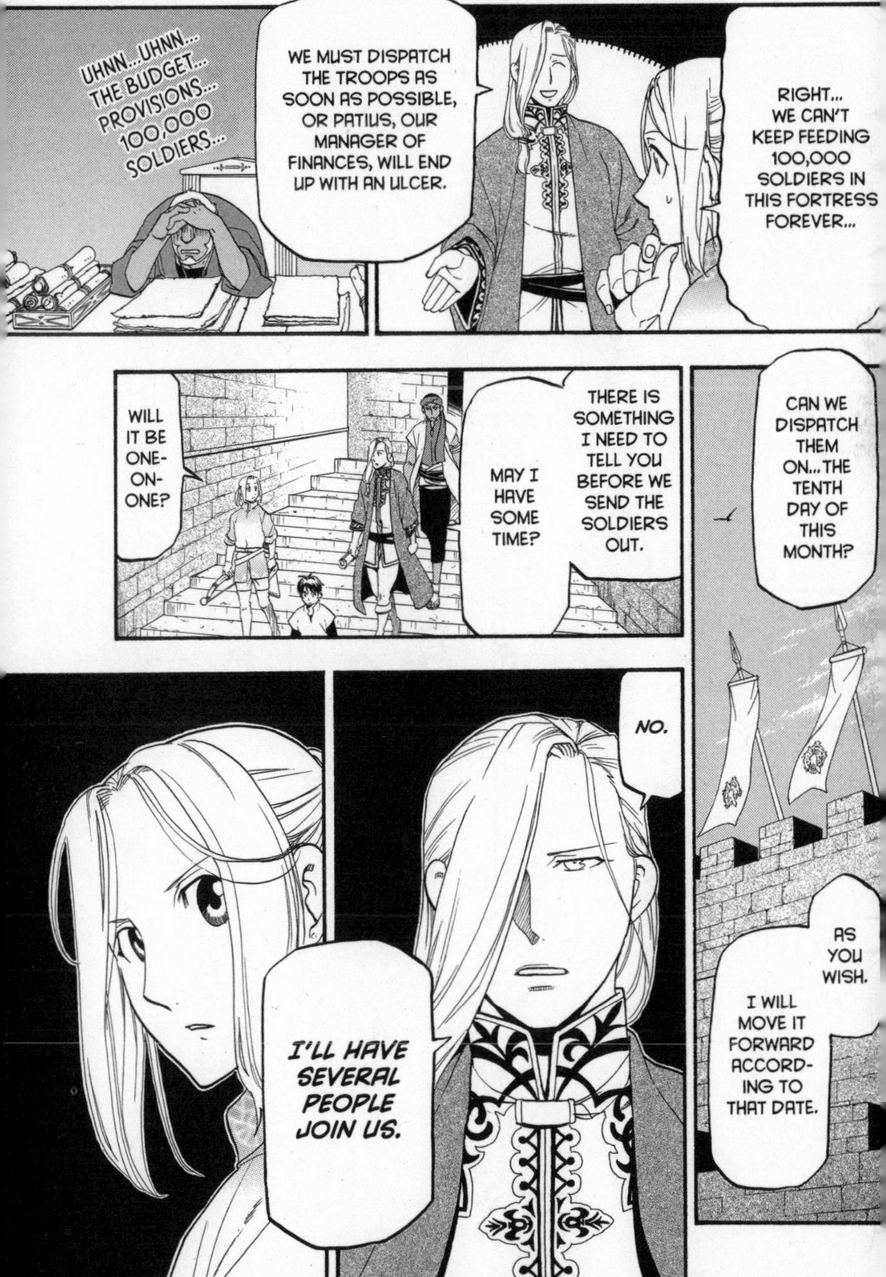
RIGHT... WE CAN'T KEEP FEEDING 100,000 SOLDIERS IN THIS FORTRESS FOREVER...
WE MUST DISPATCH THE TROOPS AS SOON AS POSSIBLE, OR PATIUS, OUR MANAGER OF FINANCES, WILL END UP WITH AN ULCER.
UHNN...UHNN... THE BUDGET... PROVISIONS... 100,000 SOLDIERS...
CAN WE DISPATCH THEM ON...THE TENTH DAY OF THIS MONTH?
AS YOU WISH.
I WILL MOVE IT FORWARD ACCORD-ING TO THAT DATE.
THERE IS SOMETHING I NEED TO TELL YOU BEFORE WE SEND THE SOLDIERS OUT.
MAY I HAVE SOME TIME?
WILL IT BE ONE-ON-ONE?
NO.
I'LL HAVE SEVERAL PEOPLE JOIN US.

THE HEROIC LEGEND OF
ARSLAN

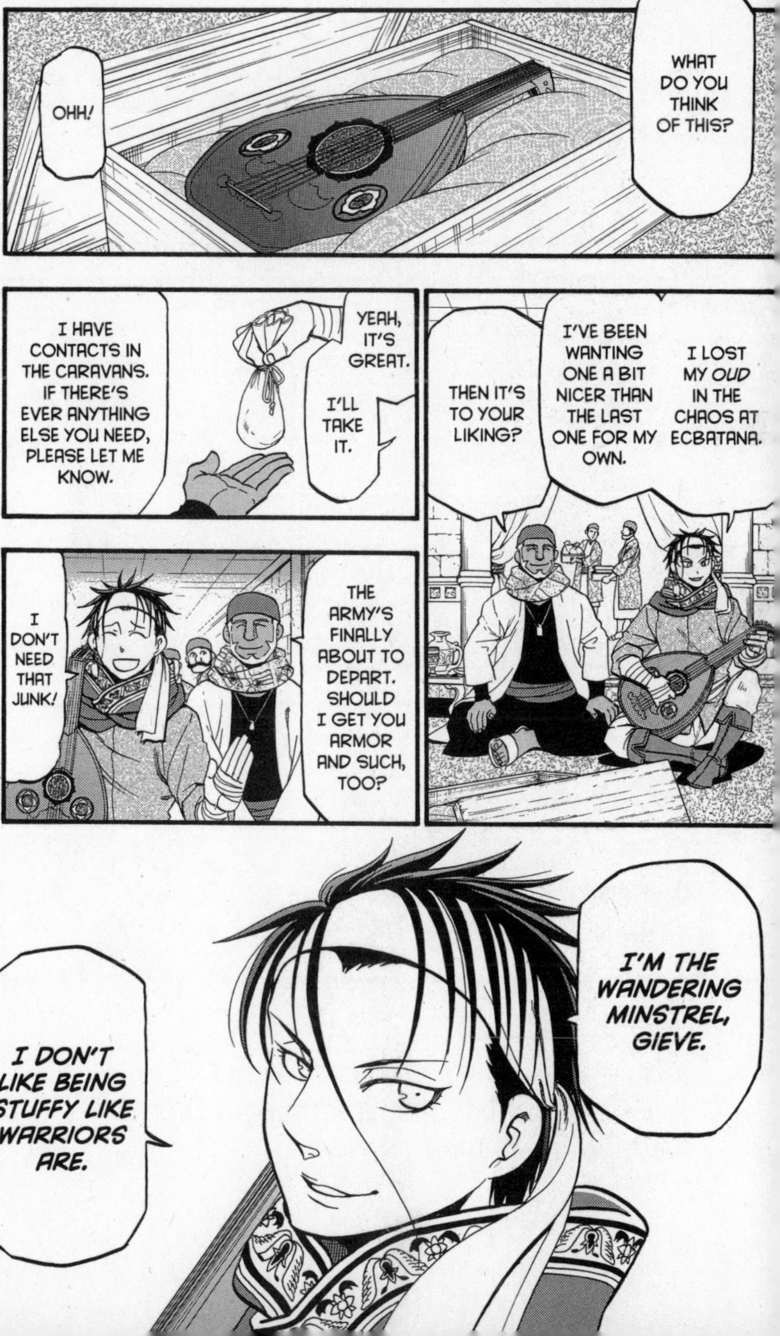
WHAT DO YOU THINK OF THIS?
OHH!
I LOST MY *OUD* IN THE CHAOS AT ECBATANA.
I'VE BEEN WANTING ONE A BIT NICER THAN THE LAST ONE FOR MY OWN.
THEN IT'S TO YOUR LIKING?
YEAH, IT'S GREAT.
I'LL TAKE IT.
I HAVE CONTACTS IN THE CARAVANS. IF THERE'S EVER ANYTHING ELSE YOU NEED, PLEASE LET ME KNOW.
THE ARMY'S FINALLY ABOUT TO DEPART. SHOULD I GET YOU ARMOR AND SUCH, TOO?
I DON'T NEED THAT JUNK!
I'M THE WANDERING MINSTREL, GIEVE.
I DON'T LIKE BEING STUFFY LIKE WARRIORS ARE.

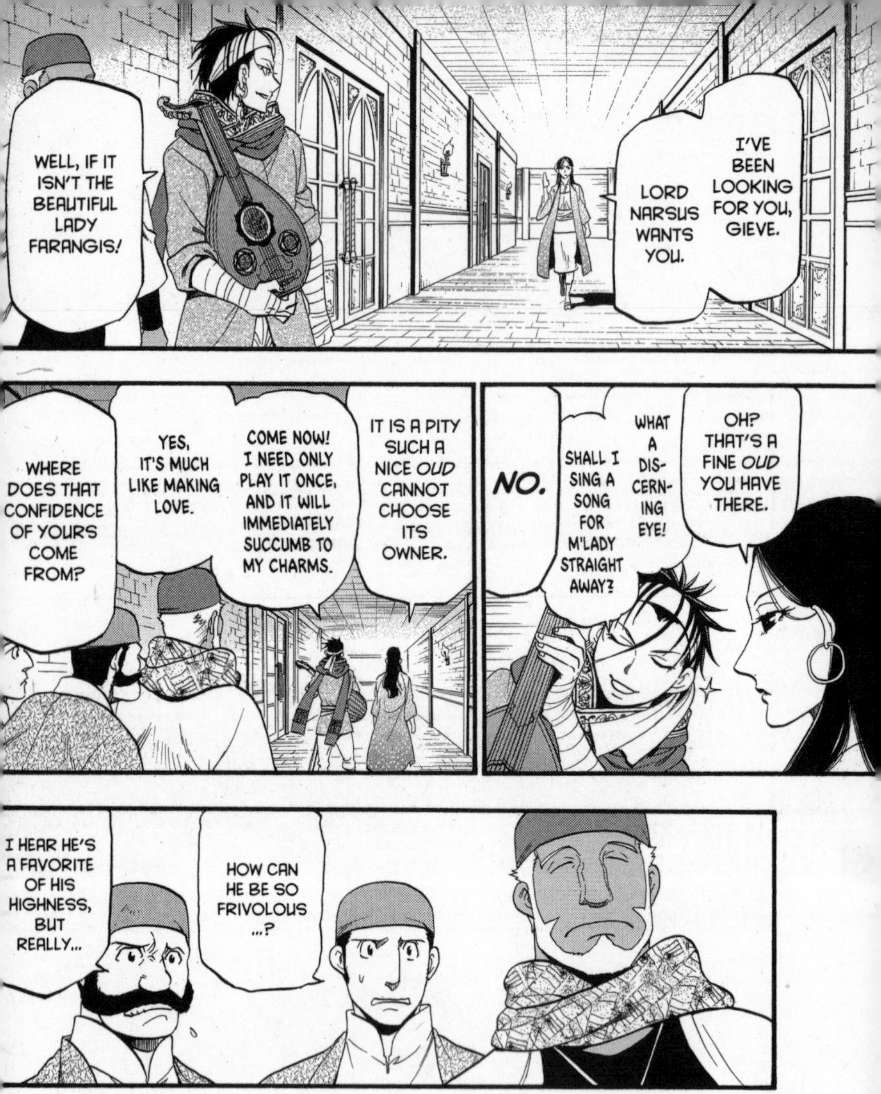
I'VE BEEN LOOKING FOR YOU, GIEVE.
LORD NARSUS WANTS YOU.
WELL, IF IT ISN'T THE BEAUTIFUL LADY FARANGIS!
OH? THAT'S A FINE *OUD* YOU HAVE THERE.
WHAT A DIS-CERN-ING EYE!
SHALL I SING A SONG FOR M'LADY STRAIGHT AWAY?
NO.
IT IS A PITY SUCH A NICE *OUD* CANNOT CHOOSE ITS OWNER.
COME NOW! I NEED ONLY PLAY IT ONCE, AND IT WILL IMMEDIATELY SUCCUMB TO MY CHARMS.
YES, IT'S MUCH LIKE MAKING LOVE.
WHERE DOES THAT CONFIDENCE OF YOURS COME FROM?
HOW CAN HE BE SO FRIVOLOUS ...?
I HEAR HE'S A FAVORITE OF HIS HIGHNESS, BUT REALLY...

Chapter 64: Shapur's Younger Brother

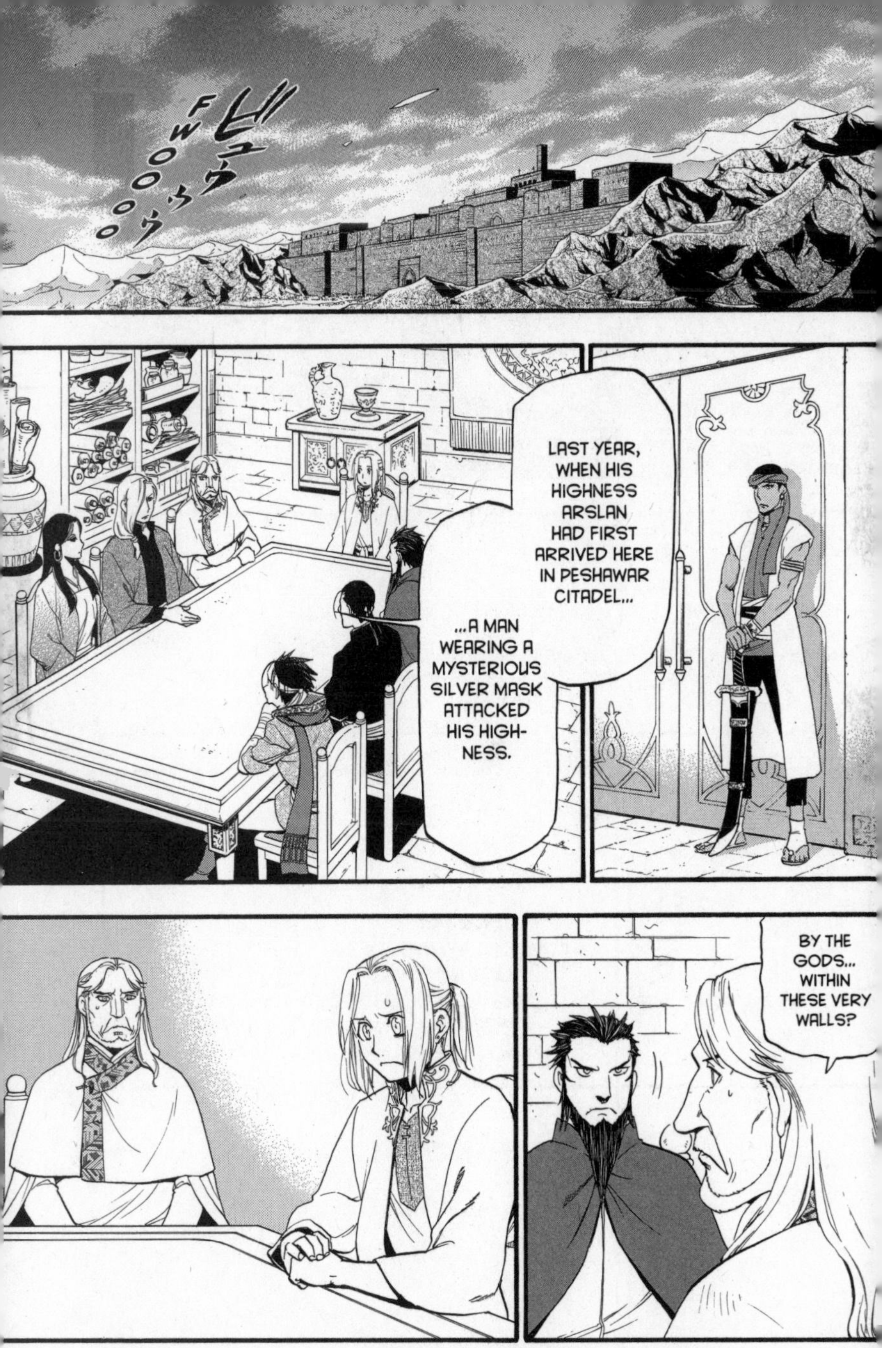
FWOOOOO
LAST YEAR, WHEN HIS HIGHNESS ARSLAN HAD FIRST ARRIVED HERE IN PESHAWAR CITADEL...
...A MAN WEARING A MYSTERIOUS SILVER MASK ATTACKED HIS HIGH-NESS.
BY THE GODS... WITHIN THESE VERY WALLS?

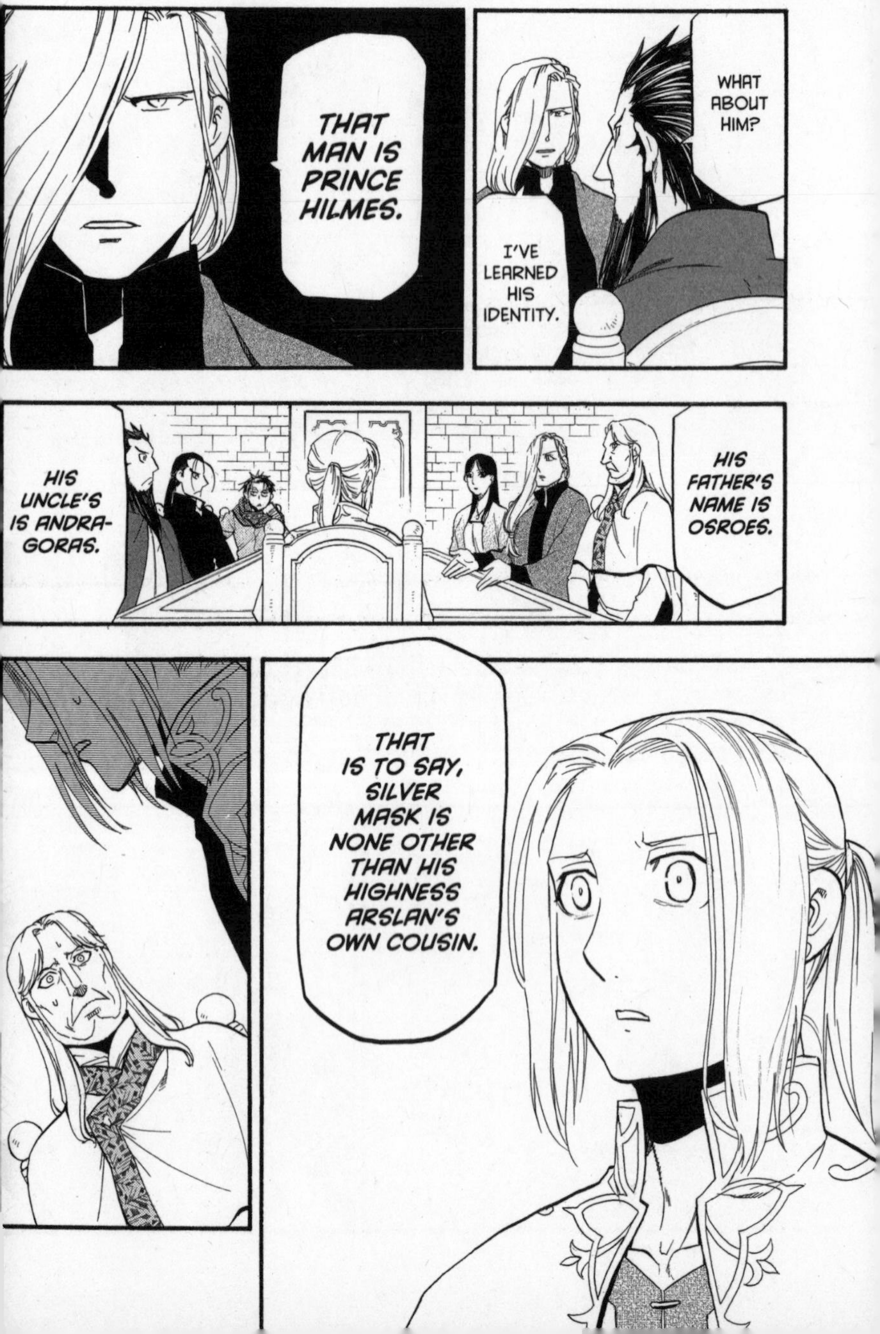
WHAT ABOUT HIM?
I'VE LEARNED HIS IDENTITY.
THAT MAN IS PRINCE HILMES.
HIS FATHER'S NAME IS OSROES.
HIS UNCLE'S IS ANDRA-GORAS.
THAT IS TO SAY, SILVER MASK IS NONE OTHER THAN HIS HIGHNESS ARSLAN'S OWN COUSIN.

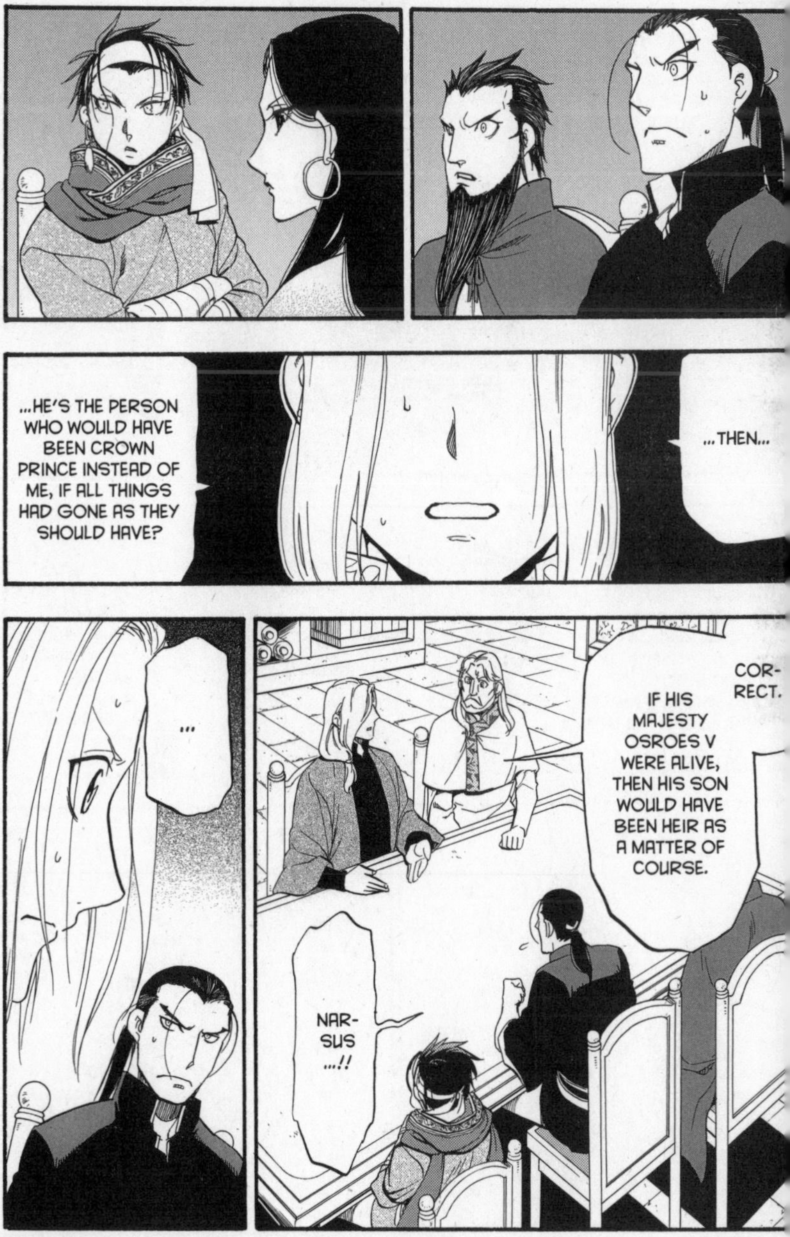
...THEN...
...HE'S THE PERSON WHO WOULD HAVE BEEN CROWN PRINCE INSTEAD OF ME, IF ALL THINGS HAD GONE AS THEY SHOULD HAVE?
CORRECT.
IF HIS MAJESTY OSROES V WERE ALIVE, THEN HIS SON WOULD HAVE BEEN HEIR AS A MATTER OF COURSE.
NARSUS ...!!
...

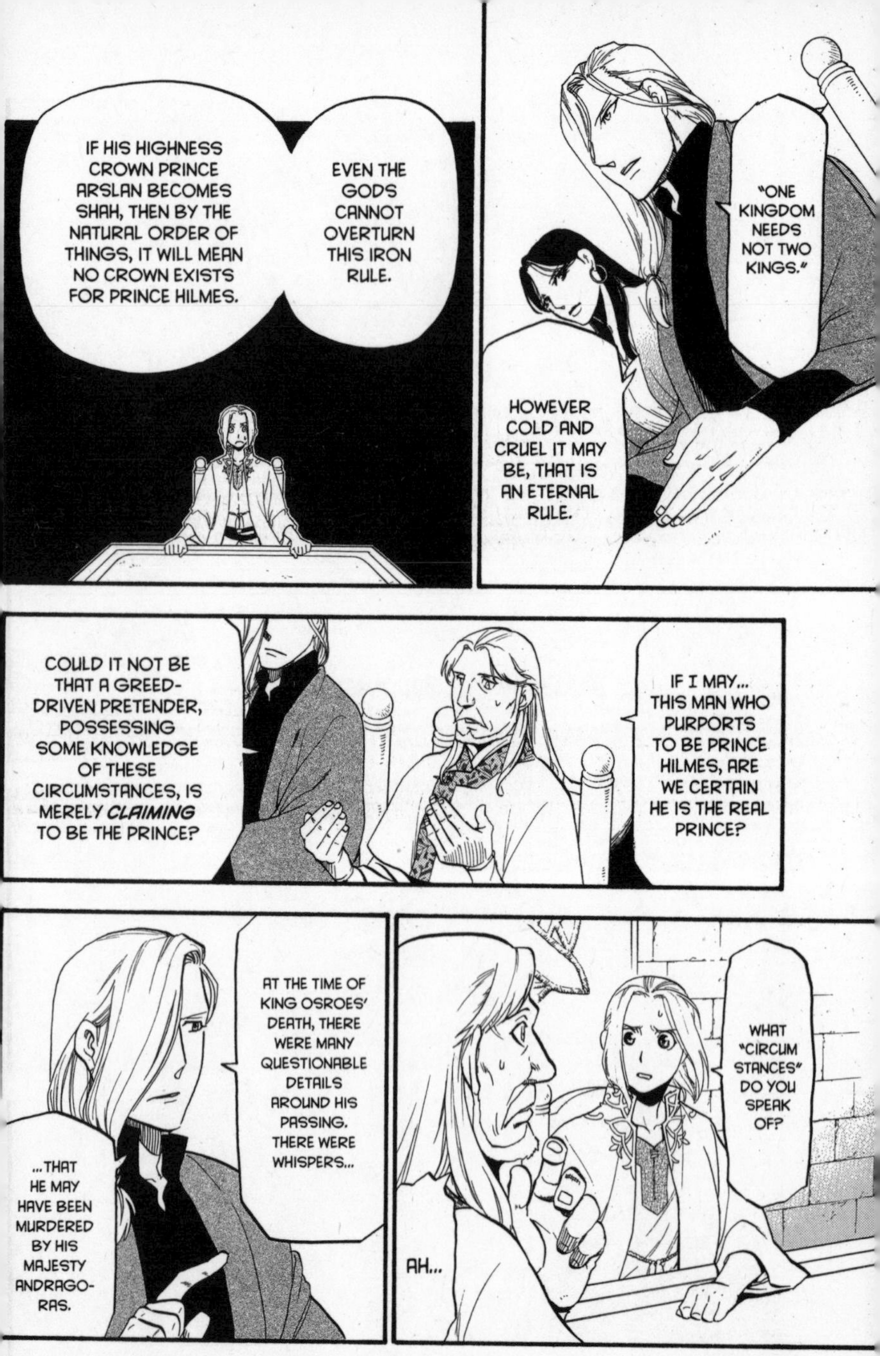
"ONE KINGDOM NEEDS NOT TWO KINGS."
HOWEVER COLD AND CRUEL IT MAY BE, THAT IS AN ETERNAL RULE.
IF HIS HIGHNESS CROWN PRINCE ARSLAN BECOMES SHAH, THEN BY THE NATURAL ORDER OF THINGS, IT WILL MEAN NO CROWN EXISTS FOR PRINCE HILMES.
EVEN THE GODS CANNOT OVERTURN THIS IRON RULE.
IF I MAY... THIS MAN WHO PURPORTS TO BE PRINCE HILMES, ARE WE CERTAIN HE IS THE REAL PRINCE?
COULD IT NOT BE THAT A GREED-DRIVEN PRETENDER, POSSESSING SOME KNOWLEDGE OF THESE CIRCUMSTANCES, IS MERELY *CLAIMING* TO BE THE PRINCE?
WHAT "CIRCUMSTANCES" DO YOU SPEAK OF?
AH...
AT THE TIME OF KING OSROES' DEATH, THERE WERE MANY QUESTIONABLE DETAILS AROUND HIS PASSING. THERE WERE WHISPERS...
...THAT HE MAY HAVE BEEN MURDERED BY HIS MAJESTY ANDRAGORAS.

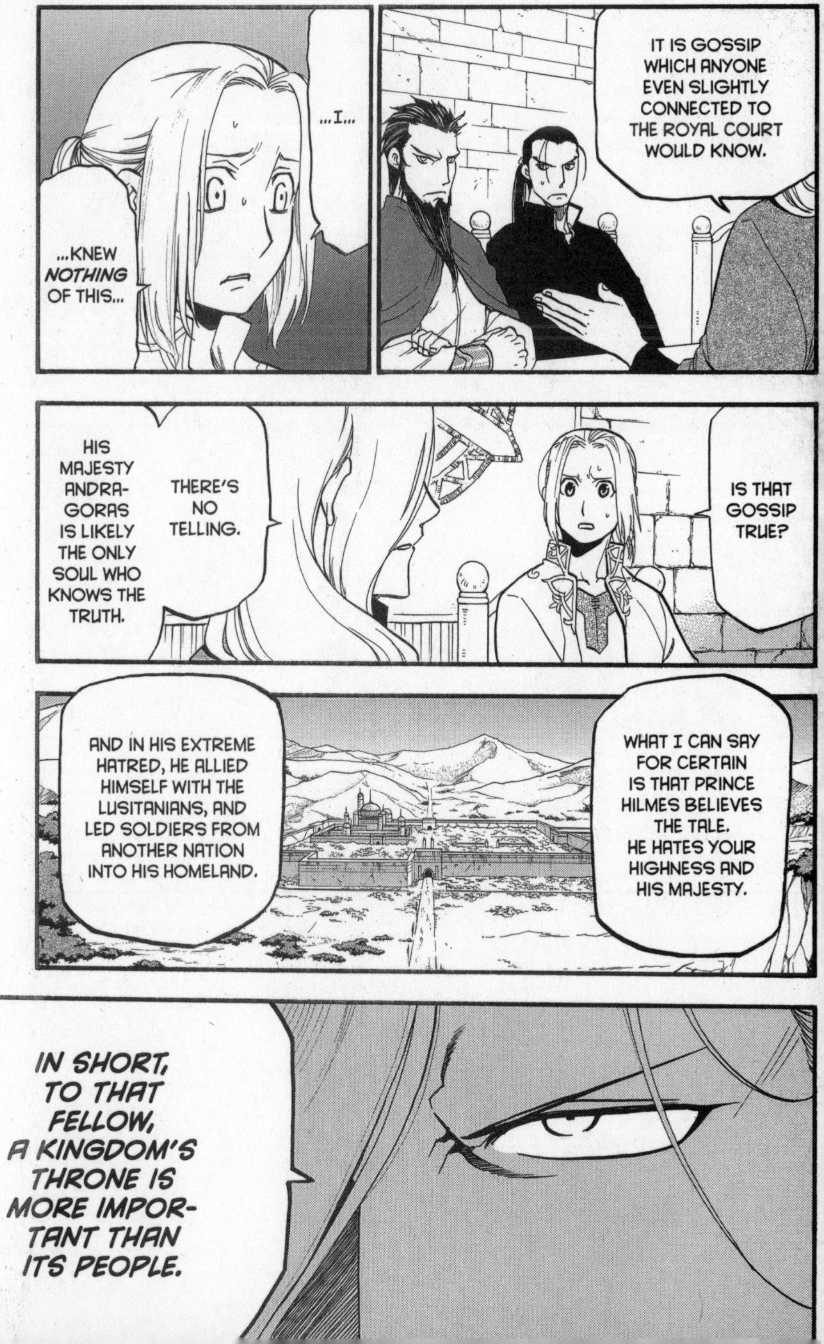
IT IS GOSSIP WHICH ANYONE EVEN SLIGHTLY CONNECTED TO THE ROYAL COURT WOULD KNOW.
...I...
...KNEW *NOTHING* OF THIS...
IS THAT GOSSIP TRUE?
THERE'S NO TELLING.
HIS MAJESTY ANDRAGORAS IS LIKELY THE ONLY SOUL WHO KNOWS THE TRUTH.
WHAT I CAN SAY FOR CERTAIN IS THAT PRINCE HILMES BELIEVES THE TALE. HE HATES YOUR HIGHNESS AND HIS MAJESTY.
AND IN HIS EXTREME HATRED, HE ALLIED HIMSELF WITH THE LUSITANIANS, AND LED SOLDIERS FROM ANOTHER NATION INTO HIS HOMELAND.
IN SHORT, TO THAT FELLOW, A KINGDOM'S THRONE IS MORE IMPORTANT THAN ITS PEOPLE.

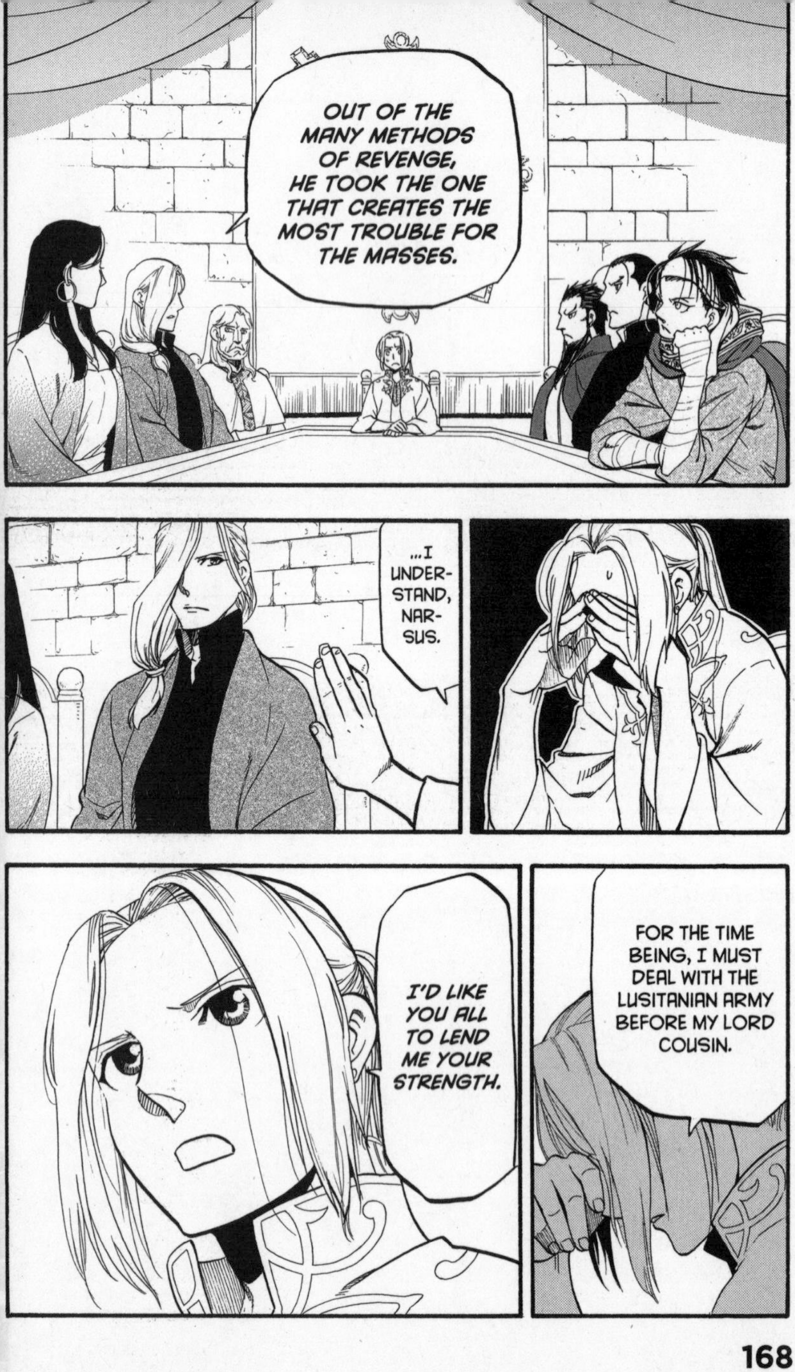
OUT OF THE MANY METHODS OF REVENGE, HE TOOK THE ONE THAT CREATES THE MOST TROUBLE FOR THE MASSES.
...I UNDER-STAND, NAR-SUS.
FOR THE TIME BEING, I MUST DEAL WITH THE LUSITANIAN ARMY BEFORE MY LORD COUSIN.
I'D LIKE YOU ALL TO LEND ME YOUR STRENGTH.

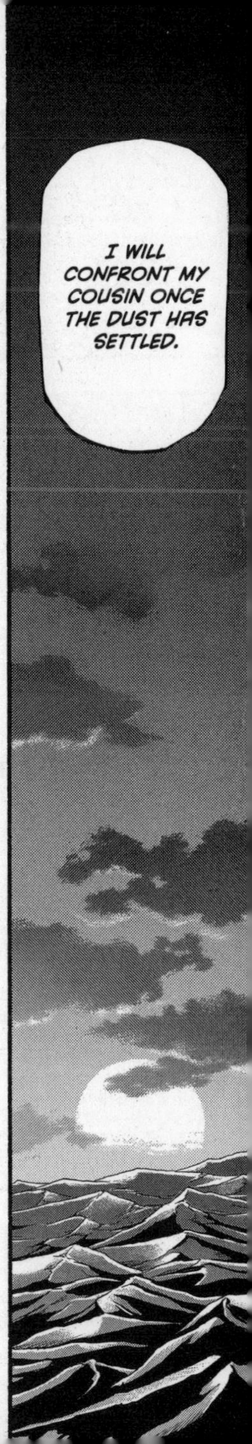
I WILL CONFRONT MY COUSIN ONCE THE DUST HAS SETTLED.

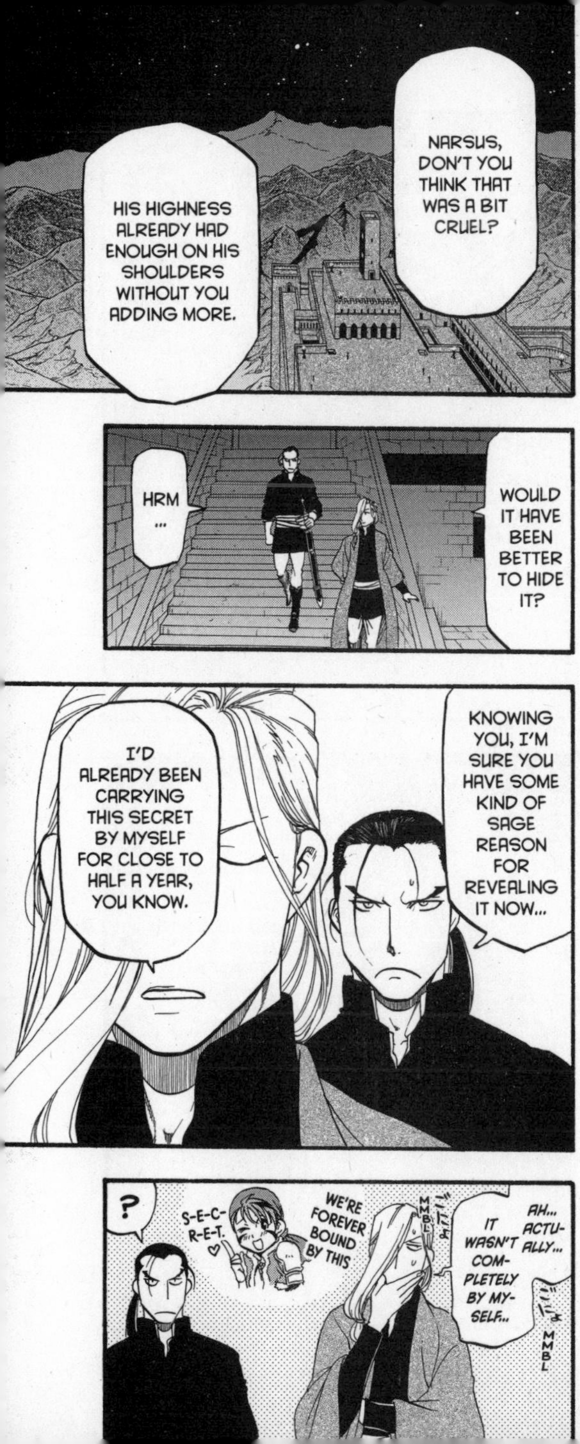
NARSUS, DON'T YOU THINK THAT WAS A BIT CRUEL?
HIS HIGHNESS ALREADY HAD ENOUGH ON HIS SHOULDERS WITHOUT YOU ADDING MORE.
WOULD IT HAVE BEEN BETTER TO HIDE IT?
HRM ...
KNOWING YOU, I'M SURE YOU HAVE SOME KIND OF SAGE REASON FOR REVEALING IT NOW...
I'D ALREADY BEEN CARRYING THIS SECRET BY MYSELF FOR CLOSE TO HALF A YEAR, YOU KNOW.
AH... ACTUALLY...
IT WASN'T COMPLETELY BY MYSELF...
MMBL
MMBL
WE'RE FOREVER BOUND BY THIS
S-E-C-R-E-T. ♡
?

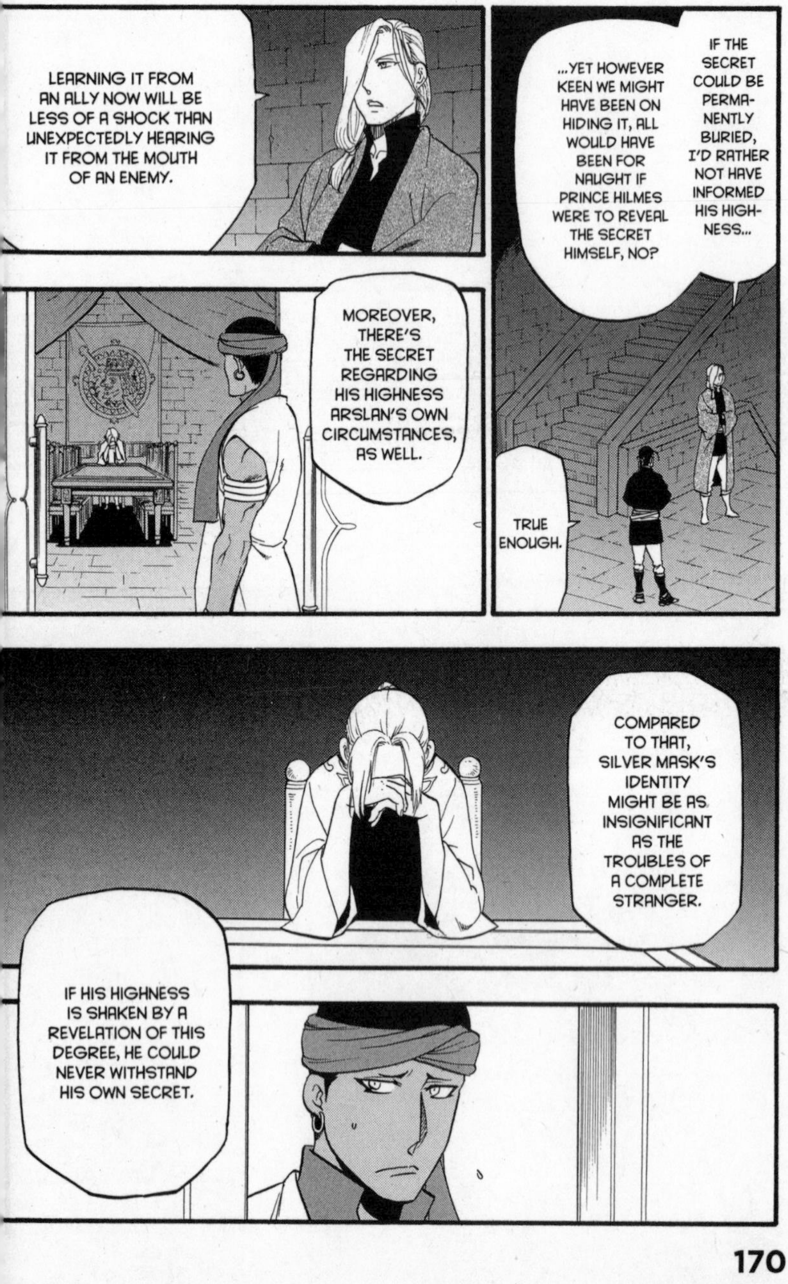
IF THE SECRET COULD BE PERMA-NENTLY BURIED, I'D RATHER NOT HAVE INFORMED HIS HIGH-NESS...
...YET HOWEVER KEEN WE MIGHT HAVE BEEN ON HIDING IT, ALL WOULD HAVE BEEN FOR NAUGHT IF PRINCE HILMES WERE TO REVEAL THE SECRET HIMSELF, NO?
TRUE ENOUGH.
LEARNING IT FROM AN ALLY NOW WILL BE LESS OF A SHOCK THAN UNEXPECTEDLY HEARING IT FROM THE MOUTH OF AN ENEMY.
MOREOVER, THERE'S THE SECRET REGARDING HIS HIGHNESS ARSLAN'S OWN CIRCUMSTANCES, AS WELL.
COMPARED TO THAT, SILVER MASK'S IDENTITY MIGHT BE AS INSIGNIFICANT AS THE TROUBLES OF A COMPLETE STRANGER.
IF HIS HIGHNESS IS SHAKEN BY A REVELATION OF THIS DEGREE, HE COULD NEVER WITHSTAND HIS OWN SECRET.

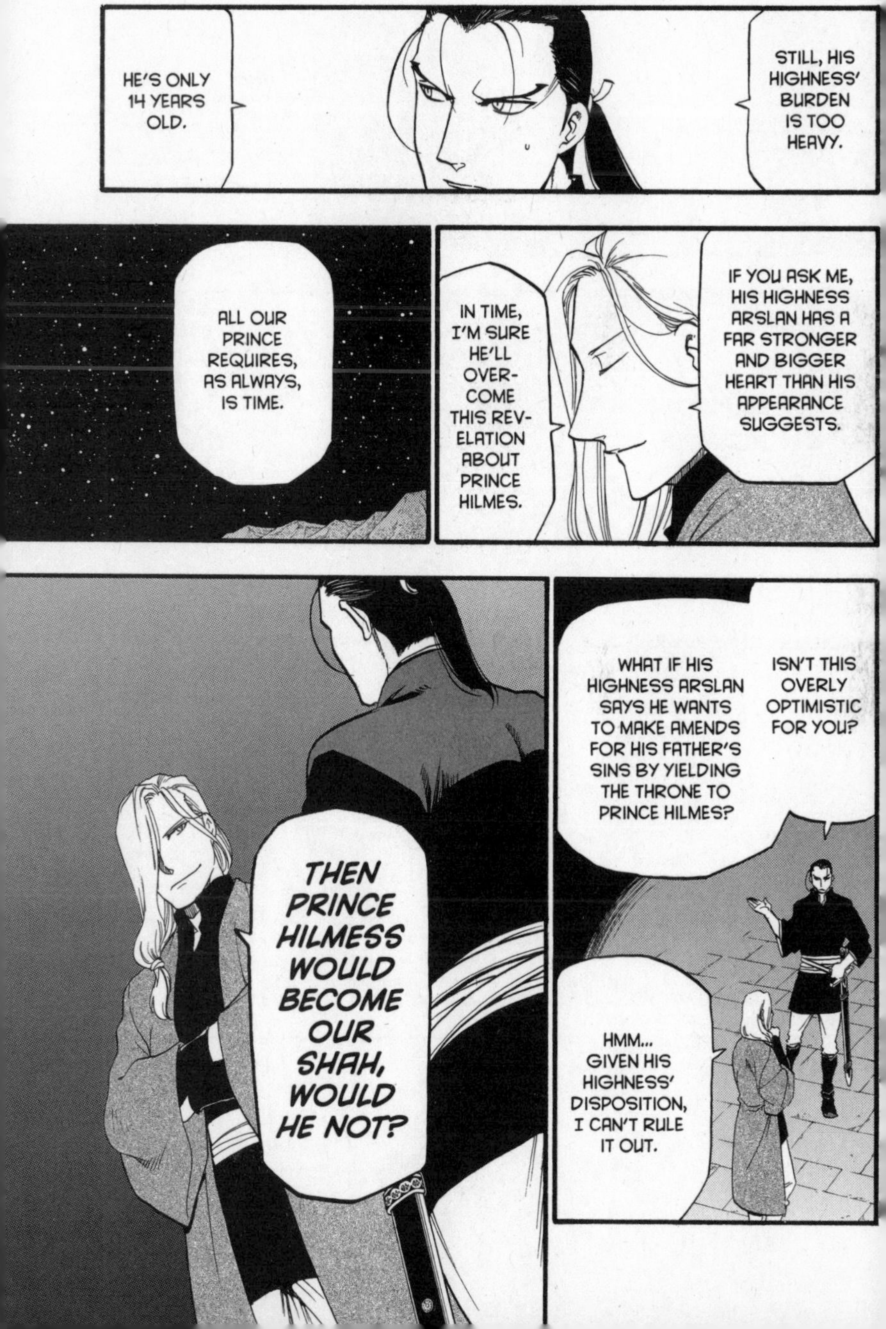
STILL, HIS HIGHNESS' BURDEN IS TOO HEAVY.
HE'S ONLY 14 YEARS OLD.
IF YOU ASK ME, HIS HIGHNESS ARSLAN HAS A FAR STRONGER AND BIGGER HEART THAN HIS APPEARANCE SUGGESTS.
IN TIME, I'M SURE HE'LL OVERCOME THIS REVELATION ABOUT PRINCE HILMES.
ALL OUR PRINCE REQUIRES, AS ALWAYS, IS TIME.
ISN'T THIS OVERLY OPTIMISTIC FOR YOU?
WHAT IF HIS HIGHNESS ARSLAN SAYS HE WANTS TO MAKE AMENDS FOR HIS FATHER'S SINS BY YIELDING THE THRONE TO PRINCE HILMES?
HMM... GIVEN HIS HIGHNESS' DISPOSITION, I CAN'T RULE IT OUT.
THEN PRINCE HILMESS WOULD BECOME OUR SHAH, WOULD HE NOT?

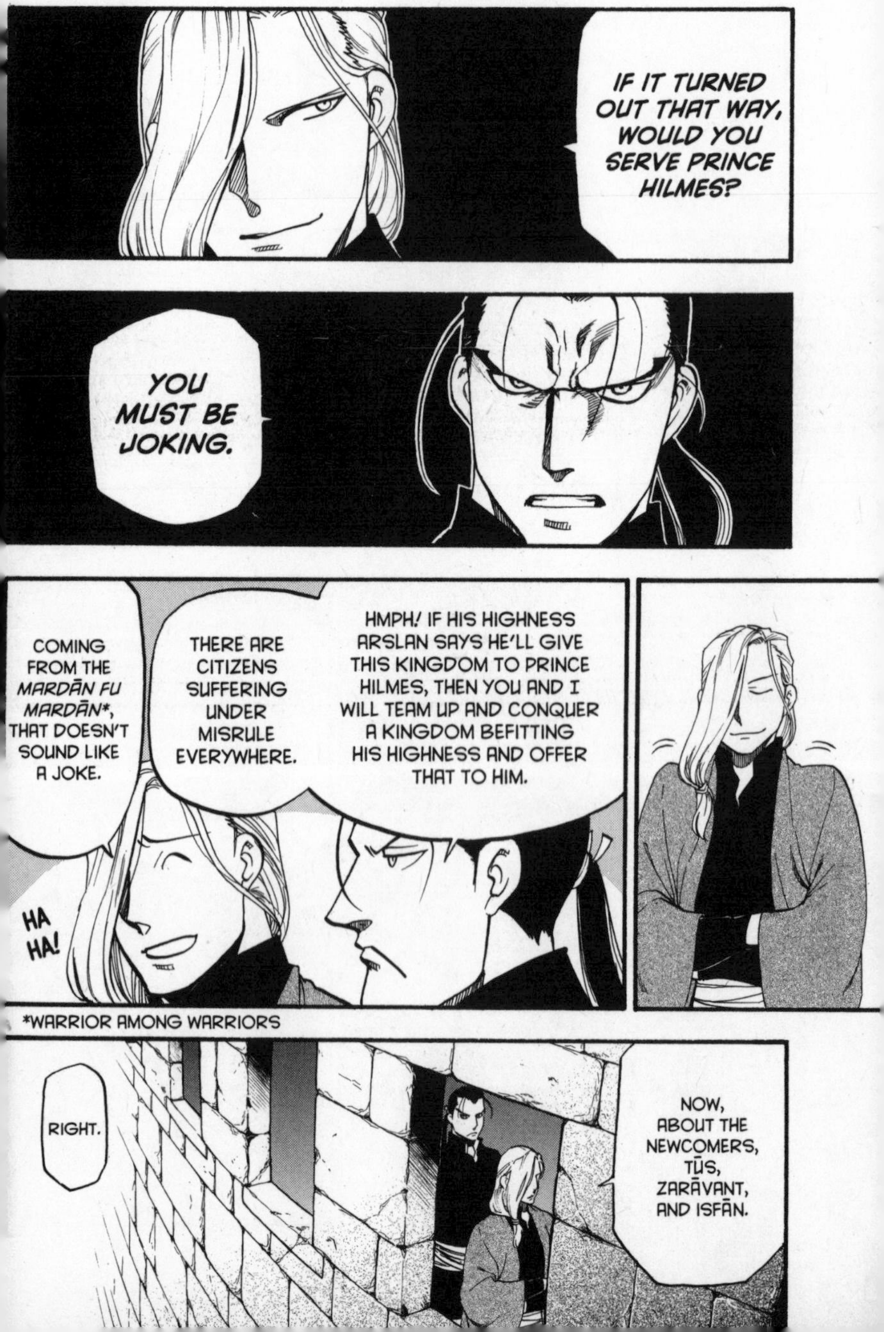
IF IT TURNED OUT THAT WAY, WOULD YOU SERVE PRINCE HILMES?
YOU MUST BE JOKING.
HMPH! IF HIS HIGHNESS ARSLAN SAYS HE'LL GIVE THIS KINGDOM TO PRINCE HILMES, THEN YOU AND I WILL TEAM UP AND CONQUER A KINGDOM BEFITTING HIS HIGHNESS AND OFFER THAT TO HIM.
THERE ARE CITIZENS SUFFERING UNDER MISRULE EVERYWHERE.
COMING FROM THE *MARDĀN FU MARDĀN**, THAT DOESN'T SOUND LIKE A JOKE.
HA HA!
NOW, ABOUT THE NEWCOMERS, TŪS, ZARĀVANT, AND ISFĀN.
RIGHT.
*WARRIOR AMONG WARRIORS

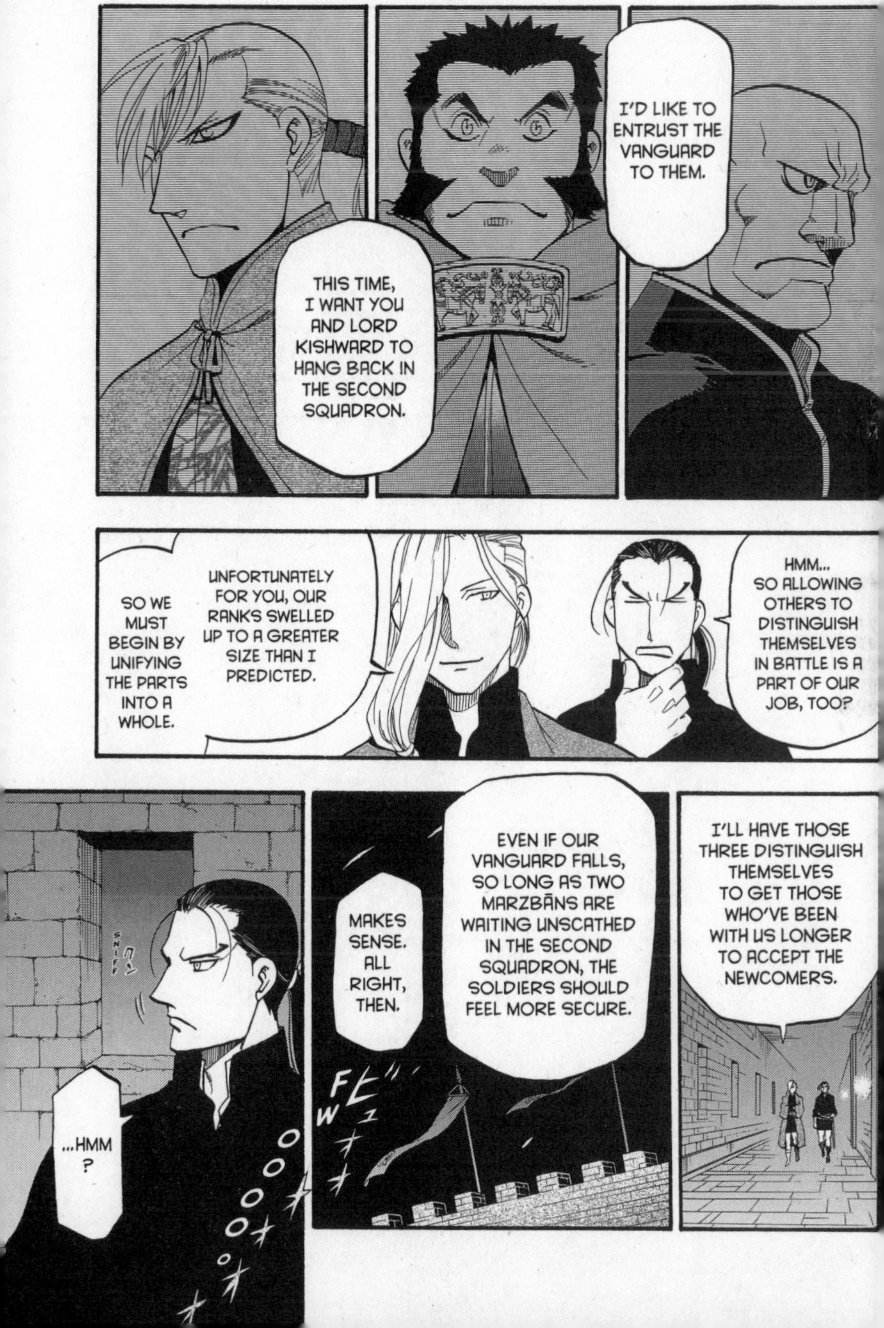
I'D LIKE TO ENTRUST THE VANGUARD TO THEM.
THIS TIME, I WANT YOU AND LORD KISHWARD TO HANG BACK IN THE SECOND SQUADRON.
HMM... SO ALLOWING OTHERS TO DISTINGUISH THEMSELVES IN BATTLE IS A PART OF OUR JOB, TOO?
UNFORTUNATELY FOR YOU, OUR RANKS SWELLED UP TO A GREATER SIZE THAN I PREDICTED.
SO WE MUST BEGIN BY UNIFYING THE PARTS INTO A WHOLE.
I'LL HAVE THOSE THREE DISTINGUISH THEMSELVES TO GET THOSE WHO'VE BEEN WITH US LONGER TO ACCEPT THE NEWCOMERS.
EVEN IF OUR VANGUARD FALLS, SO LONG AS TWO MARZBĀNS ARE WAITING UNSCATHED IN THE SECOND SQUADRON, THE SOLDIERS SHOULD FEEL MORE SECURE.
MAKES SENSE. ALL RIGHT, THEN.
SNIFF
...HMM?

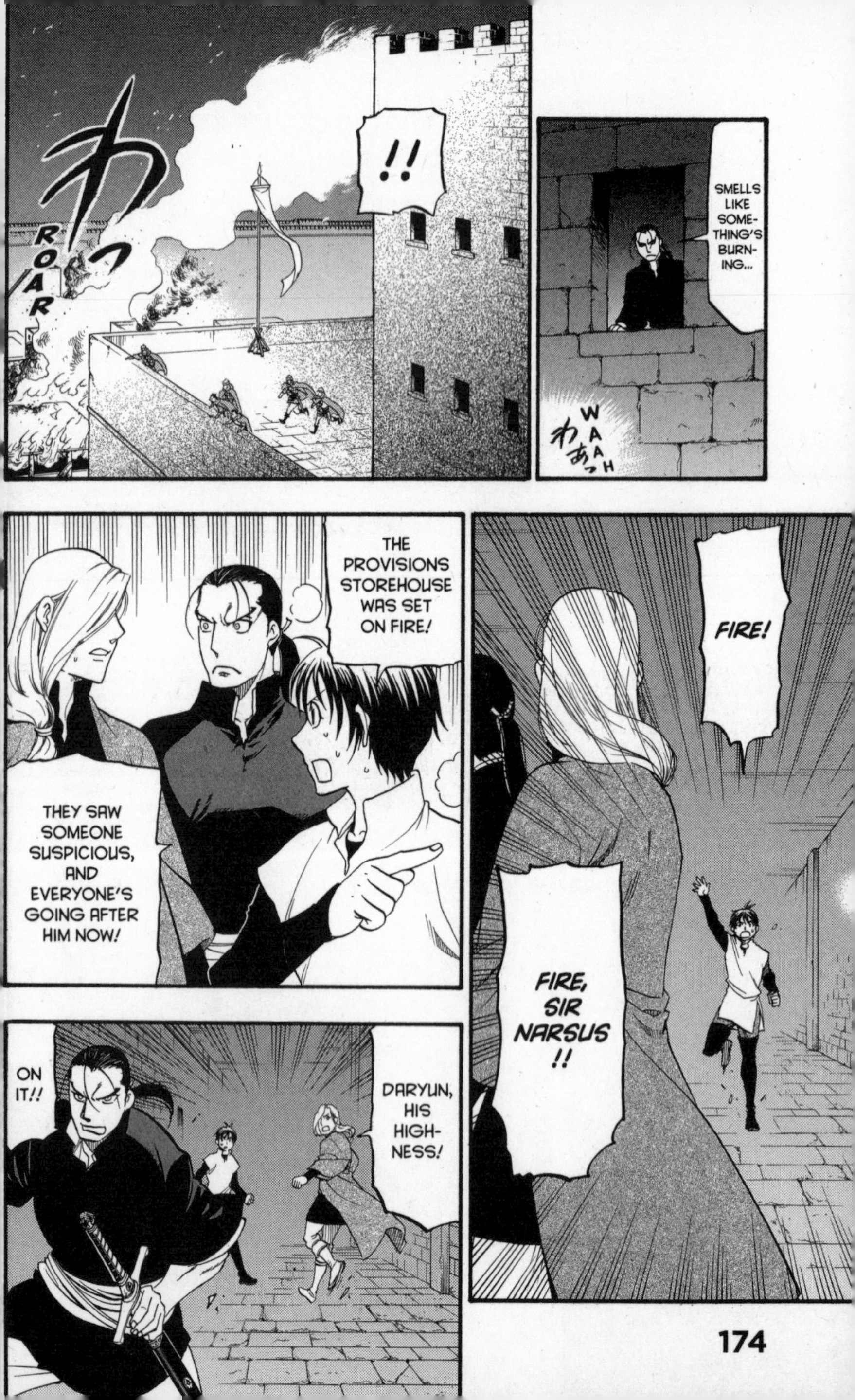

SMELLS LIKE SOME-THING'S BURN-ING...
WAAH
!!
ROAR
FIRE!
FIRE, SIR NARSUS!!
THE PROVISIONS STOREHOUSE WAS SET ON FIRE!
THEY SAW SOMEONE SUSPICIOUS, AND EVERYONE'S GOING AFTER HIM NOW!
DARYUN, HIS HIGH-NESS!
ON IT!!

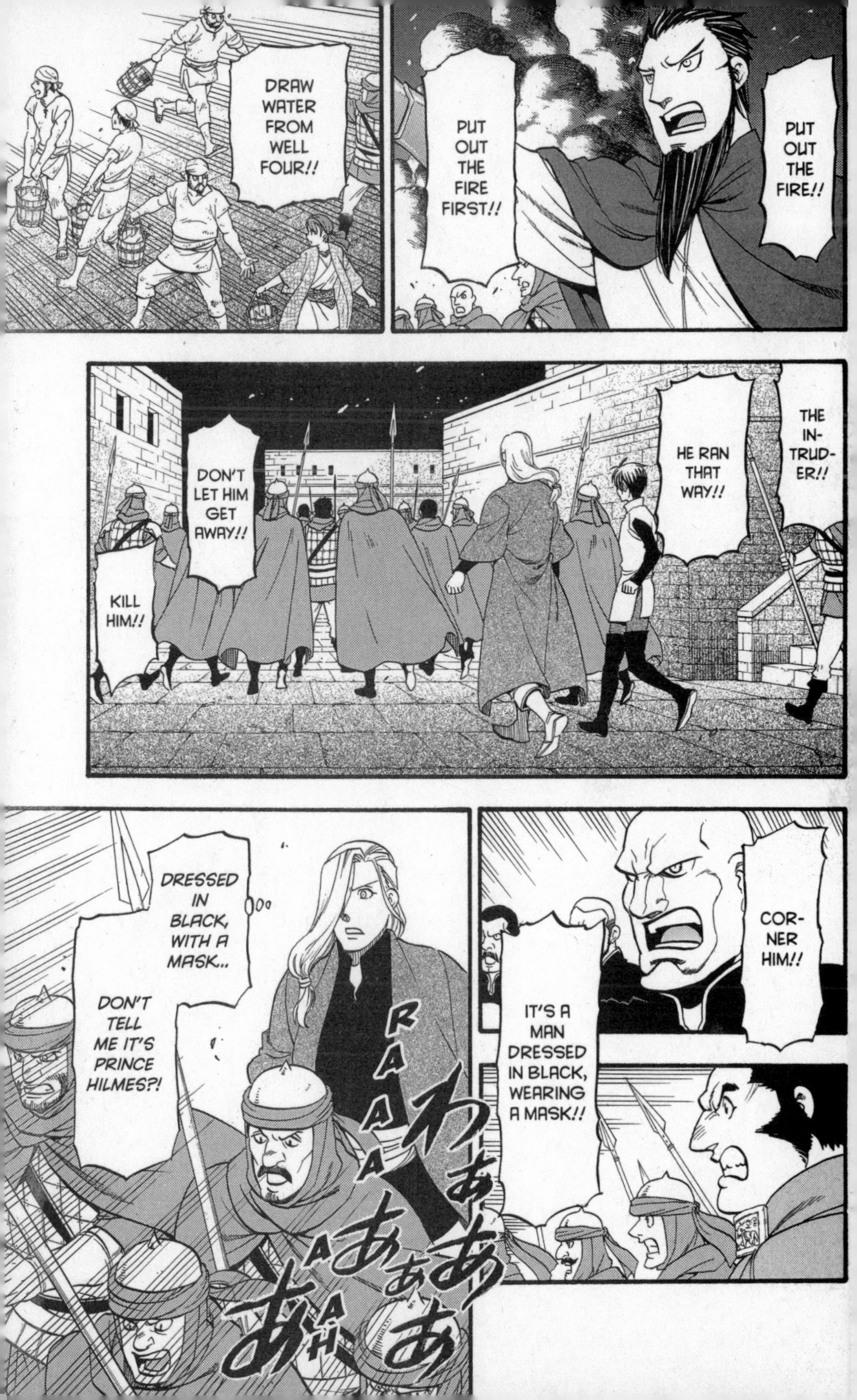
PUT OUT THE FIRE!!
PUT OUT THE FIRE FIRST!!
DRAW WATER FROM WELL FOUR!!
THE IN-TRUDER!!
HE RAN THAT WAY!!
DON'T LET HIM GET AWAY!!
KILL HIM!!
CORNER HIM!!
IT'S A MAN DRESSED IN BLACK, WEARING A MASK!!
DRESSED IN BLACK, WITH A MASK...
DON'T TELL ME IT'S PRINCE HILMES?!
RAAAAAAH
わあああああああ

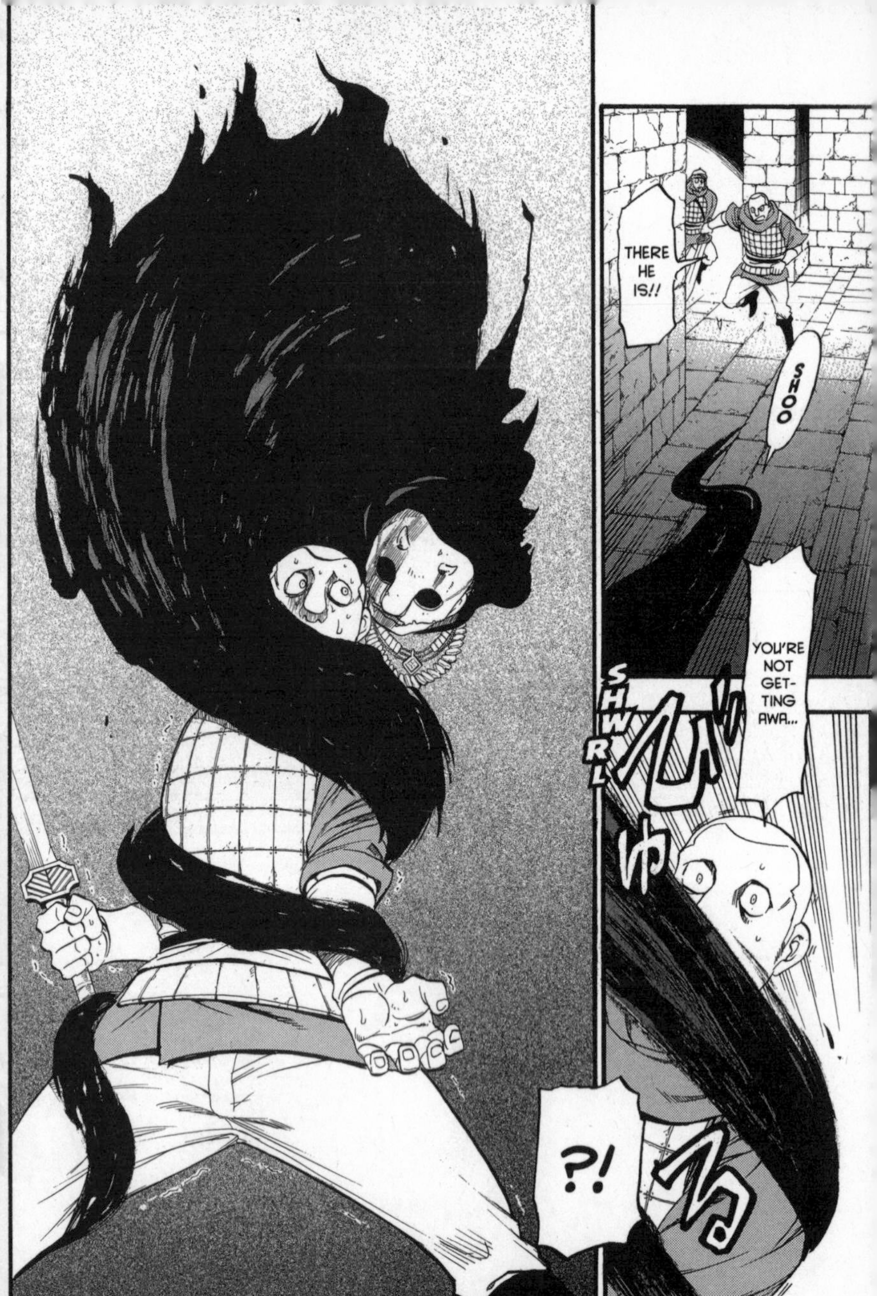
THERE HE IS!!
SHOO
YOU'RE NOT GET-TING AWA...
SHWRL
?!

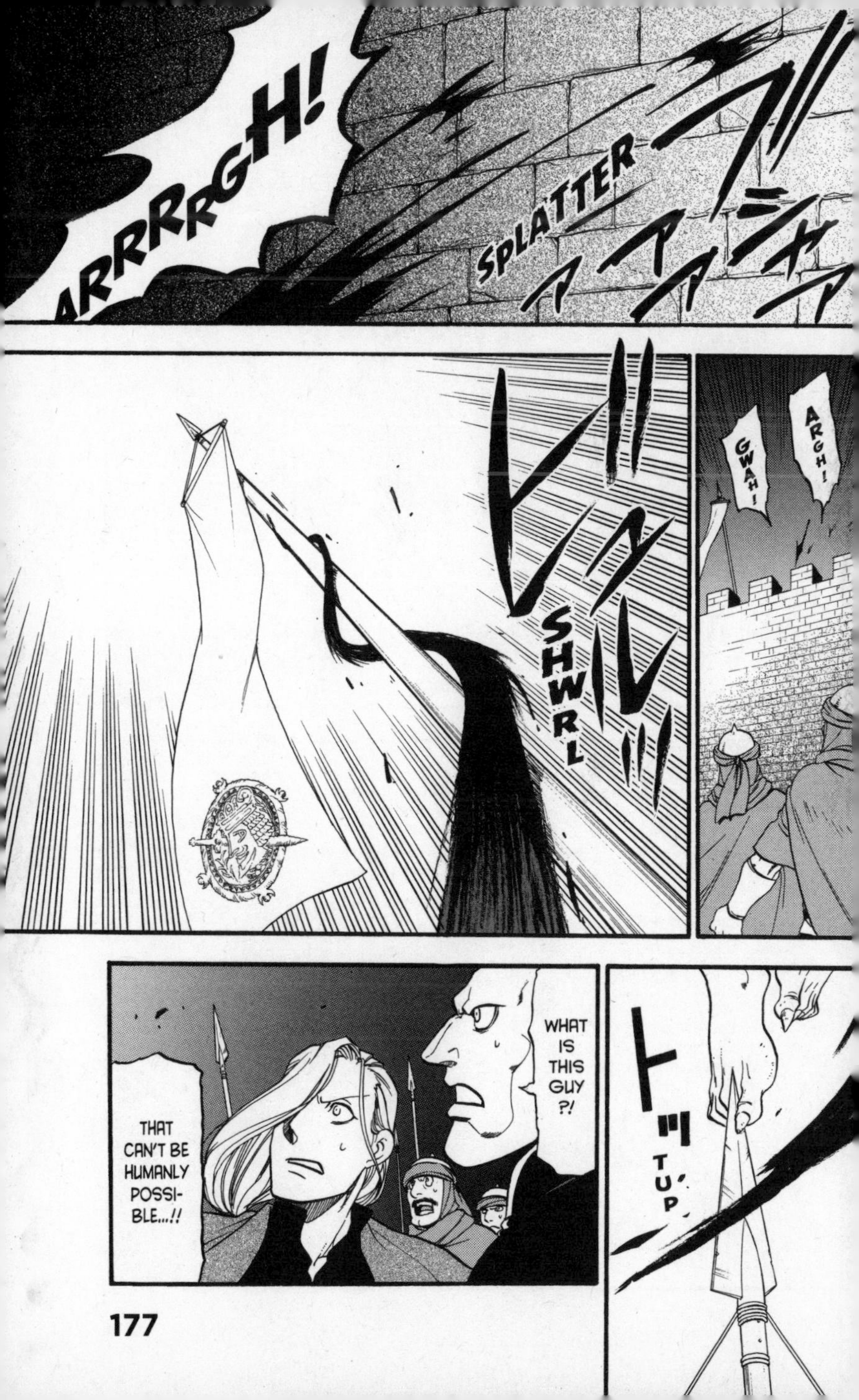
ARRRRGH!
SPLATTER
ARGH!
GWAH!
SHWRL
TUP
WHAT IS THIS GUY?!
THAT CAN'T BE HUMANLY POSSIBLE...!!

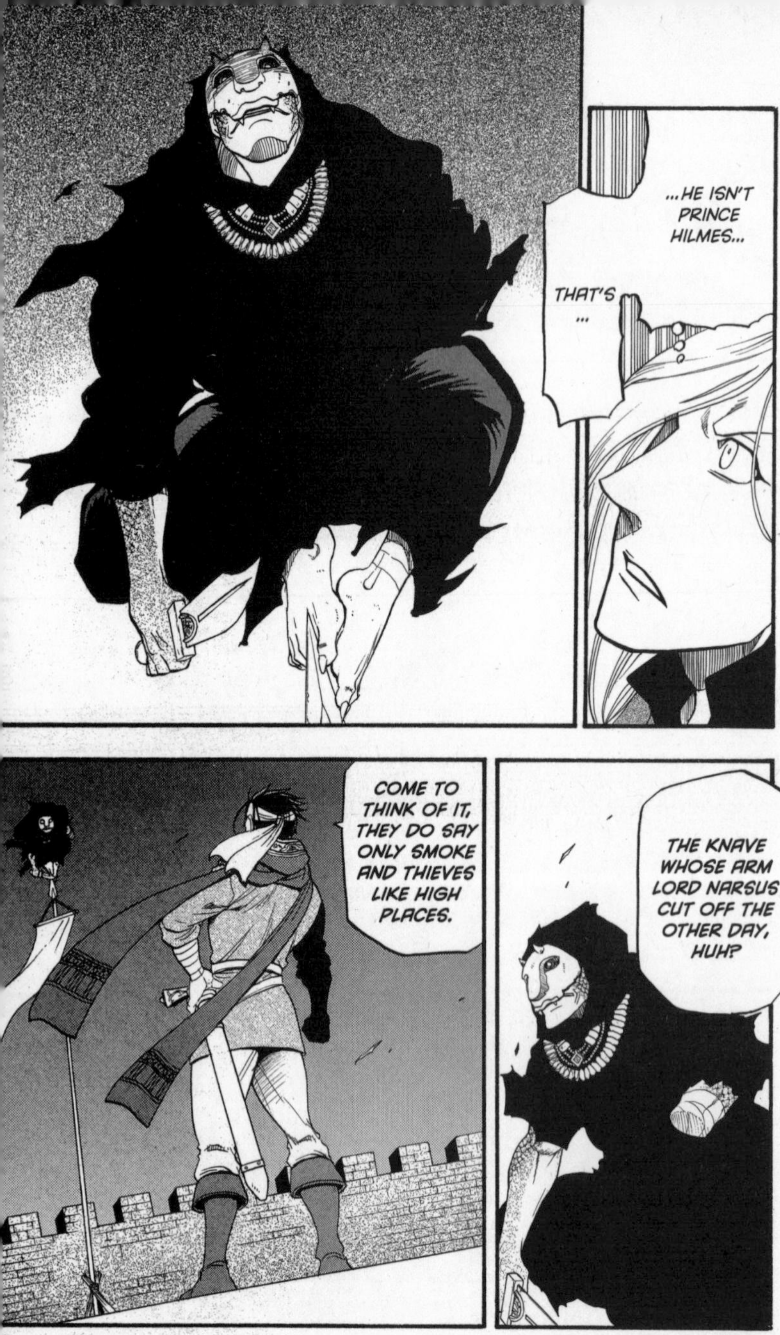
...HE ISN'T PRINCE HILMES...
THAT'S ...
THE KNAVE WHOSE ARM LORD NARSUS CUT OFF THE OTHER DAY, HUH?
COME TO THINK OF IT, THEY DO SAY ONLY SMOKE AND THIEVES LIKE HIGH PLACES.

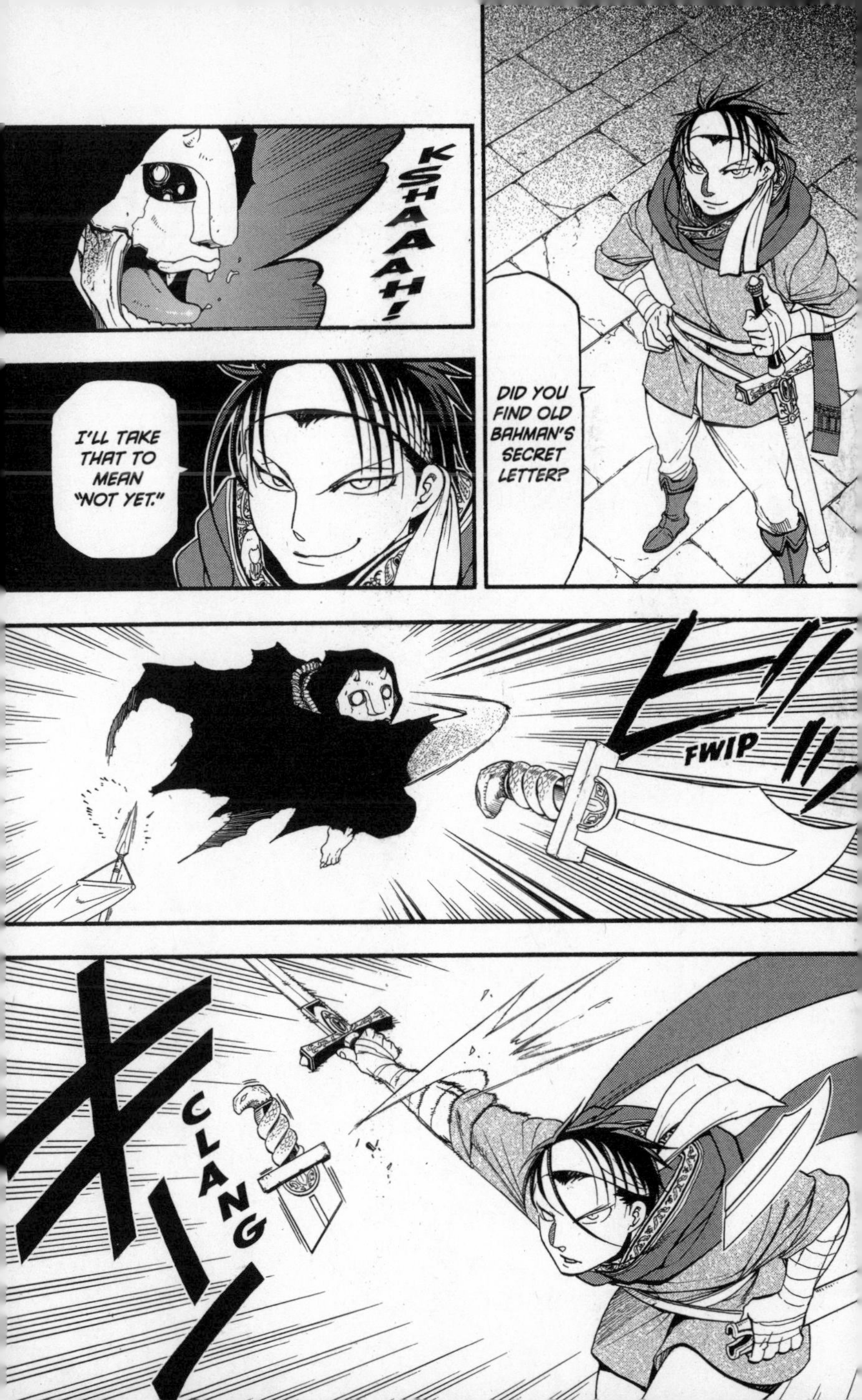
DID YOU FIND OLD BAHMAN'S SECRET LETTER?
KSHAAAAH!
I'LL TAKE THAT TO MEAN "NOT YET."
FWIP
CLANG

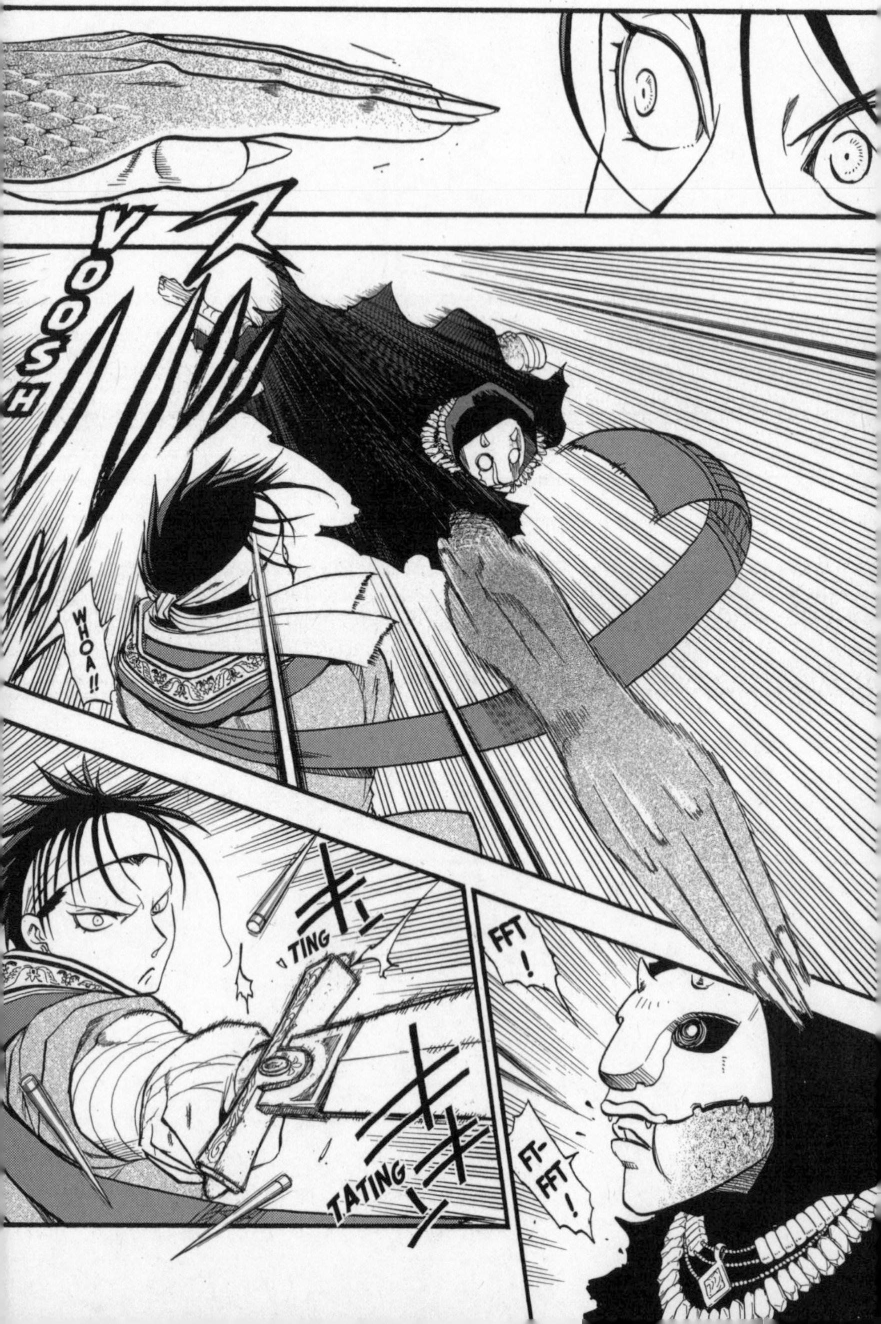
VOOSH
WHOA!!
FFT!
FT-FFT!
TING
TATING

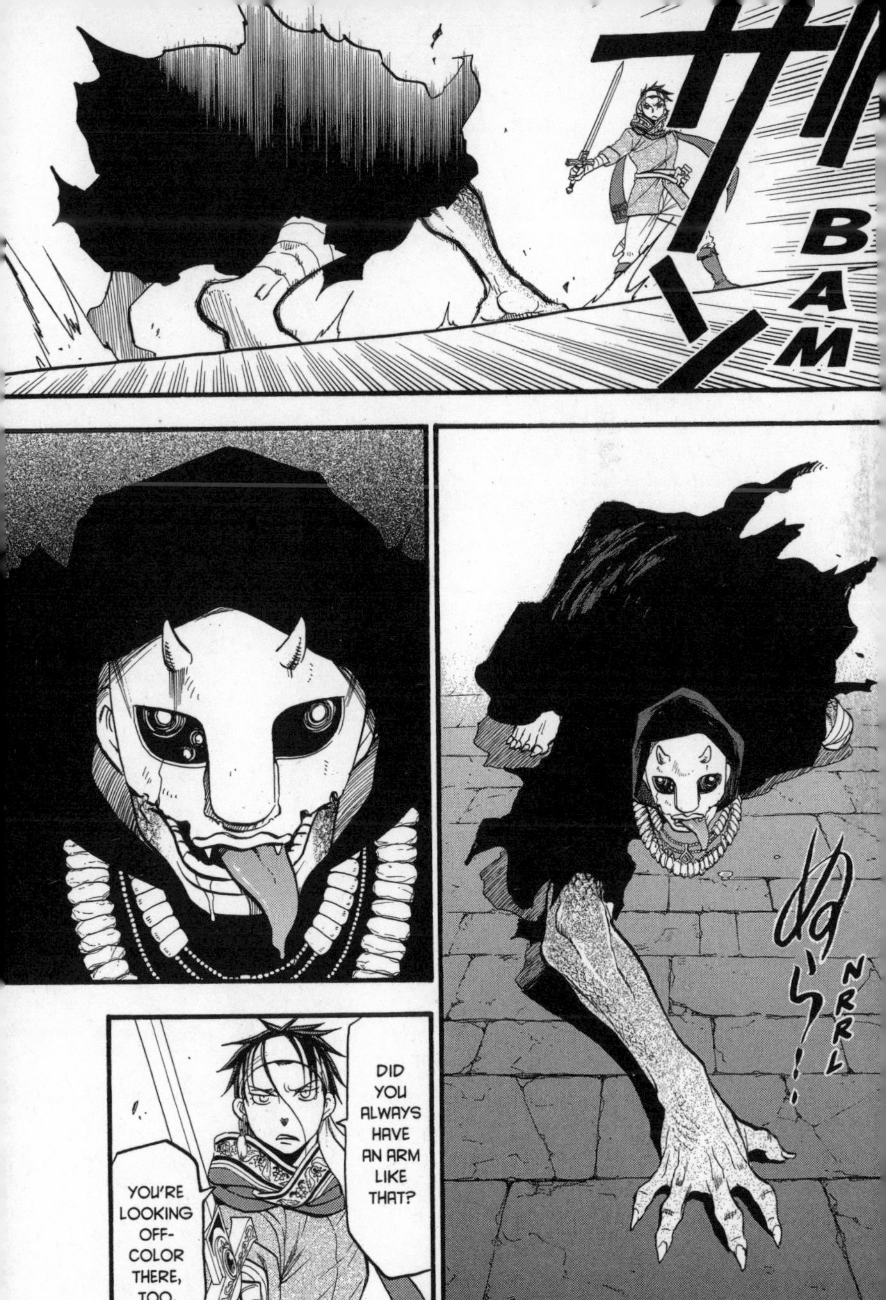
BAM
NRRL
DID YOU ALWAYS HAVE AN ARM LIKE THAT?
YOU'RE LOOKING OFF-COLOR THERE, TOO.

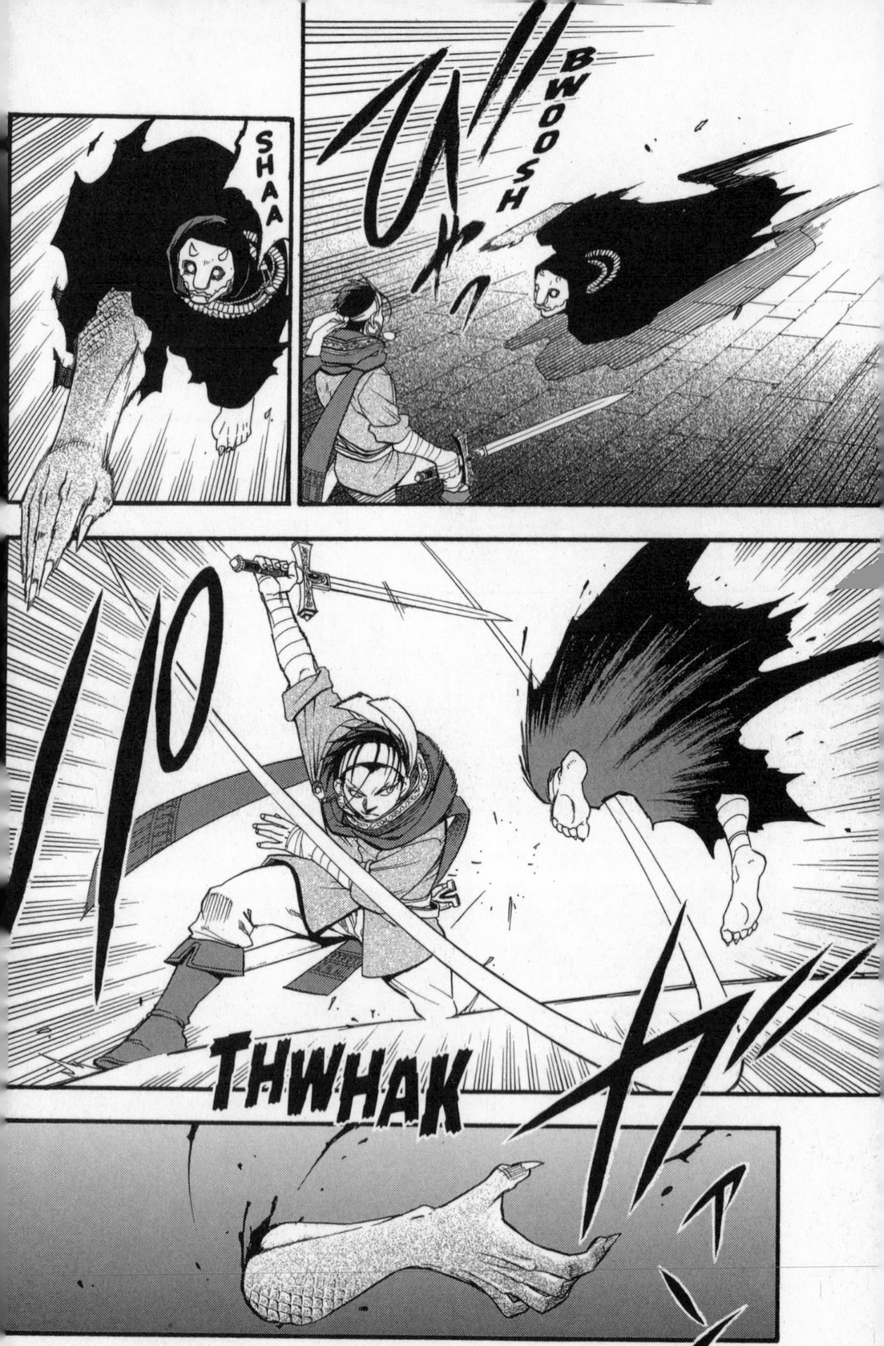
BWOOSH
SHAA
THWHAK

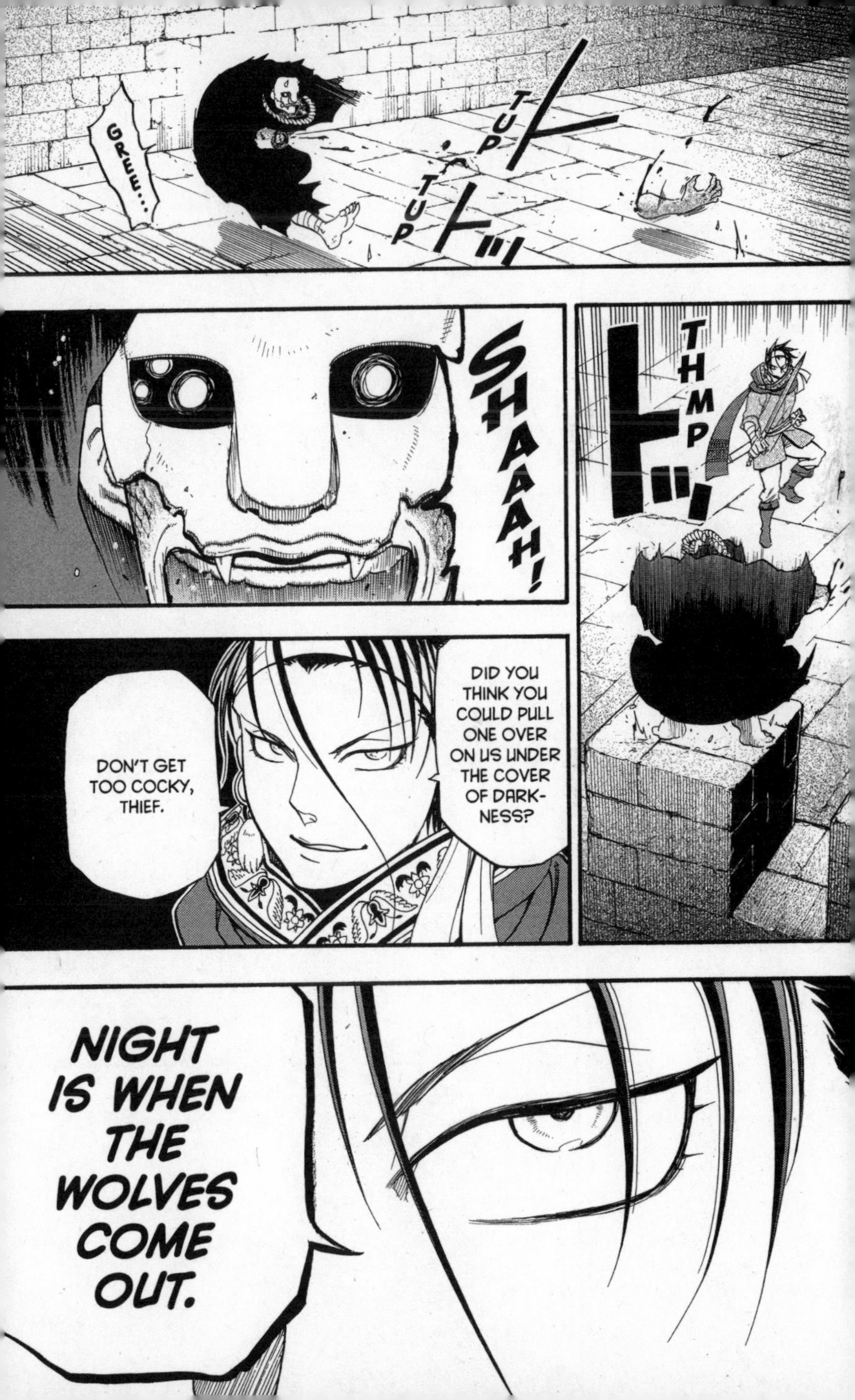
TUP
TUP
GREEE...
THMP
SHAAAH!
DID YOU THINK YOU COULD PULL ONE OVER ON US UNDER THE COVER OF DARK-NESS?
DON'T GET TOO COCKY, THIEF.
NIGHT IS WHEN THE WOLVES COME OUT.

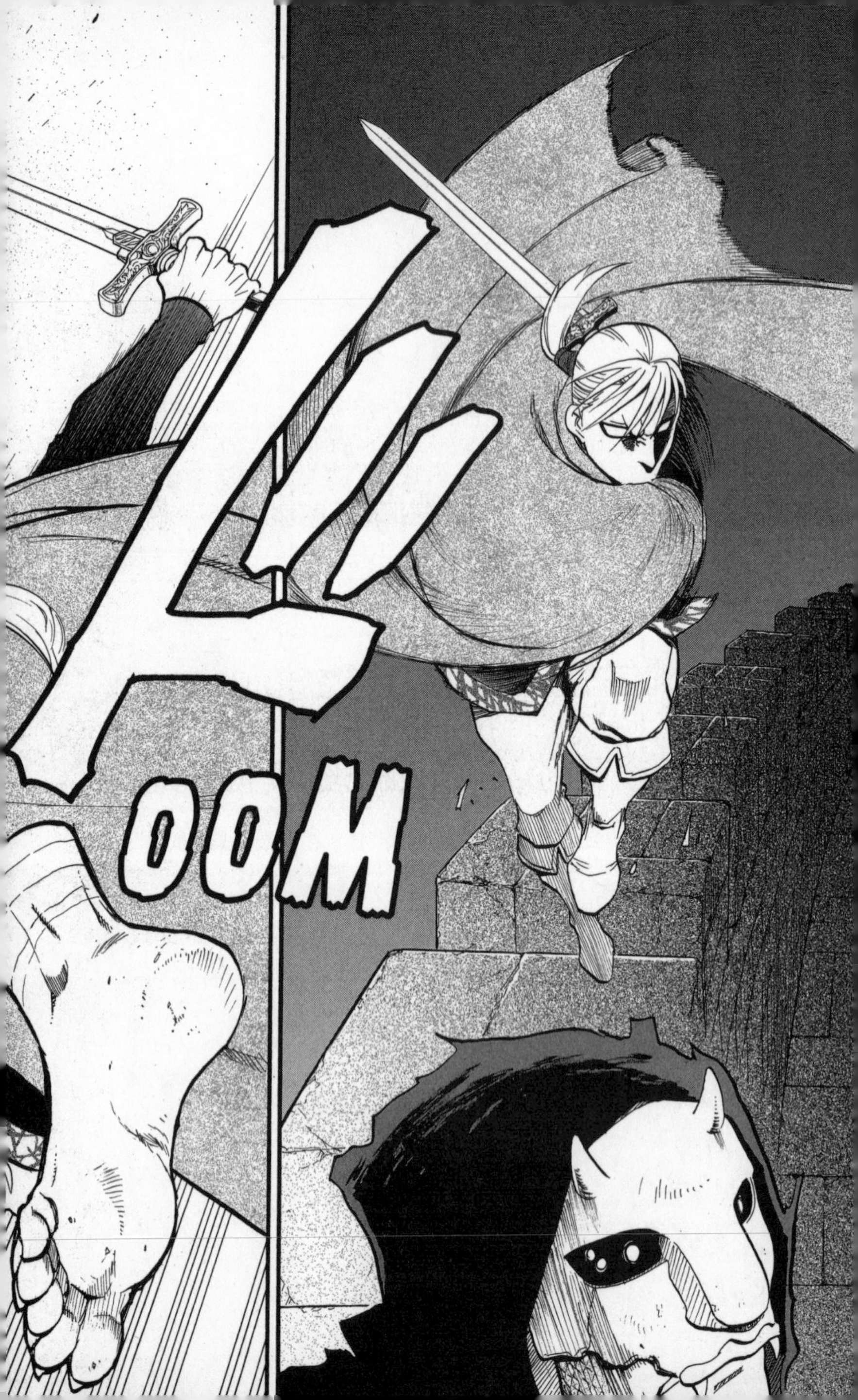
FWOOM

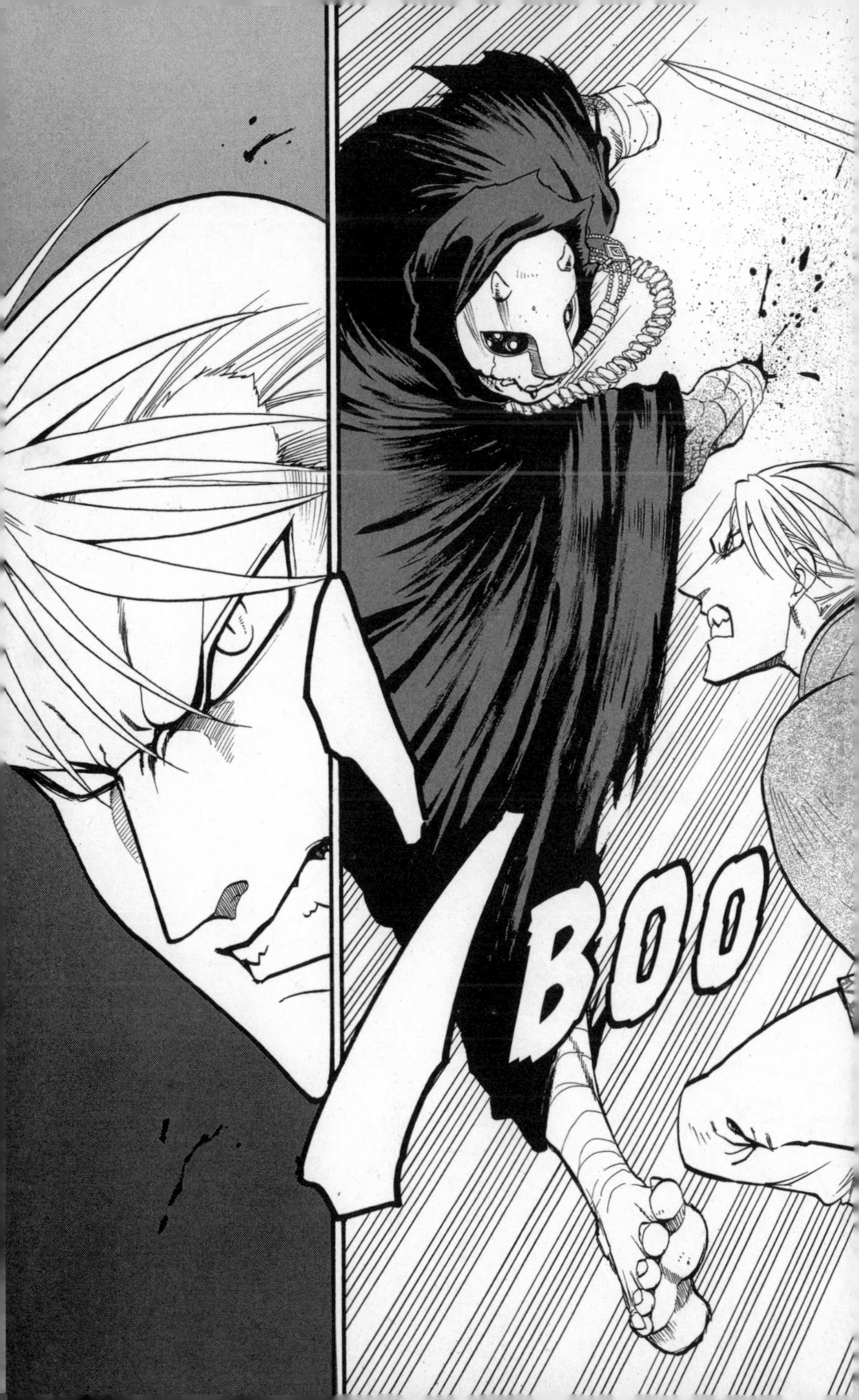
BOO

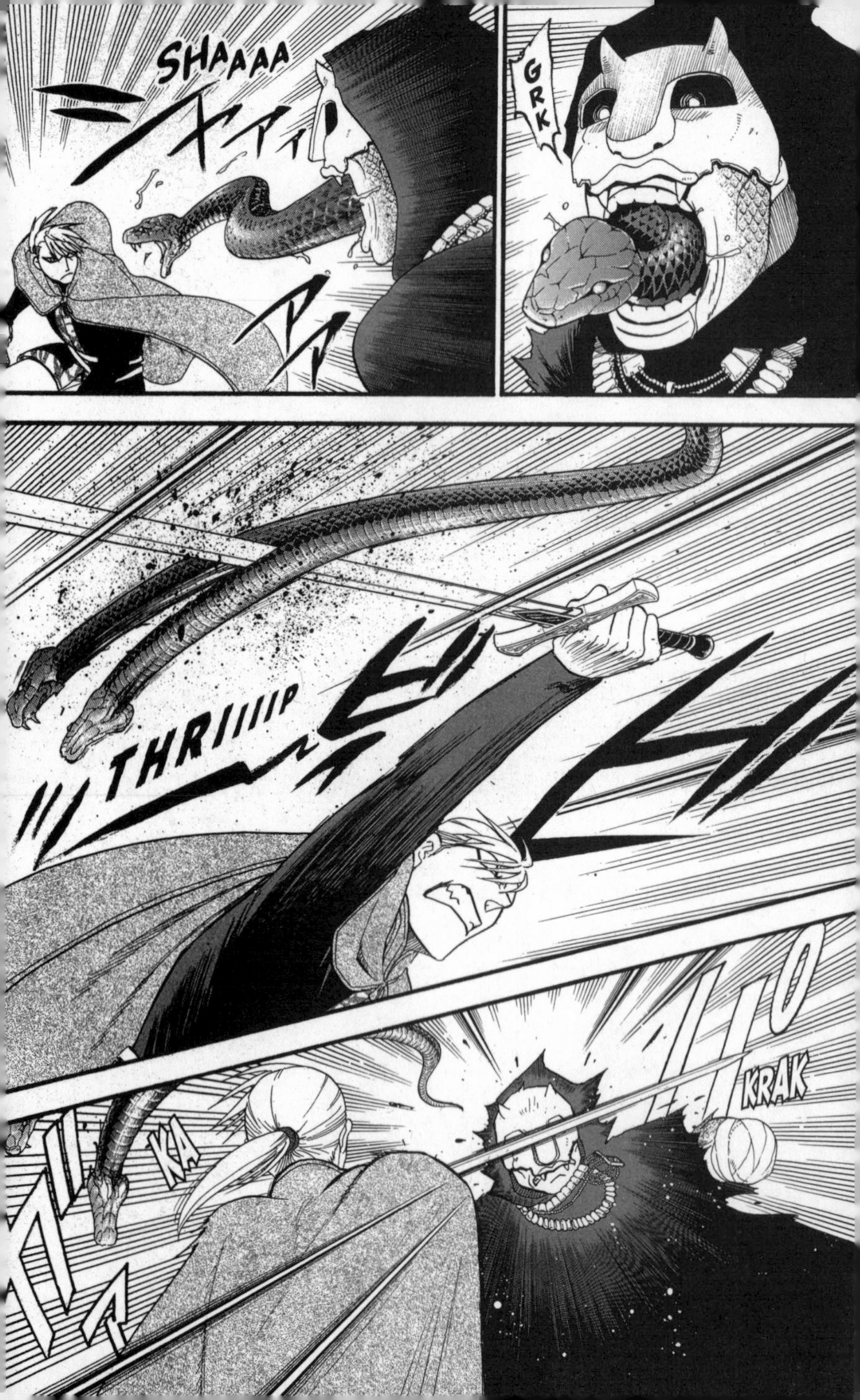
GRK
SHAAAA
THRIiiiP
KRAK
KA

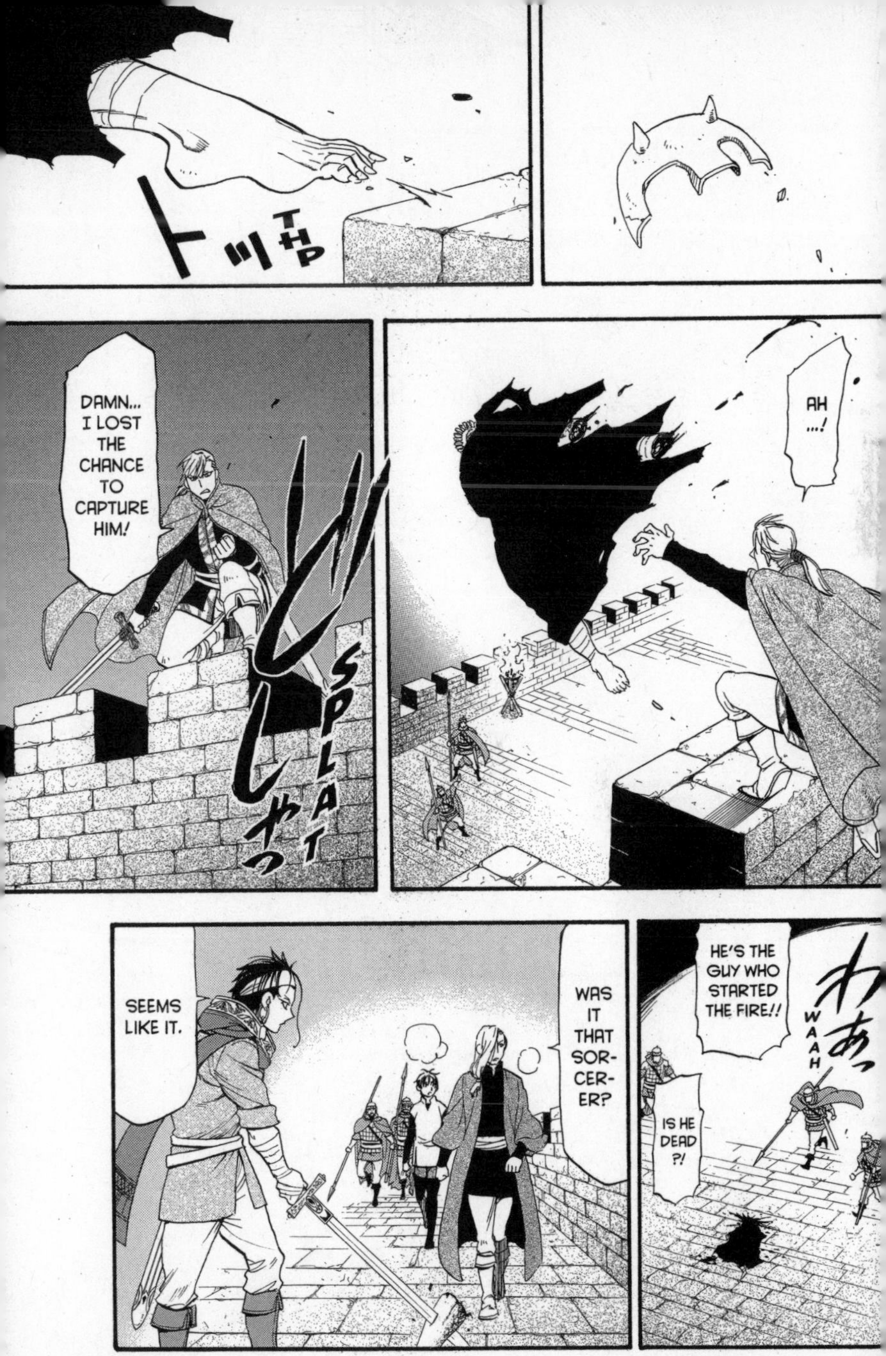
THP
AH ...!
DAMN... I LOST THE CHANCE TO CAPTURE HIM!
SPLAT
HE'S THE GUY WHO STARTED THE FIRE!!
WAAAH
IS HE DEAD?!
WAS IT THAT SORCERER?
SEEMS LIKE IT.

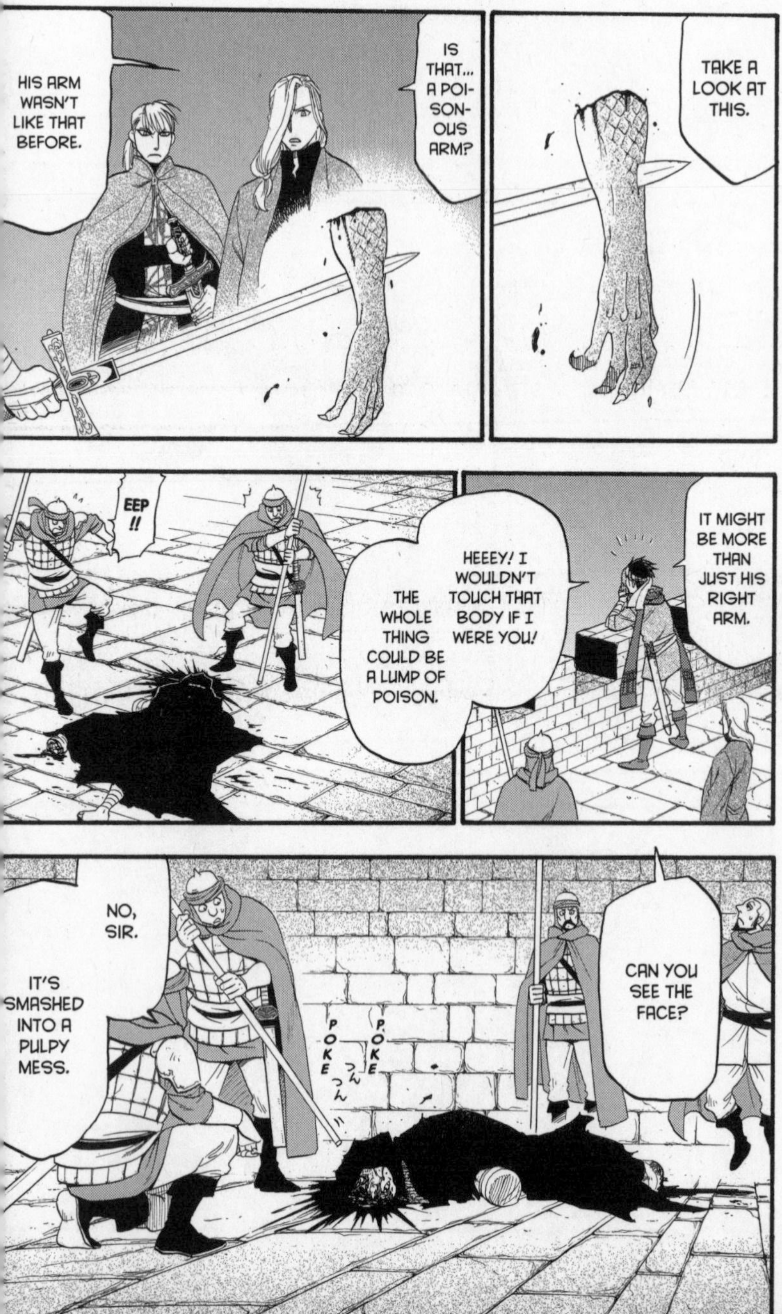
TAKE A LOOK AT THIS.
IS THAT... A POISONOUS ARM?
HIS ARM WASN'T LIKE THAT BEFORE.
IT MIGHT BE MORE THAN JUST HIS RIGHT ARM.
HEEEY! I WOULDN'T TOUCH THAT BODY IF I WERE YOU!
THE WHOLE THING COULD BE A LUMP OF POISON.
EEP!!
CAN YOU SEE THE FACE?
POKE
POKE
NO, SIR.
IT'S SMASHED INTO A PULPY MESS.

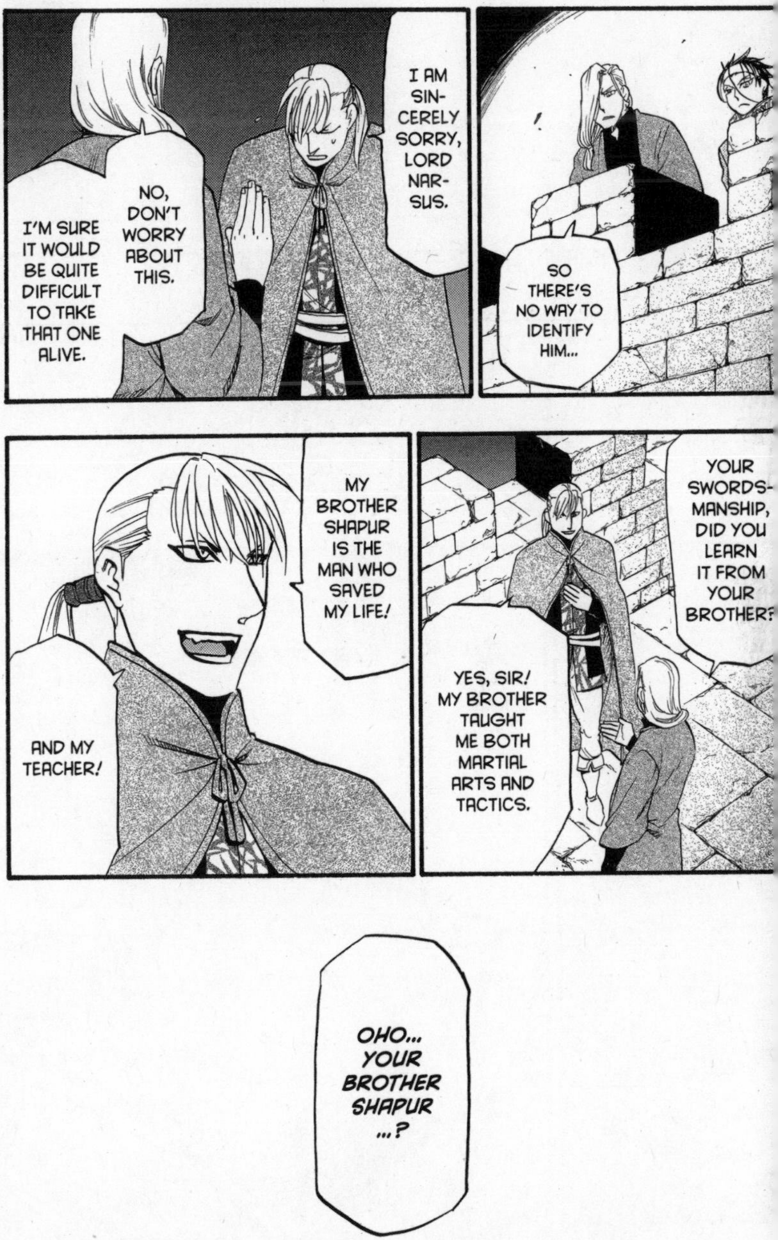
SO THERE'S NO WAY TO IDENTIFY HIM...
I AM SINCERELY SORRY, LORD NARSUS.
NO, DON'T WORRY ABOUT THIS.
I'M SURE IT WOULD BE QUITE DIFFICULT TO TAKE THAT ONE ALIVE.
YOUR SWORDSMANSHIP, DID YOU LEARN IT FROM YOUR BROTHER?
YES, SIR! MY BROTHER TAUGHT ME BOTH MARTIAL ARTS AND TACTICS.
MY BROTHER SHAPUR IS THE MAN WHO SAVED MY LIFE!
AND MY TEACHER!
OHO... YOUR BROTHER SHAPUR ...?

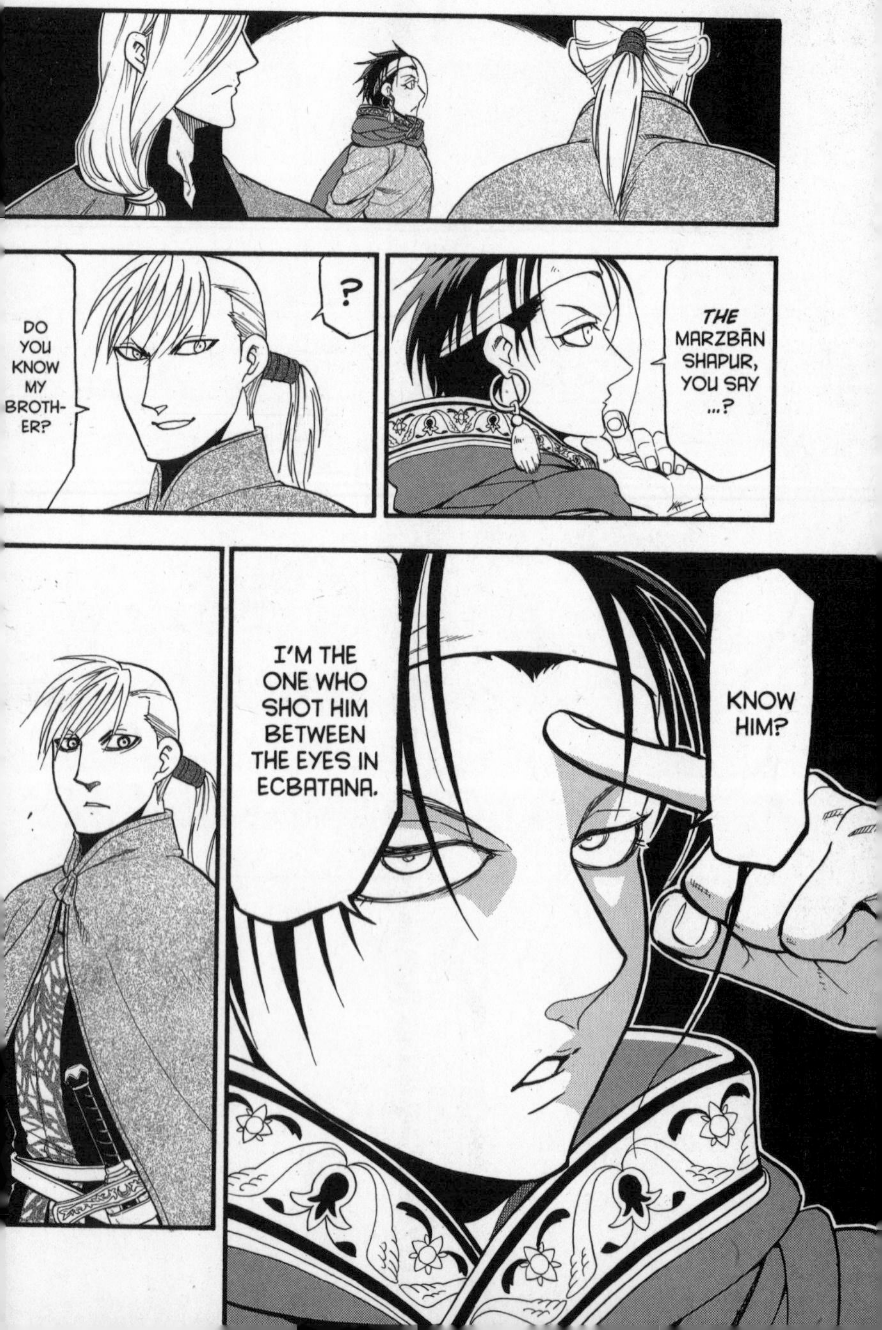
THE MARZBĀN SHAPUR, YOU SAY ...?
?
DO YOU KNOW MY BROTHER?
KNOW HIM?
I'M THE ONE WHO SHOT HIM BETWEEN THE EYES IN ECBATANA.

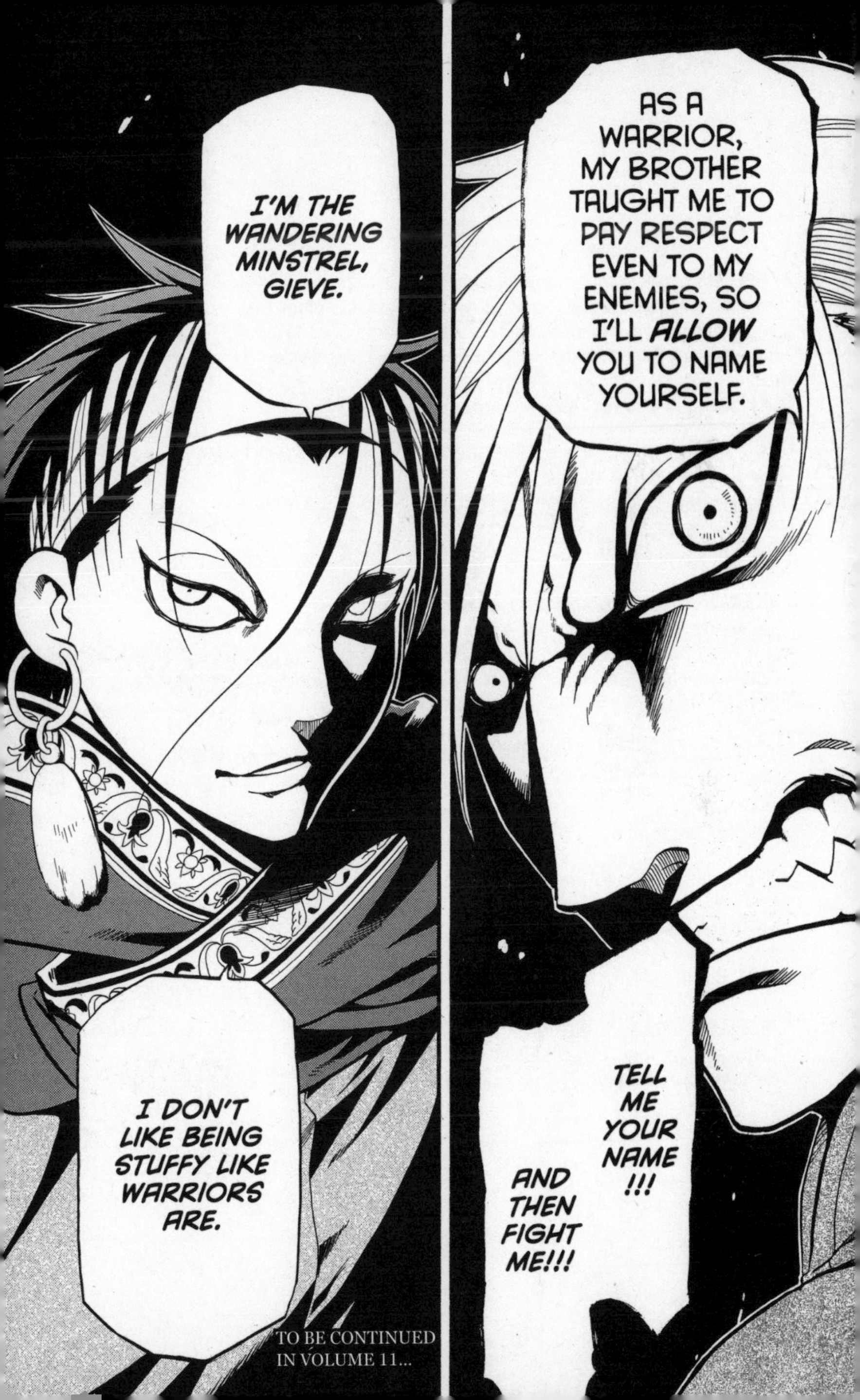
AS A WARRIOR, MY BROTHER TAUGHT ME TO PAY RESPECT EVEN TO MY ENEMIES, SO I'LL *ALLOW* YOU TO NAME YOURSELF.
TELL ME YOUR NAME!!!
AND THEN FIGHT ME!!!
I'M THE WANDERING MINSTREL, GIEVE.
I DON'T LIKE BEING STUFFY LIKE WARRIORS ARE.
TO BE CONTINUED IN VOLUME 11...

A Kodansha Comics Trade Paperback Original.

The Heroic Legend of Arslan volume 10 copyright © 2018 Hiromu Arakawa & Yoshiki Tanaka
English translation copyright © 2019 Hiromu Arakawa & Yoshiki Tanaka

Published in the United States by Kodansha Comics,
an imprint of Kodansha USA Publishing, LLC, New York.

Publication rights for this English edition arranged through Kodansha Ltd., Tokyo.

First published in Japan in 2018 by Kodansha Ltd., Tokyo, as *Arslan Senki* volume 10.

ISBN 978-1-63236-730-3

Printed in the United States of America.

www.kodanshacomics.com

9 8 7 6 5 4 3 2 1

Translation: Amanda Haley
Lettering: James Dashiell
Editing: Ajani Oloye